UNIONS
IN TRANSITION

UNIONS IN TRANSITION

ENTERING THE SECOND CENTURY

Edited by

SEYMOUR MARTIN LIPSET

ICS PRESS

ICS

Institute for Contemporary Studies
San Francisco, California

Publication of this book by ICS Press signifies that the contributions by the authors are regarded by the Institute for Contemporary Studies (of which ICS Press is a part) as valuable and responsible. The analyses, conclusions, and opinions expressed are those of the authors and not necessarily those of the Institute, its officers, directors, or others associated with, or funding, its work.

Inquiries, book orders, and catalog requests should be addressed to ICS Press, Suite 750, 785 Market Street, San Francisco, CA 94103 (415) 543-6213.

Library of Congress Cataloging in Publication Data
Main entry under title:

Unions in transition.

     Includes bibliographies and index.
     1. Trade-unions—United States. 2. Trade-unions—
Canada. 3. Trade-unions. I. Lipset, Seymour Martin.
HD.U46   1986   331.88   86−10256
ISBN 0−917616−74−X
ISBN 0−917616−73−1 (pbk.)

CONTENTS

LIST OF TABLES AND FIGURES   xi

FOREWORD   xiii

PREFACE   xv

Seymour Martin Lipset

I

The Background

1 LABOR: A MOVEMENT IN SEARCH OF A
   MISSION   3

   A. H. Raskin

   Since 1945 4   Dawn of the 1980s 9   The
   Legacy of 1955 11   Meany vs. Corruption 14
   Action for Civil Rights 16   Unions and Public
   Policy 19   The Foreign Policy Dilemma 22
   Dialogue Opens Up 23   Unions and
   Employers 26   Reliance on Politics 29
   Popular Perceptions 33

2 THE HISTORICAL ROLE OF AMERICAN
   TRADE UNIONISM   39

   Walter Galenson

   The Origins of American Trade Unionism 41
   Class Consciousness 43   The Triumph of
   Business Unionism 45   Jurisdictional
   Disputes 48   Political Action 49
   Expansion 50   The Great Depression and the
   New Deal 52   The Beginnings of a Welfare
   Society 57   The Erosion of Trade Union
   Power 59   Unions and Foreign Affairs 62
   Labor's Political Role 63   Membership
   Decline 67   Conclusion 69

3   THE RISE AND FALL OF AMERICAN TRADE
     UNIONS: THE LABOR MOVEMENT FROM
     FDR TO RR   75
     Leo Troy

     Framework for Analysis 77   The Statistical
     Record 79   Determinants of Unions' Rise and
     Decline 94   Conclusions: Consequences and
     Outlook 104

II

Comparative Perspectives

4   IS CANADA'S EXPERIENCE "ESPECIALLY
     INSTRUCTIVE"?   113
     **Christopher Huxley, David Kettler, and
     James Struthers**

     Union Density in Canada and the U.S. 116
     Disparate Developments toward Similarity:
     Canadian and American Unionism,
     1935–1964 121   Public Sector Unionism 125
     Conclusion: Law and Politics 128

5   AMERICA AND JAPAN: INDUSTRIAL
     RELATIONS IN A TIME OF CHANGE   133
     Ray Marshall

     The American System 134   Consequences of
     Internationalization and Other Trends 140
     Public Policy 148

6   UNIONISM AS A SOCIAL MOVEMENT   151
     Alain Touraine

     Industrial Society and Class Consciousness
     154   The Rise and Decline of a Class Conscious
     Labor Movement 157   The Labor Movement
     and Political Action 165   Conclusion: The
     Natural History of Unionism 172

III
Economic Analysis

7   EFFECTS OF UNIONS ON THE ECONOMY   177
     Richard B. Freeman

     The Union Monopoly Pay Effect 180   Union
     Wage Gains and Inflation 182   Structure of
     Pay: Dispersion and Composition 183   Fringe
     Benefits 188   Exit Voice: Turnover 191
     Layoffs and Concessions 193
     Productivity 194   Profitability 197   An
     Overall Assessment 199

8   COMBINATIONS OF WORKMEN: TRADE
     UNIONS IN THE AMERICAN ECONOMY   201
     Daniel K. Benjamin

     Historical Background 202   The Current
     Scene 205   An Overview of the Wage
     Bargain 207   The Effects of the Wage
     Bargain 211   The Fabled Givebacks 213   The
     New Learning: Freeman and Medoff
     Revisited 214   Conclusions 219

9   THE CASE FOR ENDING THE LEGAL
     PRIVILEGES AND IMMUNITIES OF TRADE
     UNIONS   221
     Morgan Reynolds

     The Legal Privileges and Immunities of Trade
     Unions 223   Why Unions Obtained Privileges
     and Immunities 229   The Case for
     Repeal 231   Conclusion 237

IV

The Public Sector

10 PUBLIC EMPLOYEE UNIONISM AND LABOR
    RELATIONS IN THE 1980s: AN ANALYSIS OF
    TRANSFORMATION   241
    David Lewin

    Public Sector Employment, Unionism, and
    Strikes 243   Environmental Changes and the
    Public Sector Bargaining Process 248
    Sanitation Labor Relations: The Public Sector in
    Microcosm 251   Lessons from the Sanitation
    Experience 260

11 FACULTY COLLECTIVE BARGAINING: A
    STATUS REPORT   265
    Joseph W. Garbarino

    The Extent of Organization 268   The Faculty
    Organizations 272   The Outcomes of
    Bargaining 280   Conclusion 283

V

Outside and Inside

12 LABOR UNIONS IN THE PUBLIC MIND   287
    Seymour Martin Lipset

    Lack of Confidence in Unions and Their
    Leaders 288   The Positive Social Role of
    Unions 299   The Ambivalence of Union
    Members 304   Union Power: A Source of
    Concern 309   Unions and Workers 314   The
    Effects of Unions on Inflation 316
    Conclusion 318

13   THE FIGHT FOR UNION DEMOCRACY   323
      Herman Benson

      Organization and Oligarchy 324   Levels of
      Union Government 324   The "Official
      Family" 328   Self-Image of the Bureaucratic
      Caste 330   The Organizing Staff 331   The
      Professional Staff 334   Trials, Appeals,
      Conventions 337   Normal and Abnormal
      Advantages of Incumbency 341   The Law
      347   The Roots of Insurgency 355   Union
      Democracy: The Phoenix 359   The
      Allies 362   Conclusions 366

VI

Participants' Observations

14   LABOR AT THE CROSSROADS   373
      Gus Tyler

      Troubled Times 373   Changing
      Problems 376   A "Labor Surplus
      Society" 378   A Global Setting 379   Capital,
      Labor, Mobility 381   Labor's Power 382
      "Alienation" and the Worker 383   The Need for
      Unions 385   Labor's Agenda
      Endangered 387   The Pace of Change 388
      Inevitable Adjustments 390

15   "IT HAS ALL BEEN SAID BEFORE..."   393
      Lane Kirkland

      Who We Are 396   The Future of Work 399
      Union Progress 401

16   A MANAGEMENT LOOK AT LABOR
      RELATIONS   405
      Alexander B. Trowbridge

      The Way It Was—The Good Old Days 405
      Facing Reality 407   Impact on Labor-
      Management Relations 408   Impact on
      Unions 412   The Human Resource Function
      and Growth of Union-Free Companies 414   The
      Future of Collective Bargaining in a Global
      Economy 417

VII

Conclusion

17   NORTH AMERICAN LABOR MOVEMENTS: A
      COMPARATIVE PERSPECTIVE   421
      Seymour Martin Lipset

      Structural Changes 422   The Legal
      Environment 429   Employer Policies 436
      The Impact of Public Opinion 438   Canadian
      and American Values 442

NOTES   455

CONTRIBUTORS   479

INDEX   484

TABLES AND FIGURES

Trade Union Membership as a Proportion of Employees on Nonagricultural Payrolls, 1940–1984   60

Union Density, Major Industrial Countries, Selected Years   76

Trade Union Membership and Density in the United States, 1933–1984   81

Private and Public Membership and Density in the U.S., 1962–1983   82

Composition of American Union Membership by Sector, 1933–1983   83

Union Density, Selected States   84

Occupational Composition of Union Membership, 1959–1984   86

Union Density by Major Industrial Sector, 1930–1985   87

Membership Changes, Selected Unions, Peak and Current Years   92

Canadian and American Union Densities, Selected Years, 1921–1984   118

Union Density in the United States and Canada, 1935–1980   119

The Two Faces of Trade Unionism   179

The Union Wage Advantage by Demographic Group, Blue Collar Workers, 20–65, 1979   181

Studies of the Impact of Unionism on Wage Inequality   186

Estimates of Percentage Impact of Unionism on Wage, Fringe Benefits, and Total Compensation   190

Public Sector Union Membership   242

Number and Percentage of Full-time, Organized Employees, State and Local Government, 1975–1982   244

Public Employee Work Stoppages by Level of Government, United States, 1960–1982   247

A Model of the Public Sector Labor Relations Process   250

Sanitation Service by Category of Service Recipient and
Service Provider, 1975   253

Sanitation, Police, and Fire Department Employment per
1,000 Population, 1975–1983   254

Full-Time Employment in Municipal Sanitation
Departments, 1983   256

Management Practices in Sanitation Service, by
Collection Arrangement and City Size   258

Institutions and Persons Represented, 1966–1983   269

Faculty Bargaining Units by Affiliation   274

Confidence in Leaders of Labor, Major Companies, and
Eight Other Institutions   291

Confidence in Ability of Leaders to Contribute to Society   293

Qualities Descriptive of Business and Labor Leaders   295

Ratings of Occupational Groups on Ethical and Moral
Practices   298

Ratings of Labor Unions, 1936–1985   301

Attitudes Toward Organized Labor and Business   302

Differences between Members' Expectations and
Judgments of Performance of Unions   306

Evaluations by AFL-CIO Members of Union Services   307

Attitudes Toward Power of Labor Unions   312

Evaluation of the Influence of Unions and Workers in
American Life and Politics   314

Attitude to Union Negotiating Policies   319

Service/Industrial Sector Ratios, Selected OECD
Countries, 1963, 1973, 1983   424

Rank-order of OECD Countries by Service/Industrial
Sector Ratios for 1983 and Percent Union Membership
in Total Labor Force for Selected Countries, 1960 to
1982   426

The Misery Index in Canada, the United Kingdom, and the
United States, 1970–1984   428

Correlations Between Public Approval of Unions and
Union Support, 1947–1981   439

Least-Squares Equation Predictions of Union Density   439

Relationships Between Gallup Union Approval Rates and
Union Density and Percentage Wins in Certification
Elections, and Between Predicted Union Densities and
Actual Density   441

FOREWORD

It is entirely fitting that this book should appear on the one-hundredth anniversary of the American Federation of Labor, forerunner of the AFL-CIO. Since labor unions have been important social institutions throughout the world since the late nineteenth century, an American centennial provides an occasion to "step back" and evaluate how labor unions are doing and where they seem to be going in the post-industrial democracies.

Such an evaluation is especially important because of a widespread feeling both inside and outside the labor movement that it is in "trouble," that it may have a declining relevance, both economically and socially, in contemporary society. One indication of this is that although union membership in the United States, measured in absolute terms, is about the same as it was twenty years ago, in relative terms the percentage of workers in labor unions has declined from its historic high of nearly one-third of the nonfarm work force to less than 20 percent. Union members have grown increasingly restive, dissatisfied with the services they receive in return for their union membership and dues. Workers in new sectors of the economy have resisted union organization. Perhaps most importantly, unions and union leaders are disdained by an increasing portion of the public, and unions have become ineffective in shaping a social or political consensus on labor.

To explore these phenomena, the Institute asked Seymour Martin Lipset to bring together a group of academic observers and labor practitioners to address these and other issues. Besides the distinguished group of scholars he has assembled, we are especially pleased to be able to include contributions by Lane

Kirkland, President of the AFL-CIO, and by Alexander Trowbridge, President of the National Association of Manufacturers, presenting labor and business perspectives.

This study addresses a subject of longstanding interest to the Institute. It follows publication ten years ago of one of our first studies, *Public Employee Unions: The Crisis in Public Sector Labor Relations* (1976), edited by A. Lawrence Chickering.

We hope this volume will contribute to improved understanding of the economic and social role of labor unions in modern society.

Robert B. Hawkins, Jr.
President

San Francisco, California
July 1986

PREFACE

Unions in Transition appears one century after the founding of the American Federation of Labor in 1886. The occasion calls for an evaluation of the achievements and failures of the labor movement, and the essays written for the volume try to do this. Since the role of organized labor in American society and economy has been a subject of controversy from the start, I have invited authors who vary considerably in their judgment of trade unions.

The survival of an institution for 100 years normally calls for a celebration. Yet the present situation of the AFL-CIO, the dominant force in American unionism, is not such as to invite congratulatory messages. The leaders of the federation have not arranged for any festivities since they describe their organization as 105 years old, dating the founding back to 1881 when a predecessor, the Federation of Organized Trades and Labor Unions, was formed. Yet an examination of the assorted classic histories by writers as diverse as Selig Perlman, Friedrich Sorge, Gompers' biographer Bernard Mandel, and Samuel Gompers himself in his autobiography, *Seventy Years of Life and Labor,* shows that a new organization, the American Federation of Labor, was created in December 1886. Gompers and the others emphasize that the old Federation was primarily formed to secure legislative relief and was very weak. Those who sought trade union economic action formed a new organization whose membership, unlike the previous body, was limited to trade unions.*

---

*For discussions of the formation of the AFL and the way it absorbed the Federation of Organized Trades and Labor Unions, see Samuel Gompers, *Seventy Years of Life and Labor: An Autobiography* (New York: E.P. Dutton, 1943), pp. 264–265, 268–272; Bernard Mandel, *Samuel Gompers: A Biography* (Yellow Springs, OH: The Antioch Press, 1963), pp. 74–75; Friedrich A. Sorge, *Labor Movement in the United States: A History of the American Working Class from Colonial Times to 1890* (Westport, CT: Greenwood Press, 1977), pp. 267–268; and Selig Perlman, *History of Trade Unionism in the United States* (New York: Augustus M. Kelley, 1950), pp. 111–120.

A century later, American unions are at their lowest point since the merger of the AFL and CIO in 1955 in terms of membership, labor market, and political strength. The proportion of the non-agricultural labor force organized by unions has been steadily declining, from 33 percent in 1955 to around 18 percent in 1985. One of our authors, Richard Freeman, has calculated that in absence of any change in the basic parameters affecting unionization, that percentage will drop to 13 by the year 2000.

Encompassed in the decline is an increased inability of trade unions to win labor board certification elections, contests initiated at the request of labor organizations. The union win rate declined from 74.6 percent in 1947 to 65.6 in 1954, to 60.8 in 1965, to 56.1 in 1970, and then fell below the 50 percent line for the first time to 49.6 percent in 1975. As of the last fully reported year, 1984, the win rate was 46.4 percent. Given this record, it is not surprising that the ability of unions to organize to apply for certification elections in unorganized companies has been steadily declining. There were around 3,500 such elections in 1983 and 1984, down from close to 9,000 in 1973.

Labor organizations do much worse in decertification contests, elections called in unionized companies at the request of groups of workers or the employers. During the early 1980s, trade unions lost over three-quarters of them. What is more damaging from a union perspective is that the number of such elections per year has increased from under 300 in the 1960s to around 500 in the mid-1970s and close to 900 by the mid-1980s. The ratio of certification elections to decertification ones was roughly thirty to one in 1960, it was around twenty to one in the early 1970s, it had fallen to seven to one by 1980 and stood at four to one in 1984.

The electoral defeat of Walter Mondale in 1984, following on the formal endorsement of his candidacy by the AFL-CIO, suggested to many analysts that organized labor's political influence had reached its nadir. An even lower point, however, was legislative defeat in 1978 on the issue of labor law reform under a Democratic president and Congress, an outcome which signaled the movement's weakness even within the Democratic party.

Perhaps even more troubling for the union movement is that the 1980s have witnessed an almost steady retreat with respect to its collective bargaining strength. In industry after industry, unions have signed contracts involving concessions with respect to working conditions and wages, including, in some cases, provisions for newly hired employees that are significantly less than those received by the existing labor force.

Given this background, this book is designed to deal with five fundamentally critical questions: One, why are American unions the weakest segment of organized labor in the industrialized world, why is union density less here than elsewhere? Two, what factors account for the decline in the proportion of workers organized and in the ability of unions to win certification elections? Three, what are the reasons for labor's loss of political influence? Four, can the union movement reverse these trends? Five, how consequential will labor's future role in the nation's economy and politics be? Clearly, the complexity of these questions and the gravity of the issues involved suggest that no simple answer will suffice. As we shall see, some of the most frequently advanced interpretations do not hold up when subject to the light of comparative analysis.

The chapters here range from three efforts to put the achievements and problems of American labor in historical and political perspective (Raskin, Galenson, and Troy) to comparative evaluations with the situation in other countries (Huxley, Kettler, and Struthers; Marshall; Touraine; and my concluding chapter). They include quite conflicting estimates of the effects of unions on the economy by two labor economists (Freeman and Benjamin). From a different vantage point, Herman Benson reports on the internal governance of unions. Diversity of judgments is also reflected in the evaluation of the effect of the legal environment. Much of the comparative literature on Canadian and American unionism contends that the former is much stronger because the law favors unions north of the common border and is hostile to those south of it. But this view is challenged by Morgan Reynolds, who sees American law as overly supportive of organized labor.

Labor's contemporary story includes some gains as well as major losses. The former have largely been in the public sector, although, as David Lewin notes, there have been considerable variations in achievements and some declines in this area as well. The most unique phenomenon in the recent saga of organized labor has been college faculty unionism, a story that seems worthy of a separate chapter by Joseph Garbarino. To complete the picture, I have written an analysis of the way Americans generally evaluate the labor movement, as reflected in the opinion polls. Three leaders of groups concerned with collective bargaining, Lane Kirkland, the president of the AFL-CIO; Alexander Trowbridge, the head of the National Association of Manufacturers; and Gus Tyler, a labor intellectual who is an official of the International Ladies' Garment Union, have provided views from inside. In the concluding chapter, I try to relate the weakness of American labor to the situations in other countries, and its decline since the mid-1950s to basic traits of American society. For analytical purposes the situation in the United States is contrasted with that of Canada, a North American nation in which trade unions are much stronger.

This book is obviously the product of a collective enterprise. I am grateful to the authors for the care which they took in preparing their essays. I am also particularly appreciative to various staff members of the Institute for Contemporary Studies for their assistance at different stages. These include in particular A. Lawrence Chickering and Stephen Schwartz. Janet Shaw and James Scaminaci III have my gratitude for facilitating my roles as editor and author.

Seymour Martin Lipset

Stanford, California
July 1986

I

The Background

1

A. H. RASKIN

Labor: A Movement in Search of a Mission

In the mid-1980s, organized labor is a movement in search of a mission. Replacements are needed for the building blocks put in place at a convention in Pittsburgh in 1881 by the 108 union delegates who formed what became the American Federation of Labor and Congress of Industrial Organizations (AFL-CIO). Through most of the ensuing century the principles of moderate, reformist unionism enunciated by Samuel Gompers and his fellow-founders served well as bedrock for a movement that evolved, through bitter and often bloody struggle, into a major component in every aspect of this country's economic, social, and political life.

In recent years, however, the Gompers legacy increasingly has been questioned due to major changes in workplace technology; global trade competition; industrial demographics; and the needs and wants of a better-educated, more individualistic work force. The inability of most unions to comprehend or cope with these transformations, coupled with a sluggishness of spirit making many of them prisoners of inertia, has caused a downhill slide in membership, muscle, and public regard that assumed dismaying dimensions at the start of this decade.

There is one redeeming note for those who share my conviction that a vigorous, socially responsible trade union movement is imperative to the strengthening of democratic values in this era of gigantic multinational corporations. The magnitude of labor's current afflictions has prompted the AFL-CIO to undertake for the first time those hardest of all assignments for any established institution: a candid examination of its own weaknesses and errors and a start toward restoring lost momentum.

How realistic it is to hope that this laudable venture will spark a resurgence even vaguely parallel to the revival that brought millions of unorganized workers into an even more prostrate union movement at the depths of the Great Depression in the 1930s may be somewhat easier to judge if we take a closer look at the developments that have brought labor to its present pass.

Since 1945

When V-J Day brought quiet to the fighting fronts in 1945, war between labor and management broke out all across the production front. During World War II, when the United States was the arsenal of democracy, a no-strike pact to which the still divided AFL and CIO had committed themselves maintained a high level of peace in industry. That peace enabled unions, particularly the infant CIO unions spawned by Franklin D. Roosevelt's New Deal and by the magnetic leadership of John L. Lewis, to consolidate their position under the benevolent mediatory eye of the War Labor Board.

The uncertainties of the postwar period of reconversion to a civilian economy represented a time of testing for both unions and employers. President Truman sought to head off a collision by convening a summit conference of union and industry chiefs in Washington on November 5, 1945, but it accomplished nothing. Two weeks later the most serious of the conflicts that developed out of the pent-up animosities began with a walkout of 175,000 workers at General Motors (GM).

The strike was led by Walter P. Reuther, then a vice president of the United Automobile Workers (UAW), who had come to prominence as a firebrand in the 1937 sit-down strikes at GM that gave organized labor its first foothold in the open-shop citadels of the auto industry. He sought to turn the 1945–46 shutdown, which dragged on for 113 days of siege, into the jumping-off point for an extension of the concept of collective bargaining beyond the boundaries traditional under business unionism.

Reuther's idea was that unions performed a disservice to the community if their sole concern was to win higher wages and improved conditions for their members and then allow the cost to be passed on to the consumer. As a token of the union's reluctance to enter into any contract that might feed postwar inflation, Reuther offered to keep his members at work if GM would let an arbitration board inspect its books and decide how much of a pay increase the company could reasonably afford without raising the price of its cars and trucks.

To General Motors management the Reuther proposal meant not arbitration, but abdication. It denounced as socialism and profit control any suggestion that it allow a board appointed by the President or anyone else to inquire into ability to pay as an index of what the company ought to give in wages. So profound was GM's resistance on this point that its officials boycotted hearings before a presidential fact-finding panel after Harry Truman had sent the company chairman a telegram putting the White House on record in favor of a study of the relationship between wages and prices.

The fact finders, proceeding in the absence of testimony from GM, recommended a wage increase of nineteen and one-half cents an hour, with no increase in car prices. Reuther accepted at once, but GM spurned the recommendation on the ground that it embodied the "unsound principle" that a prosperous enterprise should pay higher wages than a less profitable competitor.

The union's ranks held firm, but developments elsewhere in the labor front eroded Reuther's bargaining position as week upon week of payless paydays piled misery on his members. Philip Murray, president of both the CIO and the United Steelworkers of America, had made little secret from the start of his irritation at Reuther for having called out the GM workers instead of letting Murray's steel union set the pattern for the first postwar negotiating round. Murray was equally disapproving of what he considered the folly of the UAW leader's effort to bargain for consumers as well as auto workers.

Smoldering under these twin annoyances, Murray set January 14, 1946, as the deadline for a strike of 750,000 workers in steel and related industries. When President Truman made an eleventh-hour proposal that both sides agree on a compromise settlement of eighteen and one-half cents an hour, Murray postponed the walkout for a week in the hope that the industry would join the union in acquiescing.

The steel companies refused to go along unless the White House guaranteed a relaxation of price controls that would permit them to offset the wage boost with higher prices for steel, a reverse twist on the Reuther position at GM. Their stand touched off the biggest strike in the nation's history—a strike that ended after four weeks, with the companies granting the eighteen and one-half cent increase in hourly wages in exchange for a green light from Washington to raise steel prices by five dollars a ton.

Even before the CIO president thus undercut Reuther, both economically and philosophically, political enemies within the UAW—an unholy alliance of pro-Communists and "pork-choppers" eager to prevent Reuther from using the GM strike as a springboard to the union presidency—had put a banana peel under him by negotiating strike-free arrangements at Ford for eighteen cents an hour and at Chrysler for eighteen and one-half cents. The left-wing leadership of the United Electrical, Radio, and Machine Workers held secret talks with GM and settled for an eighteen and one-half cent increase covering 30,000 employees in the company's electrical division. When the same pattern spread to the United Rubber Workers and other key unions, GM bluntly informed Reuther that even if he struck forever it was determined not to give the UAW the extra penny an hour the Truman panel had recommended, much less a guarantee of stable car prices.

With the strike sixteen weeks old, Reuther felt he could not ask his membership to make a further sacrifice in what was clearly a lost cause. The members went back to work with a raise of eighteen and one-half cents and no promise from the company to hold the line on prices. By August, the government had approved three price increases for GM, and before the end of 1946 Congress abolished the last vestige of the war time machinery for price-wage controls.

Many of Reuther's critics in the executive suites of industry and labor alike openly gloated at the prospect that in a pragmatic, results-oriented labor movement the humiliation from the disappointing outcome of the marathon strike represented a death knell for Reuther's personal ambitions and for his brand of social engineering, as distinct from the virtues of "bread-and-butter" unionism.

That adverse judgment, it quickly developed, was not shared by the UAW membership. At the auto union's convention, which opened just after the long shutdown, Reuther challenged R.J. Thomas, the organization's jolly but bumbling president, for the top spot. Reuther squeaked through to a hairbreadth victory; then, a year later, solidified his control by winning a top-heavy majority in the international executive board.

Within General Motors, these events in addition to the solidarity its unionized employees had exhibited through the long strike, prompted a review of the company's approach to collective bargaining. GM finally recognized that the UAW was there to stay and that the sensible course for management was a live-and-let-live relationship rather than endless confrontations.

In the 1948 bargaining round, Charles E. Wilson, GM's chief executive, launched the new program by proposing the most ambitious step any major corporation had ever taken toward injecting some element of science into the hagglemaster environment that normally surrounded negotiations. The proposed formula, called "progress sharing," took much of its inspiration from the anti-inflationary principles that underlay the Reuther initiative of 1945–46.

It had two main features. The first was an "annual improvement factor" designed to give the workers a tangible stake in industry's advances in technology and productivity by raising basic hourly wages each year in line with the long-term growth in the gross national product. The second was a cost-of-living escalator, under which the purchasing power of the wage bargain would be kept steady by automatic increases or decreases reflecting fluctuations in the Consumer Price Index.

Over the next decade the GM formula became the pattern for

wage determination affecting millions of workers in auto, steel, and other industries in which a relatively few corporate giants exerted oligopolistic control over markets and prices. Out of that formula grew an *entente cordiale*, under which dominant elements in big business accepted the somewhat heretical notion that strong, secure unions could be of advantage to management by combating wildcat ("quickie") strikes and fostering cooperative relations in the workplace. Not the least of the attendant benefits, in the view of many, was the standardization of wage rates so that one company did not get an advantage on its competitors through lower labor costs.

From the standpoint of unions, the dividends of this new-found amity were even more concrete. Outside of the South and Southwest, where all forms of compulsory union membership were prohibited by state "right-to-work" laws, management became much more amenable to signing union-shop contracts under which all workers in the bargaining unit were required to join the majority union as a condition of holding their jobs. Such contracts had long been common in industries like construction, trucking, printing, and the needle trades, where most companies were relatively small. Their spread to large sections of heavy industry created a kind of pushbutton unionism, in which employers became for all practical purposes the chief recruiters of new union members and also collected the union's dues under checkoff arrangements.

Despite these pluses for both sides, several unanticipated factors contributed to frustrating the expectation of the GM plan's authors that the pay formula would function as a scientific balance stabilizing the economy while distributing the fruits of new technology equitably among shareholders, workers, and consumers. The first was the rapid climb of consumer prices, especially in the 1970s, as a result of the Vietnam War, the actions of the Organization of Petroleum Exporting Countries, and the mushrooming cost of food and health services. The steepness and sustained nature of that climb converted the escalator into a prime engine of inflation in its own right.

The second was the rapid growth in cradle-to-grave welfare benefits and other fringe protection for workers and their families, an employer-financed expenditure outside the formula, that went from almost zero in 1948 to nearly half of the basic wage bill now. Still a third destabilizing element was that the long-term improvement in national productivity, frozen into the plan at a 3 percent annual level, dropped to less than half that rate after 1965 and in the late 1970s approached the vanishing point.

Dawn of the 1980s

By the dawn of the 1980s the bloated labor costs forced upon many pacesetters in American industry by this miscarriage of the GM formula had left them vulnerable to a complex of new competitive pressures that challenged their ability to survive. Chief among these were the drastic inroads that Japan, the developed industrial nations of Western Europe, and an ever-expanding roster of low-wage economies in the Far East and Latin America were making into United States markets and jobs. Along with this savage trade competition went the deregulation policies initiated by President Carter and amplified by President Reagan, which demolished the protected positions many companies and unions had enjoyed in such fields as trucking and air transportation.

Burgeoning, aggressive new companies began to operate without unions or unwieldy administrative structures in construction, steel, mining, and other fields that had once been near-monopolies for unionism. This compelled old-line operators to embark on cost-cutting campaigns that also obliged their unions to choose between a slashing of pay rates or sacrifice of prized work rules.

The chilly climate for unionism fostered by all these conditions was made still more inhospitable by the decision of the Reagan administration in 1981 to tamp down inflation by a calculated slowdown of the economy, pushing unemployment to double-digit levels and enabling employers bent on getting rid of unions to count on a gigantic pool of hungry workers ready to go through picket lines to replace strikers.

In the years of America's industrial dominance, when it was standard practice to reflect higher wages in higher prices, entrenched unions called strikes with little anxiety that employers would even attempt to operate. In the steel strike of 1959, a half-million members of the United Steelworkers stayed out for 116 days, and the union's confidence that the mills would

remain closed was so complete that no human picket marched outside many huge plants. A picket sign tied to an empty metal drum
outside the mill gate was all the notice required to enforce the
shutdown.

No similar confidence exists in most big unions today. The precedent set by Ronald Reagan in his first year in the White House,
when he ordered 11,500 striking federal air traffic controllers
fired and put their AFL-CIO union out of business, has encouraged
many companies in private industry to take on striking unions
and even to provoke strikes in hopes of getting rid of unions
altogether. This hard line by many managements, coupled with
the frequency with which unions have found their picket lines
pierced by their own members or by sister unions, caused major
strikes called in 1984 to drop to the lowest level since World War
II—a national total of only sixty-two—involving less than one-
third of one percent of the work force.

The decline in union militancy and muscle was even more
glaringly apparent in the official figures for 1984 on the success of
unions at getting higher wages for the workers they represent.
Despite a brisk upturn in the general economy, the average annual increase in major contracts covering 2.3 million unionized
workers dropped to 2.3 percent, the lowest figure in the seventeen
years since the Bureau of Labor Statistics started keeping track of
such records. The 2.3 percent average was less than enough to
offset the sharply reduced inflation rate, and many contracts continued to call for the pay freezes or outright reductions that have
become common in these days of employer-prescribed retrenchment.

But even in a movement built on the Gompers precept of
"more," money gains are not the only measure of union effectiveness. The AFL-CIO has traditionally viewed itself as the conscience of America—the most consistent and potent force working to expand the horizons of hope and opportunity for wage earners inside and outside union ranks and for the poor and disadvantaged of all races, creeds, and nationalities.

George Meany, the iron-willed former plumber from the Bronx
who was "Mr. Labor" for a quarter-century before he stepped
down as president of the AFL-CIO in November, 1979, two months
before his death at age eighty-five, liked to recall that Gompers
himself had defined labor's goal in broad terms:

I do not value the labor movement only for its ability to give better wages, better clothes, and better homes. Its ultimate goal is to be found in the progressively evolving life possibilities in the life of each man and woman. My inspiration comes in opening opportunities that all alike may be free to live life to the fullest.

Meany's protege and successor, Lane Kirkland, focused on a similarly expansive expression of the Gompers testament when the centennial of the modern movement was being marked in 1981. "What does labor want?" was the founder's original statement which Kirkland took as keynote for the year-long celebration. "We want more schoolhouses and less jails, more books and less arsenals, more learning and less vice, more constant work and less crime, more leisure and less greed, more justice and less revenge."

In pursuing that mission of social betterment, the AFL-CIO has staked for itself so unbounded an agenda of global and parochial concerns that it amply fulfilled Kirkland's boast to delegates to the federation's 1983 convention: "Hardly a sparrow falls, here or abroad, that we do not take within the jurisdiction of the trade union movement." Inevitably, however, the duality of labor's functions in the sociopolitical arena and at the bargaining table entrap it in contradictions and crosspulls that puzzle outsiders and often make them skeptical of the sincerity of the movement's leaders.

In their primary role as representatives of their members, unions assign priority to delivering "more and better" in contract negotiations and to safeguarding workers' job and seniority rights—a mission that casts them as dedicated reinforcers of middle-class values within the capitalist system. The emphasis this aspect of union function places on jobs as the property of the workers who hold them frequently conflicts with the political alliances unions seek to build in their role as crusading social reformers. Thus, for example, environmentalists, civil rights organizations, and consumer groups have often found themselves at odds with unions over issues that arise out of labor's concern with preserving and protecting their members' jobs.

The Legacy of 1955

Because of these tensions and because many of the most critical decisions affecting the future of organized labor will be made on the political front, any realistic appraisal of the movement's chances for revival must look at least as deeply at the evolution of its social and political activities as at what it has done in organizing and collective bargaining in the three decades since the 1955 merger of the AFL and CIO ended twenty years of civil war within labor.

The merger convention rang with predictions that unity would bring a doubling of union membership within a decade plus a great burst of renewed dynamism in all aspects of union affairs. The results proved very different. One worker in every three belonged to a union when the AFL and CIO got together; thirty years later that ratio had dropped to fewer than one in every five and is still dropping. The truth was that, for all the exuberance of the 1955 convention oratory, most of the union chiefs in both camps suffered from tired blood. They were less interested in organizing the unorganized than in making sure that no other union would steal the members they already had or muscle in on the jurisdiction that, by charter, represented their sovereign turf, however slack they might be in representing their flock or seeking to enlarge it.

The cornerstone of the united house of labor was a no-raiding pact the AFL and CIO had hammered out in 1953, which committed the signatory unions in each federation not to poach on shops signed up by unions with overlapping jurisdiction on the opposite side. Established bargaining relationships were thus made sacrosanct, whatever the wishes of workers who were often disenchanted with do-nothing representation. The merger compact guaranteed that all the overlaps from two decades of conflict would be transferred unchanged into the unified federation, and that voluntary amalgamations would be relied upon to rationalize the jurisdictional jumble. The expectation was that the original total of 146 unions would shrink by the time the merged group reached its twentieth birthday to somewhere between twenty and forty, with at least a dozen in the million member class. Ten years after that milestone, the total was still ninety-six unions and more than half of them had fewer than 50,000 members. The number of Americans with jobs had climbed well over the 100 million mark and multi-billion-dollar corporations were merging on an almost daily basis into ever more gargantuan agglomerations seemingly devoid of any visible social or economic benefit and without even a pretense of concern for the welfare of the tens of thousands of employees bundled from one corporate fiefdom to another.

Other factors—some negative, some positive—contributed to the unification of labor. One was the deaths within a few days of one another in November 1952, of William Green, AFL president for 28 years, and Philip Murray, his opposite in the CIO. Both were so identified with the 1935 split that their usefulness as peacemakers was almost nil. Their passing coincided with cancellation by the electorate of the Democrats' twenty-year lease on the White House and the installation of a business-oriented administration headed by Dwight D. Eisenhower.

Reuther took over the CIO helm, but only after a bitter fight that suggested he was in command of a foundering ship. David J. McDonald, who had succeeded Murray as president of the United Steelworkers, gave increasing signs of determination to secede from the CIO unless peace with the AFL came swiftly. The CIO could ill afford the defection of a union that made up fully a quarter of its total membership, roughly the same proportion as Reuther's own auto union. The forward push had gone out of the CIO, and, even with the steel workers still inside, it had fewer than 5 million members, against 10 million in the AFL.

Most of the fundamental differences between craft and industrial unions that precipitated the division in 1935 had lost their force. The line separating those who believed all workers in an industry, from janitor to tool and die maker, should belong to the same union and those who felt jurisdiction should be rigidly compartmentalized along craft lines had been blurred. As unions in each camp reached out indiscriminately for new recruits, rivalry often meant piracy.

AFL fears that the CIO was a haven for Communists—a major obstacle to unity in the early years—evaporated when the main Communist-controlled unions were expelled in 1949 and 1950. This "purge" grew out of cleavages that developed within the CIO as a by-product of the cold war with the Soviet Union. A specific irritant to Murray was the breakaway of the Communist-dominated organizations to support Henry A. Wallace's abortive bid for the presidency on the Progressive Party ticket in 1948, a move Murray (and others) feared might cost Harry Truman the election.

Meany vs. Corruption

George Meany, the new head of the AFL, had no internal problems
of the kind that plagued Reuther, but he felt that the conservative
turn reflected in the Republican election triumph made unity a
must. He began almost at once to combat a cancer inside the AFL
that had always made the reform-minded leaders of the CIO particularly uneasy about merger on any terms. That cancer was the
dominance of underworld elements in some key unions, which the
old AFL leadership had stubbornly refused to combat on the
ground that autonomy gave affiliates ironclad protection against
federation intrusion into their internal affairs.

Meany, whose own union career had started in the New York
building trades when corruption was a commonplace, had come to
recognize that all labor was paying a high price in lost public
esteem for the refusal to crack down on unions that failed to clean
house. At the very time Meany took over the top spot, the New
York State Crime Commission was conducting a highly publicized
investigation that made it clear that the International Longshoremen's Association (ILA) had become a front for racketeer control
of the New York—New Jersey waterfront. When the ILA balked at
hauling down the Jolly Roger, Meany pushed through the union's
expulsion at the AFL convention in St. Louis in 1953.

His zeal for clean unionism did not fade after Meany became
president of the merged federation. Ethical practices codes were
drawn up as spiritual armor for the new organization and Meany
lost no time in using them vigorously for self-policing. A United
States Senate committee under the chairmanship of John L. Mc-
Clellan of Arkansas revealed that the federation's biggest and
strongest affiliate, the International Brotherhood of Teamsters,
was a happy hunting ground for organized crime. The committee's
televised hearings in the mid-1950s inspired an independent inquiry by the AFL-CIO, which culminated in a formal demand that
the giant trucking union throw off mob control or face ouster.

Meany was well aware that the strategic power exercised by the
teamsters as a make-or-break element in strikes or organizing
drives by other unions made many colleagues in labor's upper
echelon yearn for some face-saving formulation that would avert a
showdown. But Meany was unyielding. When the Teamsters under

Jimmy Hoffa thumbed their noses at the federation, he called on the merged organization's second convention in Atlantic City in 1957 to kick them out. The per capita vote for expulsion carried by a margin of more than four to one.

Beyond anything else the federation has ever done, the ouster of the Teamsters and other tainted unions in 1957—an act for which Meany deserves primary credit—ranked as its shining hour. It reflected a willingness to sacrifice in the cause of decency and idealism that has never been matched by any business organization. Regrettably, the banishment achieved none of its intended purposes. The underworld retained its iron grip on the union, and reform elements seeking to generate a rank-and-file revolt made only microscopic headway. Worse still, the Teamsters grew mightily in size and wealth while other unions withered. Attempts by Meany to ostracize the outcasts by forbidding federation affiliates from entering into mutual assistance pacts were almost universally ignored.

As if these perverse results of the federation's supreme act of moral courage were not dispiriting enough, the AFL-CIO found that it had earned few points on Capitol Hill by its ardor in self-monitorship. The 1959 Landrum-Griffin Labor-Management Reporting and Disclosure Act, establishing a bill of rights for union members and giving federal authorities extensive powers over the internal affairs of unions, was passed over the federation's vehement objections. Its passage killed the federation's enthusiasm for enforcing its ethical practices codes. Labor's current stance is that eradicating crooks from unions is a job for the law-enforcement agencies. However, the junking of its independent machinery for clean unionism has not blinded the federation to the damage all its affiliates suffer from the influence mobsters have achieved in recent years in a number of important unions. The AFL-CIO continued to demonstrate a measure of resolution in upholding the principle that unions should live by moral standards beyond those of the marketplace. For example, Lane Kirkland overrode objections by leaders of the building trades and other unions and testified in 1982 in support of legislation compelling union officials convicted of a crime involving betrayal of union trust to resign rather than hang on to their jobs through years of appeal.

Action for Civil Rights

Another field of utmost social concern in which the fusion of the
AFL and CIO resulted in a consequential broadening of labor's
horizons was civil rights. Prior to unification many AFL unions in
construction, the railroads, and the skilled metal trades had Jim
Crow locals or other forms of discriminatory or exclusionary practices against blacks and other minorities. The problem was far
less widespread in the CIO unions, in large part because the
"unskilled" workforce in mass production industries included
substantial numbers of blacks even before the unions came on the
scene.

Meany wholeheartedly backed the inclusion in the AFL-CIO
constitution of provisions making it the responsibility of the
parent organization to ensure equal sharing of the benefits of
unionism without regard for race, creed, or color. As a further sign
of his dedication to full openness within the labor movement,
Meany saw to it that two blacks—A. Philip Randolph of the
Brotherhood of Sleeping Car Porters and Willard Townsend of the
United Transport Service Employees—became vice-presidents of
the merged federation, the first time blacks had held that rank in
either the AFL or CIO.

However, the walls of racial exclusion did not come tumbling
down in labor any faster than they did in most other American institutions. In the 1960s, when John F. Kennedy came to the presidency, he was aware of the militant demand of minorities for
faster progress toward equality and assigned a top priority to the
enactment of an Omnibus Civil Rights Act. Its primary emphasis
as drafted at the White House was on wiping out restrictions on
access by blacks and other minorities to public places— buses,
railroads, soda fountains, public toilets, town halls, and the like.

Meany was totally in support of the bill, but he did not feel it
went far enough. He informed Kennedy that to accomplish its purposes the measure must also contain a strong section guaranteeing equal opportunity in jobs. The president was aghast, not
because he opposed the concept but because the ferocity of white
resistance to the equal access provisions of the bill, especially
among Congress members from the South, was so intense that the
administration faced a monumental battle even to get through the
original draft.

Meany was adamant on the need for a fair employment practices clause, one that would outlaw job discrimination in unions as well as industry. He told the House Judiciary Committee in 1963 that no amount of moral suasion on the labor leadership's part would be sufficient to bring errant unions into line in the absence of a law prohibiting discrimination. His way of summing up the need for statutory obligations was to state:

Why is this so? Primarily, because the labor movement is not what its enemies say it is—a monolithic, dictatorial, centralized body that imposes its will on the helpless dues-payers. We operate in a democratic way, and we cannot dictate even in a good cause. So, in effect, we need a federal law to help us do what we want to do—mop up those areas of discrimination which still persist in our own ranks.

The pivotal role held by union leaders as the mainstay of lobbying support for the omnibus bill finally induced President Kennedy to give reluctant assent to the incorporation of an equal employment opportunity title, but the President's fears that a measure so all-embracing would not get through Congress proved warranted. It was only after Kennedy's assassination that Lyndon B. Johnson was able to capitalize on the emotion stirred by his death to push the bill to passage with a guarantee of no bias in job hiring and promotion.

Candor requires acknowledgment, however, that fulfillment of the brave initiatives that underlay Meany's uncompromising insistence on the fair employment section has in many cases proved as disappointing as the fruits of his courageous stand to free labor of penetration by racketeers. The AFL-CIO has remained consistently out front in agitating for stronger laws against discrimination in voting, housing, or education, but enthusiasm for affirmative action in the workplace has been fitful. Indeed, unions and their white rank and file have often been conspicuous in the backlash against numerical standards or timetables to speed integration. The federal courts have repeatedly had to order reluctant unions to move faster toward eradicating exclusionary policies.

Labor's excuse is that the blame for the laggard pace of equal opportunity should be placed on government's failure to maintain full employment. In common with most spokesmen for the white middle class, labor argues that white workers and their families are being unfairly pressured to step aside for less qualified black and Hispanic job-seekers as a means of compensating for the effects of historic injustices totally outside their control or culpability. Unions did play a leading role during the Carter administration in seeking to address this problem through enactment of the Humphrey-Hawkins Full Employment and Balanced Growth Act of 1978. However, the requirement that law put on the White House to submit to Congress programs aimed at holding the level of joblessness below 4 percent became a dead letter almost before the ink dried on President Carter's signature.

The record of advancement for minorities to higher ranking jobs has not been much better within the labor movement than it has been in the executive suites of giant corporations. Not one major union has yet had a black president. Most unions count at least one black vice president, but usually in a special assignment connected with race relations. For women, white as well as black, the road to the top has been equally rocky, even in unions where women make up the great majority of the work force. When Kirkland became president of the AFL-CIO in 1979, he decided that the federation should set an example for its affiliates by increasing minority membership within its top policymaking body, the thirty-five-member Executive Council.

At that time, instead of the two black vice presidents installed at the merger convention, the number was down to one and included no woman. By August of 1980, Kirkland had persuaded his colleagues to bend the rules sufficiently to permit the election of the first woman to the hitherto all-male club of federation vice presidents. At the 1981 convention in New York, he moved to double the representation of both minorities by backing the election of a black woman to join the black man and white woman already aboard. The federation leadership called on the caucus made up of black delegates to the convention for guidance, but when the caucus proposed a black woman well-known as a rebel in the normally conformist internal politics of labor, the union establishment substituted a more complaisant candidate of its own choice. That decision prompted Frederick O'Neal of the Associated Actors and Artistes of America, at that point the only black on the council, to take the convention floor to complain that he was tired of having people make decisions for him without considering his feelings. It was, he said, "like asking the people of New York to select a congressman for New Jersey."

The 1985 convention in Anaheim, California, elected a second black man to the council. No woman was among the four new vice presidents chosen in that year. Since 1981 there has been a turnover of eighteen in the vice presidential roster, more than half the total council membership. The only minority representatives among the newcomers were one black woman and one black man. All the rest were white males.

Unions and Public Policy

In the three decades since the AFL-CIO merger, the interaction of unionism and public policy has kept multiplying the range of labor concerns and involvements in which the crucial determinants have been political. That has been especially true of the two gut issues for a "bread-and-butter" movement, wages and jobs.

Through the 1960s and 1970s inflation moved to the fore of public awareness and every president, Democratic as well as Republican, from John F. Kennedy on, felt constrained to fix part of the responsibility for the upward race of consumer prices on the degree to which wage increases consistently outran rises in productivity. The inflationary impact of basic increases far above those in earlier union contracts was heightened by the increased popularity in the General Motors formula of cost-of-living escalators, which went only one way—up.

As a brake on the wage-price spiral, the various tenants of the White House resorted to a chaotic and, in practice, quixotic cycle of devices aimed at putting a lid on wage increases. These ran a gamut from jawboning to the establishment of numerical guideposts geared to productivity to the imposition (under President Nixon) of formal price-wage controls of a type the nation had never known outside of wartime. The final phase, after all the other expedients had collapsed under the impact of union resistance, political gamesmanship, and lack of conviction by their presidential sponsors, was the negotiation by President Carter and the AFL-CIO of a "national accord" patterned in large measure after the social contracts that had brought considerable measures of both economic stability and prosperity to the Scandinavian countries and West Germany. Regrettably, the circumstances surrounding the pact's negotiation in the twilight period

of the Carter administration convinced most industrialists that it
was primarily a political ploy and they refused to become signato-
ries. The stabilization machinery created through the national accord, along with a number of tripartite instrumentalities for
cooperation by business, unions, and government to revive sick industries, died with the advent of Ronald Reagan and his philosophy of reducing governmental intrusion in industrial affairs.

No aspect of Reaganomics was more repugnant to the AFL-CIO
leadership under its newly installed chief, Kirkland, than this
negative attitude by the White House in a period when unionism's
strongholds in steel, autos, and other basic industries were collapsing under the weight of imports flooding the U.S. market and
when the administration was adding to the already high
unemployment total by deliberately throttling down economic activity to curb inflation.

So incensed did Kirkland become over what he termed a Reagan
"counter-revolution" designed to further enrich the large corporations and the wealthy at the expense of wage earners and the poor
that he was the prime mover in 1981 of a massive protest march
on the Capitol. This represented Kirkland's first truly radical
departure from the traditions hallowed by his mentor, George
Meany, in whose majestic shadow Kirkland had toiled so long and
faithfully that many observers felt he would function as a mini-
Meany when he moved up to the top seat. It was an article of faith
with Meany that American labor, in contrast with the socialist
labor movements of Western Europe, did not take to the streets to
force changes in government policy by pressure of angry numbers.
His distaste for all such fist-shaking outside the citadels of
authority was so absolute that—at the very time the AFL-CIO
was spearheading the coalition drive in Congress for passage of
the Omnibus Civil Rights Act—Meany angered Randolph,
Reuther, and other key unionists by vetoing their pleas for endorsement by the federation of the huge 1963 civil rights mobilization at the Lincoln Memorial, where the Rev. Dr. Martin Luther
King, Jr., made his famous "I have a dream" speech. It was that
gathering which Kirkland, almost two decades later, took as the
model for the Solidarity Day demonstration—a demonstration
that brought a quarter-million unionists and their allies to Washington in mid-September 1981 to form a political picket line that

stretched from the Washington Monument to the foot of Capitol Hill.

Not the least of the contributing factors in this spectacular break with the gospel as laid down by St. George was Kirkland's resentment over a quip tossed off by President Reagan in his first month in the White House. When the AFL-CIO Executive Council issued a sulphurous denunciation of the president's initial economic message to Congress, Reagan brushed it aside with the comment that the large vote he had just received from union members was all the proof anyone needed that the moguls of labor were out of touch and out of step with their rank and file. In his keynote on Solidarity Day, Kirkland made a special point of citing the vast rally as visible proof that the president was wrong in telling Americans that "he alone speaks for the working people of this country and that we do not."

It is no derogation of that impressive outpouring of protesters against Reaganomics, however, to note that its size was something less than conclusive evidence of the dimensions of organized labor's constituency or of the extent to which the new breed in the workplace, with its changed expectations, values, and life styles, subscribes to the tenets of the New Deal—Great Society programs that have remained the centerpiece of unionism's credo for a half-century.

Before turning to the 1984 presidential election as a barometer of sentiment on these points, more exploration is needed of the directions in which labor would like to see government go, of the steps the movement is currently taking to strengthen its rapport with the one-fifth of the work force now in its ranks and to recharge its dormant organizing front, and of the likelihood that labor can revive sufficiently to resume its role as hub of a progressive coalition that would reverse the conservative trend of recent years.

First on the federation's action list for government is a national industrial policy under tripartite direction to revitalize decaying industries; stimulate new ones; and rebuild cities, harbors, highways, and other public facilities. Second is a domestic content law to safeguard American jobs by requiring that all goods sold in volume in this country contain specified high percentages of U.S.-made components. These and other proposals designed to shore up existing enterprises and get away from what labor calls "the academic abstractions" of free trade help to explain why many former friends in academe, government, and the general electorate now view labor as a rear-guard force more interested in protecting past gains than in embracing the future.

The Foreign Policy Dilemma

Part of the disenchantment with labor, especially among intellectuals of the liberal-left, is a carryover from the unreserved backing the federation gave to the Vietnam War in the Meany era and to the intransigence he exhibited right up to his death toward any form of detente with Moscow, Peking, or Castro's Cuba, or toward fraternal exchanges between AFL-CIO unions and the state-dominated unions of the Soviet bloc. Kirkland is no less resolute than Meany in his abhorrence of all Communist regimes and in his distrust of their protestations of eagerness to live at peace with the West. Indeed, Kirkland's favorite taunt to the ranking executives of corporate America is that their avidity for cooperating with the Kremlin on any venture in which they see the prospect of making a dollar or a ruble represents "the soft underbelly of capitalism."

However, the foreign policy positions of the AFL-CIO have shifted substantially away from automatic support for every U.S. military excursion put forward in the name of anti-Communism. Similarly, the Pentagon can no longer count on the federation to lobby in favor of giving it a blank check for limitless expansion of the defense budget. In 1985, with the overall federal deficit mounting at an annual rate of roughly $200 billion, the AFL-CIO criticized the President for his recommendations that an additional 12 percent be spent on arms at the same time that he was demanding cuts in social and economic programs. The Anaheim convention rebuked the Reagan administration for putting emphasis on a military rather than a political solution of the conflicts in Central America.

Part of the change in AFL-CIO foreign policy is attributable to the increased influence within the organization's councils of the civil service unions and other groups that were once overshadowed by the building trades and old-line unions in the smokestack industries. The newcomers have now shot ahead as part of the transformation of the economy away from the dominance of the blue-collar and production areas toward majority status for white-collar, professional, and service employment. However, it is a mark of the suppleness of Kirkland's mind and of his skill at building consensus that the rise of these dovish elements has not fundamentally altered the federation's basic posture of antagonism toward the Soviet regime.

How pro-Western its posture still is was reflected in the adoption by overwhelming vote at its 1983 convention in Hollywood, Florida, of a resolution denouncing the shooting down over the Pacific of a Korean airliner by Russian patrol planes as an act of "barbaric mass murder" that was a precise reflection of the political system that rules in the Soviet empire. The reaction of the Reagan administration, the resolution charged, had been true to the form it displayed when the Communist government of Poland cracked down on Solidarnosc—"big talk, small deeds." The White House was reproached for its failure to cut off grain sales, declare East-bloc debts in default, or impose other curbs on business-as-usual with Moscow.

Dialogue Opens Up

The measure of change, thus, is perhaps less in substance than in a new openness and tolerance of dissent inside the AFL-CIO high command. "Lane has opened up dialogue to an unprecedented degree within the higher councils of the federation," says William W. Winpisinger, a self-styled "seat-of-the-pants" socialist, who heads the International Association of Machinists and Aerospace Workers and who began clamoring for Meany's retirement years before the patriarch was ready to go. Another long-time Meany critic, Victor Gotbaum of the American Federation of State, County, and Municipal Employees, puts the change this way: "When you disagree with Lane, it's not a mortal sin as it was with Meany."

The most remarkable instance thus far of the liberating effect of this unusual tolerance for self-criticism in what up to now has been a closed society came with the issuance of a white paper by the Executive Council at its February 1985 meeting in Bal Harbour, Florida.

It was, by all odds, the harshest appraisal the AFL-CIO has ever made of its errors and shortcomings, coupled with a list of highly unorthodox new approaches that the federation's affiliates were urged to experiment with as a means of regaining momentum. The extent of the leadership's new-found willingness to take off its institutional blinders and examine unsparingly why so many of today's workers shun unionization was perhaps best indicated by the release of some key findings—all decidedly unflattering—from an employee and public attitudes survey taken for the AFL-CIO by Louis Harris and Associates.

According to the poll, nearly two-thirds of all workers outside union ranks believe that union leaders compel members to go along with decisions they don't make and often don't like on strikes and other issues. Well over half the nonunionists are convinced unions increase the risk that companies will go out of business, stifle individual initiative, and fight change. In the population generally, fully 50 percent express the view that most union leaders no longer represent the workers in their unions. The white paper said workers who do belong to unions voiced far more positive opinions about their organizations, but no figures were made public and all requests for additional data on this point were rebuffed.

The Harris pollsters, in association with Professors James L. Medoff of Harvard and Thomas A. Kochan of Massachusetts Institute of Technology, came up with this profile of the contemporary work force:

Americans by and large see themselves as independent, self-confident, self-reliant, and skeptical of claims of authority. In line with that perception, workers, particularly better-educated workers, are becoming more insistent on securing more freedom in the workplace. It is increasingly true that the measure of a good job is high discretion as much as high pay. And despite claims to the contrary, the 'work ethic'—the personal need to do one's best on the job—is stronger in the United States than in other western democracies.

The most striking new attitudinal factor cited in the survey was "a shift in which Americans are less likely to see work as a straight economic transaction providing a means of survival and more likely to see it as a means of self-expression and self-development." In consonance with this exaltation of individual fulfillment, the Bal Harbour manifesto calls on unions to exhibit flexibility in both organizing and collective bargaining, a position sharply at variance with the rigidity of the practices that many have carried over almost unchanged from the 1930s.

These recommendations are predicated on the premise that the movement must expand its notion of what workers can do through their unions, and not merely try to do better what unions have always done. The manifesto recognizes, however, that not much will happen in this direction unless unions build stronger rapport with their own rank and file. That means convincing the members that they, not their officials, are the organization and the determiners of policy in fact as well as slogan.

Consideration is urged for creating new classes of membership outside established bargaining units. A primary target for such recruiting would be an estimated 27 million workers who once belonged to unions but no longer do—a group double the presently paid up membership of the entire AFL-CIO. Most of these ex-members, according to the report, left their old union only because they lost or left their unionized job. In addition, the federation itself is issuing credit cards and studying the practicality of offering low-premium insurance, job training and information, discount programs for purchasing consumer goods, or other services to workers reluctant to take out union cards, in the hope that these workers will eventually become full-fledged unionists.

These novel approaches to broadening the orbit of union interaction with the four-fifths of all wage earners now unaffiliated are more than matched by the proposed changes in collective bargaining that many might deem heretical in a movement whose rhetoric still rumbles with echoes of the nineteenth-century Homestead and Pullman strikes, the Ludlow Massacre, and other bygone labor wars. The white paper notes a widespread moderating of hate-the-boss attitudes among workers and urges unions, wherever employers show a disposition to deal in good faith, to shelve adversarial stances at the bargaining table in favor of mediation, arbitration, or other devices for harmonious adjustment of differences.

In place of the industrywide patterns that forced all companies into a straitjacket of identical wages, fringe benefits, and other contract terms, the manifesto recognizes that competitive pressures on the employer side and the itch for self-expression on the employee side combine to make advisable the development and effectuation by unions of multiple models for representing workers, tailored to the needs and concerns of different groups.

As one example, the AFL-CIO suggests negotiating minimum guarantees that will serve as a floor for individual bargaining on wage premiums, fringe benefits, or other deviations from the norm. The stress on giving rank-and-file workers a more assertive voice in decisions that affect their jobs finds even more striking expression in the report's recommendation that labor seek to accelerate the movement in many industries to establish quality-of-worklife programs under joint union-company auspices. The central purpose of these programs is to give workers a heightened sense of partnership in the success of their companies through employee participation in workplace decision making, but many unions have viewed them coolly as employer-fostered schemes to co-opt workers and undercut collective bargaining. While conceding that some programs have been used for purposes of avoiding unions, the report accents the positive results possible when unions make them effective vehicles for worker dignity and job satisfaction.

Unions and Employers

It would be disingenuous, however, to pretend that everything in the Bal Harbour declaration points toward a period of sweetness and light in relations with management. Far from envisaging a trend on the employer side toward "disarmament," the report estimates that 75 percent of all companies now hire professional consultants, at an estimated cost of more than $100 million a year, to guide them in keeping out unions. As a counter to such resistance, the AFL-CIO urges its affiliates to endeavor to impose employer neutrality in union organizing campaigns through more skillful manipulation of public opinion and through greater use of a sophisticated new technique known as the coordinated corporate campaign.

The first major application of this strategy brought victory to the Amalgamated Clothing and Textile Workers Union in 1980 after such traditional weapons as strikes and a global consumer boycott had proved virtually useless in effecting a cease-fire in the long war against unionization by the J.P. Stevens textile empire. In the Stevens campaign, the union turned money power, normally the boss's area of unquestioned dominance, into an instrument for isolating the company from the rest of the Wall Street community and thus forcing it to settle.

The tens of billions of dollars in employee pension funds under joint union-management trusteeship gave the Amalgamated the leverage it needed to go after major banks, insurance companies, and corporations linked to Stevens by loan arrangements or interlocking directorates. Such financial giants as the Manufacturers Hanover Bank, Avon Products, New York Life, and Metropolitan Life felt the heat in a variety of ways. Their cumulative pressure was universally viewed as the decisive element in Steven's decision to sign its first union contract after seventeen years of struggle in which the AFL-CIO had labeled the southern textile chain the number one violator of the country's labor laws. Since then somewhat similar campaigns have helped produce a turnaround toward amicable relations at two other union-management battlegrounds—Litton Industries and the Beverly Enterprises chain of nursing homes.

The federation does not delude itself, however, that the climate for unionization and collective bargaining will improve dramatically without passage of changes in the basic labor law to reduce the danger of obstructionism by a new generation of employers who, in the manifesto's words, "are bent on avoiding unionization at all costs and who are left largely free to do so by a law that has proven to be impotent and a Labor Board that is inert."

For a movement that owes a substantial proportion of the members it now has to the union security arrangements that made employers a more consequential factor in union recruitment in the 1950s and 1960s than any organizing zeal by the unions themselves, there is undoubtedly an element of paranoia in the blanket character of the federation's assessment of current employer attitudes. The report quotes as gospel an unspecified study of organizing campaigns in the private sector that purports to show that 95 percent of employers actively resist unionization.

Nevertheless, it is clear that Lane Kirkland and his associates are still traumatized by the shock they experienced in 1978 when almost all sectors of business, big and small alike, formed a united front to kill via a filibuster by their friends in the Senate a relatively mild labor reform law that had been worked out through compromise between the AFL-CIO, the Carter White House, and the leadership of the Democratic majorities in both the House and Senate. By way of tempering employer hostility to the measure, the AFL-CIO had agreed to sacrifice two of its most cherished objectives: repeal of Section 14b of the Taft-Hartley Act, which gave right-to-work laws precedence over the federal law's permit for negotiation of union-shop contracts, and certification of unions as sole bargaining representative on the basis of the signing of membership applications by 60 percent of the workers, as against the standard requirement for a majority pro-union vote in an NLRB election.

What startled the federation leadership was the refusal of the heads of companies that had cordial union relations for twenty or thirty years to break ranks and endorse the watered-down measure after a majority in the Business Roundtable, the coordinating group for the biggest of big business, had voted to join the National Association of Manufacturers and the United States Chamber of Commerce in denouncing it as a union power grab.

That closing of ranks on the industry side led to the breakup of the Labor Management Group, a summit-level think tank formed under the auspices of Professor John T. Dunlop of Harvard University when he was Secretary of Labor in the Ford cabinet. The group, operating outside the framework of government, had provided a forum for private meetings in which the top leaders of industry and unionism sought a meeting of minds on such questions of public policy as taxes, inflation, trade, unemployment, and energy. When the management members of the panel stood shoulder to shoulder with old-line union-haters in the fight over labor law reform, Kirkland, then the federation's secretary-treasurer, cited their position as proof that the field marshals of big business were using instrumentalities such as the Labor Management Group to mask behind a veneer of civility their desire to bring back the master-servant relationship in dealings with their work force.

The rupture ended in 1981 when Dunlop capitalized on initiatives from the former industry members to persuade Kirkland to join in reviving the group, with Clifton C. Garvin, Jr., chief executive officer of Exxon, serving beside Kirkland as co-chairman. The AFL-CIO head set as a pre-condition the drawing up of a formal charter subscribed to by both sides, in which each recognized the legitimacy of the other's right to exist.

From the give and take on drafting the charter—a process that often approached in intricacy the formulation of a treaty between superpowers—came a document aimed at assuring noninflationary economic growth and full employment through a new spirit of mutual trust and cooperation between management and unions. The charter affirmed that "a free labor movement and a free enterprise economy are essential to the achievement of social and political stability and economic prosperity for all." The rest of the joint pronouncement brimmed over with similarly amorphous encomia to free unions, free collective bargaining, and free enterprise as the fountainheads of well-being out of which sprang America's greatness.

Desultory meetings over the Reagan years have brought agreement by the kingpins of industry and unionism on recommendations for containing the skyrocketing cost of health care and for an ambitious fifteen-year program of governmental investment in highways, bridges, water supply, and sewage systems. But nothing concrete has come out of the project that from the outset has ranked topmost in interest for Kirkland and his fellow-potentates on the union side: the formulation of a joint statement that would define criteria designed to give substance to the pieties in the group's charter extolling the virtues of free unions and free collective bargaining.

Reliance on Politics

The Bal Harbour white paper makes plain the union establishment's conviction that it must rely much more heavily on politics than on any spread of the ecumenical spirit within industry to generate a more hospitable climate for unionism. It cites the growth of union membership in all branches of the civil service—a growth that added a million public employees to the AFL-CIO roster in the last twelve years, while membership in the private sector was declining by 2 million—as primarily attributable to favorable legislation and executive orders. Similarly, the report gives credit to sympathetic governmental policy for helping unions in Canada to grow from roughly 30 percent of the work force in 1963 to 40 percent in 1983. In the United States union membership was dropping from 30 percent to 20 percent during the same period.

The frustrations left in the wake of the AFL-CIO's unsuccessful bid for labor law reform in 1978 have been compounded by the endless round of political defeats and governmental rebuffs sustained since Ronald Reagan entered the White House. Labor's resentment was expressed in the 1984 presidential campaign by a degree of involvement that far exceeded in cost and intensity any previous effort by unions to oust an incumbent president.

In pursuance of that all-eclipsing goal, Kirkland forged an unprecedented unity among the normally fractious members of the Executive Council, behind a game plan to make the AFL-CIO the decisive element in nominating and electing its favorite, former Vice President Walter F. Mondale, as Reagan's successor. Instead of following its traditional practice of waiting until both major parties held their nominating conventions before making its own endorsement, the AFL-CIO gave its official blessing to Mondale four months before the first state primary and put its well-heeled, highly sophisticated political apparatus, the Committee on Political Education (COPE), in action to smooth his road to the White House.

The undisguised purpose was to set in motion an irresistible steamroller that would reduce the nominating process to a charade, but the heavy-handedness of the federation's maneuver made Mondale vulnerable to charges by his primary rivals that he had become a captive of the "labor bosses." Though bitterly denied by both Mondale and labor, that charge proved damaging in the early New England contests. Infuriated by the depiction of unions as a "special interest," the federation marshalled its legions in the big industrial states, notably Illinois, Pennsylvania, and New York, with consummate effectiveness. Few observers questioned that labor was the indispensable element in Mondale's designation as the Democratic nominee.

Labor's magic, however, was conspicuously absent in the main event. The Reagan forces made a decision at the start to soft-pedal the issue of Mondale's alleged subservience to the union bosses. Their private polls showed that, in the minds of many independent voters, the union label had been stamped indelibly on Mondale by the prominence given to that charge by Senators Gary Hart of Colorado and John Glenn of Ohio when they were campaigning against the former vice president in the primaries. The president's advisers felt that the support of these swing voters was safely in the Reagan column and that the sole effect of hammering away at the question of union domination would be to jeopardize the strong backing Reagan counted on receiving from rank-and-file unionists.

The election returns appeared to vindicate the G.O.P. strategy on both counts. The perception of Mondale as a mouthpiece for big labor contributed to the decision of many independent voters to line up behind Reagan, even though the president's whole record might have been expected to lend at least as much credibility to labor's charges that he was a servitor of the special interests of big business. On the union side, Kirkland's warnings to his flock that "a vote for Ronald Reagan is a vote for the worst enemies of working men and women" proved singularly unpersuasive. Experience has taught the AFL-CIO leaders that they must corral a minimum vote of 65 percent in union households if their presidential choice is to triumph over a conservative tilt in the rest of the electorate. Mondale got only 55 percent—this in the face of an incessant drumfire by labor's high command of attacks on Reagan as a champion of "union-busters and scab-herders."

More disturbing from the standpoint of the AFL-CIO hierarchy was the evidence the union vote supplied of upper-middle-class alienation within the movement, an alienation freighted with racist overtones. Support for President Reagan was strongest among white male unionists under forty and among workers in the $25,000 to $50,000 income bracket, their high earnings in important measure a testimonial to the struggles and sacrifices of labor's pioneers. Exit polls indicated that Reagan got half or slightly more of the total white union vote, even though the unaffiliated International Brotherhood of Teamsters was the only major union to endorse him.

What saved the leadership from a debacle in the union response was the tidal wave of support Mondale received from black unionists and their families. Fully 95 percent of their vote went to the former vice president, but any comfort the federation could take from that astonishing margin had to be tempered by remembrance of how completely these same black unionists had rejected their leaders' guidance on how to vote in the primaries. Before the first state tally Kirkland had set up a special task force of 200 ranking black union officials and assigned them the job of persuading the black rank and file that they would be throwing their primary votes away if they cast them for Jesse Jackson in preference to Mondale. The leader's advice did not register: black unionists voted overwhelmingly with blacks in the rest of the population—for Jackson in the primaries, for Mondale in the final election when Reagan was the only alternative. Considerations of race were clearly a much more potent spur than unionism.

The place where the labor establishment had solid basis for self-congratulations on its 1984 election performance was not the presidential race, on which it expended such extravagant attention, but the congressional and gubernatorial contests, where victory went to nearly two-thirds of those whom labor endorsed, the great bulk of them Democrats. The federation's own polls indicated that 72 percent of its members voted for Democratic Senate candidates and 69 percent for Democratic House candidates. These results encouraged many union chiefs to hope that Democrats, with union help, could win control of both houses of Congress in 1986, especially if the staggering budget and trade deficits under which the country is toiling plunge the economy into another recession, as many top unionists believe they will.

One difficulty with these expectations for the 1986 balloting is that the great majority of unions in the private sector are still bleeding from the wounds they sustained in the recession of 1980–82; their ability to withstand another crippling downturn is decidedly in doubt. An even more fundamental difficulty for labor as a national political force is reflected in an aspect of the 1984 experience that the otherwise forthright manifesto issued at Bal Harbour refuses to address, except by the most oblique indirection. This relates to the tactical implications for unions of the counter-productiveness of many of their efforts at the presidential level as contrasted with the singular success they recorded in congressional and state races.

The explanation for this disparity, in my estimation, is that designations at the local level are made by state and city central bodies and viewed by union members and the general citizenry alike as standard expressions of local civic involvement akin to the endorsements regularly made by local business and professional organizations. By contrast, at the presidential level, the demonology of American politics takes over. For large sections of the electorate, the stereotypical image of labor remains the caricature cartoonists used to the point of nausea in depicting George Meany in the quarter century of his imperious rule over the federation: a baleful figure with bulging belly and clenched cigar, hurling monkey wrenches at the White House and the Capitol. That image seems to explain why Harris polls taken over the last two decades have consistently shown the leaders of organized labor lodged in the cellar in terms of public confidence as against the leaders of all other American institutions.

Popular Perceptions

Neither the atrophy of union labor's muscle in recent years nor the gentility that is the hallmark of Lane Kirkland, a soft-spoken scion of antebellum southern plantation owners, whose own union career started as a researcher in the musty headquarters of the old AFL, has done much to alter the popular perception of the national labor establishment as a cabal of union bosses misusing their monopoly power to rule and ruin industry. In the wake of the presidential election, many leaders of the Democratic Party from the South and West began clamoring for action to convince voters that the party was not taking its orders on programs and candidates from organized labor. Even Paul G. Kirk, Jr., of Massachusetts, who was named Democratic National Chairman with labor's full backing after the 1984 voting, felt obliged to suggest publicly that the AFL-CIO hold back on any 1988 endorsement until after all aspirants for the Democratic designation had had an opportunity to employ the primary process to demonstrate the breadth of their popular base and appeal.

However, Kirkland shows no disposition to take the hint. In a news conference in mid-March 1985, he said he thought the chances were "very good" that the federation would go the same route of seeking to establish well in advance of the primaries whether two-thirds or more of its affiliates were prepared to form a united front to concentrate all energies on getting a particular candidate nominated and elected. The Anaheim convention in October formally endorsed that plan of action. Kirkland's criticisms of the 1984 campaign were directed not at labor's performance but at the "harmful" effects of the proliferation of primaries on the Democratic party and at the breakdown of party discipline that he ascribed to the so-called reforms in party structure and rules pushed through when Vietnam War resisters, feminists, gay liberationists, and other related types won control of the convention machinery and nominated George McGovern in 1972. Meany was so outraged at the capture of the party by elements he characterized as "kooks and crypto-Communists" that he kept the AFL-CIO neutral that year, a detachment that gave building trades and maritime unions all the freedom they needed to plump for the reelection of Richard M. Nixon. A principal objective ever since has been to undo the 1972 reforms and enhance the influence within the party of labor and the professional politicians with whom the AFL-CIO's political operatives have been most at ease.

That stance makes for difficulties in building the alliances the labor movement plainly requires if it is to serve as the hub of a coalition broad enough to arrest the rightward drift in national politics and install a president and Congress dedicated to an expansionist role for government in ministering to social needs and strengthening the economy. In the stridency of its rhetoric, labor matches and usually outstrips the activists advocating faster governmental action in such fields as civil rights, environmental protection, and equity for the poor and exploited. The burden of its indictment of Reaganism in 1984 was that the president was dismantling government as a shield for the powerless and afflicted while allowing the giant corporations and the overprivileged to engorge themselves.

But the very nature of a "bread-and-butter" movement operating within the enterprise system and dedicated to middle-class values causes clashes between such ultra-populist sentiments and the pragmatic dominance of pocketbook interests, which characterized so much of the rank-and-file response to the Reagan-Mondale choice. The same ambivalence accounts for the indecision unions often show on where to draw the line between antagonism and cooperation in their relations with management, both at the bargaining table and in public affairs. The unacknowledged reality behind the Bal Harbour manifesto is that all the changes the last decade of social and economic upheaval have brought in the workplace have made the labor hierarchy more aware than ever of how desperately it needs a restoration of the *entente cordiale* that prevailed without formal acknowledgment by either side through most of the period from 1950 to 1975.

The mainstream of American unionism is not turning left toward the organization of an independent labor party or other forms of what Kirkland derides as "revolutionary defeatism." Here and there grassroots rebels may embrace militant tactics of social protest in Rust Belt communities devastated by the shutdown of steel mills or factories, or in farm areas where they join with those shouting down auctioneers selling off a distressed farm, but extremist expressions get no encouragement from AFL-CIO headquarters. The Solidarity Day outpouring of 1981 stands alone as the one labor March on Washington, though smaller demonstrations have become commonplace at state houses and city halls around the country.

"Solidarity," as expressed in the sanctity of the picket line, remains an uncertain concept, ignored as often as it is heeded. Even in the airlines, where the demolition of the PATCO air controller's union and the firing of all its striking members by the president provided the most graphic evidence any labor movement ever had of the vulnerability of unions when they fail to stand together, the first test after the Bal Harbour declaration resulted in another dismal collapse of unity. Unionized mechanics struck against a second round of givebacks demanded by Pan American World Airways only to have their lines pierced by unionized pilots and flight attendants. The strikers themselves hoisted the white flag when a threat by the airline to hire permanent replacements brought unmistakable signs that the mechanics would scab on themselves if their union did not settle.

Union ranks held more firmly in a subsequent strike at United, but the most dramatic developments in airline industrial relations in 1985 involved a switch away from picket lines toward the exercise of union leverage to form alliances with labor's favorites among competing factions in battles within management for corporate control. Thus, at Trans World Airlines and Frontier, the pilots and other unions used pledges of substantial concessions in wages and work rules to make themselves the pivotal force in determining who would be boss of the two lines. In neither case were they overjoyed with the winner, but the alternative would have been much worse, in their estimation. Early in 1986 the rupturing of an ambitious experiment in power-sharing by unions and management at Eastern Airlines came close to plunging the carrier into bankruptcy and involved labor once again in a scramble to determine dominance in the corporate executive suite.

All of which brings us back to the most fundamental of labor's problems as it gropes for new approaches to reorganizing the organized and organizing the unorganized: its inability to define its mission in terms that will take the place of "more" as a spur to unionization. "What is this union business all about if it's not delivering the highest buck to our members and that's what I do," was the crisp summary of union function that Jimmy Hoffa made his watchword.

The Bal Harbour white paper correctly notes that, even where unions still can deliver by that standard, the changing priorities of the new work force have made more money something less than an adequate goal. That is not only because many young working men and women, particularly in two-income families, take high wages as their due but even more because experience in the inflationary decade of the 1970s, when unions were racking up the fattest increases in their history, taught millions of workers that such increases were illusory when higher prices ate them up faster than they could be spent. The average wage nearly doubled from $114 a week at the beginning of the decade to $224 at the end but, in purchasing power after the bite of higher prices and taxes, the typical worker wound up 3.5 percent worse off.

Today, with inflation at least temporarily in check, the holdback stems from the cost-cutting squeeze exerted by imports, deregulation, and nonunion penetration of union territory. The results extend beyond a widespread depression of wages in a period of economic upturn to the malignancies inherent in the spread of two-tier pay scales pitting young workers against old, the building up of a second-class work force deprived of job security or fringe protection through increased use by businesses of part-timers and temporaries to hold down the core force of regular employees, and the contracting out or shipment overseas of work formerly done in the employer's own facilities. With the country now seemingly reconciled to levels of joblessness nearly double those that were once taken as the outer limit of acceptability, unions confront these challenges to higher wages and living standards with knowledge that millions of workers are readily available to take over struck jobs in preference to moldering on the idle list or picking up catch-as-catch-can employment at the minimum wage. Worse still, the shakeout of facilities in declining industries or those undergoing rapid shifts in technology pushes locals affiliated with the same parent union into dog-eat-dog scrambles in which they feel compelled to compete with one another in sacrificing work rules or making wage concessions, in hopes that absentee decision makers half a world away will give their plant preference in deciding which units to keep open and which to abandon.

The inescapability of such crosspulls in the interdependent world economy of these closing years of the twentieth century helps to explain the willingness the federation displays in its white paper to move away from its historic insistence on ironclad lines of compartmentalization separating the functions of management and labor. Its endorsement of jointly conceived and administered quality-of-worklife programs represents a start toward making unions and their rank and file full-fledged partners in industrial decision making and gain sharing at every level from shop floor and office to corporate boardroom.

Such a movement in the United States is unlikely ever to take on the mandatory status it has acquired through the co-determination laws of West Germany and other Common Market countries, but the trend is toward a much more enterprise-oriented brand of unionism than this country has ever known—a trend marked by the spread of profit sharing, bonuses in place of fixed pay increases, employee stock ownership, union representation on company boards, and a widespread dismantling of authoritarian command structures in favor of more participatory democracy in the workplace. The transformation will not be easy nor is its success assured, but the new open-mindedness of the Bal Habour declaration provides the first substantial foundation in thirty years for optimism that labor will measure up to the challenges confronting it if management, with so much more at stake in the survival of free enterprise, meets it halfway.

2

WALTER GALENSON

The Historical Role of American Trade Unionism

A hallmark of a democratic country is an organized labor movement that is independent of government and employers. The traditional *modus operandi* of trade unions was to bargain directly with employers, but over time they moved toward sponsoring government legislation designed to further the interests of their members. Western trade unionism generally has been a democratic force, offsetting the accumulation of power in the hands of employers or the government. This is not always true: for example, Communist-dominated unions in France and Italy have advocated the establishment of totalitarian states that would presumably reduce them to the status of government bureaus, as in all Communist countries. Other unions have been dedicated to the replacement of private enterprise by some form of trade union hegemony, usually termed anarcho-syndicalism. Most have contributed to the formation of political parties that advocate mixed economies in which the government exercises some control of the "commanding heights," leaving the rest in private hands.

There is one great exception—the American labor movement. Despite many attempts in the past century to steer it in a socialist or Communist direction, it remains firmly dedicated to the capitalist system. This has been true despite the intense buffeting unions have received periodically from employers who preferred to deal directly with their employees without any union representation. On occasion, segments of the labor movement have been tempted to try independent labor-oriented political parties, but the American political, social, and economic environment ruled out any chance of success. The United States remains the only democratic nation that does not have a major political party allied with trade unions and professing some form of socialism.

Unions are more responsible for the enhanced economic security enjoyed by Americans than generally is realized. In preparation for the 1984 congressional elections, for example, the AFL-CIO tabulated the votes of congressmen on seventeen measures that came before the House and Senate, and although most issues were of particular interest to union members, some were more general, including affordable telephone service, the Equal Rights Amendment, fairness in taxes, federal aid to education, helping the unemployed avoid mortgage foreclosures, and community relief programs.

Some might question whether this broad concern with public welfare, often moving the unions into controversial areas, is what union members want from their organizations. Diffusion of membership loyalty is a danger, not only because of differences of opinion on some issues among members, but also because by supporting social causes, unions lose some of their thrust as defenders of parochial interests and instead become general service organizations. Paradoxically, union support for social legislation tends to reduce the power of unions as workers look increasingly to government for protection. In the full-fledged welfare states of Northern Europe, for instance, it is not always clear what functions appropriately remain with unions. While it is mainly the AFL-CIO that gets involved in social issues, some national union affiliates have also moved in this direction, and it is a question that unions will continue to face. Unions are born of social need and steeped in a progressive social tradition, and a sense of history is important in assessing what the future impact of the labor movement on American society will be.

The Origins of American Trade Unionism

The modern American labor movement received its real start in the 1880s. Why were these years favorable for union organization? A major factor was an upswing in the business cycle in the early 1880s after some years of recession. Wages in the industry and building trades had fallen almost 20 percent from 1870 to 1879. Selig Perlman writes:

> The business depression of 1873 to 1879 was a critical period in the American labor movement. The old national trade unions either went to pieces, or retained a merely nominal existence. Employers sought to free themselves from the restrictions that the trade unions had imposed upon them during the years preceding the crisis. They consequently added a systematic policy of lockouts, blacklists, and of legal prosecution to the already crushing weight of hard times and unemployment.[1]

Another major factor was the formation of a critical mass of craftsmen, who were the backbone of the new unionism. A substantial immigration of skilled blue-collar workers added to the growth of the indigenous labor force. Between 1870 and 1880, the population of the U.S. grew by 26 percent, and some 875,000 of the immigrants in that decade described themselves as skilled workers. Migrants from Britain and Germany predominated, bringing with them not only their trades but a tradition of socialism as well.

A number of evanescent unions had been established earlier, as well as several that were to remain permanent fixtures: organizations of printers, bricklayers, machinists, and railway workers, among others. The Knights of Labor, the first major attempt at a national confederation, began as a secret organization in 1869 and went public in 1878. It was not until 1881, however, that a number of craft unions, some of them newly established, formed the Federation of Organized Trades and Labor Unions, which joined with others a few years later in 1886 into the American Federation of Labor (AFL).

Many of the men who took the lead in the new organization had come to unionism through some contact with socialist doctrines. Samuel Gompers, the dominant figure in the AFL until his death in 1924, had immigrated to the United States from England with his parents in 1863. His close relationship with socialist Adolph

Strasser and others in the cigar makers' trade had left an indelible mark, giving him the grounding both in idealism and class consciousness that produced many strong leaders of American unions.[2] His closest collaborator in the early years of the AFL, Peter J. McGuire, was a native of New York City and for a period of years was an active member of the Social Democratic Party.

However, in running their organizations both men rejected any political challenge to management control and private property. They were aware that the introduction of partisan politics into the unions would have been suicidal. McGuire, who led for its first twenty years the largest union in the country, the Brotherhood of Carpenters, said in a speech at the 1898 convention of the AFL, at the twilight of his long union career:

We have never made it a test of membership in the American Federation of Labor, or in any other trade union, that a member should belong to any political party or endorse any economic creed. . . . Because some of us stand firmly by the historical uniting and cohesive character of the trade union movement, we are called "pure and simple." Better any time a pure and simple trade unionist than an impure and complex confusionist. . . . It is time we notified the men of isms and schisms in the labor movement that the trade union can never be side-tracked or befogged by economic or debatable small potato politics. In this country let us use all political parties.[3]

The immediate concern of the early trade union leaders was the labor conditions that most affected their constituents. Long hours of work were a major grievance. The standard working day was ten hours, six days a week. In some of the seasonal trades, such as construction, men worked from sunup to sundown in summer and faced long periods of idleness in winter. Many workers participated in a general strike for the eight-hour day on May 1, 1886, and though the turnout disappointed its organizers, some workers did achieve this objective. In general, working hours declined slowly, and it was not until after World War I that a fifty-hour week became the rule, although many union workers had achieved it by the turn of the century.

Raising the wages of workers also stood high on the union agenda. Wages and living standards were relatively high in the United States, drawing many immigrants to American shores. The human costs of rapid industrialization were also high, as revealed by the famous muckraking books that appeared at the time. But H.G. Wells, when he visited New York, was struck by its affluence compared to London. "Even in the congested entrances, the filthy back streets of the East Side, I find myself saying as a thing remarkable: 'These people have money to spend.'"

During the twenty-five years before World War I there was no conspicuous or concentrated change in the quality of British working life—from 1900 to 1913, real wages actually fell in Britain. In contrast, American workers enjoyed a 5 percent rise during the same years. Of even greater significance is that there were very few years from 1881 to 1913 in which both money and real wages failed to rise in the United States. This was largely a consequence of the impressive growth of the American economy. For trade unions, it meant that they could deliver to their members a steady stream of wage increases through collective bargaining efforts. The expectation of constant improvement influenced the philosophy of their leaders, as shown by the famous testimony of Adolph Strasser, Gompers' mentor, before the Senate Committee on Education and Labor in 1883:

Q. You are seeking to improve home matters first?
A. Yes sir. I look first to the trade I represent, I look first to cigars, to interests of men who employ me to represent their interests.
Q. I was only asking you in regard to your ultimate ends.
A. We have no ultimate ends. We are going on from day to day. We are fighting only for immediate objects—objects that can be realized in a few years.
Q. You want something better to eat, and to wear, and better houses to live in?
A. Yes, we want to dress better and to live better and become better citizens generally.

No Utopia, no Commonwealth of Toil, no socialist nirvana motivated these men. It did not seem necessary to transform society to achieve the objectives of the American working man. Only when the future turned black, as it did during the Great Depression, was there a serious upsurge of radical sentiment.

Class Consciousness

There were a number of obstacles to unionization, apart from the ever-present unwillingness of employers to engage in collective

bargaining. Massive immigration provided a continuous supply of
low-cost labor that could be used to undermine union standards.
American labor has always advocated restriction of immigration;
the following example from a union publication in 1889 shows that
labor's current concern about immigration has deep historical
roots:

In [New York] . . . it will probably be a tough struggle with Castle Garden
[the original port of entry] to contend against, unless Congress passes
some law to protect us . . . . No man of family with living expenses at fifty
to sixty dollars for rent and food can compete with the 'birds of passage'
from Great Britain, who hire a room for $1.50 a week and cook their
meals. Then when the dull season comes they take flight to Europe with
the earnings of several months to live comfortably, while American
citizens must walk the streets idle in search of work to keep their
families.[4]

While ethnic diversity was an obstacle to organization, the
unions did perform a positive social service by helping relieve tensions among the various groups. Immigrants tended to join fraternal and religious organizations along ethnic lines. Particularly in
smaller communities, there were ethnocentric barriers to wider
social intercourse. For example, most of the textile workers in
New Bedford, Massachusetts were Portuguese, and many of the
government offices in this city conducted their business in that
language. Trade unions were among the few social institutions in
which ethnic groups found a common interest and met with people
with whom they would not have ordinarily fraternized.

The record of American trade unions on racial discrimination
reflects the attitudes of the general public from which they drew
their members. Some national unions accepted blacks from the
start, although they were often obliged to set up local unions along
color lines, particularly in the South. National officers warned
recalcitrant unions that if they excluded blacks, they would be
creating a competitive group that could undermine union standards. Other national unions had color bars written into their constitutions. The racial integration problem was not acute until the
1920s, when thousands of blacks flocked from the South to the
North in search of jobs.

Some of the early leaders of labor may have been imbued with a
degree of class consciousness as a result of their early exposure to

socialist doctrine, but American workers were generally not affected by this psychological attribute that still prevails in much of Europe. Class consciousness facilitates union organization, as it raises the level of worker solidarity from the occupation to the entire working class, making the procurement of strikebreakers more difficult. Differences in national origin, cutting vertically through the labor force, were in large part responsible for the lack of class consciousness. Italian, German, Polish, French Canadian, and Jewish workers were just as likely to feel a community of interest with employers of the same national origin as with workers in other national groups. One way in which many unions dealt with this problem was to create locals based on language rather than skill or location. One of the largest locals of the International Ladies' Garment Workers Union, which was preponderantly Jewish in its early years, was an Italian local led by the flamboyant Luigi Antonini. Many unions published portions of their newspapers in foreign languages.

The crafts organized by the early unions were exclusively male. The first union to organize women on any scale was the International Ladies' Garment Workers Union, founded in 1900. It was established in the New York City market a decade later after a series of strikes. Most of its top officers were men despite the fact that the majority of the members were women.

The Triumph of Business Unionism

The economic instability of the early 1890s had led to a temporary setback for the AFL unions. Business picked up in 1898 and the unions had been there to take advantage of prosperity. Membership in the AFL rose from 278,000 in 1898 to 1,676,000 in 1904. This was achieved despite the first organized employer counteroffensive. Open-shop committees were set up in the major industrial centers, and employers pledged not to hire union men. A national association, the Citizens' Industrial Alliance, was established to coordinate the activities of the local anti-union groups. Eminent public figures were enlisted to back the alliance, among them President Charles Eliot of Harvard University, who referred in *Harper's* magazine to a strikebreaker as an "American hero" and urged employers to allow "no sacrifice of the independent American worker to the labor union."

To counter the anti-union drive, a group of liberal employers and public figures, together with Gompers and other union leaders, formed the National Civic Federation, headed by such dignitaries as Senator Mark Hanna and August Belmont. Gompers was severely criticized by socialists both within and outside the AFL for collaborating with capitalists, and in return he praised the liberal employers "who have concluded that antagonism to organized labor is vain and unprofitable, and who see the wisdom of a policy of conciliation."

The open-shop campaign slowed union expansion and it was not until 1911 that unions again reached the 1904 level. But growth resumed, and AFL membership reached the 3 million mark by the eve of American entrance into the European war. However, heavy industry remained solidly nonunion. After defeating a strike in 1901, the U.S. Steel Corporation systematically rid itself of all union remnants. If J.P. Morgan, Charles Schwab, and Elbert Gary had decided to live with unions, the course of American history could have been much different.

During these years, the AFL faced a challenge to its domination of the labor movement. The Industrial Workers of the World (IWW) was formed in 1905 by the Western Federation of Miners, an independent union of metal miners, and several East Coast-based socialist factions. Both the Miners and the socialists eventually dropped out, leaving an organization that catered to migratory and unskilled workers of the West—lumberjacks, farm workers, seamen, longshoremen. The IWW favored direct strike action rather than collective bargaining. In its view, capitalism would eventually be brought down by a nationwide general strike and replaced by a federation of trade unions, a doctrine called syndicalism. In the meantime, strikes were to be used to improve working conditions. Formal contracts were to be eschewed; the IWW simply posted its wage list. Members were urged not to participate in elections or any other activities of the government. To do so, the IWW believed, would have represented acquiescence in the capitalist system.

This philosophy was well suited to IWW constituents—rootless, unmarried men who worked seasonally in the forests, on the farms, and on the waterfront, and wintered in flophouses in San Francisco and other western cities. Labor relations shared the western tradition of violence, and the collective bargaining tactics of the skilled workers represented by the AFL were alien to IWW members. The AFL unions warned their members to have nothing to do with the IWW, but there was little direct conflict between the two organizations since there was little overlap between the groups to which each appealed.

The IWW led some major strikes, including several in the East, but they left little in the way of organization behind. The IWW leaders were excellent strike tacticians but weak administrators. Their militancy and their refusal to cooperate in the war effort after 1917 led to their undoing. A combination of employer violence and government repression decimated their ranks. Frank H. Little, a member of the IWW executive board, was lynched in Butte, Montana, in 1917. Hundreds of members including their top officer, the charismatic William (Big Bill) Haywood, were indicted under espionage and criminal syndicalism statutes and many were jailed. Haywood left the country while out on bail and made his way to the newly established Soviet Union, where he was hailed as a labor hero. But he soon found out that Communism and syndicalism were irreconcilable, and he lived out his years in a dingy Moscow apartment, ignored by the Communists. When he died, however, his status was raised and his remains were interred in the Soviet pantheon, the Kremlin Wall, an honor accorded only one other American, John Reed.

By the end of the first World War, the IWW had virtually ceased to exist. Even if it had not been subject to persecution, its days were numbered simply because its constituency was fading away. The migratory workers were settling down and eventually their places were taken by Mexican migrants who were more difficult to organize. The IWW did leave a legacy of some importance: the leaders of some unions that were formed in the 1930s—lumber workers, seamen—had been brought up in the IWW and imparted to the new organizations something of an IWW flavor. The philosophy of the IWW was a purely pragmatic response to specific conditions that prevailed on the western frontier of the United States. It is not surprising that recent books and movies have romanticized it; it was, after all, a part of the Old West.

Jurisdictional Disputes

One aspect of American trade unionism that has often been condemned but never well understood is the emphasis American unions placed on the principle of exclusive jurisdiction. The AFL was reluctant to charter a new union when its proposed area of work was already claimed by an existing organization. "That work belongs to us" was a constant refrain. It was Selig Perlman, in his famous *Theory of the Labor Movement*, who first pointed out that deprived of class consciousness as an organizing device, American unions had to rely on job consciousness. The craft unions staked out a particular area of work and claimed that they had what amounted to a property right in it, which they were willing to defend with whatever weapons were available to them. Jurisdictional disputes were simply a reflection of this principle.

When unionism was in its infancy and organization was minimal, there was little cause for conflict. As the unions grew and craft lines became blurred, particularly because of new technology, interunion disputes became a major problem. The public could never understand, for example, why a large construction project could be closed down by a controversy between two of a dozen unions on the job over which had the right to install certain materials. There have been interunion disputes over jurisdiction in Britain and other European countries, but they have been much less frequent and easier to settle than in the United States. It is not at all uncommon in Britain to find that workers in a factory who are doing essentially the same job belong to different unions, with little friction between them. The important thing is that they are all fellow members of the working class. When the National Labor Relations Act was being debated by Congress in 1934 and 1935, there were advocates of proportional representation in industrial relations, particularly employer groups hoping to maintain divisions among employees. The AFL fought this proposal with all the vigor it could command and succeeded in having majority rule enshrined in the law. Dual unionism has always been a cardinal sin for American organized labor, and it would have preferred no law to one that made it inevitable.

Political Action

During the first part of the twentieth century the AFL began to develop an approach to political action. A so-called Bill of Grievances was presented to President Roosevelt and the principal officers of the House and Senate in 1906. It contained demands for an eight-hour day, barring the sale of goods manufactured by convict labor, reducing immigration, exemption from the anti-trust laws, and the issuance of injunctions in labor disputes by the federal courts. Nothing came of this, and the AFL decided in 1906 to oppose the reelection of a Maine congressman whose voting record was strongly anti-labor. Gompers and other unionists campaigned against him in his district and succeeded in substantially reducing his winning margin. Similar efforts in 1908 and 1910 bore more fruit, but the first real victory came in 1912 when the AFL, without formally committing itself, supported Woodrow Wilson for the presidency. Part of its reward was the Clayton Act, which exempted union activities from the operation of the Sherman Anti-Trust Act.

This type of political action had been foreshadowed as early as 1884, when Peter J. McGuire, commenting on the elections held that year, observed that "wherever organized labor has asserted itself [by voting] it has helped its friends and defeated its enemies." This meant that AFL unions were prepared to support or oppose individual candidates for national, state, or local office on the basis of their votes on issues of importance to organized labor, regardless of party affiliation. The men who guided the labor movement through its formative years were fully aware of the political differences among their members and of the consequent danger of taking positions on any but purely labor issues. As a resolution adopted at the 1896 AFL convention put it, "party politics, whether they be Democratic, Republican, Socialistic, Populistic, Prohibition, or any other shall have no place in the convention of the American Federation of Labor." This certainly did not mean, as many Europeans assumed, that American unions were apolitical. In fact, the unions were mindful from the start of the importance of electing their friends to public office. Governors and state legislators could do much to improve labor conditions by state legislation. Mayors and city councils could control entrance to many skilled trades by licensing, as in the case of plumbers and electricians, and building codes could prevent the introduction of craft-destroying new technologies, such as dry wall for plaster. For instance, as far as the Firefighters Union (AFL) was concerned, it was more important to elect a friendly mayor than a president of the United States.

Expansion

Wartime economies tend to provide favorable conditions for union expansion: labor is scarce, demand is high, and patriotic sentiment reduces industrial conflict. The main concern of the government is to ensure a steady flow of war matériel, and it is not disposed to tolerate work stoppages, whether initiated by acts of management or labor. In 1916, AFL membership was 2.1 million. By 1920, it had risen to 4.1 million, a figure higher than for many years to come. As it has done in every war in which the United States has been involved, the labor movement strongly supported the war effort. Woodrow Wilson addressed the 1917 convention of the AFL, the first time a president had done so, and Gompers and several national union leaders served as members of the War Labor Board, which laid down the principle that workers should have the right to bargain collectively through representatives of their own choosing, an important landmark in federal government labor policy.

The war years provided only a temporary lull in employer opposition to unionization. After the end of hostilities prices rose sharply, and lagging wages led to an increase in strike activity. A national steel strike in 1919 was financed by the AFL and led, interestingly enough, by William Z. Foster, then an organizer for the Brotherhood of Railway Carmen and some years later the general secretary of the American Communist Party. The strike was broken, and it was almost two decades before any of the major steel companies accepted collective bargaining.

A prosperous economy normally provides a favorable background for trade union progress. The 1920s were a glaring exception to this rule. By 1928, membership in AFL unions had fallen to 2.9 million. Some major unions suffered catastrophic membership losses. The Machinists' Union, for example, experienced a decline from 331,000 members in 1920 to 74,500 in 1928. The cause was primarily a second concerted employer offensive against unions. Open-shop associations sprang up once more in 1920, and a national convention of these groups was held the following year, adopting as the name for its drive the "American Plan." Employers who had been dealing with unions broke off relations. Symptomatic of contemporary attitudes was a strike by the Boston police force; Calvin Coolidge, then the governor of Massachusetts, called out state troops to maintain order, and proclaimed that none of the strikers would be rehired. He made good on this threat; a completely new police force was recruited. This episode raised Coolidge to national prominence and eventually the presidency. It is generally believed that it was the inspiration for a later Republican president who was faced with a strike of government employees shortly after assuming office and took similar action.

The 1920s also saw an attempt to deflect unionism by what has been termed welfare capitalism. Some of the less bitterly anti-union employers—who nevertheless did not want unions in their shops—attempted to enhance worker loyalty to the company by improving working conditions; protecting workers from arbitrary discharge; and providing fringe benefits in the form of group insurance, pensions, and stock purchase plans. Company-dominated unions were established, and though they did not engage in bargaining, they were consulted on some matters. They preached the doctrine that the welfare of the individual worker was closely bound up with the progress of his company and that personal grievances should be subordinated to the common enterprise. The following statement by a company union official epitomizes this approach:

The final recourse we, as employees, have is to strike. Membership in the trade union or the company union does not change this. Certainly we want no strike, and I believe Mr. General Manager will play fair with us in the future as he has in the past. A strike would make us lose wages and the company lose production. It would put them in wrong with their customers and mean a loss of business, which would mean that when the difficulty was straightened out there would be less jobs and some of us would be out of luck.[5]

An employer weapon that was used with great effectiveness during the 1920s was the labor injunction. The federal courts extended the scope of judicial intervention in labor disputes to an unprecedentedly high level. They issued orders without hearing the defendants and included in them detailed provisions regulating the conduct of disputes that were drawn up by lawyers for the plaintiff. They were particularly deadly when used in conjunction with the so-called yellow dog contract—a commitment from an employee that he would not join a union for the duration of his employment. If a union approached him, it could be enjoined for inducing a breach of contract. Organizing campaigns could be stopped in their tracks.

These abuses of the judicial power were catalogued in a very effective piece of social science research embodied in a book entitled *The Labor Injunction* by Felix Frankfurter and Nathan Greene (Frankfurter was then a professor at Harvard Law School). The authors included in the book draft legislation to correct the abuses. With few changes it was enacted by Congress as the Norris-LaGuardia Act in 1932 and signed into law by President Hoover. Republicans as well as Democrats acknowledged that the courts had overstepped the bounds of legitimacy. The Act took the federal courts out of most labor dispute situations, and many states adopted similar legislation to curb their courts.

The Great Depression and the New Deal

No episode in American history had more influence on the labor movement than the Great Depression. Unemployment rose steadily from 3.2 percent in 1929 to a peak 25 percent in 1933, by far the highest level ever recorded in this country. Average hourly earnings fell from 57 cents an hour to 44 cents during the same period. Strikes called to resist wage cuts were invariably lost. Dues-paying membership in unions affiliated with the AFL fell to 2.1 million, the lowest figure in almost two decades. Many unions were forced to call off their conventions and stop their publications for lack of funds. The fortunes of organized labor had never been at a lower ebb.

But at the same time the prestige of American businessmen, which had been greatly enhanced by the economic expansion of the 1920s, also declined. President Hoover tried to commit the large corporations to maintenance of wages in order to keep purchasing power up, but in 1931 the line was broken and wages tumbled. The business community had no remedies for the catastrophe that had overtaken them, any more than the government did. The result was the Roosevelt electoral sweep in 1932 in which not only the presidency but Congress as well, was captured by the Democratic Party.

It is not generally appreciated, however, that Roosevelt owed nothing to organized labor. The AFL remained neutral as an organization. The two most powerful members of its executive council, John L. Lewis of the Miners and William L. Hutcheson of the Carpenters, endorsed Hoover. Hutcheson agreed to act as director of the Republican Committee Labor Bureau. Only two prominent labor leaders supported Roosevelt—Daniel Tobin of the Teamsters' Union and George L. Berry of the Printing Pressmen—both of whom were interested in becoming Secretary of Labor.

Roosevelt was not unaware of the AFL's lack of enthusiasm for his cause. William Green, president of the AFL, urged Roosevelt to appoint Tobin labor secretary, but Roosevelt selected Frances Perkins, who had worked with him when he was governor of New York, leading Green to issue the following statement:

Labor has consistently contended that the Department of Labor should be what its name implies and that the Secretary of Labor should be representative of Labor, one who understands Labor, Labor's problems, Labor's psychology, collective bargaining, industrial relations, and one who enjoys the confidence of Labor. In the opinion of Labor the newly appointed Secretary of Labor does not meet these qualifications. Labor can never become reconciled to the selection made.[6]

As things turned out, Madam Perkins turned out to be strongly sympathetic to the aspirations of organized labor and played an important role in its subsequent advances.

The New Deal and its first piece of major legislation, the National Industrial Recovery Act (NIRA), caused a spurt in organizing activity. John L. Lewis sent organizers into the coalfields preaching, "The President wants you to join. Your government says, 'Join the United Mine Workers.'" And the miners did: in 1932, the Mine Workers had between 100,000 and 150,000 members; by 1935, the number had risen to 541,000. Other unions, however, were less successful. Strikes were lost and the mass-production industries remained nonunion. When the Supreme Court ruled the NIRA unconstitutional in 1935, employers were no longer required to guarantee workers "the right to organize and bargain collectively through representatives of their own choosing." With the Depression and 20 percent unemployment, the outlook for unions seemed bleak.

One problem was that the craft unions were unwilling to cede any of their traditional jurisdiction over skilled workers. They insisted that when large factories were organized the skilled workers should be divided up by occupations—molders, pattern makers, machinists, building craftsmen, and so on. The unions were skeptical of the possibility of organizing semi-skilled workers, due to past failures. But Lewis' union had considerable experience with the industrial form of organization, and Lewis was willing to gamble that the time was ripe for a general movement in this direction. He created the Committee for Industrial Organization (CIO), backed by a $2.5 million war chest from the Mine Workers' organization. An important political development was the 1935 National Labor Relations (Wagner) Act, which not only reinstated the NIRA declaration of union organization and collective bargaining rights, but also set up a government agency to prevent employers from interfering with employees' organizational efforts and to require them to bargain with unions that represented a majority of their employees. This was probably the most important piece of labor legislation ever enacted by Congress, and was of inestimable value to union organization.

Lewis' strategy was to attempt to organize the basic industries that had provided the core of resistance to unionism—steel and automobile manufacturing. The steel companies attempted to set a backfire by creating company-dominated unions, but these were infiltrated by the CIO and turned against them. Secret negotiation between Lewis and Myron C. Taylor, chairman of the U.S. Steel board of directors, led to an agreement without a strike call. But most of the other steel companies decided they would fight, and it was not until 1941 that they were forced to recognize the union under a great deal of pressure from the federal government, which was concerned that disruption of steel production would interfere with the massive wartime buildup of armaments.

The campaign to organize the auto industry was climaxed by a sit-down strike at key General Motors plants in December, 1936. Production at GM was completely halted, but the company would not even meet with union representatives until its plants were vacated. The union refused to do this before negotiations, and the deadlock was broken only after intervention by President Roosevelt and the governor of Michigan, Frank Murphy, who refused to use state troops to force the strikers out. GM finally met with the union and recognized it as the bargaining agent for its members, signaling one of the most important victories for the CIO. Chrysler followed suit after a brief sit-down strike, but Henry Ford refused to go along, holding out until 1941 when the combined pressure of a federal government threat to withdraw defense contracts and a national boycott of Ford cars (partly because of Ford's expressed sympathy for the Nazis) brought the last of the major auto makers under union contract, completing the most successful union drive in American history.

Faced with the mounting success of the CIO, the AFL unions began an organizing drive of their own. They had superior experience and financial resources, and faced employers who preferred dealing with them rather than with the more radical CIO. As a result, several AFL unions achieved phenomenal growth. The Teamsters grew from 150,000 members in 1936 to 530,000 in 1941; the Machinists from 90,000 to 285,000. Thus, despite the tremendous publicity generated by the CIO drive, the AFL remained the country's dominant labor federation.

An unforeseen result of the CIO organizing campaign, which was extended with some success to the rubber, textile, and lumber industries, among others, was that it enabled the Communist Party to gain a foothold in the labor movement. The CIO had to build up a staff of organizers, lawyers, and journalists in a very short time, and Communists, most of them secret members, offered their services. When aides remonstrated with Lewis about this infiltration, he is reported to have replied: "Who gets the bird, the hunter or the dog?"

In this case the dog received a substantial chunk of the bird. At the height of their power the Communists controlled about 25 percent of total CIO membership and had some influence over another 25 percent. They mounted several political strikes in 1940 and 1941, the period of the Hitler-Stalin pact, and led a campaign against any U.S. participation in the war or aid to the embattled British under the slogan "the Yanks are not coming." The non-Communist CIO was a strong supporter of Roosevelt's program of assistance to Britain (except for Lewis, who joined the neutral America First organization), and an incipient split in the CIO was averted only when the Soviet Union was invaded in June, 1941. The Communist unions made an overnight switch to all-out support of war production and participated in what had been transformed from a capitalist war into a war against fascism.

Many of the AFL leaders remained distrustful of government intervention in the labor market, although the Federation did support some New Deal legislation. A powerful group within it opposed minimum wage legislation on the grounds that "the enactment of such legislation would very materially interfere with the free functioning of the trade union movement," and it succeeded in preventing the creation of a permanent wage-fixing board as part of the Fair Labor Standards Act. As the AFL executive council stated in 1936, "If we give one Congress the authority to enact legislation favorable to labor, we cannot prevent another Congress passing legislation unfavorable to labor." This was a prophetic statement, although it is necessary to add that the Wagner Act was of inestimable help to the unions for a decade.

On the political front the AFL maintained its policy of neutrality during the 1936 presidential campaign, although several of its national union leaders joined in the formation of Labor's Non-Partisan League, which belied its name by working for Roosevelt. For the first and only time in his long career, Lewis supported Roosevelt. The AFL remained neutral in 1940 once again, but Lewis returned to the Republican fold with a dramatic radio speech in which he urged the election of Wendell Willkie and threatened to leave the presidency of the CIO if Roosevelt were reelected. He must have been surprised by the alacrity with which his former lieutenants accepted his refusal to run at the next CIO convention; he must have anticipated a cry of "No" and a unanimous draft. The fact is that his political positions and dictatorial rule had antagonized his colleagues, and they seized upon this opportunity to get rid of him. Thus ended the role of this remarkable man as a national figure; he finished his life as head of the declining Mine Workers Union, and when he died, he left a vacuum that took the union thirty years to fill.

In contrast to the AFL, the CIO was firmly in the Roosevelt camp in 1940 and played a major part in the selection of a vice-presidential candidate at the 1944 Democratic national convention. Its political action committee, led by Sidney Hillman of the Clothing Workers, raised $70,000 for Roosevelt. The Republicans charged that Roosevelt had directed his campaign managers, when faced with controversial issues, to "clear it with Sidney," and attempted to make political capital out of alleged domination of the Democratic Party by the CIO. William Green, on behalf of the AFL, repeated that "the nonpartisan political policy of the American Federation of Labor is based on the principle that the workers should elect the friends of labor and defeat its enemies regardless of their political affiliation."

The labor movement's support of civil rights for racial minorities began during this period. The AFL chartered an all-black union, the Brotherhood of Sleeping Car Porters, in 1936. It was headed by A. Philip Randolph, a pioneer of the civil rights movement. It was he who planned the first mass march on Washington that induced President Roosevelt to issue Executive Order 8802, mandating nondiscrimination clauses in defense contracts and establishing a Committee on Fair Employment Practices to police it.

Randolph also applied pressure within the AFL by threatening to denounce unions that engaged in discrimination unless they could demonstrate some progress toward its elimination. National union officers were induced to go before their executive boards and seek to bring about changes that may have been politically unpopular. The CIO had no problems on this score. When it was organized in the 1930s, any course other than full equality for blacks would have made impossible the unionization of the mass-production industries.

The Beginnings of a Welfare Society

World War II provided a favorable milieu for trade union expansion. Combined AFL and CIO membership rose from 8.9 million in 1940 to 14.8 million in 1945 despite a decline in the civilian labor force. Unemployment, which had remained high before 1940, fell to almost zero. The War Labor Board and other government agencies virtually forced employers to deal with unions in return for a no-strike pledge by the unions. When Sewell Avery, the chairman of Montgomery Ward and a determined foe of unionism, refused to do so, Roosevelt sent federal troops to take possession of the company's headquarters in Chicago. Avery would not leave his office so he was carried out by several soldiers and dumped on the sidewalk outside the building, in full view of press photographers. This lesson was not lost on the nation's employers.

The War Labor Board by no means gave the unions everything they wanted, but it did provide protection against predatory employers who may have sought to weaken them. Collective bargaining supplemented by compulsory arbitration became the standard method of conducting industrial relations in wartime America. The success of a price-control program in restraining inflation despite shortages of goods contributed to labor peace. Prices rose by only 22 percent between 1941 and 1945.

The end of the war and the release of the purchasing power that had been accumulated led to a chaotic economic situation. Prices began to rise rapidly and the unions reacted in a militant fashion to protect their wartime gains. There were more man-days idle due to work stoppages in 1946 than ever before or since. The unions had learned that the best time to strike is on the upswing of the business cycle. Public attitudes began to move against the unions for the first time since the onset of the Depression. Employers gained ground with their argument that while the Wagner Act might have been appropriate to help incipient unions, it was too one-sided now that they had become powerful. After long hearings, Congress passed the Taft-Hartley Act in 1947 over President Truman's veto. It declared certain union practices to be unfair along with those stipulated for employers in the Wagner Act, and thus deprived labor of one of its most potent weapons, the secondary boycott. This marked an end to the halcyon days of the New Deal and the War Labor Board.

The full implications of the change in public sentiment were not appreciated immediately. The Automobile Workers pioneered the winning of pensions for their members, benefits that had theretofore been restricted largely to management personnel. Employer-sponsored health insurance plans soon followed. When the Bureau of Labor Statistics made its first comprehensive survey of fringe benefits in 1959, employer expenditures for private pensions and health insurance constituted 5.2 percent of total labor compensation, rising to 11.9 percent two decades later. The most recent survey (1981) revealed that 71 percent of all employees in medium and large establishments were covered by private retirement plans in addition to Social Security.

The labor movement played an important role in moving the country toward a welfare society. The original Social Security and Unemployment Compensation laws did not owe a great deal to the still-weak labor movement. But once these programs and others were in place and had gained general acceptance, the unions became the principal advocates for their liberalization. They lobbied for extension of Social Security to cover ten million additional employees in 1950. They were instrumental in widening the coverage of the minimum wage law and provided the main impetus for periodic congressional increases in the minimum rate. Medicare, Medicaid, housing subsidies, and government training programs received strong union support.

The welfare states of Western Europe were created by social democratic parties allied with the trade unions. In the absence of a socialist party, American unions operated in both the collective bargaining and legislative arenas to achieve their objectives. The result is a bifurcation in the welfare network not found abroad. There is no national health scheme in the U.S., apart from Medicare; private schemes instead provide the basic coverage. Social Security provides minimal retirement benefits, which are supplemented by the private plans to provide a reasonable living standard. Unions spend a good deal of their time and money policing the health and safety standards set by government.

The Erosion of Trade Union Power

The enactment of the Taft-Hartley Act marked a watershed in American trade union power, but its impact was masked temporarily by the quasi-wartime economy of the Korean War period. Prices and wages came under government control, and what amounted to compulsory arbitration was imposed upon defense industries. President Truman seized the nation's steel mills in 1952 when the companies refused to accept the recommendations of a government board. Although the Supreme Court held that the president lacked the authority to take this action and a strike was called after the government vacated the mills, further pressure by the Truman administration brought a settlement.

Government controls were lifted in 1953 and normal collective bargaining relationships were resumed. If one examines the data in Table 1, where union membership is shown as a percentage of the labor force, it would appear that the unions achieved their greatest increases in 1945 and 1955, and that their subsequent decline was a consequence of government policy. While this may be true in part, structural changes in the labor force complicate the conclusions that may be drawn about causation.

One major event of the 1950s strengthened the labor movement and another weakened it. The first was the merger of the AFL and the CIO in 1955. The CIO had expelled all of its Communist-dominated affiliates a few years earlier, thus eliminating a source of friction with the strongly anti-Communist AFL. After World War II, the Communists used their unions to advance the foreign policy goals of the Soviet Union; they opposed the Marshall Plan and

Table 1
Trade Union Membership as a Proportion of Employees on Nonagricultural Payrolls, 1940–1984

Year	Percent
1940	26.9
1945	35.5
1950	31.5
1955	33.2
1960	31.4
1965	28.4
1970	27.3
1975	25.5
1980	23.0[a]
1984	19.1[a]

[a]The data for these years are not exactly comparable with those for earlier years since they were derived from a different source, but the magnitude of the discrepancies is not believed to be great.

Source: Bureau of Labor Statistics *Handbook of Labor Statistics,* 1980, Table 165; *Monthly Labor Review,* February 1985, p. 25.

tried to punish Truman for his role in furthering it by persuading Henry Wallace to run against him on a third-party ticket in 1948. Another factor behind the merger was a split within the CIO. Philip Murray, who had succeeded Lewis as CIO president, died in 1952, and a fight to replace him ensued. Walter Reuther, the head of the Automobile Workers, was elected in a close race, but differences with the more conservative Steelworkers' leadership persisted.

The AFL was twice as large as the CIO when the merger took place. The two top posts in the united federation went to the AFL. The AFL had maintained its position as the mainstream of the labor movement. By this time, however, there was little to distinguish the two wings that had fought so bitterly for two decades. Many AFL unions had widened their jurisdictions to include semi-skilled workers. Some CIO unions had organized skilled workers over whom the AFL crafts claimed jurisdiction. The hallowed principle of exclusive jurisdiction had given way to new realities.

The second event was the creation of a congressional Committee on Improper Activities in the Labor Management Field, chaired by Senator John L. McClellan, with Senator John F. Kennedy as one of its members and Robert F. Kennedy as its chief counsel. Hearings extended over two years, and the committee found that the leaders of several national unions had engaged in corrupt practices, extorting money from employers and denying their members any vestige of democracy. The worst offender was the International Brotherhood of Teamsters, the largest union in the country. As a consequence of these revelations, Congress enacted the Labor-Management Reporting (Landrum-Griffin) Act of 1959. It was designed to reduce the opportunities for corruption by guaranteeing union members the right to participate in union affairs and by permitting closer scrutiny of union financial transactions.

While the unions were not happy about this legislation, they could hardly oppose it. In practice, the law has been instrumental in upgrading the quality of internal union practices. Elections are conducted with greater care lest they be overturned by government action. Union constitutions have been made more democratic. The cost to the unions has been an increase in litigation, but it does not appear to have weakened them. On the contrary, it may have improved their public image by ensuring that they are held to a standard of conduct required of few other organizations in American society. Although it will never be possible to eliminate all corrupt practices, the gross abuses of the past are not likely to be repeated.

Unions and Foreign Affairs

While foreign policy issues have not been a matter of major concern to members of American trade unions, their leaders have spoken out often on foreign affairs. The average worker does not look to his union as a means of influencing American foreign policy. Union members, like the general public, rank foreign policy fairly low on their list of concerns. However, the spokesmen for the labor movement have displayed a remarkable degree of consistency over the years. Anti-Communism is their main focus. The AFL strongly opposed U.S. recognition of the Soviet Union, and submitted a brief against it when the Roosevelt administration was considering such action. The AFL also did what it could to oppose Italian and German fascism, helping to organize a boycott of German goods in 1933, and urging American sports organizations not to participate in the 1936 Olympic games in Berlin.

The AFL and the CIO split on whether to join the new World Federation of Trade Unions in 1945, in which the Soviet trade unions participated. The AFL refused, while the CIO joined, only to withdraw a few years later when it became clear to Western trade unions that the Federation had fallen under Communist control. Both wings affiliated with a new body, the International Confederation of Free Trade Unions, in 1949, and apart from a temporary break in the 1970s, the AFL-CIO has remained a member.

It has been a cardinal point of AFL-CIO policy not to have any contact with Soviet trade unions on the ground that they were government bodies with no power to protect their members. The AFL-CIO has been able to prevent representatives of Soviet trade unions from securing visas to enter the United States. When Richard Nixon made his historic visit to China in 1972, George Meany is reported to have remarked, "I used to be the number two anti-Communist in the United States. Now I am number one." The unions have been highly critical of American businessmen for their willingness to establish commercial relationships with the USSR, even when union jobs were at stake.

The anti-Communist views of American labor leaders are reflected in their stands on particular issues. They supported American participation in the Vietnam war; a resolution introduced at the 1969 AFL-CIO convention that called for U.S. withdrawal failed to get any support. Increased defense expenditures have been favored. The AFL-CIO has been in the forefront of efforts to assist Soviet dissidents, and acted as host for the Soviet writer Aleksandr Solzhenitsyn when the White House declined to receive him for fear of offending the Russians. It mounted a major campaign to help the Polish trade union Solidarity, and has been critical of softening U.S. government attitudes toward Poland after Solidarity was crushed. In addition, American unions have been consistent in backing the state of Israel. Close ties are maintained with Histradut, the Israeli labor federation. The AFL-CIO has also established missions in developing countries to assist democratic unions that were struggling for existence. Non-Communist totalitarian regimes have been threatened with boycotts unless they permit trade unions to function independently of government and employers.

Labor's Political Role

The aftermath of Taft-Hartley was the abandonment by the labor movement of its traditional neutrality in national politics and its alliance with the Democratic Party. The Democratic candidate in 1952, Adlai Stevenson, promised that he would work for repeal of the Act, while Eisenhower favored retaining it. The AFL-CIO endorsed Stevenson once more in 1956 and Kennedy in 1960. There was no question about the 1964 election: Goldwater was considered strongly anti-labor whereas President Johnson had close working relationships with the unions. Nor was there any hesitation in backing Hubert Humphrey, whose political record was perfect from the union standpoint.

Humphrey lost the 1968 election despite an intensive campaign by the Committee on Political Education, the political arm of the AFL-CIO. The election was very close and was complicated by the third-party candidacy of George Wallace, who drew blue-collar votes by raising racial issues. In 1972, faced with a Democratic candidate, George McGovern, whom many in the labor movement regarded as being too far to the left on both domestic and foreign policy issues, the AFL-CIO remained neutral. They were back in the Democratic fold in 1976. President Ford, who was running for reelection, had promised to sign legislation liberalizing the rules of picketing at construction sites if Congress enacted it. When the measure came to his desk, however, he vetoed it under what he subsequently admitted was an intense pressure campaign from conservative business interests, which threatened to oppose him for the Republican nomination if he let it go through. Had he approved the bill, there is a good chance that the unions would have remained neutral since Jimmy Carter, the Democratic candidate, had won the primaries without any union backing and was not their favorite. The election was very close, and Ford might very well have won with the support of the construction unions.

While the unions were not happy with the record of the Carter administration, they saw no alternative but to support him in his 1980 bid for reelection. Ronald Reagan was reputed to be ultra-conservative, pro-business, and anti-labor. Nothing that occurred during the first Reagan administration seemed to alter this assessment. Reagan's first Secretary of Labor was a businessman rather than a union representative, and unions considered his policies inimical to the labor movement. Appointees to the National Labor Relations Board, which administers the Taft-Hartley Act, were drawn from the ranks of lawyers engaged in fighting the unions. One of Reagan's first acts as president was to discharge government-employed airport controllers who had gone on strike and to direct their replacement by an entirely new staff. What made the unions even more bitter was that Reagan once had been president of an AFL union, the Screen Actors' Guild, and had a much greater knowledge of labor affairs than any of his predecessors. One must go back to the early 1920s to find a federal administration that the unions saw as more hostile.

As a result, the AFL-CIO plunged itself more deeply into the 1984 campaign than it ever had done before. Unhappiness with the last two Democratic nominees, McGovern and Carter, led the leadership to conclude that it had to intervene at an earlier stage in the election process, the primaries, in order to guarantee a satisfactory candidate. The AFL-CIO decided to back Walter Mondale, a Humphrey protégé who had been vice-president under Carter, and they helped him gain the nomination despite a vigorous challenge by Senator Gary Hart. But in doing so, they alienated many Democrats and allowed the Republicans to label Mondale as the tool of the unions. The Reagan victory represented one of the greatest political defeats in the American labor movement's history.

It would be wrong to leave the impression that American trade unions have come to occupy the same position vis-à-vis the Democratic Party as European unions have with their socialist allies. There is much more diversity at the state and local levels than at the national level in the U.S. Regional labor organizations are more concerned with local issues when deciding whether to support a candidate for office and less worried about party labels. For example, when Arthur Goldberg, a trade union lawyer who negotiated the AFL-CIO merger and who later became a justice of the U.S. Supreme Court, ran against Republican Nelson Rockefeller for the governorship of New York, a large segment of the labor movement in New York supported Rockefeller, who won handily. Although he was one of the richest men in the U.S., Rockefeller, in his first term as governor, had maintained cordial relations with the unions and was helpful to them in many ways. As far as they were concerned, Goldberg was an outsider, and Rockefeller a proven friend.

A union endorsement does not guarantee that the members will follow along. Somewhere between 30 and 40 percent of blue-collar workers tend to vote Republican in presidential elections. In the 1984 elections, after the vigorous campaign that the AFL-CIO had waged on behalf of Mondale and with every union except the Teamsters solidly behind him, an AFL-CIO poll indicated that 39 percent of AFL-CIO members and 43 percent of AFL-CIO households had voted for Reagan. Forty-six percent of union members under thirty-five years of age voted for Reagan, while 52 percent of white male union members under forty voted for him. The overall majority among union members for Mondale was attributed to the votes of older men, women, and racial minorities.

On the other hand, two-thirds of the candidates for congressional and gubernatorial office endorsed by labor—most but not all Democrats—won their contests. Some 72 percent of AFL-CIO members voted for Democratic candidates for the Senate and 69 percent for the House of Representatives, indicating that many had split their tickets to vote for Reagan. There are different ways of interpreting this result—one explanation is that the personal popularity of an incumbent president, on the one hand, and a greater knowledge of local issues and politicians, on the other, worked in opposite directions. Despite the sweeping Reagan victory, the House of Representatives remained firmly in Democratic hands, as did a substantial majority of state governments.

The failure of a large number of American workers to follow the recommendations of their unions may be due to a factor that was appreciated by the founders of the labor movement: the labor force is split along ethnic lines and is likely to have divergent views on various issues that may transcend parochial trade union issues. Many Polish workers may have voted for Reagan because of U.S. support for Solidarity. Catholics may have been concerned with the abortion issue, on which Reagan took a position consonant with that of the Church. Jews were influenced by policy toward Israel, and blacks on civil rights. There are closely knit ethnic groups—Irish, Italian, Latin American, among others— which tend to support compatriots regardless of party affiliation or union endorsement. Absent is the class consciousness and ethnic homogeneity that makes possible the working-class parties of Europe.

The AFL-CIO's decision to involve itself so deeply in the 1984 presidential campaign is quite understandable considering its relationship with the Reagan administration. However, after the most intensive political efforts in its history, the labor movement had to face the fact that almost 40 percent of its own members voted against the advice of their unions. In view of the overall results, it is clear that the great majority of those whom labor would like to bring into its ranks voted for the candidate strongly opposed by the unions.

This does not mean that the unions will have to abstain from political action. As we have seen, they did fairly well in the election of state and local officers, as well as congressional elections. But the presidential race is both the most conspicuous and the one in which voters have the least personal comprehension of the issues involved. It is also the one which most clearly stamps the partisan stance of the unions. A choice may have to be made between the potential gain from a more friendly national administration against the loss flowing from the alienation of the many workers who support candidates opposed by the unions.

The labor unions may not in fact be giving up very much if they were to maintain a lower profile in national elections. Their gains have not been outstanding since 1952, when the AFL first began formally endorsing Democratic candidates. (The then-independent CIO had followed this practice earlier.) Of the nine presidential elections held since then—or eight if the failure to endorse a candidate in the Nixon-McGovern race is excluded—in only three were the union-endorsed candidate successful, and in the case of the Carter victory it is not clear what advantages the unions gained. The Kennedy and Johnson administrations were certainly friendly to unions, though the union's backing of Johnson was of only marginal importance in his election. But in general, the labor movement has given up the political neutrality that served it well over a good part of its existence for fairly meager rewards over the past three decades. And it is possible that less identification with organized labor might improve the electoral fortunes of the Democratic Party.

Membership Decline

Since 1935, trade union membership as a proportion of employment has dropped steadily, as the data in Table 1 demonstrate. From 1968 to 1980, the number of union members remained fairly stable at 20 million, but it fell to 17.4 million at the end of 1984. At the same time, the number of those working for salaries or wages increased from 67.9 million in 1968 to 91.3 million in 1984. Recent changes in union membership can be explained, in part, by declines in the American economy, particularly in the smokestack industries, centers of union strength. And the long-term decline of union membership reflects the changes that have been taking place in the labor force.

This pattern has been reflected in individual union memberships. The one-time giants of the union world—the Auto Workers, the Steelworkers, the Machinists—have suffered substantial reductions in memberships. At the same time, there has been a massive shift in employment toward the service industries, and unions in these areas have grown. The National Education Association, for instance, is now the largest union in the country. But only 10.6 percent of all service employees were union members in 1984, compared with 24.5 percent for the goods-producing industries.

Unions may have to make some fundamental changes in policy in order to attract groups of employees whose outlook and interests are in many ways different from those of the blue-collar workers who constitute the core of present union membership. If the unions are to succeed in organizing service employees on any scale, for instance, in all likelihood they will have to rethink their political roles. Where these groups have been unionized in Europe, it has often been in bodies independent of the traditional federations that supported socialist or labor parties.

Another cause of declining union fortunes has been the resumption of employer militancy. Beginning in 1980, taking advantage of the pro-business stance of the Reagan administration, many employers began not only to resist union organization, but also to displace unions where they were already entrenched—to create what was called a "union-free environment." This movement was not as highly structured as the open-shop drives of 1901–1905 or the 1920s, but it made up for that in sophistication. Providing legal advice on how to keep unions out became an expanding and lucrative occupation.

Some indication of the success of this effort is provided by the outcome of representation elections held by the National Labor Relations Board (NLRB). During the 1950s unions were winning 65 to 70 percent of these elections. In the early 1980s they were down as low as 45 percent. Increased delays in processing unfair labor practices charges as well as a pro-employer shift in NLRB personnel contributed to union defeats. The NLRB had been established in 1935 to protect workers from employer interference with their free choice of bargaining representatives. A half century later it appeared to be doing just the reverse.

This is certainly the perception held by the labor movement. Lane Kirkland, the AFL-CIO president, declared at a recent press conference that the NLRB "has become an instrument not just of employers generally, but of those employers who have most aggressively engaged in practices contrary to the spirit of the law to deny working people the right to self-organization, self-representation." He went so far as to suggest that if by boycotting the Board, the unions could get rid of all government regulation of industrial relations and "go to the law of the jungle," they might be better off. One can almost see the ghosts of Samuel Gompers and William Hutcheson rising up and saying, "We warned you that what the government gives, it can take away." The trouble with the Kirkland prescription is that when the political wheel turns once more and labor comes out on top, it can hardly be expected to deny itself the assistance of a friendly administration.

Conclusion

When living standards were low and workers had little protection against arbitrary employer actions, the union emphasis was on higher wages and job protection. White-collar workers began to perceive that they were being left behind the organized blue-collar workers, and some organized for defensive purposes. But as countries became more affluent, and as welfare programs began to provide a safety net, concerns shifted to employment security and to employee participation in corporate decision making as a means of enhancing that security—on the part of blue-collar as well as white-collar workers. Safety and health also took on added importance.

The economic events of the last decade, with two recessions and continuing high unemployment, plus the structural adjustments that have led to what appears to be a permanent decline of several major industries, have raised concern for employment security to a high level. Workers have been willing to trade off wages for some modicum of job security. Wage increases in major collective bargaining agreements during 1984 were the lowest since the Bureau of Labor Statistics has been tabulating such data. There seems to be no real demand for shorter working hours. In fact, 20 percent of all employees are working part time, and many would like full-time work.

If unions were able to say to workers, "We are in a position, if not to guarantee you lifetime employment in your present jobs, at least to guarantee that you will not be discharged without a full discussion of alternatives in which your representatives will participate," they would have a powerful appeal, judging from European experience, an appeal that might be particularly attractive to the many white-collar employees who are not as accustomed to employment fluctuations as their blue-collar brethren.

There will have to be some reorientation of traditional trade union thinking if such a position is to be achieved. Union leaders, and particularly their members, will have to gain a full understanding of the link between employment and wages. Some have learned the hard way when faced with the prospect of bankrupt employers. But if this contingency is not present, it is not easy to convince individual groups of employees that immediate wage demands may affect their jobs adversely. Local unions in the construction industry have priced themselves out of the home building industry and have only begun to realize that commercial construction has a limited ability to pay. State and municipal workers have come to believe that an endless cornucopia of public funds will be available to them. National leaders are much more aware of the problem, but internal political considerations may make it difficult for them to act with restraint.

Seniority clauses in collective agreements, the earliest form of job security provided by unions, contribute in a perverse way to magnification of the difficulties involved in readjusting ideas. Unions tend to be controlled by older workers who are willing to see employment reduced as long as their jobs are safe. An extreme expression of this attitude is a recent trend toward two-tier wage agreements under which new employees are paid less than current employees. It would be difficult to conceive of a policy more likely to discourage unionization.

If unions are to accept greater responsibility for the employment consequences of their wage policies, it will be necessary at a minimum to provide them with more information about the enterprises with which they deal. About all that most unions have now are statements to stockholders plus whatever their staff members can piece together. The Japanese and German models are often cited as examples of systems in which unions do have access to company records.

The Japanese model has little to offer. The most important unit in the Japanese trade union structure is the so-called enterprise union, one for each company. These organizations resemble the company unions that were set up in the United States in the 1920s to frustrate independent unions. Although most are affiliated with national unions, they have little real power and are basically subservient to management. Their officers, many of whom are lower or middle management personnel, may discuss problems with top managers, but they are not in a position to participate in making important decisions.

German co-determination is of much greater relevance. It has two basic elements: work councils that are elected by vote of all employees regardless of union status and formally divorced from the unions, and employee representatives on corporate boards of directors. The latter are normally designated partly by the work councils and partly by the unions that represent the firm's employees. They can be either union officials or outside financial experts. Work councils are entitled to a full range of information on all matters affecting the operation of the plants in which they are located, while the labor-designated board members have the same rights to participate in decisions as those representing stockholders, including the appointment of managers. The labor board members are in a minority, but it is rare that major decisions affecting employees are taken over their objections.

How the system works may be exemplified by a typical procedure for plant closure. If the corporate officers decide that a particular plant is no longer profitable and should be shut down, the matter would be brought before the board of directors. The employee directors might argue that closure would burden the workers with undue hardship and impact too heavily on the community. Efforts might be made to adopt actions short of closure— transfer of work from other plants, reduction of personnel, installation of new machinery, postponement of closure until employees could find other work. Only after all alternatives had been canvassed would a final decision be made. In practice, many plants have been saved by this procedure.

In the United States, such decisions are usually made unilaterally by management with little or no notice to employees or their unions. Steady income, fringe benefits, and all the protections afforded by collective agreements disappear with no redress. The current wave of corporate raiding and the use of bankruptcy laws to escape contract obligations exacerbate the problem. And it is a problem that affects all employees alike, regardless of occupation or skill.

There have been a few well-publicized cases in which unions have been given representation on boards of directors—Chrysler and Eastern Airlines are examples—but this has usually happened when the company involved was near failure and needed extraordinary concessions from the unions. Generally speaking, American management remains resolutely opposed to the whole idea of co-determination. Union leaders are also hostile to the arrangement, fearing that involvement in managerial decisions might impair their ability to represent their members. How can one be on both sides of the bargaining table?

Suffice it to say that the system has worked well in Germany. It appears to have had no adverse effect on the productivity or profitability of German firms.[7] Co-determination has been accepted and both parties have learned to live with it. The unions would like equal representation on corporate boards rather than the minority voice they now have, but there is little likelihood of this happening under the present government.

American unions have been a force for social change even as they have been a means for increasing workers' wages. A strong labor movement performs vital functions in a democratic society. It helps impose work discipline upon the labor force without arousing the resentment and tension accompanying employer control. Instability of industrial relations, characterized by wildcat strikes as in France and Britain, is a manifestation of union weakness. American trade unions have been important allies of capitalism. They have helped limit extremism. They provide the most important institutional links among our many ethnic groups. They have been instrumental in preventing the "them" and "us" syndrome that bedevils other societies. They have been proponents of a strong national defense and a firm foreign policy. Even if it were possible for anti-union employers to weaken the labor movement so that its economic role was negligible, the employers would most likely find the social outcome undesirable.

A sense of history is important in assessing the future impact of the labor movement on American society. American unions have survived and prospered because they understood what was possible, given the philosophy of American employers and the needs of their members. They were flexible enough to alter their strategies to meet the demands of the time. When they faced hostile governments, both national and local, they espoused the doctrine of free and unregulated labor markets. As they gained strength, they moved toward an acceptance of more government intervention, particularly in the interest of those nonmembers as well as members who were in need of outside assistance. The present soul-searching that is going on within the labor movement suggests that some new approaches may emerge, particularly if unions are to move beyond the bounds of their present sectoral confines.

One must recall that unionism in the United States has faced much more critical situations in the past and survived. The AFL claimed 2.1 million members in 1933, down from 4 million in 1920. Even this total, representing about 4 percent of the labor force, probably overstated dues-paying membership by a substantial amount. Yet within five years, the country experienced the greatest burst of unionization in its history.

Lane Kirkland, the president of the AFL-CIO, remarked recently that "one thing our history tells us is to be patient. The greatest virtue of our system is that it is self-correcting over time. If the passing judgment of the public is not always infallible, there is always another chance; no social or economic experiments can escape the test of lively opposition." That has been the attitude of American labor, and in the end it proved to be a successful formula. There is no reason to believe that a first century of progress and growth will not be followed by a second.

3

LEO TROY

The Rise and Fall of American Trade Unions: The Labor Movement from FDR to RR

As the American labor movement begins its second century, it apparently has entered a new stage in its history, a stage of permanent decline. Organized labor has lost millions of members since its peak in 1975, while its grip on the labor market has dropped to the levels of the Great Depression. The proportion of union members employed in nonfarm industries including government—a standard measurement of union "density"—has fallen to fewer than one in five, the lowest since 1937–1938. Membership in 1985 is the same as twenty years ago, about 18 million, while the number of union mergers is unparalleled in union history. The market seems to have rejected unions in large sectors of the private economy and in growth areas of the country.

Indeed, growth in employment is associated with little or no unionism, while stagnant or declining industrial and geographic sectors are associated with high union penetration. Unions have failed to benefit from one of the longest peacetime expansions in post–World War II history, a growth which began in November 1982 and continues into the spring of 1986, the time of this writing. The national polity holds union leaders in low esteem and, with significant support of union members, rejected unions' political policies in the presidential election of 1984. It is no exaggeration, therefore, to characterize the current state of unions as a crisis. The reversal in the fortunes of organized labor—its march upward and slide downward during the past half-century—is of major significance not only to the union movement but to the future of collective bargaining, the labor market, and the economic and political life of this country. The decline of the American union movement, a decline which I believe is a permanent one, is the focal point of this chapter.

Significantly, the decline of unionism in this country is not unique among industrial nations—it is also occurring in Britain, France, West Germany, Italy, and Japan (Table 1). The parallel behavior of unionism in the major industrial nations is significant because it suggests that the causes of union decline may be com-

Table 1
Union Density, Major Industrial Countries, Selected Years
(Percent)

	1962	1970	1975	1981	1982
France	20.5	23.1	22.9	19.0	n.a.
Italy	20.5	33.1	44.2[a]	41.4	39.6
Japan	46.2[a]	35.4	34.4	30.8	29.7
W. Germany	37.1	36.3	37.9	39.3[a]	37.1
U.K.	43.8	48.5	51.1	54.6[a]	48.9

[a]Denotes peak rate of union density. Italy's peak rate occurred in both 1976 and 1978 and is the figure reported in the table. Japan's peak year was 1950 at 46.2% and is the figure reported in the table. Also, the figure for 1983 is shown instead of 1982. The peak year for both West Germany and the United Kingdom is 1979 and the figures shown in the table are for that year.

Source: Leo Troy and Neil Sheflin, *Union Sourcebook* (West Orange: IRDIS, 1985).

mon to industrial economies making the transition to service-dominated labor markets. Except for Japan, where the decline in density preceded the American decline, the developments in Western Europe are trailing those in the United States, and the decline is not yet as steep. At the same time, these countries trail the United States in the evolution of the service-dominated labor market, a factor that I regard as one of the keys to understanding the long-run decline of unionism in this country.

My purposes in this chapter are to detail the statistical record of union organization beginning in the 1930s, offering an explanation for the flow and ebb in the fortunes of American unions from Franklin D. Roosevelt to Ronald Reagan. I also argue that as a result of its historical experience over the past half-century, organized labor in the United States has switched its philosophy of "more" for its members to a philosophy of "more government intervention" in the economy and society. In tracing the record of public sector unionism, particularly since 1962 when its "boom" began, I believe that the rise of public sector unionism has produced a philosophical split between the private and public sectors of American unions (albeit not yet publicly acknowledged) over the meaning and application of the new philosophy. Finally, I analyze and speculate on recent trends in the labor movement, looking toward the balance of this decade and to the end of the twentieth century.

Framework for Analysis

Economic theories explaining the aggregate flow and ebb of unionism—similar, for example, to theories explaining changes in aggregate employment and output—have eluded scholars of industrial relations. As an alternative, econometric models have been developed in an attempt to provide a compact, empirical explanation of changes in unionism. Two leading examples, studies by Ashenfelter and Pencavel, and Bain and Elsheikh, claimed to have captured the primary determinants of union growth in the twentieth century.[1] Both were reexamined by two colleagues and me using revised and extended membership data and, more importantly, both were investigated for structural stability.[2] Contrary to the claims of the models' stability, we found evidence of a break in the structure of each. In addition, we estimated that the breaking points occurred in 1937–38. We believe this reflected the impact of the National Labor Relations Act (Wagner Act) adopted in 1935, but not upheld by the Supreme Court until April 1937. Neither econometric study had been able to capture the determinants of union growth in a single equation;[3] consequently, we questioned whether either study added much to understanding the process of union growth in the twentieth century.

In the absence of a general theory or an empirical model explaining union behavior, I propose a framework based on the role of public policy toward labor organization and collective bargaining. The framework falls into three fairly distinct periods. In the first, public policy, fashioned principally by the judiciary, at best tolerated union organization. During this period, which spanned nearly the entire century from the legalization of unions in *Commonwealth of Massachusetts v. Hunt* in 1842 to the New Deal, union behavior was governed principally by economic factors; organization developed and was concentrated in skilled occupations as implied by Alfred Marshall's theory of joint demand[4] and moved with changes in employment. Public policies strengthened unions in general during the First World War, particularly the railway unions. Statutory support of railway unionism and bargaining was extended by the Railway Labor Act (RLA) of 1926. In fact, the wartime policies and RLA became the blueprints for labor relations policies of the New Deal in the 1930s. However, the labor policies of the Wilson administration were short-lived, and except on the railways, union organization from about 1920 to 1932 basically remained subject to the public policies and economic forces that prevailed prior to the war.

This epoch ended with the enactment of the Federal Anti-Injunction Act of 1932, which limited the role of the judiciary in fashioning public policy for unions and bargaining. Bloom and Northrup characterized the Act as establishing "laissez-faire" labor relations.[5] However, what soon followed was not "laissez-faire" but government intervention. By legislative mandate, government intervened on a massive scale and in behalf of unions in the private sector of the labor market. The National Labor Relations Act of 1935, which essentially remains intact today, ushered in a new stage of the evolution of unions in this country.

In this stage unionism spread to millions of workers in occupations and industries, notably manufacturing, which had hitherto proved beyond the power of unions to organize. The special labor policies of the Second World War and the Korean War gave additional impetus to union growth, as they had during World War I, but in contrast to the post–World War I era, unions held their gains, culminating in the peak rate of unionization attained in 1953. From that time on, however, membership in the private sector was governed far less by public policies than by economic factors. In effect, private sector unionism had reached a saturation point by the early 1950s. Its membership peaked in 1970 and but for the Vietnam War doubtless would have done so earlier. (In 1953 it hit 15.5 million; in 1965, as American involvement in Vietnam began to grow, it was 15.6 million.) Meanwhile, the share of the private sector labor market organized fell steadily from 1953 to the present.

Obscuring the unions' saturation of private sector employment was the spectacular growth of union organization in the public sector. This, the third step in public policy development, was initiated in 1962 by President Kennedy's Executive Order 10988. Coupled with similar policies in important cities and states (New York City and Wisconsin anticipated the federal policy), these pro-union labor policies stimulated the growth of membership in the public sector as the Wagner Act had done earlier for unions in the private sector. The peak of public sector organization, in both number of members and extent of the labor market organized, came in 1976. While it may be premature to argue that government unionism has also reached a saturation point, ten years have elapsed since its peak and no breakthroughs are on the horizon.

The Statistical Record

The data base. The figures for this paper come from a new and unique computerized data bank on union membership and finances developed by myself and a colleague.[6] We revised Leo Wolman's 1936 study covering the years 1897–1934;[7] revised my 1965 study, which extended Wolman's statistics to 1962,[8] and extended that series from 1962 through 1984. The data bank incorporates every known labor organization from 1897 on, identifies the year in which the organization's membership series began and peaked, and notes the year an organization dissolved, merged, or was absorbed by another union. Each organization is coded for such characteristics as the sector of the labor market, public or private, in which it functions and its historical affiliation status (AFL, CIO, independent, or other federation). Each union's membership record was adjusted from a fiscal year to a calendar year measure, which made all the values comparable. Only those few unions for whom financial information—dues and per capita receipts—were not available remained unadjusted. The sources of most unions' financial data are the financial reports they filed with the Department of Labor under the Labor-Management Reporting and Disclosure Act of 1959. Prior years, to 1935, were obtained from the financial reports of unions published in their respective journals.[9] Wolman's figures came mainly from the per capita dues paid to the American Federation of Labor by affiliates.[10] In addition, I use selected data from the Bureau of Census. Based on this, I believe that the record of unionism in this country reviewed here is reliable and fairly consistent.

Overview of membership and density, 1933–1984. Table 2 summarizes the general trends in union membership and density, 1933–1984.[11] Three distinct periods emerge: the first twenty years are years of growth in *both* membership and the percentage of the labor market organized. The year 1953, which marked the end of the Korean War, also marked the peak of the two traditional measures of union density, the percentage of union density, the percentage of union membership in the civilian labor force and nonfarm employment. During the following thirty years a steady erosion in union density occurred. Total membership continued to rise after 1953, reaching a peak in 1975. Since 1975 (to the beginning of 1986) the union movement has lost nearly 4 million members, dragging union penetration of nonfarm employment down to levels of the 1930s.

However, the totals reported in Table 2 obscure significant and conflicting trends within the union movement: the ebb of private sector membership and a meteoric rise in public sector membership. At the peak of union penetration in 1953, unions represented nearly 36 percent of private sector, nonfarm employment, while

Table 2

Trade Union Membership and Density in the United States, 1933—1984

Year	Membership (000's)	Density	
		Labor Force	Nonfarm Employment
1933	3,491.0	6.8	14.7
1939	6,491.3	11.8	21.2
1945	12,254.2	22.8	30.4
1950	14,294.2	23.0	31.6
1953	16,310.0	25.9[a]	32.5[a]
1962	16,893.2	23.9	30.4
1965	18,268.9	24.5	30.1
1975	22,207.0[a]	23.7	28.9
1983	18,633.6	16.6	20.7
1984p	18,306.0	16.1	19.4

[a]Denotes historic peak.

p: Preliminary.

Excludes membership of American unions in Canada.

Source: See Table 1.

union penetration of government employment was less than 12 percent. Private sector membership fluctuated from 15.5 million in 1953 to a low of just under 14.5 million in 1961, and then climbed to its all-time high of nearly 17 million in 1970. As already indicated, much of the limited growth of unions from 1965 to 1970 may be attributed to the war in Vietnam, paralleling similar experiences during the First and Second World Wars and the Korean War.

On the other hand, union membership in the public sector, consisting of slightly more than 3 to 4 million members in 1953, began an unparalleled rise in growth, both in numbers and penetration, after 1962. By 1976, public sector membership rose to its record level, just under 6 million, which amounted to over 40 percent of government employment, also a record. The magnitude of this accomplishment may be gauged by comparing it to the growth of the Congress of Industrial Organizations: at no time in its history did the CIO ever have so large a membership. In effect, the public sector union growth was equivalent to the formation of a major new labor federation.

After 1976, both membership and density in the public sector declined, though much more slowly than in the private sector. By 1983, public sector union membership had fallen by more than half a million and the penetration rate had declined to 34 percent. Even so, public sector union density was nearly double that of the private labor market in 1983 (34.4 percent compared to 17.8 percent). Preliminary information for 1985 indicates a continuing decline in both sectors and thus for the entire union movement, despite the resurgence of the economy since the end of 1982. The data on private and public sector union membership and density are reported in Table 3.

However, I wish to point out that the sudden jump in public sector membership commencing in 1962 is to a great extent the result of including the membership of the National Education Association (NEA) in the series for the first time. The NEA, as is well known, has historically denied that it was a labor organization, claiming instead that it has always been a professional association. In fact, a court order was required in the late 1970s to compel the organization to file financial and other reports with the Labor Department. The NEA is included from 1962 because the organization became involved in representation disputes with the American Federation of Teachers at about that time and abandoned its no-strike policy in the 1960s. President Kennedy's landmark executive order encouraging organization and bargaining in

Table 3
Private and Public Sector Membership and Density in the U.S., 1962–1983

Year	Membership (000's)		Density (Percent)	
	Private	Public	Private	Public
1953	15,540.2	769.8	35.7[a]	11.6
1962	14,731.2	2,161.9	31.6	24.3
1970	16,978.3[a]	4,012.0	29.1	32.0
1973	16,803.5	5,077.8	26.6	37.0
1976	16,166.8	5,980.3[a]	25.1	40.2[a]
1983	13,142.6	5,410.7	17.8	34.4

[a] Denotes historic peak.

Source: See Table 1.

Table 4

Composition of American Union Membership
by Sector, 1933–1983

(Percent)

Year	Private	Public
1933	91.5	8.5
1939	93.4	6.6
1945	95.6	4.4
1953	95.3	4.7
1961	94.1	5.9
1962	87.2	12.8
1976	73.0	27.0
1983	71.0	29.0

Source: See Table 1.

the executive departments of the federal government was issued in 1962, the watershed for public sector unionism in this country. While some might dispute the exact date of the NEA's transition from professional association to labor organization, whatever date is chosen would result in a sharp increase in public sector membership in that year because the NEA is so large—currently second only to the Teamsters in size.

Because of their rapid growth in the 1960s and 1970s, and their slow decline since 1976, public sector unions now represent a larger percentage of the labor movement than ever. Their increased importance is bound to move organized labor further to the left politically and lead to increased demands for more government intervention in the economy and society. In 1961, on the eve of its rapid growth, public sector unionism accounted for less than 6 percent of total membership; currently, it accounts for nearly 30 percent, a record high (Table 4).

In sum, the statistical record demonstrates that there has been a precipitous decline in union penetration of the labor market from the peak in 1953 and a massive loss in total membership since the peak in 1975. Today, union penetration of the labor market has slipped to levels prevailing almost a half century ago in terms of nonfarm employment and about forty-five years ago as measured relative to the civilian labor force. Membership at the beginning of 1986 stands where it was approximately twenty

Table 5
Union Density, Selected States

State	1939	1953	1982
California	23.8	37.0	25.4
Florida	11.9	16.5[a]	9.6
Illinois	27.3	40.7	27.5
Massachusetts	16.2	30.4[a]	19.7
Michigan	21.2	44.6	33.7
New Jersey	17.7	35.9	19.9
New York	24.7	35.6	35.8
Ohio	25.5	38.0[a]	27.4
Pennsylvania	29.0	40.6[a]	27.0
Texas	10.9	17.4[a]	12.5

[a] Denotes historic peak.

Source: See Table 1.

years earlier. Although the bulk of the unions' membership decline has been in the private sector, membership and the percentage organized have fallen in the public sector of the labor market as well, a fact not widely known.

Regional changes, 1939–1982. The overall changes in unionism just sketched had significant effects on the geography of membership among the states (Table 5). In general, states that have experienced significant growth in employment since World War II also had sharp declines in the percentage of nonfarm employment organized. Thus, California, Texas, and Florida, three states with large gains in employment, showed large declines in union density. As Table 5 shows, the percentage organized in these states fell sharply from their peak rates in 1953 or 1960. In Florida, union density in 1982 had even dropped below the rate of 1939; California's rate in 1982 was only slightly above the 1982 national average. Texas' rate was slightly higher in 1982 than in 1939 and well below the national average in 1982.

In contrast, the "smokestack" states: Michigan, Ohio, Pennsylvania, and New York—states that lagged in employment growth compared to the sunbelt states—showed much smaller declines (in New York, a rise) in union density between 1953 and 1982. Each was substantially higher than the national average in union density and each had a much higher rate of unionism in 1982 than in 1939. New York's higher rate in 1982 compared to 1953 is largely attributable to its very high rate of public sector union density. In fact, New York currently is the most unionized state in the country because of its high union density in the public sector and in manufacturing. Massachusetts' decline in union penetration 1953–1982 is explained by the replacement of organized and declining industries such as shoes and textiles with unorganized and growing high-technology industries. New Jersey had a similar exchange, losing organized manufacturing jobs while gaining large numbers of unorganized white-collar jobs, which lowered the state's union density.

The impact of public sector union growth among the states reported in Table 5 has been substantial. In all the states reported, union density in the public sector greatly exceeded private sector unionization, as might be expected from the national comparisons of the two groups. Nevertheless, it is striking that even in states which have had a history of limited unionism, such as Texas and Florida, the percentage organized in government employment significantly exceeds organizational rates in the private sector. The extremely high rates of public sector unionism within states that have historically ranked high in organization, states such as Michigan, Ohio, Pennsylvania, and New York, are also remarkable.

The higher public sector union penetration in both groups of states indicates that the process of unionization in the public sector differs from that in the private labor market. One factor is clearly the role played by professional associations of government employees, particularly at the state and local level. Challenged by established unions, the associations either joined unions or transformed themselves into collective-bargaining organizations. In many instances they abandoned their historic position of eschewing the right to strike and became *de facto* unions[12] just as the National Education Association did. Another reason that huge membership gains were made so swiftly was the encouragement union organization received from public sector management and officials. Indeed, given the pro-union attitudes of many elected officials, this was not a surprise.

Occupational and demographic changes. The shift in the private/public composition of membership also significantly

Table 6
Occupational Composition of Union Membership, 1959–1984
(Percent)

Year	White Collar	Blue Collar	Service & Other
1959	19.1	79.5	1.4
1966	17.5	77.7	4.8
1970	22.5	69.3	8.2
1973	27.8	63.0	9.2
1977	33.9	55.8	10.3
1980	37.8	52.3	9.9
1984	37.7	50.4	11.9
1985	38.5	49.6	11.9

Source: 1959, Leo Troy, "Trade Union Growth in a Changing Economy," *Monthly Labor Review* (September 1969), p. 5; 1966–1984, Bureau of the Census, Current Population Survey.

altered the occupational makeup of the American union movement. Beginning in 1985 and for the first time in its history, blue-collar workers no longer comprise the majority of union members (Table 6). White-collar unionists now account for nearly two of every five union members, primarily as a result of the enormous and rapid growth of organization among public employees. This reinforces my contention that the compositional shift in union membership in this country must be expected to move organized labor, or at least its leadership, toward demands for increased government intervention in economic and social policy.

Women members of unions now comprise a much larger share of the union movement than before. Census data show that women accounted for 22 percent of membership in 1966, and today account for more than one-third of the total. Although women now hold more positions in the leadership and bureaucracy of American unions, they have not had an impact commensurate with their increased importance in the union movement. The census data also show that union density among white-collar and women employees has risen steadily, again reflecting the growth of membership in government. White-collar workers, about 10 percent organized in 1966, increased to 13 percent by 1984; union density among women was 12.7 percent in 1966 and 13.8 percent in 1984. Meanwhile, the percentage of blue-collar workers unionized fell dramatically from 39.3 percent in 1970 to 30 percent in 1985.

Table 7

Union Density by Major Industrial Sector, 1930–1985

(Percent)

Year	Mfg.	Mining	Constr.	Transport All	Rwy.	Servcs.	Govt.	All Nonfarm
1930	7.8	21.3	64.5	22.6	39.0	2.3	8.5	12.7
1935	16.4	54.4	71.5	25.8	44.0	2.6	9.0	13.5
1939	22.8	65.4	77.3	50.0	50.3	6.0	10.8	21.2
1940	30.5	72.1	77.0	47.3	56.5	5.7	10.7	22.5
1947	40.5	83.1	87.1	67.0	75.8	9.0	12.0	32.1
1953	42.4	64.7	83.8	79.9	91.2	9.5	11.6	32.5
1966	37.4	35.7	41.4	n.a.	n.a.	n.a.	26.0	29.6
1970	38.7	35.7	39.2	44.9	78.6	7.8	31.9	29.6
1973	38.8	37.6	38.1	49.3	82.6	12.9	37.0	28.5
1975	36.6	32.0	35.4	46.6	78.6	13.9	39.5	28.9
1977	35.5	35.1	35.7	47.6	80.3	n.a.	38.0	26.2
1980	32.3	32.1	31.6	48.0	81.8	11.6	35.0	23.2
1983	27.8	20.7	27.5	42.4	n.a.	7.7	34.3	20.7
1984	26.0	17.7	23.5	38.7	n.a.	7.3	n.a.	19.5
1985	24.8	14.6	22.3	37.0	n.a.	6.6	n.a.	n.a.

Sources and Notes: All Nonfarm and Government, 1930–1984, from *Union Sourcebook;* all other industries, 1930, 1935, 1940, and 1947 from Leo Troy, unpublished tables; 1939 and 1953, Leo Troy, *Distribution of Union Membership Among the States, 1939 and 1953* (New York: Nat. Bur. of Econ. Res., O.P. 56, 1957). From 1930 to 1953, Services include Trade, Finance, Insurance, and Real Estate; from 1966 to 1985 all figures are from the Bureau of Census.

Industrial density and composition. Unions have never represented more than one-third of the labor market and, at most, just over one-quarter of the civilian labor force (in 1953), but the density, of course, has varied substantially among industries. Unions' industrial penetration not only shapes the character of labor relations within and among industries, but also reveals a great deal about the internal trends of the organized labor movement and suggests factors responsible for general trends. In Table 7, I have summarized data on unions' penetration of major industrial sectors from 1930 to 1985. Before commenting on the results, I wish to call attention to the eclectic nature of the figures. The figures for all industries except government, 1930–53, are from unpublished or published data by the author, while those from 1966–85 are from census reports, most of which were prepared for the Department of Labor but nevertheless are not consistent throughout. Despite these limitations, I believe the results accurately reflect the trends among major industrial sectors over the last half-century.

Manufacturing, formerly the largest industrial sector in employment until it was surpassed by services in 1982, had been predominantly nonunion before the rise of the Congress of Industrial Organizations in the 1930s.[13] By 1939, the percentage of unionized employees in manufacturing had nearly tripled over the 1930 level. The density rate nearly doubled again by 1953, the year in which unions most likely attained their highest penetration of manufacturing at 42.4 percent. From that time on, the degree of unionization in manufacturing has slipped steadily to the current level of 25 percent. Nevertheless, the decline in manufacturing has not shrunk to 1930 levels as it has for two other centers of industrial union strength, mining and construction.

Even more dramatic turnarounds in union penetration rates have occurred in mining and construction. As Table 7 shows, mining unionization rose sharply during the New Deal era, and by 1947 had approximately quadrupled its 1930 density. From that peak, union penetration has fallen sharply and steadily and currently accounts for less than 15 percent of the sector, a percentage even below its 1930 depression rate. Construction unions, probably the labor movement's strongest industrial center over much of its history and the backbone of the old American Federation of Labor, also grew during the 1930s and continued to increase their penetration rate in the post–World War II era. After 1947, however, such a precipitous decline ensued that at the beginning of 1985, construction unions had dropped far below the 1930 rate of 64.5 percent of employment unionized to 22.3 percent.

Transportation unions traced a record of growth similar to the other industrial sectors reported in Table 7, gaining sharply during the New Deal period and continuing to increase their strength until peaking in 1953. However, the sector differs from the other industries in that much of it was subject to government regulation in *addition* to the National Labor Relations Act, as in the case of railway and airline transportation, to the Railway Labor Act. Under the Railway Labor Act union shop agreements were made legal and, as a result of a Supreme Court decision, are not subject to right-to-work laws, a factor undoubtedly contributing to the high unionization rate of the industry.

In addition to regulating labor relations, government also regulated prices charged by interstate rail and road carriers and airlines. The pricing of these services has been deregulated only recently. For unions, regulation brought not only greater wages and benefits, but until at least 1953, increased organization. Thereafter, the penetration rate fell, but transportation union membership is still substantially higher than all other private major industrial sectors. Railways, which have had the longest and probably the most comprehensive regulation of their labor relations, are still about 80 percent organized, and are only outranked in density by the U.S. Postal Service, a government enterprise in which government involvement in labor relations dates from the early part of the century. In 1983, the USPS was 87 percent unionized, although the rate has declined from its all-time high of 95.5 percent in 1976.

Services, the most rapidly growing major industrial sector, historically has been very low in the percentage of employees unionized, as Table 7 shows. Indeed, in 1982 services surpassed manufacturing as the largest major industrial sector in employment (services include such categories as hotels, personal services, business services, auto repair, motion pictures, amusements, health, and private educational services). Rates for the 1980s show a declining trend and are already below post–World War II and Korean War levels. In fact, they are only just above the rates of the late 1930s. The weak position of unions in the service industries underscores the crisis of American trade unionism now and for the foreseeable future: unions are slipping sharply in the declining industries, the historic mainstays of union organization, and have failed to take hold in the growth portions of the labor market. Until 1976, government was the only sector in which density (and for that matter, membership) continued to increase. At that time, the unionized proportion of government employment— federal, state, and local—topped out at 40.2 percent. Since 1976 the proportion of employees organized in the public sector has fallen, as reported in Table 7.

Variability in the rates at which membership and density among industrial sectors rose and fell quite naturally changed the *industrial composition* of American unionism. From unions' inception to the eve of the founding of the Congress of Industrial

Organization in the 1930s, virtually three-fourths of all membership was in the nonmanufacturing industries. After 1935,
manufacturing unionism surged, but never accounted for one-half
or more of total membership. Since the end of the Korean War,
when it accounted for 45 percent of total membership (probably
the peak share), manufacturing union membership's share of the
total has shrunk steadily, currently to about 29 percent, a proportion less than in 1939. However, the renewed dominance of nonmanufacturing unionism in the 1980s is different from that which
prevailed from the beginning of the modern union movement until
the 1930s. The growth of public sector unionism, which is included
in the nonmanufacturing total, is the reason. Whereas the dominance of the construction and other nonmanufacturing unions of
the 1930s led the philosophy and policies of organized labor (identified as those of the AFL) in a conservative direction, the weight
of the public sector group in the AFL-CIO is redirecting organized
labor toward a more leftist philosophy, a matter that I will examine below.

Mergers. The declining fortunes of American unions have accelerated mergers, especially since the late 1960s. "Merger"
means either the fusion of two or more national or international
unions, or the absorption of one or more smaller unions into a
larger national or international union. In the latter case, the
smaller unions may or may not retain an autonomous identity, but
even if an autonomous identity is retained, the parent union is still
in administrative control. In some cases, small organizations
affiliate with larger ones, but do not surrender their identity; these
are not regarded as mergers here, but as secondary affiliations.
For example, the ill-fated Professional Air Traffic Controllers
union was affiliated with the Masters, Mates, and Pilots, AFL-
CIO, but functioned independently.

One of the expectations of the merger of the AFL and the CIO,
which occurred in December 1955, was that affiliates with overlapping jurisdictions and parallel interests would merge. Very little came of this, but what the merger of the two federations failed
to achieve, adverse circumstances did. An acceleration of union
mergers beginning in the late 1960s encompassed labor organizations outside the AFL-CIO as well as those within the federation.[14]

Merger activity picked up even more speed in the late 1970s when the factors spurring combination became more severe.[15] Factors responsible for the recent increase in mergers include greater foreign competition, technological innovations, recessions (1973–75 and 1981–82), weakness of unions in the private service economy,[16] costly jurisdictional disputes, attempts at shoring-up collective bargaining strength, and survival in the face of dwindling membership.[17] Over one-third of all mergers recorded by the Bureau of Labor Statistics from December 1955 to April 1984 have occurred since 1979.[18] Not all takeover attempts are friendly, however, as exemplified by the Teamsters' aborted attempts to absorb the International Typographical Union. The record of mergers does not include those which are not consummated nor the number of those seeking amalgamation openly or covertly. Furthermore, the large number of small national unions presages still more merger activity in the future. The AFL-CIO is expected to take a more active role in arranging marriages, and perhaps the Federation will now be more successful than it was in its first decade of existence, given the more intense economic pressures many of its affiliates confront.

Mergers sometimes function as a substitute for organizing the unorganized. Many unions have turned their organizing attention to absorbing independent state public-employee associations rather than organizing previously unorganized workers. For many of these independent associations, joining an AFL-CIO union has many attractions, not the least of which is insulation from raids by other AFL-CIO unions under Article 20 of the Federation's constitution. This protection does not apply, of course, to powerful independents such as the Teamsters or the NEA. An additional inducement for many associations to merge is that they are in states without legislative provisions protecting a certified bargaining representative from a raid for one year after a representation election or for a longer period under a contract bar rule. Finally, takeovers are a low-cost way of reviving their fortunes, given the declining circumstances confronting many unions. Even though conditions are markedly different, such maneuvers are reminiscent of national and international unions' takeovers of company unions in manufacturing during the 1930s, such as the CIO's Steelworkers Organizing Committee organizing drive against U.S. Steel and other companies.[19]

Unions in the forefront of the acquisition movement come from both the private and the public sector. The most successful appears to be the Service Employees International Union (SEIU), AFL-CIO, hitherto an organization primarily in the private sector. Because of its remarkable success in acquiring public sector groups, the SEIU is becoming a new form in union structure, what I term a "joint" union, that is, a union with members from two distinct segments of the labor market and often with significant occupational differences. However, it is unlike the "amalgamated" union of earlier times which combined skilled and less-skilled workers from the private labor market only. Whether the "joint" public-private sector union will be a stable structural form merits future attention. Instability is a possibility, I believe, because of the competing goals and policies of organized public and private sector employees, a subject that I have yet to examine in this chapter. Because of the SEIU's growth-through-merger, it is not possible to assert with certainty that its core private sector membership has declined along with the general union movement, but this is very likely to have been the case.

The pressure on major unions to take action to retrieve losses is underscored by contrasting peak-to-current membership of leading unions. The hardest hit is the United Steelworkers of America, AFL-CIO. From its 1973 peak of nearly 1.1 million members in the United States, in ten years the union had lost more than 50 percent of its membership (Table 8). Indeed, the losses were even greater than indicated because in September 1972 the Steelworkers absorbed District 50, which had over 200,000 members in

Table 8

Membership Changes, Selected Unions, Peak and Current Year
(000's)

	Peak (1)	Current (2)	Peak Year	Ratio (2)/(1)
Teamsters	1946.0	1523.4	1974	83.8
NEA	1817.6	1444.2	1976	79.5
Auto Workers	1425.7	903.8	1969	63.4
Steelworkers	1069.9	496.6	1973	46.4
Machinists	859.9	475.3	1969	55.2

Note: Membership figures are for the United States only; membership figures of Canadian affiliates are excluded. The current year is 1983.

the United States. No wonder, therefore, that the *Wall Street Journal* could report that the Steelworkers "recently set its sights on 20 unions, each with under 100,000 members as merger candidates."[20] It is no surprise that it has been rumored that the Steelworkers are considering a change in name. Even the mighty Teamsters, pressed by deregulation, has seen its membership shrink in excess of 400,000 between the peak year of 1974 and 1983 (Table 8). Another heavy loser, surprisingly, is the NEA. Independent, whose average full-time dues-paying membership is down more than 370,000 from its peak year, 1976. On the other hand, it is not surprising that the Auto Workers and the Machinists have taken very large membership losses between their peak and current years.

Since membership losses stem principally from disappearing employment, a significant and interesting response of a few unions and their members is to take over ownership of the company. While historically, employee-operated enterprise has had a poor record, this has not discouraged contemporary efforts. One that apparently has been successful is the Independent Steel Workers Union's acquisition of National Steel's plant in Weirton, West Virginia. The union is a local independent that over the years successfully resisted incorporation into the United Steelworkers Union.

The statistical record I have presented paints a somber picture of American trade unionism. In general, the decline—perhaps even what might be characterized as the decay—of the modern union movement in this country is the result of long-term forces. Are there any current data and developments that might point to a reversal of the long-run decline? In brief, I believe the answer is no. True, there is a small number of unions that made gains in recent years, such as the Food and Commercial Workers, the American Federation of Teachers, and the American Federation of State, County and Municipal Employees, all affiliates of the AFL-CIO, but some of their gains stem from mergers rather than previously unorganized workers. More importantly, the failure of the union movement to participate in the economic recovery underway in this country since November 1982 is an extremely ominous sign for the future. While the cyclical sensitivity of membership is difficult to track because the figures are annual data, union membership generally rises after an improvement in business conditions. Yet total numbers fell in 1983, 1984, and 1985, and the bottom is not yet in sight.

Determinants of Unions' Rise and Decline

Market forces. By far the most important forces driving down membership and the percentage of the labor market organized appear to be economic, both long and short term. One key long-run factor has been the shift to a labor market dominated by employment in industries furnishing services: the switch from a goods to a service labor market has meant the decline of union and the expansion of nonunion employments and industries. Adopting Victor Fuch's definition of the goods industries, the transition took place about thirty years ago, or roughly coincident with the peak union penetration of the labor market in 1953.[21]

Many of the characteristics of the private-service sector pose severe obstacles to the spread of unionism, and unions were unsuccessful in coping with them even before services came to dominate the labor market. Among the principal reasons for the private-service sector's resistance to unionism are the prevalence of smaller, owner-operated businesses; greater personalization of work; extensive employment of youth, part-timers, and women; self-production of some services by consumers; greater industrial heterogeneity and dispersion of employment; the educational requirements of many occupations essential to the service industries; and perhaps most significant of all, the very large number of white-collar occupations found in the services. Because these factors are continuing to grow in importance while employment in the services is also continuing to expand, the barriers to the spread of unions will also become larger.

The switch in the economy also has important long-run spillover effects on the goods sector of the labor market itself and therefore on unions. Within the goods industries there has been a radical change in the composition of employment, a relative reduction of blue-collar coupled with a rise of white-collar occupations. In 1953, one-fifth of manufacturing employment consisted of nonproduction workers; in 1983 the proportion had jumped to one-third. Even more telling than the radical change in the composition of manufacturing is that there are the same number of production workers in manufacturing today as thirty years ago. In construction, mining, transportation, communications, and public utilities, the proportion of blue-collar production workers has also become smaller.

In union terms, the compositional exchange of nonproduction for production employment has meant an exchange of nonunion for union jobs and therefore constitutes another source of "leakage" in union ranks and density. Decertification elections might also be thought a factor in the ebbing of union penetration of some of the industries reported in Table 7, but this is not the case because these are too few in number and involve too few workers to account for the declines shown. They do reflect, however, employee opposition to unions, a factor of great importance in explaining the poor record in organizing the unorganized. Other key long-run factors are: changes in the methods of production, the substitution of capital for labor, and in the industrial life cycle of industries.[22] Unions have suffered from this switch but also have stimulated the change because of higher-than-market wages and benefits. Again, unions are both a victim and a cause of such changes.

One way the substitution of nonunion for union production workers occurs is in plant relocation. When companies relocate organized plants to nonunion areas of the country, often to states with right-to-work laws, membership and union density are reduced. Another way is through corporate mergers and acquisitions in which the survivor company breaks relations with unions and substitutes nonunion for union labor. The impact of these varied economic forces (and employer opposition is such a force) on union ranks can be gauged from census data from the period 1980–84. Thus, between 1980 and 1984, employment in durable-goods manufacturing fell by 500,000, while union membership in these same industries plummeted by double that number, one million.[23] During the same period, nondurables lost 300,000 jobs and 400,000 union members.

One way to gauge the long-run impact of the service-dominated labor market and the substitution effect on union membership is to estimate how much larger it would be in the private economy if the shift from goods to services had not taken place. Thus, if employment in 1983 had the same structure as in 1953 and the percentages organized in each major private industry were those actually prevailing in 1983, union membership in the goods industries would have been 3.4 million greater, and 700,000 fewer in the services, for a net of 2.7 million more than actual 1983 membership. Although this is speculative, I believe that it suggests just how powerful the impact of the new service labor market and the long-run substitution effect has been on unionism.

Increased foreign competition, business cycles, industrial migration, the rise of new industries and companies—frequently nonunion, the decline of older more organized firms and industries, and deregulation have hewed large chunks out of the ranks of unions. The breakup of the American Telephone and Telegraph Corporation and the ensuing competition in telecommunications and in communications equipment manufacturing and service are bound to injure the unions in these industries, notably the Communications Workers of America (CWA) and the International Brotherhood of Electrical Workers (IBEW). The IBEW has had a small reduction in its membership between 1983 and 1985, a decline that I believe can be attributed in part to the breakup of AT&T. The impact on the CWA has thus far been obscured by the union's absorption of some public-sector associations.

Foreign competition has dealt devastating blows to union membership and is the principal reason for the depletion in the ranks of the Steelworkers, Auto Workers, and Machinists (Table 8). Deregulation must be held responsible, in part, for the loss of more than 400,000 members by the Teamsters from their peak in 1974 (Table 8). The data on the extent of unionization by state (Table 5) reflect the consequences of the migration of industry from more-organized to less-organized parts of the country, as well as the fact that many new firms and industries which have moved to the Sunbelt states—or even when they have located in previously well-organized states such as Massachusetts and New Jersey—originate as and remain nonunion.

Business downturns typically reduce union membership while upturns usually bring with them a rise in membership. During the most recent cyclical experience, union membership fell with the downturn but, significantly, failed to revive during the upturn. Between January and July of 1980 the economy turned down, then it revived until July 1981, after which it turned down severely until November 1982. Since then, business conditions have improved markedly: real GNP in 1984 grew at a rate not experienced since 1951, and the expansion continued through 1985 and into 1986, albeit at a much reduced rate. Nevertheless, unions not only failed to make a comeback during the last three years, but contrary to previous experience they lost membership. Between 1980 and 1982, a period dominated by recession, unions lost nearly 1.4 million members; between 1982 and 1984, a period of strong economic recovery, unions lost yet another 1.25 million members. Census data show that the decline in membership continued in 1985, although at a much reduced pace. This episode may be the largest non-cyclical-associated loss in union annals; certainly it is atypical and reinforces my judgment that American trade unions are in a permanent state of decline, certainly as measured by the percentage of the labor market organized.

Public policy. As I mentioned previously, tests showed two leading econometric models that attempt to explain American union behavior as being structurally unstable. My colleague Neil Sheflin has noted that contrary to the models' conclusions, "the process of union growth in the United States has not remained unchanged during the twentieth century."[24] Furthermore, the break point—the shift in the process—occurred in 1937 in one model and 1938 in the other, in tandem in one instance and virtually so in the other with the April 1937 validation of the National Labor Relations Act by the Supreme Court. In other words, the nature of the process governing the growth of unions specified in each econometric model began to change coincident with the Wagner Act.

After finding that the Wagner Act influenced the process of union growth, Sheflin went on to consider how long it took the Wagner Act to change the processes specified in the two models. He found that the duration of the transition period from one "regime" governing union growth to another depended on which year one considered that the National Labor Relations Act became effective. Should it be 1937, when the NLRA was upheld by the Supreme Court, or 1935, when it was enacted? If 1937 is selected, then the transition from one growth process to another occurred quickly; that is, the transition to a different growth process was completed by early 1938. If the analysis uses the enactment year, 1935, then the transition took three to four and one-half years, implying completion of the transition somewhere between mid-1938 and the end of 1939. The results of the two procedures are not inconsistent, however, because for the first two years of the NLRA—from July 1935 when it was enacted, to April 1937 when it was declared constitutional—it was largely ignored in the belief that the Supreme Court would invalidate the statute.

Even in the absence of econometric indications of the significance of the Wagner Act, qualitative analysis has identified the NLRA as a critical and significant factor on the process of union growth. Unions certainly regard public policy that fosters organizing and collective bargaining as important to their well-being. When the Taft-Hartley Act amended the NLRA in 1947, redirecting the objective of that law from one-sided support of labor organization to one of balance, the amended law was denounced by organized labor as a "slave labor act." In 1977–78, the labor movement unsuccessfully attempted to have the NLRA drastically amended to extend and deepen government intervention, in favor of organizing and bargaining. In the interim they obtained an Executive Order from President Kennedy in 1962, which launched public sector unionism in this country. In 1977, Title VII of the Civil Service Reform Act was enacted, codifying federal policy on federal employee unionism and bargaining. Previously, under the Postal Reorganization Act of 1970, postal employees were transferred to the jurisdiction of the National Labor Relations Board (NLRB), and the scope of bargaining between the postal unions and the USPS was extended to include wages. Although strikes and compulsory membership agreements for all federal employees continued to be forbidden, the legal changes in federal labor relations which the unions won in the 1970s brought federal-employee union practices much closer to those in the private sector. This was a major step toward the unions' goal of what I term "convergence": the elimination of differences in the legal status of public and private sector unions in bargaining, making public sector labor relations like those in the private economy.[25]

What about the NLRB? Recently, organized labor, with some academic support, attacked its practices, claiming it a major factor contributing to the decline of union strength in this country.[26] Criticisms of the NLRB are not new, cropping up whenever Republican presidents appoint majorities to the board. During the Eisenhower years, when unions began their long-run decline as a percentage of the private sector labor market, pro-union critics blamed both the Taft-Hartley amendments to the NLRA and the board.[27] In the 1960s and 1970s the decline in private sector density continued, even though board majorities were appointed by Democratic presidents during much of the period; with the recent massive decline in membership among private sector unions, severe attacks on the board and its policies have resumed.[28]

These criticisms of the board and its policies minimize the fact that the right to organize and to bargain collectively are legally protected activities and that employer interference with those rights still violates the law. Indeed, if the Act and its applications are toothless, as its critics contend, why do unions continue to file charges under it? Moreover, where is it ordained that the application of public policy must be wielded solely on behalf of one group in an open society? More importantly, both the Act and the board, in my judgment, are responding to the reascendancy of market forces. The goal of the New Deal labor policy was to contain or suppress market forces in industrial relations, and this it did successfully for quite some time. However, market forces have reemerged and have chipped away at the monopoly powers bestowed by the labor policies of the 1930s. Public policy had a great deal to do with the rise of unions, but market forces are primarily responsible for its decline.

Because it is still widely believed that the NLRA and its administration bring net benefits to unionism, it was a great surprise when the president of the AFL-CIO, Lane Kirkland, suggested repealing the nation's labor laws and letting business and labor battle it out "mano a mano."[29] According to Kirkland, repeal would speed up the organization of the unorganized. However, most union leaders and labor lawyers reject laissez-faire labor relations. Meanwhile, a thoughtful and expert proposal to do just that by abolishing the NLRA and the Federal Anti-Injunction Act (the Norris-LaGuardia Act) has been made.[30] Richard Epstein proposed replacing them with a "coherent theory of private law, with well-developed principles of contract and tort, [which] can govern labor relations."[31] Because current public policy still confers benefits on unions, the proposal was rejected by union supporters.[32] Nevertheless, it is an idea that may have a future, given the reemergence of public belief in the market system.

Employer opposition. As for employer opposition, whoever said that labor-management relations is not a game of hardball? From the inception of unions in this country, employers, or most of them, have opposed unionization of their employees; this is a rational economic response on the part of employers and not a new element in the process of organizing the unorganized. In the 1930s, unions made their most spectacular gains in the private economy despite the bitterest employer opposition in union history. As Freeman and Medoff (among the archetypical advocates of employer opposition as the cause of union decline) stated, "when unions are most costly to employers, employers are most hostile to unions."[33] At the same time it is important to remember that unions are declining in other major industrial countries (Table 9) where employer opposition is less of a factor, if a serious factor at all.

Advocates of the employer opposition argument fail to distinguish adequately between union losses in established units and new organization to compensate for these reductions in membership. While employer opposition plays a role in thwarting the organizing of the unorganized, most of the decline in membership is associated with losses in employment. Economic factors, such as those already noted, are primarily responsible for declines in union membership, not employer ejection of unions from established units. Thus, Dickens and Leonard pointed out that decertification elections played no major role in accounting for the decline in union membership in the period 1950–80.[34] How much the unions could have made up for their membership losses due to economic factors in the absence of employer opposition is a matter of speculation and of course is a "non-sense" question, since employers usually oppose unionization of their employees. The relevant question is whether they do so within the law and its administration by the NLRB, matters on which there can be wide divergence of judgment.

What of the other side of the coin, the opposition of workers to unionization? The charge that employer opposition is mainly responsible for unions' inability to organize the unorganized assumes that American workers are completely cowed by their employers, that workers who vote against unions are mindless automatons completely manipulated by their employers. In this view, only when workers vote for a union are they acting rationally. Yet there is evidence that most nonunion workers reject unions for their own reasons. In a December 1984 report to the AFL-CIO, Medoff found that "only 30 percent of the nonunion work force in a survey conducted in 1977 responded yes to the question, 'Would you join a union if one existed in your workplace?'"[35] In an analysis of the preference of unorganized workers toward union representation, only one-third would vote for a union in an election with a secret ballot. In a demographic breakdown of the results the only subgroup with a majority that would vote for a union was nonwhite workers, 69 percent.[36] This finding is especially significant because minority workers must surely regard themselves the most vulnerable of all workers and therefore most susceptible to employer pressure not to join unions. Are we to assume that all other workers, presumably more secure than nonwhites, nevertheless feel more susceptible to employer pressure?

Other data in the Medoff report indicate that nonunion workers may, indeed, hold their own views on what serves their best interests. Coincident with a fourfold increase in charges of employer unfair labor practices, Gallup polls showed, according to the Medoff report, "that the public approval of unions declined steadily during the entire 1965–1981 period" and that the public's attitude was never less favorable than in 1981, the latest year available at the time of the report.[37] It is reasonable, therefore, to conclude from these results that nonunion workers' opposition to unions is part of the public's disapproval of unions, not *sui generis* simply a product of employer manipulation. But the Medoff survey does not end there. In response to the survey query, "Which do you think is a bigger problem—companies that unfairly deny their workers a chance to join a union, or unions that do not fairly represent their members?" more than two-thirds of the general population (68 percent) identified the unions, 17 percent identified the company, and the remainder gave no response.[38]

Another recent study on the attitude of nonunion workers toward unions reported that only one-fourth of unorganized male workers between the ages of twenty-eight and thirty-eight favored a union. By industry, only in public administration did more than one-half (54 percent) support a union.[39] This should not be surprising in view of the close collaboration of public officials and union officials in many state and urban jurisdictions. The same study showed that in the historic strongholds of unions—mining, construction, and manufacturing—the proportions of nonunion workers favoring unions were 20 percent, 34 percent, and 19 percent, respectively! These startling results parallel the sharp declines in the penetration rates of unions in these industries over the past three decades, as indicated in Table 7. In general, the findings on nonunion worker attitudes coincide with the decline of union representation in NLRB elections, especially over the last decade. It seems reasonable, therefore, that the failure of nonunion workers to join unions goes beyond a simplistic analysis that places the bulk of the blame on employer opposition while ignoring employee opposition.

Unions. The employer opposition explanation exonerates unions themselves from responsibility and gives the leadership a convenient scapegoat. But what of the unions themselves? Are not unions themselves a factor in their decline? It may be that American unions are in the grip of forces beyond the control of any union managerial force, and, indeed, I do believe this is largely the case. Nevertheless, the management of unions is doubtless a factor also. Business failures or declines usually lead to the replacement of the incumbent management, and yet criticism of union leadership is muted and officers at the national level are infrequently challenged. Moreover, given the defeat organized labor suffered in the presidential election of 1984, it is remarkable that the leadership that engineered the political involvement of the AFL-CIO apparently escaped any challenge for their failure. Yet at its latest convention in October 1985 the leadership of the AFL-CIO again decided to endorse a candidate for the Democratic Party's nomination. A. H. Raskin caustically characterized this decision as follows:

The Anaheim convention of the AFL-CIO, in dutiful response to the strongly expressed wish of the federation's high command and in contemptuous disregard of the reservations expressed by virtually all segments of the professional leadership of the Democratic party, decided that three years in advance of the 1988 presidential elections was none too soon to affirm its eagerness to duplicate next time around every suicidal step in the approach to nominating and electing a President of the United States that backfired so disastrously against labor in 1984.[40]

There may be other mistakes in judgment. The financial resources of unions are, to say the least, respectable. The most recent statistics available, those for 1982, showed unions had net receipts of $135 million and consolidated net assets of $6.3 billion, a record high. Despite such healthy financial resources, a study by Paula Voss reported by Freeman and Medoff showed that union expenditures on organizing declined sharply into the 1970s. Although stating that their estimates might be crude, Freeman and Medoff concluded that, " . . . possibly as much as a third of the decline of union success through NLRB elections is linked to reduced organizing activity."[41] Depending on the figures one uses to determine *employer* responsibility for the unions' decline in organizing success, unions' *own* responsibility for the decline could exceed that which they attribute to employer opposition.[42]

Two other important factors responsible for the decline of unions deserve at least brief mention, disinflation and the substitution of government services for many of those provided by collective bargaining. Disinflation coupled with the rising share of the unorganized labor market have reduced negotiated increases and have prompted union concessions. Milton Friedman pointed out nearly forty years ago that "it is not so much that strong unions will produce inflation as that inflation will produce strong unions."[43]

Paradoxically, governments at all levels, actively encouraged by unions, are providing substitutes for union organization and collective bargaining.[44] By enactments and judicial interpretations limiting employers' right to discharge at will, establishing safety and health laws and regulations, and creating pensions, government is offering workers benefits competitive with union benefits. Currently, the Secretary of Labor has a commission considering the employer right to close plants, after a bill regulating their right to do so narrowly missed passage in the House of Representatives.

Conclusions: Consequences and Outlook

Philosophy and policies. Clearly, reduced union strength will contribute to weaker unions at the bargaining table, as already indicated. A report by the Labor Department on employment costs in 1985 showed that its "most striking feature ... was a slowdown in compensation gains for union workers," rising 2.6 percent compared to 4.6 percent for nonunion workers.[45] This continues a slowdown in union-negotiated gains since the beginning of the decade. Coupled with declining union membership, extent of organization, organizing activity, and smaller gains at the bargaining table, unions are compensating by markedly increasing their political activity. This is shown by their unprecedented action in supporting a candidate for the Democratic Party's presidential nomination in 1984, and their intention of repeating that process for the 1988 election.

Beyond the unions' increased political activism lies something more profound: a change in union philosophy between the presidencies of Franklin Delano Roosevelt and Ronald Reagan, from that expressed by the traditional philosophy of "more" to one that I call "more government intervention" in the economy and society of this country. The shift will make the union movement much more political than ever before in its history, and in this sense, will become more like union movements in Western Europe. Thus, the very character of the American union movement has changed since the New Deal, its politicization accelerated by its steady and deep decline.

Yet current interventionist philosophy and policies are not actually a complete break with historic positions: "more intervention" is an evolutionary extension of "more." The rise of public sector unionism has accentuated the interventionist philosophy and practices of organized labor, but more importantly is also changing the nature of the intervention.[46] The traditional philosophy of American unions expressed in the single word "more" simply meant that trade unions wanted more real income for their members; it came to be known as "bread and butter" unionism. The labor movement's policies for achieving its goal were straightforward—acceptance of the market system and the reliance on collective bargaining. Hence, organized labor's philosophy and policies were characterized as pragmatic and empirical.

Because American unions rejected socialism (despite the Marxist rhetoric in the preamble of the AFL, which remained until its merger with the CIO in December 1955) and relied principally on collective bargaining to gain "more," there is the mistaken impression that organized labor was essentially apolitical. However, from their inception, unions were always engaged in political activities. Again, it was practical and empirical, and was best expressed by Samuel Gompers' credo of rewarding political friends and punishing political enemies. Intellectuals frequently contrasted this unfavorably with the Western European union movements' commitment to socialism—that is, the allegedly more sophisticated strategy of restructuring society as the way to get "more" for workers.

Instead of undertaking a master project of social engineering, American unions applied their political efforts to make collective bargaining more effective. They sought and eventually secured a wide measure of legal sanction of their activities in organizing, striking, picketing, and boycotts. Indeed, they became very successful in switching government policy from the protection of property to the protection of union activities. Legal protection of these activities strengthened unions' abilities to get "more," and therefore was concomitant with that philosophy. With the enactment of the Federal Anti-Injunction Act in 1932 and the National Labor Relations Act in 1935, organized labor's efforts to gain legal immunities were largely won.

As a result of the Great Depression, organized labor shifted its emphasis to a new form of government intervention, the exercise of macroeconomic policies to "fine tune" the economy in the interests of high employment and high wages. In the post–World War II era, organized labor shifted its focus from the battle over legal immunities (Taft-Hartley notwithstanding) to government intervention to manage the economy. In brief, full employment displaced legal rights as the unions' primary concern.

That the advent of large-scale, public sector unionism accelerated government intervention in the economy and society is not surprising. But not as evident is public sector unionism's impact on the *nature* of that intervention, putting public sector unions on

a collision course with private sector unions. On one hand, private
sector unions want government to vigorously apply macroeconomic policies to stimulate economic growth and avoid depression; on the other hand, public sector unions want a *redistribution*
of the national income from the private to the public sector in the
form of social services and transfer payments. In this sense, public
sector unions are as much the offspring of the Great Society as the
New Frontier.

The redistributionist goal of public sector unions and their
members puts them at odds with the goals of private sector unions
and their members, especially in the long run. This is because private sector unions, with the help of government intervention,
want to raise members' income; to the extent they are successful,
their members become subject to higher taxes, which their fellow
public sector unions will want to push even higher. Anecdotal evidence of this recently came from the leader of a Teamster
organization with both public and private sector membership, who
was reported as saying that his union will soon discuss higher
taxes in some areas to support wage increases for its public sector
members. "The issue," he continued, "could be explosive internally...."[47] For unions with a close balance between public and
private sector members, such as the Service Employees, the internal dissension could be so severe as to raise the question of
whether the "joint" union of public and private sector members is
structurally stable.

In the short run, the two wings of organized labor are likely to
see their goals as complementary. Public sector unions have the
same goal in the short and long run. Private sector unions take the
Keynesian view that only the short run counts. During depressions they want government spending increased and financed out
of deficits, not taxes, and on this the two groups could agree.
However, during good economic periods and over the long run, private sector members will resist the tax increases demanded by
public sector unions to expand the public economy. As for the
clash on taxes, can there be any doubt that a large proportion of
the union vote which helped reelect President Reagan in 1984
came from private sector members?

The summary account of the differing uses to which government intervention should be put by public and private sector

unions does not fully span all the issues and implications. However, three important observations are in order: First, although public sector unions may claim they too favor economic growth (so as to enlarge their share of resources), their redistributional objectives can be expected to have a contrary effect. And although private sector unions may emphasize macroeconomic policies to stimulate growth, they too welcome government spending on output and services that employ their members, as for example, the construction unions. Finally, to the perennial question of whether American unions will one day embrace socialism, the experience of the past half-century with Keynesian policies of economic intervention has made that option obsolete. And at the same time, unions are unlikely to abandon their current attachment to Keynesian economics despite many economists' and intellectuals' disenchantment with it.

Outlook. Based on the record of trends in density and membership and on my analysis of the factors responsible for this record, I would argue that the American union movement is in a permanent state of decline. Decline does not mean extinction. It means that the union movement will continue to represent workers in the industries in which they are entrenched, but that new organization will be minimal and density will continue to slide. Overall, the nonunion sectors of employment are growing while the union sectors are declining or at best holding their own in employment. Moreover, within historically high-unionized industries like manufacturing, there is an exchange going on, an exchange between disappearing union jobs and new, unorganized jobs.

Additional information on union movements in other countries indicates that the decline of unionism may be becoming characteristic in industrialized societies, although Canada, Scandinavia, and Switzerland differ. Since the phenomenon is occurring in highly varied countries that differ in important ways in social and political structure, this suggests that economic factors are the common denominator in the decline. The data in Table 1 show that well-entrenched unions in Great Britain, West Germany, France, Italy, and Japan have also lost ground. Except for Japan, union density declined well after the American, but the direction

is clear and will likely deepen as the service-dominated labor
market emerges in these economies. In Japan, union penetration
of the labor force fell from 46.2 percent in 1950 to under 30 percent by 1983.

Is there anything that could reverse this declining pattern? Recently, the AFL-CIO undertook a self-study of its dilemma, and
recommended some new approaches to gain members.[48] One key
proposal is to attract the unorganized through associations, rather
than full-scale unions. Why a partial membership should appeal to
nonunion workers more than full-scale identification with unions
suggests a distinction that perhaps its academic proposers can dis-
cern, but whose subtlety is likely to be unappreciated either by
union organizers or unorganized workers. Apparently, the intent
is to apply to the private sector the experience of the public sector
of the 1960s and 1970s, when many associations, like the NEA,
transformed themselves into unions. However, the analogy does
not apply. First, the associations in the public sector were established well before collective bargaining. For example, the NEA
was established in the nineteenth century, and many state associations go back several decades if not further. Moreover, these
organizations were formed as professional associations to further
the welfare of groups with common interests. They were functioning entities and brought with them the know-how of a functioning
unit when they made the shift to unionism and bargaining.

In the private sector, unions would have to build associations
from the ground up. If successfully established, the theory is that
such "union-friendly" groups would eventually make the transition to full-scale unions. Such organization by the back door is
unlikely and cannot be attractive to unions. Why should they gamble valuable resources to establish a group that may never become
a union? For the same expenditure, they might just as well attempt full-scale organization. There is a gap here between the
academic and the union mind, and I doubt that the recommendation will attract support from experienced union organizers.
Moreover, in promoting such associations, unions may run afoul of
the NLRA's protection of the right-to-organize; they could find
themselves in the position of employers in the 1930s who set up
employee representation plans in order to thwart trade unionism.

Another recent AFL-CIO proposal to reverse membership

decline is to offer consumer benefits to the unorganized, such as low-cost credit cards. This smacks more of desperation than a serious effort to meet the challenge. A more serious and direct approach to organizing, adopted by the Executive Council of the Federation at its annual meeting in 1986, is a plan for organizing a targeted company through pressure on other companies doing business with the target, an approach similar to the illegal secondary boycott. The method was employed in the 1986 Hormel strike with no success. However, it has been reported that such tactics did help organize the giant J. P. Stevens textile company several years ago. The Federation is reported to be planning to establish a new office known as the office of Comprehensive Organizing Strategies and Tactics (COST) to carry out this policy.

In my judgment, only massive government intervention in labor relations can reverse the decline of unions, and even that reversal would be short-lived. It would require amending the NLRA along the lines of the proposed Labor Reform Act of 1977 to reverse the decline in the private sector. In the public sector, legislation to establish a national labor relations policy for state and local employees could revive union growth among public employees. The recent Supreme Court decision mandating that local authorities in San Antonio, Texas, pay federal minimum wages opens the constitutional way for federal legislation governing labor relations at the state and local levels of government. However, such enactments are unlikely for the foreseeable future. Most likely, therefore, the American labor movement will continue into its second century a much smaller movement than it is even now. The American labor movement always has been a minority movement in this country, and it will be a smaller one as it enters the twenty-first century.

II

Comparative Perspectives

4

CHRISTOPHER HUXLEY, DAVID KETTLER,
AND JAMES STRUTHERS

Is Canada's Experience
"Especially Instructive"?

In its labor relations as in many things, Canada has often been
considered, since the Second World War, little more than an ap-
pendage to the United States. Patterns of union organization, collective bargaining, and labor law appear essentially similar in
both countries, and, indeed, many of the unions and large employers are the same. The Americans have provided models and,
often, the leadership. But the past few years have brought about
some interesting changes. Starting in the late 1950s, the extent of
unionization in the United States first stagnated and then started
to decline, while all measures of union involvement in labor relations in Canada began a steady increase, which continues. Not

Research for this study was supported by the Frost Centre for Canadian Heritage and Development Studies, Trent University. David Kettler's contribution also benefited from a grant from
the Social Sciences and Humanities Research Council of Canada and a fellowship in the Bard
College Center.

surprisingly, a number of American unionists and academic
specialists have become curious about differences between the two
situations.

The AFL-CIO Committee on the Evolution of Work, in a widely
publicized report on the causes and possible remedies for the
failure of the American trade union movement to keep up with the
expansion of the work force, well illustrates this interest. "The
Canadian experience is especially instructive," the Committee
remarks. With "roughly the same kind of economy," "many similar employers," and comparable changes affecting the labor
market, "the percentage of the civilian labor force that is
organized increased in the period 1963–1983 from roughly 30 percent to 40 percent, at the same time that the percentage of
organized workers declined in the United States from 30 percent
to 20 percent."[1] Following an analysis developed by several of its
most influential economic advisers, the Committee saw differences
in public labor policy as the principal cause for the divergence. "In
Canada, unlike in the United States," it maintains, "the government has not defaulted in its obligation to protect the rights of
self-organization."[2]

The AFL-CIO Committee refers, here, mainly to legal and administrative policies concerning certification of unions as bargaining agents and to sanctions against unfair labor practices by
employers. There is no doubt that differences in these respects are
important. But a statement by a different union organization on
another occasion suggests a complementary approach to the
differences between American and Canadian developments.

At the end of 1984, the Canadian section of the United Auto
Workers (UAW), the sixth largest union in Canada, comprising
about 10 percent of the parent international union, made demands for autonomy that were so sweeping that they led to separation. In explaining and justifying his proposals, the Canadian
UAW Director, Robert White, repeatedly stressed that the Canadian union had to gain the freedom to pursue its "separate program." And this program was said to include not only a distinct set
of bargaining priorities for the automobile industry but also a
"Canadian labour movement program" in which the UAW had "a
responsibility to play a lead role."[3]

White stressed the rejection by the Canadian UAW and the

Canadian Labour Congress of the "concession era" in collective bargaining and their determination to "address the issue of jobs through political action" and through collective bargaining efforts to shorten the working day.[4] His union had already parted company with the international in the 1982 auto industry negotiations, refusing to accept profit sharing in lieu of regular increases, and in 1984 it had carried its disagreement to the point of a strike against General Motors rather than accepting the lump sum increases negotiated in Detroit.

It would be a journalistic oversimplification to trace differences that also involve pragmatic readings of distinctive market situations to a contrast between "business unionists" at the head of the American union, and the Canadian "social democrats." Yet, White and the Canadian UAW do represent a conception of the relationship between collective bargaining and broader political aims, as well as of strategies, which is more prevalent and influential in the Canadian labor movement than it has been in the American, especially during the past two decades.[5]

We suggest that the differences in governmental policies and practices noted by the AFL-CIO Committee, in its brief allusion to Canada, must be seen in conjunction with differences in the outlook and activities of unions, epitomized by the Canadian UAW's reasons for separation. Some commentators have spoken of the greater "militancy" of Canadian auto workers. Indeed, more generally, Rose and Chaison's study of the contrasting contemporary states of American and Canadian unions has suggested that the greater militancy of many Canadian unions—as measured, for example, by major indicators of overall strike activity during the years of growing divergence in density rates—cannot be ignored as a possible factor in the divergence itself.[6]

We relate American and Canadian union membership patterns to differences between the two labor regimes, defining the latter term as the "principles, norms, rules and decision-making processes around which actor-expectations converge in a given issue-area,"[7] along with the constellation of power upon which the arrangement rests.

Canada maintains adversarial collective bargaining within legal constraints that limit but also normalize the pattern. In the U.S., by contrast, the adversarial relationship within the labor regime has been moved back a step, in the direction of struggle over the legitimacy and normality of the collective bargaining pattern itself. This does not imply a "pro-labor policy" in Canada. Like other modern states, Canada is conditioned by public economic policies to manage the labor market in the interests of economic growth. Compared to the U.S., however, this management has proceeded more frequently through negotiations at the highest level or through *ad hoc* interventions that regulate or supersede collective bargaining, especially in the public sector, rather than through a weakening of the competitive position of organized labor within the adversarial system.[8]

Employers in America are more apt in general to pursue the goal of "union-free organizations," especially in new and growing sectors, and unions accept limitations imposed by employer resistance. Canadian employers and unions are both more willing to accept one another, and commit themselves more directly and blindingly to political parties. Although the labor-funded, socialist New Democratic Party (NDP) has never threatened the preponderant electoral position of the other two parties (Liberals and Progressive Conservatives) in federal elections, it has occupied a strategic "balance-of-power" position during periods of minority government, and it has been the governing or official opposition party in several of the more important provinces, whose governments in Canada control the bulk of labor policy. Unlike the American trade union movement, which has been divided from an important segment of its historical political support since the 1960s, the NDP has remained intact.

In short, the stronger position of Canadian unions has nothing to do with "mutualism" or long-term cooperation, which some have urged upon American unions as a new direction.[9] It seems doubtful that the lessons of this experience—if any can be transferred—are compatible with the American unions' preference for alternatives to the "adversarial collective bargaining relationship" or to the extreme caution with regard to political alliances implied in the AFL-CIO report.

Union Density in Canada and the U.S.

Data on unionization in Canada and the U.S. have been available since the early 1920s.[10] Table 1 shows changes in union density for each country for selected years between 1920 and 1984, and Figure 1 graphically compares union densities for the two countries from 1935 to 1980, giving union membership as a percentage of non-agricultural employment.

For more than half of the past sixty years, union membership density in Canada has exceeded that of the U.S. The major exception occurred in the long period of rapid union growth in the U.S. beginning in 1933. A corresponding breakthrough in union organization in Canada was not achieved until the end of World War II. This illustrates the uneven patterns of union growth in the two countries and raises a question about the most recent developments.

The most dramatic periods of union growth in the U.S. and Canada have taken place at different times, with different durations. Bain and Price note that over the years 1921–1977 the annual rate of change in union density fluctuated considerably more widely in the U.S. (ranging between −16.1 percent and +38.8 percent) than in Canada (where the range was between −13.8 percent and +19.0).[11] But if allowance is made for this difference in the amplitude of fluctuations in union growth, the similarity between the general trends in union density in the two countries for the first two-thirds of the period since the early 1920s becomes apparent. This similarity came to an end by the early 1960s. Since then, as noted by the AFL-CIO committee, the two patterns of union growth have diverged sharply.

The question nevertheless arises whether this continuing and increasing difference in union densities represents another expression of unevenness, and this question leads us to look carefully for signs of a return to similarity. Comparison between the two countries reveals no other instance of opposing tendencies at work for so long a period. For almost twenty-five years now, the two labor movements have been progressing along quite different trajectories. The longest period of sustained union growth in the U.S. extends from 1933 to 1947, although, as we shall show later, this is more correctly viewed as two distinct phases, the New Deal and World War II, with the union growth of the latter being followed shortly in Canada. Most other periods of union growth in the U.S. comprise gains over relatively short periods of time. For the years covered by our comparisons, Derber points to the periods

Table 1
Canadian and American Union Densities,[a]
Selected Years, 1921–1984

	Canada (Labour Canada) %	United States (BLS)	
1921	16.0	18.3	
1924	12.2	11.9	
1927	12.1	11.3	
1930	13.1	11.6	
1933	16.7	11.3	
1936	16.2	13.7	
1939	17.3	28.6	
1942	20.6	25.9	
1945	24.2	35.5	
1948	30.3	31.9	
1951	28.4	33.3	
1954	33.8	34.7	
1957	32.4	32.8	
1960	32.3	31.4	
1963	29.8	29.1	
1966	30.7	28.1	
1969	32.5	27.0	(29.5)[b]
1972	34.6	26.4	(29.4)
1975	36.9	25.3	(28.9)
1978	39.0	23.6	(26.2)
1980	37.6	N/A[c]	(24.6)
1981	37.4	N/A[d]	
1982	39.0	N/A[e]	
1983	40.0	20.7[e]	
1984	39.6	19.5[e]	

[a]Union membership as a percentage of nonagricultural work force.

[b]Starting in 1968, the BLS statistics add data on both unions and employee associations. Figures in parentheses include members of both types of organizations.

[c]Separate statistics for union members were unavailable in the 1980 survey.

[d]Data have not been collected by the BLS since 1981.

[e]Data supplied by Troy (see his chapter 3 in this volume) are drawn from a different series from that of the BLS and are not strictly comparable. They are, however, indicative, and correspond to the figures which the AFL-CIO Committee appears to have available.

Table 1 (cont'd)

Sources: Canadian union density: G.N. Chaison, "Unions: Growth, Structure, and Internal Dynamics," in John Anderson and Morley Gunderson, eds., *Union-Management Relations in Canada* (Don Mills, Ontario: Addison Wesley, 1982), p. 149, for the years 1921–1980. Minister of Labour (Labour Canada) *Directory of Labour Organizations in Canada, 1984,* (Ottawa: Minister of Supply and Services Canada, 1984), p. xxvi, for the years 1981–1984.

United States union density: G. S. Bain and R. Price, *Profiles of Union Growth* (Oxford: Blackwell, 1981), pp. 88–89 for the years 1921–1975. J. B. Rose and G. N. Chaison, "The State of the Unions: United States and Canada," *Journal of Labor Research* 6:1 (Winter 1985), p. 99 for the years 1976–80. L. Troy, "The Rise and Fall of American Trade Unions: The Labor Movement from FDR to RR" (see chapter 3 in this volume) for the years 1983–1984.

Figure 1

Union Density in the United States and Canada, 1935–1980

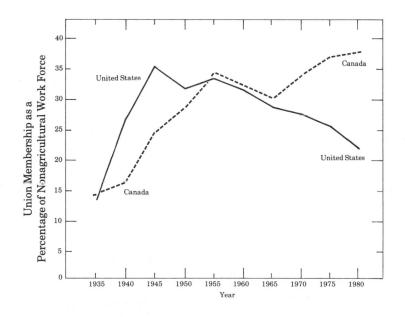

Source: Reproduced from Paul Weiler, "Promises to Keep: Securing Workers' Rights to Self-Organization under the NLRA," *Harvard Law Review* 96 (June 1983), pp. 1769–1827, p. 1818.

1950–1953 and 1965–1970 (although the latter spurt in membership did not suffice to interrupt the decline in union density, since
the nonagricultural work force grew faster).[12] In Canada, comparable periods of abrupt union expansion occurred during both
world wars. In contrast to continuing union decline in the U.S.
since the late 1950s, the Canadian upturn in the early 1960s has
been sustained and represents a longer-term phenomenon deserving explanation.

Divergences in union growth in the U.S. and Canada might be
understood by looking at the overall industrial distribution of
employment in the two countries. Meltz finds, however, that this
will not explain matters. He reports that if the pattern of employment in Canada in 1980 had been the same in the U.S., and if existing Canadian rates of union organization had pertained, the
overall level of union density for Canada would have been about 10
percent higher than its actual figure. In sum, he writes, "if Canada
were more like the United States in its employment distribution
there would be a greater difference in the overall rates of
organization".[13]

A related argument, which Meltz also considers, is that particular occupational groups can account for most of the difference in
union densities. More extensive unionization of the public sector
in Canada, for example, might provide an explanation. While this
is an important factor, it does not stand alone. Meltz reports that
by 1980—in contrast to the mid-1960s, when industry groups such
as construction, transportation, communications, and public
utilities, for example, were more unionized in the U.S.—all broad
occupational sectors were more highly unionized in Canada than
in the U.S. Weiler concludes that "Developments in the public sectors of the two countries . . . cannot explain the divergent . . . union
density in the two countries."[14] An indicator of private sector
union growth in Canada noted by Rose and Chaison is that Canadian sections of "international" unions have been increasing as a
proportion of the overall membership, while American memberships have fallen or at best held steady.[15]

Structural changes in the composition of the labor force in both
the U.S. and Canada since World War II have been well documented, with a similar relative decline in the manufacturing sector and a relative growth of government and service related sec-

tors. But the patterns of unionization in the two countries still reveal a sharp contrast. As Meltz observes:

In both countries, had there been no other changes, the shift in employment towards trade, finance, and service employees would have lowered overall rates of unionization. A decrease did not occur in Canada because membership rates grew in these industries and remained unchanged in the others. A net decline occurred in the United States because the growth of unionization in trade, finance, service and government was not sufficient to offset the declining rates of organization in the other sectors.[16]

The data are strong and consistent. Like the other observers who have considered them, we do not see any promising purely economic explanations. We believe, rather, that the historical differences between the labor regimes provide the most promising starting point.[17]

Disparate Developments toward Similarity: Canadian and American Unionism, 1935–1964

During and for the three decades immediately following World War II, the relations among labor, business, and the state stabilized within the U.S. and Canada. In both nations this "settlement" was supported by similar legal frameworks, deriving from the design of the U.S. National Labor Relations (Wagner) Act of 1935. In return for government recognition of workers' rights to collective bargaining, trade unions in both countries agreed to institutionalize labor conflict within conditioned terms of entry, collective agreements, and tactics. The corresponding agreement by business groups seems more reluctant, qualified, and by no means universally accepted; and the history of settlements has been marked by efforts by some parts of the business community—and intermittent efforts by many—to undo it. The labor regimes, accordingly, are characterized by political conflicts, notwithstanding their settled appearance.

Despite similarities in the shape of the labor "settlements" in Canada and the U.S., the process by which they were achieved and their subsequent durability differed significantly. In the U.S., the evolution of a *more regulatory* labor regime took place in three distinct stages between 1935 and 1952. During the first stage, lasting from 1935 through 1937, industrial unionism achieved its initial breakthroughs in America's mass production industries. After 1937, however, this initial organizing impetus was stalled by a new recession and employer resistance. Only the onset of World War II completed the dramatic recovery of American trade unionism. By virtue of full employment, expanding business profits, effective organization, and vigorous regulatory protection by the National War Labor Board, mass production unionism broke through the last barrier of "open shop" resistance. CIO membership more than doubled, and by the war's end approximately 35 percent of the American nonagricultural work force were union members.[18]

The years 1946–52 marked the third stage of the American labor settlement. The postwar strike wave of 1945–47, combined with a political reaction against wartime controls associated with labor's political allies, fostered legislative responsiveness to business campaigns against union power. The 80th Congress passed the Taft-Hartley Act, placing substantial new limits on trade unions—including restrictions on the closed shop, a ban on secondary boycotts and sympathy strikes, the provision of sweeping new federal labor injunctions, the prohibition of strikes in cases of national emergency—and granting state governments the authority to outlaw union shops for employees otherwise under federal jurisdiction.[19]

Despite a concerted campaign, the American labor movement was unable to secure the repeal of Taft-Hartley. Union membership grew modestly during the early 1950s, but organized labor, in an increasingly unfriendly political environment, was unable to recover the organizing momentum of the 1941–46 era. Reaching a postwar peak in 1953–54 of nearly 35 percent of the nonagricultural work force, union density in the U.S. began a slow decline, which continues to the present.

Within Canada, a broadly similar labor settlement emerged during the 1940s, but the process was telescoped within a much shorter time period and did not come up against as sweeping a legislative backlash as Taft-Hartley. Canada's labor situation is also conditioned by a difference in constitutional doctrine. Under a 1925 decision, Canadian federalism was interpreted to place labor law jurisdiction over 90 percent of the work force in the provinces.

During the 1930s, Canadian trade unions enjoyed no legislative protection. Federal labor legislation remained oriented towards the avoidance of work stoppages, not union recognition. The Industrial Disputes Investigation Act of 1907 provided elaborate procedures for conciliation, including compulsory "cooling-off" periods before strikes could lawfully occur. Although this legislation ceased to apply to cases placed under provincial jurisdiction after 1925, it continued to set the tone. As a consequence, Canadian unions, for the most part, failed to achieve major breakthroughs equivalent to the 1937 recognition drives of the CIO in the U.S. On the eve of World War II, unionization in Canada was making gradual headway, compared to the American experience of a steady steep climb (see Figure 1).

World War II transformed Canadian, as well as U.S., labor. During the first three years of Canadian involvement, the federal government attempted to manage the war effort without significant reform in labor legislation. Through the legislative authority of the War Measures Act, which superseded provincial jurisdictions, it enforced compulsory conciliation, wage controls, and compulsory allocation of essential labor. However, it refused to establish compulsory union recognition or collective bargaining.[20] The gains of Canadian unions during much of the war were less dramatic and more uncertain as collective bargaining relationships than in the U.S.

Yet there was a breakthrough. It was directly linked to labor unrest, unprecedented until that time. Denied legislative protection, Canadian unions refused to agree to a wartime no-strike pledge, unlike many American unions to which some were affiliated. By 1943, a larger proportion of workers was on strike than in any years since 1919. Equally important was the growth in support for the socialist Co-operative Commonwealth Federation (CCF)—the electoral organization that would later, with official labor backing, become the NDP—outside of its prairie heartland in Saskatchewan. A 1943 Gallup Poll revealed that it was Canada's most popular party, and during the same year, the CCF came within four seats of forming the government of Ontario, Canada's most industrialized province.

Faced with evidence of working-class militancy, Canada's provincial and federal governments rushed to implement a new labor settlement. In 1943, Ontario passed a collective bargaining act which closely duplicated the main provisions of the American Wagner Act. Quebec followed suit a year later. But because of the sweep of wartime powers, temporarily shifting jurisdiction to the center, the framework for Canada's postwar labor settlement was laid down by Mackenzie King's government through federal Privy Council Order-in-Council 1003. Borrowing heavily from the Wagner Act, P.C. 1003 established procedures for union certification and a modest conception of unfair labor practices, as well as national regulation. Under P.C. 1003, key industries such as steel were successfully organized for the first time, and "recognition" strikes ebbed for the remainder of the war. In some contrast with the U.S., legislative protection for trade unions was extracted from a reluctant state through a combination of strike activity and the growth of a socialist party.

During 1945–47, Canada experienced a postwar strike wave similar to that in the U.S.: unions fought for security clauses and substantial wage increases once wartime controls were lifted. In contrast to the U.S., however, the postwar strike wave did not provoke an immediate backlash against the power of trade unions. In 1948, the Industrial Relations and Disputes Investigation Act put into statute form the wartime provisions of P.C. 1003 by grafting American Wagner Act certification and recognition onto Canada's procedures for strike avoidance. More importantly, the provinces had regained primary jurisdiction over labor relations, and all nine provinces moved to duplicate P.C. 1003.

In Canada, as in the U.S. during the 1950s, organized labor appeared to approach a high-water mark. Trade unionism continued to make modest gains in existing sources of strength, reaching a peak in 1956 similar to that achieved in the U.S. two or three years earlier. Despite this growth, Jamieson observes that by 1956, "virtually all the workers that were organizable in terms of prevailing union techniques, finances, ideologies and policies, had been enrolled."[21]

After 1956, escalating unemployment and anti-union provincial legislation frustrated union hopes for expansion. Unemployment in Canada between 1957 and 1962, which was more prolonged and severe than in the U.S., increased the pressure for restrictive legislation and facilitated its passage. Unemployment also took its toll. Despite an outburst of strikes in 1958, unrest had ebbed by 1960 to its lowest point since the war.

Economic recovery combined with new political leverage for labor, thanks to the reorganization of the old CCF with official labor support as the NDP, to reverse dramatically this pattern of union decline during the remainder of the decade. From 1961 onward, Canada experienced a cycle of union growth and militancy, culminating in strikes during 1965–66 far beyond any level of unrest in the U.S. Rank-and-file frustration with contracts negotiated during the 1958–62 recession, which failed to keep pace with inflation, and anger at attacks on union rights, particularly injunctions against strikes and picketing, produced bitter disputes across Canada. During 1965–66 large extra-legal walkouts by Sudbury nickel miners, Hamilton steelworkers, Montreal longshoremen, and railway and postal workers across Canada, suggested that Canada's postwar settlement was coming apart.[22]

Out of 617 Canadian strikes in 1966, involving 411,459 workers, almost one-third were "wildcats."[23] A number of these, including the longshore, railway, and postal disputes, were only settled by legislative intervention, as the minority federal government of the time, under pressure from the New Democrats, conceded annual wage increases in excess of 18 percent. Mass picketing in the 1960s and early 1970s ended use of *ex parte* injunctions, as provincial governments, in the face of such widespread unrest and rising support for the NDP, adopted conciliatory approaches. Under these new conditions, unionization in the private sector began a sustained new growth.

Public Sector Unionism

Between 1956 and the early 1960s, there was a parallel decline in union density in Canada and the U.S., although the Canadian level did not drop as steeply. In both countries, public sector unionization during the 1960s and 1970s provided the main impetus for revitalization. But public sector unionism in Canada and the U.S. has differed significantly, with impact upon the shape of the labor movement in each. While the decline in union density continued in the U.S. after 1964, with new gains failing to compensate either for losses or the growth of the nonagricultural labor force, the

Canadian curve moved sharply upward, surpassing all previous peaks by the early 1970s. Public sector unionism made a greater quantitative difference in Canada than in the U.S., and it also appears to have made a greater qualitative difference, strengthening the elements of aggressiveness and competitiveness in the movement. The Canadian labor mobilization of the mid-1960s, which changed the condition of private sector unionism as well, is unthinkable without the activities of employees in the public sector.

In both countries, the rapid expansion of public sector employment, particularly at the provincial or state and local levels, in the two decades following World War II, provided a major impetus to public sector unionization. By the mid-1970s, one in every five U.S. wage and salary earners worked for some level of government; and in Canada, the proportion reached one in four.[24]

In both Canada and the U.S., the conditions of closely contested political changes during the 1960s provided organized labor with opportunities for extending bargaining rights into the public sector. During the closely fought presidential election of 1960, organized labor's support of John F. Kennedy proved decisive. In 1961, federal employees gained the right to unionize but not to strike or to bargain collectively over wages and benefits, which remained within the exclusive purview of Congress. As a result, federal public sector unionism in large measure remains confined to "the development of a grievance and advisory arbitration procedure,"[25] keeping unions cut off from many aspects of the employment relationship, especially compensation issues. A majority of state governments followed the federal lead. By 1977, thirty-eight states had extended collective bargaining rights to their employees; however, many state and local governments also extensively restricted the scope and conditions of collective bargaining.

Despite these limitations, the result of these reforms was that American public sector unionism achieved considerable growth in the 1960s and 1970s, particularly at the state, county, and local levels, which had a later start and vast numbers. By 1978, 23.5 percent of America's total public work force belonged to unions and 39 percent belonged to unions and employee associations combined.[26] The AFL-CIO Committee on the Evolution of Work claimed in 1985 that "approximately 50 percent of full-time state and local government employees are organized."[27]

In Canada, public sector unionism also achieved major break-throughs in the 1960s, but the extent of unionization and scope of bargaining rights moved far beyond that of U.S. public workers. Indeed, it seems plausible that the greater unionization, militancy, and bargaining rights of Canadian public employees, by virtue of their indirect effects on the union movement as well as by their direct effects on membership figures, account for at least some present-day differences between the two countries. Public sector bargaining in Canada has a longer history than in the U.S. More importantly, as was also the case with collective bargaining in the private sphere, public sector unionism burgeoned in Canada during the 1960s through a more contentious process of political confrontation and engagement at both the provincial and federal level. By the late 1950s, the growing intrusion of federal and provincial governments into labor disputes was unintentionally paving the way for public sector unionization. As Jamieson argues:

> Where governments were directly or indirectly recommending standards and influencing rates of pay, hours and conditions of work and fringe benefits in industries operating under "free enterprise" and "free" collective bargaining, via compulsory conciliation procedures, they provided a strong and growing inducement for employees of public utilities or publicly regulated enterprises and of governments themselves to seek comparable gains through collective bargaining and, if need be, by strike action.[28]

During the early 1960s, the politics of Quebec's "Quiet Revolution" took this process even further. Throughout the late 1950s, Quebec's national trade union movement, led by Jean Marchand, had backed the provincial Liberal Party in its efforts to overthrow the quasi-authoritarian, clericalist "anti-labor" Union Nationale government of Maurice Duplessis. When the Liberals successfully took power in 1960, Marchand's influence was soon apparent. In 1965, as part of its concessions to labor in the period leading up to a new election, the Liberal government enacted a new labor code granting full collective bargaining rights, including the right to strike, to almost all public employees in the province.

During the summer of 1965, postal workers in most major Canadian cities staged an illegal "wildcat" strike demanding pay and

benefit increases. The Quebec developments, postal walkout, and
the parliamentary position of the NDP convinced the minority
Liberal federal government to extend collective bargaining to its
own employees. Under the Public Service Staff Relations Act of
1967, federal employees were given not only the right to bargain
collectively over wages and benefits and most other aspects of the
employment relationship but also the right to choose between two
bargaining routes: one leading to compulsory arbitration and the
other to the strike option.[29] Within a decade, other Canadian jurisdictions once again followed the federal lead. Between 1962 and
1977, government employee unionism had grown by 150 percent,
accounting for a large proportion of Canada's overall union
growth.[30] Coincident with the legal transformation of the collective bargaining status of public employees, restrictions on private
sector unionization were eased. The new wave of organization
brought heightened influence and energy, strengthening the more
socially minded and political elements of labor.

It is arguable that the greater extent, scope, centralization, and
militancy of Canadian public-sector unionism has provoked the
most recent cycle of exceptional legislation in Canada, notably
temporary "emergency" wage controls, beginning in 1975, and
more recently, comparatively frequent back-to-work legislation to
end strikes. If the pre-1962 interventionism of the Canadian state
played a major role in stimulating the growth of public sector
unionism, so too, paradoxically, has labor's very success since the
1960s provoked an even higher level of interventionism during the
1970s and 1980s, as Canadian governments at all levels attempt to
contain public sector spending.[31] Public sector unionism may have
rounded out the postwar labor settlement, while at the same time
putting it in jeopardy.

Conclusion: Law and Politics

The cumulative effect of the differences between the Canadian
and American labor regimes, overall, is to give the adversarial
system of collective bargaining greater weight in Canada, and this
difference helps importantly to account for the declining membership and coverage of American trade unions. Paradoxical as it
may seem, collective bargaining is not losing ground in the United

States because unions are less attractive, but unions are less attractive because collective bargaining is losing ground.

A brief summary of the differences between the current state of the two regulative schemes, so similar in basic features, will substantiate this contention. It will also show why the AFL-CIO Committee on the Evolution of Work stressed legal policy and administration in its analysis. First, Canadian jurisdictions have a more categorical prohibition on strikes during the life of a collective agreement than most American law, and they back this up with legislative provision for mandatory grievance arbitration, whether the agreement includes it or not (and recently, in several key jurisdictions, with provision for quick and comparatively inexpensive arbitration). Unions commonly cannot legally strike after an impasse has been reached in negotiations until there has been an attempt at conciliation by a public official and a finding by the minister that further conciliation efforts will not bear fruit. As a practical matter, this means above all that there must be considerable notice given before there can be a legal strike or lockout. In addition, the strike must be supported by a majority vote of the entire bargaining unit in a secret ballot (and recent legislation in some jurisdictions also allows the employer to demand one secret ballot on his last offer at any time before or during a strike). But there is some reason for believing that these requirements may do more to establish a bargaining ritual, involving mutually supportive interplay between union negotiators and members and culminating in a solemn strike authorization, than they do to deter strikes. In any case, many negotiations go to the conciliation stage, and settlements that wait for the last minute or brief strikes are common. On the whole, the adversarial style of the Canadian trade union movement appears to be reinforced by this regulation of the strike decision.[32]

A second significant difference between Canadian and American labor law during recent decades, as noted earlier, concerns the collective bargaining rights of employees in the public sector. Since the mid-1960s, most jurisdictions provide these employees with rights and procedures that approximate those of workers in private employment, especially with regard to the forms of organization and the scope of permissible collective bargaining. Not all jurisdictions allow public employees the right to strike, and none allows that right to all categories, but even where alternative modes of impasse resolution are mandated, arbitrators usually have been given a much freer hand to adjudicate interest issues than is possible under comparable American law.[33] Expansion of collective bargaining in this sector has also been a prominent feature of American developments during the past two decades, but the extent, scope, and conflictual character of public sector unionization in Canada make the legal differences worth underlining.

The third important area of difference concerns the divergent legislative, administrative, and judicial implementations of the shared principles of voluntary choice, certification of exclusive bargaining agents, and good faith bargaining, as well as the remedies provided. These are different enough to be seen by several observers as the principal cause of the differences in unionization trends.[34] In no Canadian jurisdiction is it the case at the time of this writing, as in the United States, that all certification applications which are not voluntarily consented to by employers must be approved by majority decision in a secret ballot of everyone in the bargaining unit, with the elections preceded by a campaign that may last months, during which time the employer enjoys guaranteed privileges of "free speech" regarding the choice to be made. The most common rule in Canadian jurisdictions is automatic certification where more than 55 or 60 percent of the bargaining unit are shown to have signaled their adhesion to the union by the signing of membership cards and the payment of a nominal sum for dues. Where certification elections are required (including in Nova Scotia, which has been exceptional in requiring elections in all cases), they occur within a few days of the formal request for certification and, in many jurisdictions, interventions by employers are restrained by express legislative provisions for automatic certification where employee preferences cannot be clearly ascertained because of employer action.[35] Canada has seen nothing like the dramatic expansion of active management opposition to unionization that is indicated by the growth in the United States of consultancies specializing in preventing certification, the rise of discriminatory dismissals of union supporters during organizing campaigns, the decline of consent certifications, and the consistent failure of unions to win more than half of the certification elections.[36] In contrast to the existence of numerous states with "right-to-work" laws outlawing important forms of union security, the most important Canadian jurisdictions now eliminate free-riding by nonunion members of certified bargaining units by making the agency shop universal.[37] Although the policy is not universal, there have been well-noted labor board decisions limiting the power of companies to shift operations away from unionized sites.[38] Canadian law is moving toward increased backing for the actual establishment of a collective bargaining relationship after the preliminary step of certification. Four jurisdictions already have legislation allowing the imposition of a binding first agreement by governmental action if negotiations fail, and there is a strong likelihood that several others will follow suit.[39] In sum, it is fair to say that the Canadian legal design overall serves in greater measure to encourage, as the Ontario legislation purposes, "the practice and procedure of collective bargaining between the employers and trade unions as the freely designated representatives of employees," and that it is prepared to limit some of the otherwise preponderant power of employers in order to achieve this, without interfering with the effects of the power disparity, especially in a weak economy, *within* the collective bargaining relationship. While the similar language in the preamble of the American National Labor Relations Act has never been repealed, it would be more accurate to say that the American legal scheme now *allows* rather than *encourages* such bargaining, and that it also allows comparatively free play to the very considerable forces opposed to it.

But the most striking difference between the Canadian and American movements during the past two decades is the increasing importance of more adversarial and political unionism in Canada, marked above all by the interdependence and effective mutual aid between key unions and the New Democratic Party in English Canada, and analogous developments in Quebec involving a more electorally amorphous and even an extra-parliamentary left. This occurred at a time when American unions found their distinctive concerns only intermittently of interest to the presidential and much of the congressional Democratic Party, notwithstanding AFL-CIO attempts to broaden legitimacy by attempting to represent all socially-disadvantaged or even "con-

sumer-class interests" in general.[40] In view of the differences between the two political cultures and institutional frameworks, and
as noted by Lipset in the concluding chapter of this volume, in
some major social values, as well, it is not clear whether the Canadian experience can be of much help to American unionists and
others who are troubled by the decline of American unionism.

5

RAY MARSHALL

America and Japan: Industrial Relations in a Time of Change

The American and Japanese industrial relations systems have developed to fit the political, economic, and social environments in each country, but they also have influenced each other. The systems in both countries have been, and are being, shaped by common trends, especially *internationalization* and *technological change.* Because the Japanese system was revamped after World War II, its basic features reflect postwar conditions and therefore are not as deeply embedded as the American system in the economics of the 1930s. There are, however, similarities. Japanese industrial relations were shaped by American occupation forces and modeled after the legal framework of the National Labor Relations Act.

The American System

The traditional American industrial relations system had some characteristics in common with those in Western Europe: both were supported by a Keynesian demand management approach to macroeconomic policy; had a commitment to "free" labor movements—free from control by outside political or religious organizations and emphasizing democratic control, as well as the right to strike; and both were structured so that representatives of labor, management, and specialized government agencies were the main actors in the system.

Since an industrial relations system is likely to be shaped by a country's dominant economic institutions and policies, it is not surprising that there were close interrelationships between traditional European and American industrial relations systems and Keynesian ideas, which dominated the economic policies of these countries until the 1960s. Keynesian policies conceived the main national economic problem to be achieving a level of aggregate demand adequate to maintain high levels of growth and relatively low rates of unemployment. Growth strengthened companies and unions, and collective bargaining was justified in part because it helped maintain aggregate demand by sustaining wages.

The main microeconomic objectives of the traditional American and European industrial relations systems were the establishment of wages and other work rules and assuring sufficient flexibility to respond to changes affecting the system. The basic relationships between labor, management, and specialized government agencies were shaped by such contextual forces as technology, budget or market constraints, and the power status among the systems' principal actors. An implicit ideology—the body of common ideas holding the system together—involved management's recognition of the right of workers to organize and bargain collectively, and the unions' acceptance (at least temporarily in the European case) of the prevailing economic and political system.

In addition to these features, which it had in common with other industrial nations, the American industrial relations system was distinguished by the following:

1. Exclusive representation, whereby the union recognized as the

bargaining agent represents all employees whether or not they are members of the union. The legal right of workers to vote for or against unions in government-supervised elections has had an important influence on the American industrial relations system, creating competition between the union and nonunion sectors and between unions and employers for the workers' allegiance. In some ways this process extends the industrial relations system from union to nonunion firms. There is little doubt that the behavior of both unions and employers has been influenced by this legal right; nonunion employers treat their workers better and unions have modified such practices as race and sex discrimination in order to appeal to minorities and women in representation elections.

2. Decentralized bargaining with heavy emphasis on wages, hours, and working conditions in particular firms, industries, and labor markets. But pattern bargaining has been very important—wage comparisons between companies and occupations have been major elements in wage determination—with only a loose connection in the short run, with economic conditions in particular firms or industries. Pattern bargaining, cost-of-living adjustments, and wage structures within enterprises were strongly influenced by equity, as well as product and labor market, considerations.

3. American employers probably are more hostile to unions than their counterparts in other industrial nations. The reasons for this greater employer hostility here are not clear, but undoubtedly relate to the greater political power of unions in other countries (which causes these labor movements to be more of a threat to hostile employers) and the greater individualism and fluidity in the American economy. The traditional American industrial relations system also was characterized by an authoritarian management system and adversarial, confrontational relationships between labor and management. This system was rooted in American industrial history. The "scientific management" system developed in the beginning of America's industrial revolution for relatively uneducated and inexperienced (often immigrant) workers in goods-producing activities and subdivided work into discrete tasks. This man-

agement system assumed that workers had little other than brawn to contribute to the work process, that there was one best way to do a task, and that management's responsibility was to determine what that one best way was and to impose it on employees. This model provided little security for or participation by workers, and workers had little commitment to or identification with the enterprise. Workers often assumed that a major function of unions was to protect them from exploitation by elitist managements more interested in profit maximization than workers' welfare. This adversarial, confrontational industrial relations system tended to produce detailed rules that carefully specified such matters as "management's rights," job content, promotion and layoff procedures.

4. The American system has a nonsocialist political orientation. As noted frequently in this book, American unions are unique among major industrial market economy countries in not having formed a labor party. A lower degree of class consciousness has caused the American labor movement to be organized mainly around the job for economic purposes rather than around the working class for political purposes.

5. Conflict resolution is highly developed, with private as well as public dispute settlement mechanisms. Other countries rely much more on labor courts and other public dispute settlement processes.

A major objective of American and European unions was to take labor out of competition. Labor movements considered labor market competition to be bad for individual workers, whose bargaining power is weak relative to employers. Unions also are concerned that labor market competition does not guarantee "living wages" and worker protections. There was, moreover, a strong inverse relationship between the traditional American industrial relations system and the degree of product market competition. Unions were strongest in large oligopolistic firms, urban areas, regulated industries, the skilled trades, and among male blue-collar workers and workers who occupied strategic locations in the economy—such as transportation. A number of features aided the unionization of oligopolies (control of a commodity or service in a given market by a small number of companies): the size and location of oligopolies in key labor markets, public opinion (which turned against the oligopolies in the 1930s), and oligopolistic profits. After the National Labor Relations Act, oligopolies resisted wage increases less than competitive firms because they had greater control over their prices and therefore could pass wage increases through to consumers in the form of higher prices—indeed, by justifying price increases for antitrust purposes, oligopolies could even make money on wage increases.

In other strongly unionized industries, such as trucking, airlines, and railroads, *regulations* limited competition. These unions and noncompetitive companies accommodated each other within the framework of adversarial relations. The unions helped companies regulate markets, and companies recognized the right of unions to represent workers. This informal "social compact" lasted at least until the 1960s.

The American system, as it was established in the 1930s and matured in the 1940s and 1950s, was partly justified as a stabilizing system that took wages out of competition, thus reducing product market competition. At the beginning of this period excessive competition—or at least the simultaneous existence of industries characterized by competition on the one hand and various degrees of monopoly power on the other—was widely regarded as a major cause of the Great Depression. The American industrial relations system, along with social security, unemployment compensation, and minimum and prevailing wage legislation, helped sustain aggregate demand. In fact, the National Labor Relations Act specifically acknowledged this demand-creating role for collective bargaining.

The federal government consolidated the "traditional" American system during World War II through the War Labor Board. Recalcitrant companies and unions were brought in line by the military. The economy's performance during the war also strengthened and justified the assumption that Keynesian policies could achieve full employment.

There were a number of economic consequences of the traditional American industrial relations system:

1. Keynesian economic policies and the expanding international economy facilitated by the Bretton Woods institutions contributed to a long period of relatively high growth in produc-

tivity, real wages, and total output. Collective bargaining made it possible for most union members to achieve middle-class incomes. Moreover, the participatory features of collective bargaining and the "shock effects" of unions on employers tended to increase productivity in unionized firms.

2. Industrial relations systems in the United States and Europe have traditionally contained inflationary biases, with inadequate attention to productivity and efficiency. The decentralized American system was conducive to whipsawing (raising wages by playing one employer off against another) and leapfrogging (union leaders escalating wages in competition with each other). Long-term contracts with cost-of-living adjustments and annual improvement factors tended to cause temporary factors to increase the wage base and therefore ratchet compensation upward. The "safety nets" of unemployment compensation and income maintenance programs for those who were unemployed or not expected to work reduced the impact of unemployment on wages, as did the growth of families with multiple wage earners. The "full employment" policies pursued by governments created less incentive for employers to resist wage increases or for unions to hold wages down because wage and price increases were likely to be offset by government monetary-fiscal policies.

3. The American system is not as flexible in adjusting to change as the Japanese system, but is more flexible than in most of Europe. The main indication of flexibility in the American system relative to the European was the greater decline in real wages and increase in employment in the United States during the 1970s and the greater increase in long-term unemployment in Europe during the 1970s and 1980s. Greater flexibility in the United States relative to Europe was based on the principles of exclusive bargaining rights, a more decentralized bargaining system, lower income support for those not working, lower unionization rates, and greater competition between union and nonunion companies. In addition, the American economy is more open to immigration and imports, and there is greater internal displacement of labor from American agriculture (creating pools of underemployed workers). American employers

may also close plants and lay off workers more easily because of the "employment at will" doctrine and the absence of plant closing legislation.

The evidence of more flexibility in the Japanese system is suggested by higher growth in productivity, total output, and real wages than in either the United States or Europe. The Japanese achieved flexibility and security mainly through enterprise management systems supported by closely related and reinforcing national economic policies. Relatively low levels of unemployment were achieved and the system exhibited greater ease in bringing inflation down after the oil price shocks of the 1970s without generating high levels of unemployment. In general, large Japanese enterprises have adjusted to declining demand by maintaining output and by flexible labor compensation and price policies.

Many factors have made for greater flexibility in the Japanese system than either the U.S. or European models. These include: highly interrelated consensus-based economic policies that have emphasized the upgrading (in terms of productivity and value added) of the Japanese industry mix. Enterprise management stresses labor-management cooperation, participation, and consensus. Mechanisms exist to absorb shocks in demand, including a bonus compensation system, production sharing (whereby low-wage work is done in Third World countries), subcontracting, and the use of temporary workers. Japan has one of the world's most effective positive adjustment programs to shift resources from noncompetitive to more competitive industries. Its industrial relations system emphasizes relative job stability for junior standard employees and continuing education and training on the job for an already well-educated work force. Collective bargaining is concentrated at the enterprise instead of the industry or sectoral levels, and the annual adjustment of wages through a "spring wage offensive" that minimizes whipsawing and leapfrogging. Japan relies heavily on consensus mechanisms at every level rather than the detailed regulations that characterize the American and European systems. A bonus compensation system has prevented wage increases based on temporary factors from becoming embedded in the wage base, thereby avoiding the Amer-

ican practice of ratcheting wages up, and flexibility in job assignments and training has been made possible by the "lifetime
employment" system. The Japanese stabilize inputs and outputs
and let prices and rules vary. Americans and Europeans stabilize
rules and prices and let inputs and outputs vary. The European
and American systems assumed steady growth would justify
relatively rigid prices and wages; the Japanese relied on flexible
wages and prices to stabilize production. The Japanese system
causes key workers to have *employment* security rather than *job*
security, with the consequence that workers are less concerned
about protecting particular jobs, and companies are more willing
to finance long-term education and training for their employees.

Consequences of Internationalization and Other Trends

A number of trends have disrupted the traditional American and
European industrial relations systems. The most important of
these have been related to the emergence of a more integrated
world economy. However, other simultaneous trends have altered
the relationships between the actors in the industrial relations
system. Productivity growth declined after the middle of the 1960s
(which made it much more difficult to sustain increases in output
and real wages), and stagflation upset the Keynesian economic
policy framework supporting the industrial relations system.
Technological changes have enhanced the multinationals' ability
to operate on a worldwide basis and shifted employment out of
heavily unionized industries, companies, and places into smaller
rural firms and the sunbelt (where unions are weaker). Women
are generally less unionized than men, and their presence as a
permanent, integral part of the work force has put pressure on
work rules and compensation systems oriented to male heads of
households and based on the assumption that women were temporary, peripheral labor market participants. Today, of course,
women are participating in the labor force at increased rates. In
1950, 70 percent of American households were headed by men
whose income was the sole source of income; by 1984, less than 15
percent of households fall into this category. Moreover, between
1950 and 1984, the proportion of the work force in the information
occupations had increased from less than 20 percent to about 60
percent.

All of these trends tended to interact with internationalization to weaken unions and domestic goods-producing oligopolies and erode the traditional industrial relations system. As the multinationals' position in relation to labor has strengthened, it has become apparent that unions are no longer as able to help stabilize product markets by taking labor out of competition. In economies characterized by stagflation and declining real wages, the public's price consciousness has led to economic deregulation and a removal of the regulatory structures that limited competition and supported collective bargaining in the transportation industry.

Because of the mobility of capital relative to labor, multinationals can engage in international whipsawing or playing workers of different countries against each other. Worldwide unemployment and nationalism limit organized responses by unions or governments. Although unions have turned to such international agencies as the International Labor Organization, these organizations—while very important—have limited power relative to the multinationals.

Keynesian policies have important limitations in an internationalized information world. These policies give limited attention to price and wage flexibility, productivity, and efficiency. They contain inflationary biases, and assume a closed national economy—or at least work best under those conditions. Moreover, the Keynesian system assumes downwardly inflexible wages, which have reduced the international competition of European and American industries. The basic policy objective of Keynesian economics—low levels of unemployment—means that wages and prices can escalate, but cannot fall very much.

Of course, most of the inflation of the 1970s originated outside product and labor markets, resulting mainly from the external energy price shocks. The American industrial relations system, however, did not permit the wage and price flexibility needed to produce the real wage reductions required to achieve *external* equilibrium in the face of low or declining productivity growth and external energy and commodity price shocks. Real wage cuts therefore were achieved mainly through inflation, followed inevitably by rising unemployment. Unfortunately, the American enterprise management and industrial relations systems *accelerated* these exogenous inflationary pressures and caused external shocks to be absorbed by employment and real output and not by prices and wages.

Internationalization, moreover, makes it more difficult for the United States to carry out monetary-fiscal policies of whatever variety. Efforts to stimulate the economy are much less effective if other economies are not also growing. In such cases, immigration and imports create "drag" effects which tend to limit the expansion of our economy. Similarly, with floating exchange rates, checking inflation through restrictions on the growth of the money supply when demand is increasing raises both interest rates and the value of the dollar, leading to worldwide economic problems. In an increasingly interdependent global economy, these worldwide dislocations boomerang back to the United States. An overvalued dollar makes it more difficult for American employers to sell in international markets, increasing domestic unemployment; however, the overvalued dollar reduces the price of imports and therefore helps with inflation. The limitations of Keynesian policies opened the door for political and intellectual alternatives—monetarism and supply-side economics—which were hostile to the traditional American industrial relations system.

Thus, the main impact of internationalization has been to transform a system that was geared primarily to the American product and labor markets into one that must address the requirements of international competition. This competition has not only influenced wages and prices, but also has called into question the effectiveness of traditional management and industrial relations systems. Other countries, especially Japan, have developed governance mechanisms that appear to be much more competitive than those used in the United States.

While the Japanese system has received a lot of attention, its aggregate economic performance should not be exaggerated. Productivity is still higher in the United States than in Japan and most American companies (outside the basic industries where oligopolies predominated) have been fairly competitive. Moreover, some Japanese sectors like agriculture and consumer distribution are not very efficient. No more than 15 to 20 percent of the work force has "lifetime" employment to age fifty-five or sixty, and older workers and women have less security than either prime-working-age males in Japan or their counterparts in the United States.

Nevertheless, the Japanese have developed a very competitive system in the industries they have targeted—like automobiles, steel, consumer electronics, and computer chips. The Japanese system provides rising real incomes and security to all, even though some people have more security than others. The Japanese system is more egalitarian than the American, in the sense that the income differentials between managers and workers are much smaller. The Japanese also have developed a system where workers perceive their benefits to be much more closely related to productivity improvements than is the case with American workers. For example, a Public Agenda survey found that only 9 percent of American workers thought that higher productivity would benefit them; 93 percent of comparable Japanese workers thought they benefited from increased productivity.

Finally, the Japanese provided an economic environment for their enterprise that is conducive to flexibility and productivity growth. Coordinated economic policies based on public-private cooperation and consensus creates greater stability, predictability, and flexibility. Japanese public policy socializes much economic risk, making it possible for enterprises to be satisfied with lower rates of return. The Japanese financial system is particularly beneficial to economic activity. Consumer credit, social security, compensation, consumer price and tax systems all encourage a high level of savings; the government has kept interest rates relatively low to producers; and Japanese corporations rely much more heavily on debt financing than their American counterparts, who rely more heavily on equity. Government-supported bank financing socializes risk and relieves the Japanese of the need to be concerned about short-run stock market quotations, enabling them to develop longer-term strategies based on the latest technologies. Moreover, Japanese banks and related companies are likely to be the enterprises' main stockholders. These related companies are less likely than individual or institutional investors to be concerned about short-run returns on their stock. They are more interested in their long-term business relations with the enterprise than in their stock dividends. Finally, Japanese corporations are likely to give higher priority to the concerns of their

workers than to their stockholders. This, along with the importance of size in the Japanese economic value system, makes the
Japanese firm more interested in market share than profit maximization, the main driving force of the stockholder-oriented
American enterprise. In order to enlarge market share, the
Japanese firm gives much greater attention to quality and productivity than has been the case with large oligopolistic American
firms in basic goods-producing industries.

Some observers also believe the Japanese education system,
especially at the elementary and secondary level, to be a major
source of advantage to the Japanese firm. The Japanese elementary and secondary school system appears to be much better than
the average American school system, especially in science, mathe-
matics, and language training. The large Japanese firm continues
this education process after the graduate enters the firms'
employment.

Thus, the scarcity of energy and other physical resources has
caused the Japanese to emphasize human resource development.
Indeed, some observers even believe human resource development
to be the Japanese's main economic advantage—more important
than its management and industrial relations systems. However,
the components of the Japanese system are so closely interrelated
that it would be very difficult to single out any one of them as *primarily* responsible for the overall outcome. I am persuaded,
however, that the Japanese's main advantage relative to the
United States is their comprehensive consensus-based economic
policy, though their industrial relations system gives them important advantages in the basic industries.

Are the Japanese and American systems converging? This is
an interesting question and the answer is far from obvious. There
clearly has been considerable international borrowing by both
systems. The demonstrated successes of the Japanese system,
though often exaggerated, have been the object of considerable
emulation by managers in other countries, especially in the
United States. On the other hand, many American companies
already had features similar to those that have come to be
regarded as the "Japanese model." These features include job
security, bonus and other incentive systems, and employee involvement; attention to productivity, quality, and customer needs;

technological innovation; and emphasis on goals other than short-run profit maximization.

The Japanese system was not as deeply embedded in Keynesian demand management and public income support systems as either the American or European systems. In part, this was because the Japanese system, like the German, was able to jettison institutional obsolescence in the postwar period; its institutions and procedures therefore were shaped more to the economic requirements of the 1950s and 1960s.

Japan, like other developed nations, formulated a full employment strategy, but the system depended more on flexibility, growth, and international competitiveness and less on public income maintenance systems and demand management. The Japanese system therefore appears to be more adaptable than either the American or European. Nevertheless, Japanese society is being subjected to stresses created by an aging work force, a less supportive international economic environment, and changing attitudes by Japanese citizens. It remains to be seen if the Japanese can maintain sufficient flexibilities in their systems simultaneously to accommodate the demands for change and retain their international competitiveness.

It is not clear, moreover, whether the apparent convergences in the Japanese and American systems are due to *emulation* or to common *responses* to the same competitive economic realities. The latter will have more lasting impact on the systems. Indeed, many American business efforts to emulate such Japanese practices as quality control circles appear to be artificial transplants and not organic adaptations that will have long-run viability. The Japanese, American, and European systems will acquire common features in the sense of adapting to the viability requirements of the internationalized information world, but they also will have diverse features reflecting their unique histories, cultures, and institutions.

The implications of international competition for the American industrial relations system include:

1. As the U.S. faces increased international competition in a relatively open trading system, it is more difficult to remove labor from competition and maintain oligopolistic pricing.

2. Because technology can be standardized and capital and material prices are determined mainly by international markets, unit labor costs become more important and strategic elements in the viability of economic enterprises. The oligopolistic wage premium becomes less tenable, as do long-term contracts, pattern bargaining, and fragmented work assignments.

3. Competition with the more flexible and productive Japanese industrial relations system reveals weaknesses in the American system. The lessons to be learned include the following:

   • Quality and productivity are related. Quality affects management and worker morale, market share, the ability to maintain steady production, and is a key to optimal resource mixes and utilization levels.

   • Domestic and international competitiveness depends heavily on productivity, quality and flexibility, all of which weaken such traditional American collective bargaining procedures as pattern and industry bargaining and compensation systems that rely exclusively on long-term contractual wages. Compensation systems that combine wages and bonuses provide greater flexibility and worker involvement in (and identification with) the enterprise.

   • Maximizing market share rather than profits gives the Japanese firm a competitive edge. It is very difficult for oligopolies to compete with the Japanese model which adjusts to declining demand with flexible price and compensation systems and attempts to increase market shares. The oligopolist, by contrast, attempts to keep prices fixed and adjusts to declining demand by reducing output. This means that the oligopolist loses business during recession and has inadequate capacity to take advantage of increased demand during recoveries. It could be, however, that employee-owned enterprises would be more competitive because of higher productivity resulting from greater employee involvement and motivation and lower profit requirements because workers are likely to be more concerned with employment preservation than profit maximization.

- Cooperation and consensus building (labor-management, public-private) are related to productivity, quality, flexibility, and stability.

- Consensus-building processes can improve the *amount* and *quality* of information available to government, labor, and management representatives; reduce conflict; facilitate adjustment to change; and strengthen market, management, and governmental decision making. Indeed, those economies with superior performance on most change indicators supplement market, collective bargaining, and other decision processes with national and subnational consensus mechanisms.

- Employment security, worker commitment, and good management are highly correlated. Employment security provides greater flexibility. With labor as a fixed cost, education, training, and job rotation allow more flexibility. As some American companies have discovered, employment security strengthens management by making it more difficult for managers to shift the costs of change to workers in the form of unemployment, forcing management to better plan production and labor utilization.

- The adversarial/confrontational mode of labor relations places American enterprises at a disadvantage when competing with more cooperative models like those in large Japanese firms. Adversarial/confrontational relations make it difficult for labor and management to establish the kind of cooperation and mutual trust required for quality output, productivity, and flexibility in adjusting to change. In the internationalized information world where workers have higher levels of education, authoritarian, adversarial management systems deprive enterprises of the productivity and creativity of workers who know their jobs better than anyone else in the organization. Moreover, the production requirements of high tech processes often diminish the need for close management supervision, increase worker discretion, and put a premium on trouble shooting and knowledge rather than physical performance, all of which reduces the need for supervisors and blurs the lines between workers and management. There are strong visible links between the viability of enterprises, labor-management cooperation, employment security, and worker participation. In this new environment, *unions* therefore must give greater attention to the enterprises' economic viability and managers must give greater attention to workers' security and involvement in decision making. A logical division of labor appears to be emerging between cooperative labor-management relations to improve an enterprise's competitiveness and adversarial collective bargaining systems to fix rules and share gains.

Public Policy

Public policy with respect to industrial relations systems must be concerned about creating the environment within which enterprises can compete. The Japanese keep prices and interest rates low and encourage flexible systems in order to absorb shocks, while maintaining output and employment in a continually growing economy. Small, open European systems (like the Austrian) have developed wage and price policies that keep prices competitive in the sectors that depend on exports, as well as those that are most affected by import competition. Public policy must therefore be concerned with maintaining an economic environment that permits and encourages productivity and flexibility. This requires some consensus-building processes, balanced macroeconomic policies, and selective measures to deal with inflation, labor market problems, and industrial upgrading through more explicit industrial policies.

Finally, the economic and political health of the American system requires the strengthening and preservation of the right of workers to decide for themselves whether or not they want to be represented by unions for collective bargaining purposes. I am persuaded that worker participation systems are not likely to be very viable unless workers have independent power to protect their workplace interests. Moreover, a free and democratic society requires a free and democratic labor movement just as much, if not more, in an internationalized information world than in a more national, goods-producing system. Those politicians, employers, and employer organizations that attempt to take advantage of the unions' temporary weaknesses to create a "union-free" environment by denying workers the free and unfettered right to organize and bargain collectively, in the long run, will probably strengthen more militant and more political labor organizations whose procedures and objectives are less compatible with labor-management cooperation and a relatively free and open market economy.

I can understand the American unions' frustration with the present legal apparatus which is supposed to protect the workers' rights to organize and bargain collectively. Legalisms and tactical maneuvers delay workers' timely exercise of these rights. Weak penalties make it possible for recalcitrant employers to violate the National Labor Relations Act with virtual impunity. The law has taken away the right of workers to help each other through secondary boycotts while permitting companies to help each other defeat unions, even through outright boycotts of unionized companies. I think a strong case can be made that unions and workers who want to be unionized are helped little, if at all, by the present legal apparatus. Nevertheless, it would not be in the national interest to return to the law of the jungle in resolving union recognition issues.

This is not to imply, of course, that the law has been a fundamental or basic determinant of the incidence of collective bargaining. Collective bargaining results from the relative power positions of unions, workers, and employers. Most economic and technological trends are against unions as traditionally organized. The unions will therefore need to develop new procedures to deal with the internationalized information world. There are signs that some of them are doing that. Because of the importance of collective bargaining and free labor movements for the nation's economic, political, and social health, it is in the public interest to encourage these adjustments and strengthen the workers' right to decide for themselves whether or not they want to be represented by unions.

6

ALAIN TOURAINE

Unionism as a Social Movement

Sociological studies of labor unions are dominated by a focus on three causes of labor conflicts: economic conditions, the nature of the political system, and the ideological orientations of union actors. The first two have been studied definitively by Clark Kerr and Abraham Siegel, while the latter two have been dealt with by Charles Tilly and Seymour Martin Lipset.[1] This chapter addresses the third problem and examines the factors that have influenced how unions define their broad social objectives—when they limit their role to collective bargaining and when they aim, much more radically, at transforming the foundations of the entire society.

The most fundamental issue addressed here is that of "class consciousness," historically an important determinant of union action. It is important to note that the expression "labor movement," is used here to refer *only* to union activity based on class consciousness, which is distinct from political radicalism. The proceedings of the conventions of the American Federation of Labor in the 1920s, for example, reveal a low level of doctrinal political radicalism, but a very high degree of consciousness that focuses on the class character of the conflicts between labor and management. Similarly, moderate unionists may believe firmly in a basic conflict of interest between employers and workers, while rejecting political conflict or even the intervention of the state. An example of this was observed by Heinrich Popitz in his well-known survey on worker attitudes in Germany: he found that only 3 percent of respondents were "revolutionary," but at least 38 percent were strongly class conscious and 25 percent viewed society as divided between distinct classes.[2]

Further, there is no organic link between "class consciousness" and "revolution." Victoria Bonnell in her study of the Russian prerevolutionary unions clearly demonstrates the discontinuity between unions and revolutionary—in this case Bolshevik—political activity.[3] The origins of class consciousness and of the transformation of unions into a "labor movement" do not stem from the crises of economic or political institutions, but, on the contrary, from the defensive occupational solidarity of some categories of workers against the trends of modern industrial organization. Political radicalism originates in the lack of political participation, while class consciousness is the product of *occupational* problems, involving the defense of the worker from the forces that impose specific constraints. Difficult "proletarian" conditions do not necessarily lead to class consciousness, a point made fifty years ago by Leon Trotsky. The defense efforts are much stronger among skilled workers. There are, however, very few examples of national union movements led by semi-skilled workers. The most conspicuous contemporary exception was Italian unionism after 1969, but its actions were more politically radical than class conscious.

Class conscious workers accept the basic cultural values of an industrial society (such as belief in progress through improved industrial productivity) but see themselves as victims of the social control of economic activities. In a French survey, in which I was involved, we asked the question, "Are the consequences of mechanization good or bad for workers?" Some respondents said good; others, bad. But a more significant third group said mechanization could have positive effects if it helped to improve working conditions, not if it only served increased profits. This combination of an awareness of social conflict with acceptance of social values shared by both workers and managers is a practical definition of class consciousness.[4] In a more elaborate way, workers' attitudes and union actions may be characterized by the degree to which social conflicts are related to the acceptance of institutionalized cultural values, which are accepted equally by the opposing social actors, labor and business.

Historically, union activities have been categorized into three types. The first, "business" unionism or "economism," defends labor's economic interest in the market. It does not involve any specific model of social conflict and makes no judgment about industrial society. The second, "professional" or "guild" unionism, defends workers against entrepreneurs or managers as a stratum. It presupposes a clear definition of the opposing camps and tries to influence institutional practices and decision-making systems. Finally, "labor movement" or "class conscious" unionism clearly sets the "working class" in opposition to a society that is seen as dominated by management or capitalists, and proposes a reallocation of the resources created by industry.

Class conscious unionism can be found both in market-capitalist and state-socialist countries. Miklos Haraszti's study in Hungary and my own research in Poland have revealed widespread class consciousness among workers who feel exploited by managers in the *nomenklatura*, who accuse them of being irrational and incompetent and of acting against the people's interests.[5] Such feelings tend to diminish either when workers come to reject the overall social reality of industrialism and social conflict then gives way to cultural crises, or conversely, they begin to view management as a partner, not an adversary, in the efforts to improve living conditions. This analysis of class conscious action, very different from both Marxist analyses and the main orientations of academic labor economics, is based neither on the assumption of contradictions and crises in capitalism or on the presumed social effects of a worsening economic situation. It posits the capacity of a "collective actor" to transform a situation. We speak of a social movement when a collective action challenges not only relative levels of participation—as expressed by wages or amounts of political influence—but the overall system of social control of economic resources. When unionism reaches this level of action, it becomes a labor movement.

Industrial Society and Class Consciousness

If a class conscious labor movement is based on promoting the interests of those who see themselves as "workers" as opposed to management, different levels of class consciousness must correspond to various stages of industrial organization. In the early 1960s, a study carried out in seven industrial sectors in France measured responses to the statement that "industrialism" is good for management, not for workers, as an indicator of "class consciousness."[5] The percentages expressing agreement were

Building trades	28
Coal mining	34
Foundries	31
Mass production manufacturing	43
Non-mass-production manufacturing	40
Gas and light (nationalized)	26
Oil refineries	21

Responses referring to the economic (rather than general) consequences of industrialism indicated a high level of discontent in coal mining, but even higher expressions of class consciousness in non-mass-production manufacturing industries. The highest level was found among skilled workers employed by large companies and paid through incentive systems. Class consciousness appears to result from a defense of workers' occupational autonomy—their craft, in extreme cases—against a "scientific" management symbolized by the names of Frederick H. Taylor and Henry Ford. Class conflict sets workers as autonomous producers in opposition to industrial management, centralized and imposed upon workers who feel "de-skilled" more by new methods than by new machines. This view corresponds to the classical analysis of industry made by observers like Karl Marx or Andrew Ure, who viewed industry more as a social form of production relations than as a form of technology.

Class consciousness reaches its highest level when skilled

workers are directly threatened by rationalization and their interests are defined by economic policies linked to the division of labor. Skilled workers paid by piecework are more directly dominated by scientific management than those paid on an hourly basis, which explains why they often reach a higher level of class consciousness than unskilled workers. In the 1950s, large companies were more likely to adopt scientific management methods than small enterprises; as a consequence workers were more often class conscious in the former. Industrial sociologists, beginning with Fritz Roethlisberger in the Hawthorne Plant of Western Electric Company, showed that restriction of output served as a form of collective defense against imposed production norms.[7] The strength of the labor movement during the main period of industrial growth stemmed from its ability to unite skilled workers, deprived of autonomy, with semi-skilled workers. The latter on their own would have found it difficult to oppose "scientific management."

Unionism reached the level of a social movement—became a labor movement—during the period of industrialization—the factory system—and has operated at a lower level both before and since. Although it is wrong to equate historical eras with specific types of occupational situations, we can relate the maximum strength and importance of social movement unionism to the long period that began symbolically with the expansion at Henry Ford's plant and ended with the development of new forms of production—especially automation and the growing importance of office work and data processing technologies from the 1970s on.

A recent study using the "sociological intervention" method buttresses this conclusion with evidence secured in discussions with groups of unionized workers in steel, chemical, and automobile production; railway repair shops; and data processing companies.[8] Diverse opinions to union goals were expressed, but each group referred to the kind of consciousness described here as the only way to see unionism as a labor movement. Some said unions should *not* act as a social movement, but rather should limit themselves to defending wage levels or to obtaining a better contract; others were convinced that political parties, not unions, should lead what they felt was a necessary transformation of society. No group put forward an alternative to "class consciousness" as a preferred image of the "labor movement." All were aware that the model "belongs to the past" and corresponds more to the reality of a declining steel industry than to the growing high-tech enterprises or service industries. Still these French workers chose to maintain this nontraditional emphasis as their central reference, even though the idea was expressed with some nostalgia.

Does this mean that worker attitudes and union actions are determined by technological changes? Some observers argue that an extreme division of labor encourages high levels of protest because workers are defined not by a particular craft or guild but by their limited participation in a collective production process. Others think that the progressive "loss of autonomy" by workers and the development of new technologies that leave them with a less crucial role in the production process depresses their aspirations and transforms "labor" into an interest group whose action is increasingly dependent on larger political and economic factors. Both approaches reflect technological determinism. In contrast, I would define "the industrial situation" in *social* rather than in *technological* terms. Thus, mechanization should be seen not simply as a technique but socially, as a process involving the loss of workers' autonomy and the strengthening of management. Workers' behavior is explained not by the occupational situation but by specific power relationships rooted in the workplace. *Behavior* may not be explained by a *situation*. To analyze the "political capacity"—to use Pierre Joseph Proudhon's words—of a social category, it is necessary to investigate how that category or stratum becomes able to challenge patterns of power, influence, and authority.

A quite different Leninist view has been influential in Europe and even more so in recently industrializing countries. This approach asserts that the working class cannot free itself through its own efforts both because it is dominated and alienated and because the state and processes of cultural control lock workers into tradition, repression, and submission. Unions alone cannot hope to attain more than limited reforms; only a revolutionary party can break the power system and allow a social movement to develop. The logical consequence of this view is to subordinate the labor movement to "the party" and, when the party becomes the party-state, to further subordinate it to an absolute State.

The main purpose of my analysis, on the contrary, is to define the conditions in which a movement can become a central and autonomous agent of social transformation. This process is threatened by two opposite dangers: subordination to political action on one side and self-limitation to piecemeal claims and monetary gains on the other.

The Rise and Decline of a Class Conscious Labor Movement

Movements such as unionism have a life history: infancy, youth, maturity, old age, and death. Historically, they have evolved from a focus on pure economic objectives—described at the turn of the century as business unionism—to more radical and more encompassing "class conscious" actions.[9] After this latter phase, in part a result of success, they turned to economic and political "bargaining," and finally, with the crisis of industrialization, to the defense of occupations or industries in decline. But such a view is oversimplified. The first phase of this evolution, for example, cannot be defined entirely by the simple concept of business unionism; it was also a period of socialist theorizing and community-oriented strikes. The simultaneous presence of these orientations demonstrates that unionism is not defined by one element, but by the integration of three components: defense of the specific interests of workers, attack against an enemy identified through an economic situation, and active participation in the values of industrial society—faith in the positive social consequences of higher productivity. These three elements are always present in union activity, but they are often separated. A "class conscious" labor movement can appear when the three are tightly linked; unionism does not always result in a class conscious labor movement. It is only in certain very specific situations that organized labor has been able to reach this stage of development and play a central role in the social and political processes of industrial societies.

Craft unionism and utopias. Unionism rose from a lower to a higher stage of integration as a result of the destruction of occupational autonomy by "scientific management," which allocated workers to unskilled jobs and limited roles. Before this transformation, the activities of unions were separated into three elements: (1) business unionism, (2) communitarian defense, and (3) utopian politics.

Historically craftsmen were able to negotiate their working conditions. Their bargaining strengths enabled them to impose the union label on employers and successfully to boycott anti-union companies. Skilled workers were highly mobile: a good proportion of those in the printing trades, for example, had the option of opening their own shop or company. Semi-skilled or unskilled workers, on the other hand, lacked autonomy, were extremely dependent, and their unions were frequently subordinated to local politics. In France, Italy, and Spain, radical unions frequently formed alliances with local politicians and could be manipulated by demagogues.

The move from business unionism to a higher form of labor action has been studied by historians and sociologists such as E. P. Thompson and Richard Hoggart in Britain, and Yves Lequin and Jacques Ranciere in France.[10] The defensive struggles of local communities, threatened by low wages, unemployment, and repression, were frequently *violent* but far from *revolutionary*. There is no continuum between communitarian defense and mobilization for general political goals. Regions or crafts historically have defended their interests separately from, and often against, other groups of workers as much as against employers or governments. There have also been strong communities of workers, such as coal miners, that remained isolated and were not easily integrated into broader instrumental and political action.

The third phase in the development of a nonintegrated labor movement, which never developed in the United States, is one that fosters the utopian ideal of a "labor-dominated" society, in which workers will be recognized as the only productive and progressive force, while capitalists will be eliminated as wasteful, speculative, irrationally greedy, and sometimes war-mongering. The conditions for such a utopia are usually projected into the future: anarchists, for example, believe in science and education as the main instruments in the construction of a rational world completely free of religion, war, and profit. Sometimes the utopia is oriented to the myth of a "golden past," to the revival of the integrated community, which had been destroyed by capitalism, proletarianization, and uprooting. Georges Sorel, influential in France and Italy at the beginning of the century, expressed such a pessimistic view, believed in regressive evolution.[11]

As noted, the early stage corresponds to business unionism and is characterized by a strong separation of union organization from political action and ideology. Intellectuals and politicians play a very prominent role in the mobilization of workers who, at the craft or community level, organize strong *autonomous* economic action but fail to produce political action or a class-oriented ideology. Such a labor movement can be observed both in moderate and radical political environments. The American social and political systems are different from the European; nevertheless, while unions on both sides of the Atlantic developed different political orientations, they have been basically similar with respect to "workers' consciousness." At the beginning of this century, Samuel Gompers, head of the generally moderate AFL, and Victor Griffuelhes, Secretary General of the revolutionary French General Confederation of Labor (CGT) did not have any common political conceptions, but both were convinced of the deep conflict between workers and capitalism, rejected state intervention, defended the idea of a working-class culture, and believed in industry, progress, and reason.

Forms of limited integration of a labor movement. The first great transformation came with the First World War, again, in similar terms in different countries. Samuel Gompers and William Green in the United States "discovered" industrial management and sought to negotiate workers' participation, just as Communist union leaders in France, with a completely different outlook, followed a similar evolution from a unionism concentrating on job security to one that focused on *conditions of work* at the shop level. The two main consequences of this change were to make possible the integration of skilled and semi-skilled workers into the same unions and to give more political and ideological autonomy to workers. The separation of the three components of the labor movement gave way to a partial integration of union activity and socialist ideas. The first consequence made collective bargaining more important, even in unfavorable situations in which management hired scabs and created yellow (company) unions. The second aimed at some form of "co-determination" or workers' control. The Weimar period in Germany, for example, featured a long debate between radical and moderate labor leaders over co-determination. Nevertheless, in this period, as Adolf Sturmthal correctly observed, unions almost everywhere were unable to create a lasting link between social reforms and proposed solutions to economic problems.[12] The German case and the 1936 French Popular Front are dramatic examples of the almost complete ignorance by union leaders of economic facts.

The central phase. The New Deal, the Wagner Act, and the wave of strikes culminating in the creation of the CIO in the United States, the 1936 Popular Front and sit-in strikes in France, and the triumph of socialist policies in Scandinavian countries— especially in Sweden and Norway in the 1930s—historically represent the highest point reached by labor movements. During this period organized labor played a central role in the development of new economic policies and identified itself with democracy and its defense against fascism. Historians provide various interpretations of this progress of unionism in various countries, contrasting it with the relative decline of the British trade union movement after the 1926 general strike. But analyses of economic and political situations should not prevent us from understanding the general social conditions underlying this new role of organized labor. After the successes of a widespread anti-union policy in the 1920s, especially in the United States with the "American Plan" as well as in France, a "new unionism" emerged that incorporated the mass production industries of automobiles and rubber. Detroit and Akron, and the Brillancourt industrial suburb of Paris, became symbols of a unionism that united workers' grievances and political action more tightly than the earlier forms. This integration of occupational and political problems presupposed the fusion of skilled craftsmen and semi-skilled mass production workers in industry-wide unions. Skilled workers brought to unionism "positive" goals, the reconstruction of social and economic life; mass production workers were the backbone of the "negative," the defensive, aspects of union behavior. The growth of mass production industries before and after the Second World

War gave a central role to organized labor, from Detroit and Paris in the 1930s to Gdansk in the 1980s. For fifty years North American and European countries have defined themselves as industrial nations, and the central actor in their protest movements has been organized labor—usually with a reformist political orientation but sometimes with a radical one, either linked to a revolutionary anti-capitalist political movement or directed in Eastern Europe against the dominance of the Communist party-state. Beyond this diversity of political situations, the core of the labor movement everywhere has been the workers' struggle against both management and a system of social organization that appeared to embody the political and cultural domination and exploitation of the working class by a power elite. Formulations of this sort were accepted by American CIO leaders, as well as by Norwegian Laborites, French Communists, and even the Czech and Polish anti-Soviet protest movements.

Disintegration and transformation. A long period of economic growth, Keynesian policies, and international tensions help to explain the contemporary decline of working-class-based radical movements. But again, the determinants of radicalism or its falloff should not be confused with the conditions affecting the extent to which a labor movement is class conscious, which by definition is different from political radicalism. The main reason for the decline of a class conscious labor movement is the disintegration of the "classic" working class. On one side, a growing number of employees, blue-collar as well as white-collar, will have *communicative* rather than *productive* functions. They emit, receive, and transmit information rather than intervening directly in the production process. More than craft or skill, they have status and function. In the service industries, such as data processing, occupational roles are defined either in professional or hierarchical terms. Employees defend a status and a career, their relative positions in a complex organization, rather than their "rights" as "producers" of goods. The very basis of class consciousness is disappearing and the labor movement is being replaced by interest group unionism.

Still, both in industry and services, a large number of individuals are technically and economically marginalized: unskilled and semi-skilled people working in maintenance or non-manual production jobs and workers with temporary contracts or employed by subcontractors. The expression "new working class" has been increasingly used to describe both the new interest group unionism and the newly marginalized workers. Some observers, like Serge Mallet and the Italian followers of "workerism," conclude that the growing importance of technicians and very highly skilled workers has allowed the labor movement to extend its efforts to influence policy from the job and shop level to the company and national levels.[13] These ideas have gained some importance among American and Canadian auto workers. The more workers are incorporated into industrial organizations the less autonomy they possess, the more they are able to attack the system of economic management and to develop an alternative policy.

This interpretation is in many ways quite different from the historic analysis presented here. During the early 1970s, especially in reaction to a long strike at the Lip watch company in France during which workers not only occupied the factory but also sold the existing supply of watches to pay themselves wages, the concept of "self-management" became influential and was adopted as a goal by one of the main French union organizations, the Confederation Francaise et Democratique du Travail (CFDT), of Catholic and Socialist origin. Sometimes, as particularly in the Lip case, this social philosophy has been linked with a Christian communitarian orientation. But it rapidly became obvious that this objective flew in the face of the objective reality. Radical labor tendencies were actually merged at Lip with counter-cultural ideas, but the labor movement had not been able to develop support for a new self-management industrial policy. On the contrary, most unions have become more and more defensive. The increase in such "defensive unionism" has occurred in tandem with the unionization of the rapidly increasing number of civil servants and salaried professionals, but at the same time the labor movement has been severely challenged by economic crises and technological developments that have undermined its traditional industrial strongholds and unions have failed to organize the new growing high-tech industries.

The most interesting example of new union initiatives has emerged in Italy. The labor movement led by skilled workers lost ground, but between 1969 and 1975 a new type of unionism, headed by mass production workers and politically radical groups, came into existence.[14] Union locals were dissolved and were replaced by factory councils. The unions proposed a pyramidal "articulated" action program ranging from workplace grievances to national economic policies. The three main unions (CGIL, CSIL, and UIL) seriously considered a merger, one that was nearly achieved among the metal workers. But this transformation, probably the most important in the Western world during this period, cannot be viewed as a new successful form of a class conscious labor movement. On the contrary, the Italian situation witnessed a growing subordination of "mass" movements to political actors, who became more radical in reaction to a deep state crisis, and eventually produced terrorism. Ideologists have formulated the nature of this new type of union action in precise terms.[15] The ideologist of terrorism, sociologist Antonio Negri, concludes that *il operaio sociale* (the worker as social unit) is no longer primarily dominated by the company owner but is directly controlled by State power and a societal system of "reproduction" or social control, which maintains the capitalist system through repression and results in widespread alienation. Under such conditions union action by itself cannot achieve anything. Collective action must be directly political. Negri was not a member of the Red Brigades, but his neo-Leninist analysis was widely perceived as a defense of violence. It is quite far from the ideology underlying a class conscious, autonomous, and workplace-centered labor movement.

Unions have acted less and less like a social movement and more and more like parts of a political decision-making system. In social-democratic countries like Sweden and West Germany, unions negotiate at the national level and are closely allied with the left parties. In France, negotiations are often still held at industry level, but since 1968 the most important decisions have been made in the national agreements negotiated by the government with unions and national management organizations. In the United States, however, collective agreements are generally signed at the company level.

Today, the unions' capacity for social mobilization has decreased and has been subordinated to the negotiation process. In an extreme case, the Japanese "spring offensives," spectacular actions are taken which are essentially symbolic. The union leaders know what the new agreement will be even before the demonstrations occur.

In this situation unions have seemed more influential in the determination of working conditions. Often the union delegate or shop steward is equal to the foreman, and many material arrangements may be made through formal grievance procedures or in formal agreements between supervisors and union representatives. When unions are very strong, as in the Scandinavian countries, autonomous *teams* are organized at the shop level, but their behavior is very far from "class conscious" craft unionism: their autonomy means a growing separation of workplace problems from general economic and political options.

Back to "business unionism"? During the earliest stage in the formation of the modern labor movement, employment was a more important issue than working conditions and wages. The same holds true for the current stage of *extreme disintegration*. Beyond the effects of an economic depression, employment continues to fall in many Western European and some North American industries, sometimes striking whole industries and regions. Facing this change in the labor market and the effects of what can amount to deindustrialization, unions try their best to protect workers. But they fail to achieve this goal for two opposite reasons. Radical unions, like the French CGT, refuse to negotiate a reallocation of labor because they consider capitalism to be responsible for its own general crisis. But a close identification with the Communist Party has weakened this position, and French workers are abandoning essentially ineffective unions. In an opposite way, U.S. unionism, mostly limiting itself to collective bargaining at the company level, is neither able to control the waves of economic change buffeting its old strongholds or to organize new high-tech industries where the old strategies do not work. In Sweden, however, the Landsorganisasjon (LO) has succeeded in merging job protection, including programs for retraining discharged workers, with new mainly public investment strategies.

But in almost all cases, union policies remain essentially defensive. Unions no longer aim at *controlling* management's economic decisions, despite some confused attempts at workers' control in Sweden. Socialist programs have become more popular among intellectuals and other highly educated elites than among workers. In France, proposals to denationalize major companies have not provoked mass demonstrations to retain government control. In some countries, like the Scandinavian ones, unions are strong and have organized as much as three-quarters of all wage-earners; in others, like the United States and France, less than 20 percent are unionized, although a much higher percentage in the latter vote for the Socialist and Communist parties.

Class conscious union movements have not been able to maintain themselves anywhere. There has been a general decline in Europe of collective efforts aimed at "transforming industrial society in the interest of the working class." Even the militant sometimes violent 1984–1985 coal strike in Britain was not linked to a socialist or class program. Rather, on one side, it was presented as a community defense against the threat represented by the decline of coal extraction, and on the other side it was a political confrontation between two strong personalities, Mrs. Thatcher and Arthur Scargill. The strike was a typical example of the outcome of a process of disintegration that was not compensated for by increased radicalism.

In conclusion, the history of the modern labor movement can be summarized as the formation of a class conscious social movement, followed by the collapse of its core. This breakdown reflects the separation of class consciousness from the positive orientation of workers toward some industrial values such as production and progress. Organizationally, it means a widening gap between skilled, technical, or professional categories and unskilled or marginal workers or masses.

The Labor Movement and Political Action

A "class conscious" labor movement is centered around workplace conflicts and deals with the structural problems of an industrial society, conceived as a civil society. This image is directly counter to the Leninist view in which Marx's "class for itself," *Klasse für sich,* is identified with political vanguard parties that give the working class a revolutionary orientation and organize its collective action, rejecting reformist or pure unionist tendencies. But a "class for itself" can express itself through a revolutionary strike or through limited collective bargaining, through either a strong bond or a loose alliance between unions and political parties. Thus, following the analysis of the labor movement itself, it is necessary to consider its relationship to political action. Ironically what gives strength to the labor movement is at the same time the source of its weakness. Its action is concentrated on only one level of economic life: the division of labor and industrial management, which the early French socialist Saint-Simon called the "domination of organizers" upon workers. In pre-industrial societies, the major conflicts took place between craftsmen and merchants. Their specific forum was the market and the city, while the forum for industrial conflicts is the factory. In pre-industrial societies, social conflicts were limited because production as such remained untouched by collective conflicts. Politics stood well above social movements. This distance is much reduced in industrial society: the labor movement deals with aspects of social relations of production within the limits of industry. In the end, perhaps, the Leninist model is correct in a certain sense: unions cannot transform strength developed in industrial conflicts into a political force that will construct a post-industrial, or post-capitalist society. The other face of "class conscious" labor, in a strict sense, is its subordination to political action; in most cases, to socialist parties.

Labor and socialism are neither synonymous nor wholly distinct forms of class activity. They are both complementary and opposed. They are complementary because socialist parties are supposed to lead the way out of the capitalist system within which the labor movement fights its class enemies. But when economic and social change supposes the overcoming of fundamental cultural or political obstacles, socialism becomes more radical and more distant from union activities. Such was the case historically in Austria, where the central political problem was the conflict between the Austrian monarchy and the nationalities struggling for their independence. It was also true in France, where political movements have always been more advanced and active than the social movements, partly because of the maintenance of some aspects of the old regime and partly because of the political triumph of a middle class that opposed big business and the Catholic church and incorporated the labor movement into the struggle for its democratic program.

Where organized labor is strong, socialist parties are weak in power, though not in electoral terms. Socialist parties predominate where political and cultural obstacles to modernization are more important than structural conflicts within an industrial society. Labor movements always limit themselves to social problems of industrial production and leave to political parties the main responsibility for historical change. An extreme form of this separation between social movements and political action is seen in the "syndicalist" movement or "revolutionary unionism," also known as direct action unionism: the French CGT, the Irish movement associated with James Larkin, or the American Industrial Workers of the World (IWW), are well-known examples of militant labor movements between 1900 and 1920 that refused to participate in socialist party politics. Even more extreme were the explicitly anarchist movements, especially strong in Mediterranean countries, in the main Atlantic ports, and on the north and south Pacific coasts of Latin America. The separation of unions from political action can be used by various political forces, including those of the right wing; but when the labor movement gets nearer its central model it returns to an alliance with left and liberal (in the Anglo-Saxon sense) parties, according to the political situation in different countries. But even where very strong links exist between unions and socialist or labor parties, the labor movement and political organizations often remain distant.

Attempts at unification. The decline of a class conscious labor movement may stimulate attempts to unify social movements and political action, but in contrasting ways. On one side, we have already described the post-1969 Italian example, based on a deep crisis of the political system and the joint efforts of management and labor at the national level to reform a disorganized State, combining industrialization and social policy. Bruno Trentin, on the union side, and Giovanni Agnelli, on the management side, came together in collective bargaining agreements that amounted to a global economic and social policy. Similarly, the French CFDT has proposed general political programs opposing the "dualiza-

tion" of society and the growing distance between the employed
and the unemployed, developing measures of "work-sharing,"
which it hopes will lead to a new type of industrial democracy.

Unions have become more and more incorporated into political
action in both social democratic Sweden and the French Communist Party. In these cases, the main reason for the "transformation" is that unionism is focusing less on working conditions
and wage problems and more on employment and social security
systems—on general economic policies. In Scandinavian countries, unions have become more and more closely linked with
Social-Democratic governments, especially in Sweden where the
Social-Democratic Party has been almost constantly in power. In
France, where the Communist Party was strong until 1981, when
the Socialists came to power, the most important union has identified itself more and more openly with the Communist Party political strategy at the cost of a *decreasing* capacity for mass
mobilization and bargaining.

From collective bargaining to the "social contract." The
attempts discussed above have proven of limited value for reasons
that have already been mentioned. The growing distance between
technical and professional categories and the marginalized
masses has made it more and more difficult for the labor movement to elaborate a general economic and social program. The
result has been a strong tendency of unionism to limit itself to interest group politics and direct bargaining with management.
Especially in Britain and the United States after the Second World
War and during the period of economic growth, unions were active
at the company level and tried to exercise direct control over
working conditions. In Britain and Scandinavia, collective agreements were complemented by informal pressures, wage drift, and
sometimes "dual" or informal militant organization: in Britain,
radical shop stewards, often influenced by the Communist Party,
led strikes and protests that were opposed to the national or industry-wide agreements signed by the union. In the United States,
where agreements are signed at the company level, this
phenomenon was much more limited.

But the almost total separation of unionism from politics, widely
hailed as the most stable form of labor organization, appeared to

be increasingly unsatisfactory when the postwar period of economic expansion came to an end. Industrial relations, important as they are, cannot be considered synonymous with trade unionism: the role of the State herein must be recognized. In the United States, the expansion of the unions in the 1930s was linked to the New Deal and especially to the role of the National Labor Relations Act (Wagner Act), which played a role similar to the Matignon agreements of the 1936 French Popular Front and the Swedish Saltsjobaden agreements in 1938. State intervention became a central factor in industrial relations, so that the earlier period of direct management-labor relations at the company level can almost be considered a long preface. The collective agreements that were signed during the 1930s could not prevent or even limit the consequences of the economic crisis. Conversely, today collective bargaining in many countries has been progressively complemented or replaced by a "social contract," to use the British expression. From the Grand Coalition in the early 1960s through the subsequent Social Democratic administrations, the German DGB (union confederation) discussed with government and industry the conditions for economic growth. The Swedish LO has been involved even in tripartite negotiations.

The British Trade Union Congress refused to sign general agreements with the Conservative government but negotiated with the Wilson Labor government in 1975. Trade union leaders hailed the British Joint Production Consultative and Advisory Committee and many other forms of participation in economic decision making as new steps forward on the road to industrial democracy. As recently as 1977, the Bullock Report was still considering "workers' control" as the final aim of these measures. Nevertheless, few steps were made in that direction. On the contrary, British unions were integrated into official committees in which the defense of workers' interests was only one among many preoccupations. New objectives became predominant—the economic recovery of the country, its defense against foreign competition, breaking the rigidities imposed upon employment practices by union or legal regulations. In the past, British unions had evidenced little interest in macroeconomic problems; during the 1970s, by contrast, they began integrating economic policies and social demands.

The situation varied on the Continent. The Italian trade unions have consistently negotiated general economic issues with government and business leaders. In France, only one union, the CFDT, was favorable to a social contract policy even if many of its members did not support this orientation. Another, the CGT, identified itself with the Communist Party, while the smaller Force Ouvriere favored a pure collective bargaining orientation. To be "class conscious" is too high an ambition for today's unions, which no longer focus on the occupational experiences of "producers" dominated by industrial management. To be no more than an interest group is, however, too low an aspiration for labor unions, especially in countries where they represent half or more of the wage earners. Unions, during the early stage of their evolution, were interest groups; then they became a social movement; now throughout Western Europe they are a political force. No major economic policies can be worked out without the active participation of unions. It is no longer possible for unions to defend workers' interests without relating social goals to economic situations, especially in countries where production strongly depends on international markets.

Neo-corporatism. The contemporary choice for unions is not between reform and revolution or between wage bargaining and political action, but between the "social contract" and "neo-corporatism": to negotiate with the State or to be incorporated into it. Social democracy originally was perceived as the political expression of a labor movement and defined itself primarily as a class-oriented party. More recently in some European countries, it has been subsumed into a neo-corporatist State, the expression of a national consensus and the agent of social integration and equality. Thus, unions have become part of the State apparatus. Such "corporatism" should not be confused with the neo-fascist Spanish-Portuguese model, which was mainly anti-labor, an instrument of political control over workers. The new corporatist State, according to Philippe Schmitter, negotiates with organized groups that no longer defend the interests of a social category or class, but claim to represent a sector of national life.[16] Their representatives try to convince the government, the parliament, and public opinion of their usefulness in serving the common good and the future of the nation.

Latin America provides a series of examples of corporatist regimes that fall between the old Spanish/Portuguese neo-fascist model and the "second generation" social democratic regimes. The government-controlled Confederacion de Trabajadores Mexicanos (CTM) has mainly been an instrument of political control whose leadership is challenged by independent, radical unions, especially among railway and electrical workers. In Brazil, unionism expanded greatly during the Vargas government, assisted by direct state intervention. Union life was organized and regulated by labor laws. The link between unions and the State was more positive in Brazil than in Mexico, at least before the 1964 coup. In Argentina after 1945, Peron destroyed the old anarchist and socialist unions and created a Peronist unionism which remained so closely linked to the political power and opposed to parliamentary government that it finally participated in post-Peron military regimes.

But beyond these profound differences among Latin American countries, unions basically became part of the broad process of national mobilization under the direct control of nationalist States. In Europe, even in Scandinavia, the degree of incorporation of unions into the State has been much more limited; still unions for the most part are no longer independent social actors. Some receive financial help from governments, many are part of the decision-making system, and almost all act in a "responsible" way. The distance is not wide between a neo-capitalist state, a "social contract" policy, and a purely redistributive welfare government. Nevertheless, these three reflect real differences among countries, while "liberalism" and "socialism" have become empty words, sometimes useful during political campaigns, but no longer corresponding to real choices (even Prime Minister Margaret Thatcher was unable to reduce the role of the welfare state in Britain). Economic and political systems in today's Western world are less defined by class relations than by the link between the State and civil society, between problems of economic development and the internal conflicts of an industrial society. The more urgent the problems of economic development or national economic survival the more unions and management are incorporated into the State,

which acts as the main policy setter in a situation of fierce international competition and tensions with powerful multinational
corporations. Unions are involved in management policies in the
most dynamic industrial countries, Japan and the United States.
And as noted, the European industrial countries maintain
trilateral systems of economic decision making in which unions
are both independent social forces and responsible participants in
the economic and political decision-making system.

Conclusion: The Natural History of Unionism

The labor movement was never merely a pressure group. Both in
autocratic and democratic countries, in favorable and unfavorable
economic conditions, it acted and was considered as a central
agent in the functioning and transformation of industrial
societies. Labor laws, collective agreements, and finally the
welfare state resulted from the protests and proposals of the labor
movement. In Western Europe, unions are influential in all
aspects of national life, even when they are in conflict with
governments—a situation that has become increasingly common
with the victory during the last decade of conservative parties in
many countries. Their role is more limited in the United States.
That does not mean that unions act as a core social movement in
industrial countries. They often have a more limited scope of action, but no other collectivity has been able to replace the role that
the labor movement was able to assume as the representative of
the less privileged.

In the advanced industrial countries, some of which appear to be
in a process of deindustrialization, the labor movement no longer
plays a central role in the economy, even when unions retain a
large political influence. But there is no serious reason to believe
that unions everywhere will lose ground permanently. The loss of
strength of American or French unions, the serious problems met
by British and Italian ones, are in the end no more significant
than the effectiveness of the Swedish and German labor organizations, the current expansion of Brazilian unions, and the central
role played by the Solidarnosc union in the Polish democratic,
social, and national liberation movement. Unions may remain important, but what appears to have declined permanently is the

"labor movement" as such—the capacity of organized labor to *challenge* the system of social and economic organization. Trade unionism was, at a given time, a social movement; it is now a political force that is necessarily subordinated to political parties and to governments because it tends to defend specific interests, much as most of the American unions always have been doing. Gone is the link between unions and alternative images of a reconstructed society.

III

Economic Analysis

7

RICHARD B. FREEMAN

Effects of Unions on the Economy

The impact of trade unionism on the economy has long been an area of contention among economists. There are those—Alfred Marshall, Sumner Slichter, Lloyd Reynolds, John Dunlop—who come up with generally favorable assessments of unions. There are those —Milton Friedman, Henry Simons, Fritz Machlup, Gottfried Haberler—with generally negative assessments.[1]

To buttress their beliefs analysts can, and have, cited various instances in which unions have been a positive or negative factor in the economy. A reading of the case study literature, ranging from the immense Slichter, Livernash, and Healy volume to smaller studies of individual bargaining situations, suggests that everything anyone has said—good and bad—about unions is true. There are situations in which unions and the collective bargaining process raise wages, improve personnel practices, lower turnover, and induce management to improve productivity. There are also cases in which unions harm the operation of individual companies, reduce productivity, and have a generally deleterious effect on the economy. There are unions that are democratic social institutions and unions that are nondemocratic and corrupt.

To provide a realistic assessment of the economic effects of unionism it is necessary to go beyond the recitation of good and bad cases to a broad statistical analysis that permits one to reach generalizations about the institution as a whole and to specify the conditions under which the positive or negative effects of the institution are likely to dominate.

In recent years the availability of computerized data files that contain vast amounts of information on thousands of individuals, establishments, and companies has for the first time offered students of unionism the opportunity for such broad quantitative analyses. While an overall assessment of what unions do to the economy requires one to weigh positive and negative impacts on diverse outcomes—on which reasonable persons may differ—it is possible to determine the direction and magnitude of union effects on key economic variables.

In this chapter I present evidence indicating that in addition to well-advertised effects on wages, unions alter nearly every other measurable aspect of the operation of workplaces and enterprises, from turnover to productivity, wage inequality, profits, and fringe benefits. The evidence indicates that unions have "two faces": a "monopoly wage-setting" face, with generally harmful effects to the overall efficiency of the economy; and a "collective voice/management response" (voice/response) face with generally positive effects on the operation of the economy (Table 1).

In the United States in recent years the empirical evidence suggests that the voice/response face of unions dominates the monopoly face, with unions in most settings associated with greater efficiency, lower earnings inequality, and generally more desirable workplaces. The widely stressed monopoly effects of unions on resource allocation and on such macroeconomic factors as wage inflation are found to be relatively modest in quantitative terms, and the voice/response effects of unions on turnover, wage inequality, provision of fringe benefits, and productivity are found to be somewhat larger.[2]

Evidence suggesting that, on net, unions are a positive economic

Table 1
The Two Faces of Trade Unionism

	Union Effects on Economic Efficiency	Union Effects on Distribution of Income
Monopoly Face	Unions raise wages above competitive levels, leading to too little labor relative to capital in unionized firms.	Unions increase income inequality by raising the wages of highly skilled workers.
	Union work rules decrease productivity.	Unions create horizontal inequities by creating differentials among comparable workers.
Collective Voice/Institutional Response Face	Unions have some positive effects on productivity — reducing quit rates, inducing management to alter methods of production and adopt more efficient policies, and improving morale and cooperation among workers.	Unions standard-rate policies reduce inequality among organized workers in a given company or a given industry.
		Union rules limit the scope for arbitrary actions in the promotion, layoff, and recall of individuals.
	Unions collect information about the preferences of all workers, leading the firm to choose a better mix of employee compensation and a better set of personnel policies.	Unionism fundamentally alters the distribution of power between marginal (generally junior) and more permanent (generally senior) employees, causing union firms to select different compensation packages and personnel practice from those of nonunion firms.

Source: Based on R. B. Freeman and J. I. Medoff, "The Two Faces of Unionism," *The Public Interest* 57 (Fall 1979), p. 75.

force does not, of course, mean that unions are beneficial to individual companies. Indeed, the opposite appears to be the case on average. The gains of unionism accrue to their members. The costs show up in lower profitability for many organized companies. The paradox of American unionism is that it is at one and the same time a plus on the overall social balance sheet (in most though not all circumstances) and a minus on the corporate balance sheet (again, in most though not all circumstances).

The Union Monopoly Pay Effect

That unions raise the level of pay of their members is hardly news. Some early observers of unionism, indeed, expressed fears that the union monopoly wage effect constituted "an attack on the competitive system" (Lindblom), "the rock on which our present system is most likely to crack up" (Simons), or "the most important domestic economic problem" (Haberler). Empirical estimates of union wage effects and historical experience (including the successful operation of highly unionized economies throughout the free world) show these fears to be groundless.[3]

They are not groundless because the union impact on wages is slight. A seemingly endless number of empirical studies of union wage effects, which compare the pay of union and nonunion workers (establishments) with similar economic attributes, or which compare pay of workers before and after they have been unionized, show that the union effect on wages is quite sizable, 15 to 25 percent on average in post–World War II years.

The effect is not, of course, uniform across workers or industries. In general, the union wage effect has been larger in historically regulated sectors (such as trucking and air transport) and in sectors in which unions organized larger portions of the work force. It has been larger for workers who tend to be lower paid and less skilled than for those who tend to be higher paid (Table 2).

The effect is, moreover, not constant over time. In the 1970s, when the economy performed particularly poorly, the union wage premium rose, as unions maintained or increased the *real* (inflation-adjusted) pay of their members, while other workers suffered from increases below the rate of inflation. During this decade the

Table 2

The Union Wage Advantage by Demographic Group, for Blue-Collar Workers, 20–65, 1979

By Education

27%	19%	17%	6%
Less than High School	High School	College 1-3	College 4+

By Region

10%	18%	22%	22%
Northeast	Central	South	West

By Sex

19%	15%
Male	Female

By Age

21%	17%	13%	19%
20-35 Years Old	36-45	46-55	56-65

By Race

17%	25%
White	Nonwhite

By Occupation

19%	12%	27%	28%
Craftsmen	Operatives Except Transport	Transport Operatives	Laborers

By Tenure

27%	17%	8%	9%
0-3	4-10	11-15	16+

Service Workers 12%

Source: R. B. Freeman and J. L. Medoff, *What Do Unions Do?* (New York: Basic Books, 1984), p. 49.

union wage effect rose by as much as 9 to 10 percentage points (from about 15 to 25 percent) putting significant profit pressure on organized companies. The concession bargaining of the 1980s represents a return to more traditional union wage premium.

While the union wage premium is sizable, the adverse economic effects on resource allocation tend—virtually all analysts agree—to be slight. Indeed, empirical studies find only modest misallocative effects because the value of the output loss due to the monopoly increase in wages depends on the product of that increase and the number of workers whose employment is lost due to higher wages, which tends to be modest. Estimates based on the standard economic formula for evaluating the social loss due to monopolies suggest that union monopoly wage gains cost the economy 0.2 to 0.4 percent of gross national product (GNP), which in 1980 amounted to about $5 to $10 billion dollars or $20 to $40 per person.[4]

Recent theoretical work on union contracts suggests that even this modest estimate may be too large. This work stresses the impact of union contracts on employment levels as well as wages and argues that an "efficient contract" would redistribute company income from profits to workers without causing any social misallocative loss. A smart union leader and company bargainer could rewrite an existing contract to eliminate the social loss and raise either pay or profits or both. Consistent with this argument are studies which find union employment effects, (as opposed to wage effects) difficult to estimate in data.[5] As analysis of the "efficient contracts" view of unionism has just begun, the safe conclusion is simply that traditional estimates of union misallocative effects which are modest probably overstate the true effects somewhat.

Union Wage Gains and Inflation

It was once widely believed that union wage increases were a primary cause of cost-push inflation. Until the "stagflation" of the late 1970s and early 1980s, the facts contradicted this belief. Far from outpacing other wages or salaries, union wages increased more slowly in inflationary periods, so that the union wage premium tended to fall. The usual explanation was that by negotiating contracts that set wages over extended periods, typically three years, union wage gains caused periods of inflation to last longer than they would have otherwise, but one could not reasonably blame unions for initiating cost-push inflation.[6]

The increase in the union wage premium in the highly inflationary late 1970s and early 1980s lent new life to the argument that unions cause inflation. In this period, union cost-of-living adjustment clauses may have created a new situation in which union wage policies tended to augment rather than to reduce inflationary wage pressures.

Just how important might the union wage gains have been to the inflation of the past decade? If union wage increases have no effect on the wages of other workers, it is relatively easy to demonstrate that unions can be blamed for only a miniscule share of inflation. To see this, note that:

Contribution of union wage increases to percentage change in unit costs, and thus in prices	=	Union labor's share of costs	×	Percentage change in union wage premium

Unionized labor accounts for about 25 percent of total cost of national output, and the union wage premium rose over the entire 1975–81 period by a total of about 9 percentage points. The result was to add 2.3 percentage points of inflation to the observed 68-point increase in the GNP deflator. While it is still possible that union wage increases adversely affected inflation through "spillovers" on other workers, no serious student of inflation believes this to be a major cause of the stagflation of the period. There simply is no evidence for such an assertion.[7]

Structure of Pay: Dispersion and Composition

The impact of unions on pay goes far beyond altering the level of pay in organized jurisdiction. Anyone who compares union and nonunion firms is almost immediately struck by two marked differences in the structure of pay: the unionized sector evinces greater equality (less dispersion) of wages for comparable workers and it pays a larger proportion of compensation in the form of fringe benefits.

The effect of unions on equality of pay has long been at the heart of economists' evaluations of the institution. In *Capitalism and Freedom* Milton Friedman laid out the case that, for all the talk of worker solidarity, unions increase inequality:

If unions raise wage rates in a particular occupation or industry, they necessarily make the amount of employment available in the occupation or industry less than it otherwise would be—just as any higher price cuts down the amount purchased. The effect is an increased number of persons seeking other jobs, which forces down wages in other occupations. Since unions have generally been strongest among groups that would have been high-paid anyway, their effect has been to make high-paid workers higher paid at the expense of lower-paid workers. Unions have therefore not only harmed the public at large and workers as a whole by distorting the use of labor; they have also made the incomes of the working class more unequal by reducing the opportunities available to the most disadvantaged workers.[8]

By contrast, industrial relations experts, beginning with the Webbs, have stressed union standard rate policies favoring "equal pay for equal work," within and across establishments, as a likely force reducing inequality of wages.[9]

The issue is an important one. Many people champion unions in the belief that they are an egalitarian force, and if in fact unions increase inequality, the case for a positive role of unions in the economy would be greatly weakened.

The modern empirical analyses of union effects on inequality, summarized in Table 3, show the claim that unionism increases inequality to be wrong; on the contrary, unionism tends to be a powerful force for equalization of earnings in the economy. The earnings inequality claim is wrong not because the effect to which it directs attention—raising wages of some workers at the expense of other workers—does not occur. It does. The claim is wrong because the increase in inequality induced by monopoly wage effects is dwarfed by three other union effects on wages that reduce inequality: union wage policies favoring lower inequality of wages within establishments; union wage policies for equal pay for equal work across establishments; and union wage gains for blue-collar labor which reduce inequality between white-collar and blue-collar workers.

The effect of unions on inequality of wages within establishments results in large part from policies designed to force employers to pay workers on the basis of specified job rates, in which all workers classified in a given category are paid the same wage, as opposed to paying personal rates that depend on the supervisor's perception of workers. Unions favor job rates for three reasons. First, as a political organization whose policies reflect the preference of average workers, unions can be expected to adopt wage policies benefiting the majority of the work force. In most situations the majority of workers have earnings below the mean level, suggesting that the majority will favor pay policies that accord greater gains to the lower paid. Second, unions are likely to favor single-rate policies because they replace managerial discretion and power at the workplace with more objective decision rules. Because the value of a worker's contribution to a firm is extremely difficult to measure and different supervisors may read the same facts in different ways, the union will seek to protect the membership from the uncertainty of arbitrary supervisory decisions by pressing for a one-rate-per-job pay policy. Third, unions are likely to seek equalized wages among workers doing similar tasks for reasons of worker solidarity and organizational unity. As the mid-1980s debates over two-tier wage systems indicate, unions are fearful that policies other than equalization will erode their organizational strength, dividing the higher paid from the lower paid.

Comparisons of wage policies and inequality of wages within establishments show that unionism has a significant impact toward equalization of pay. One study of thousands of plants has found that 68 percent of union workers are paid by a single rate or automatic progression in pay compared to 35 percent of nonunion workers, with a resultant lower inequality of wages in the union plants.[10]

Unions try to standardize wages in an industry or local product market in order to "take wages out of competition." While there are notable exceptions in the form of concessions given to companies in trouble, multi-employer bargaining (which in 1980 was the practice in agreements covering 43 percent of the major contract work force) or multi-plant bargaining (the practice relevant to an additional 40 percent) tend to produce uniform or near-uniform rates across establishments. The result is a distribution of pay among plants in a given sector that paradoxically seems to

Table 3

Studies of the Impact of Unionism on Wage Inequality

Study	Nature of Data	Finding
1. Freeman (1980)	May current population survey data on individuals and expenditures for employee compensation data for firms.	Unionized workers have 15 percent lower standard deviation of log earnings than otherwise comparable non-union workers; unionism reduces white-collar/blue-collar differential by 10 percent. These effects produce a 2-3 percent reduction in inequality among comparable workers.
2. Freeman (1982)	BLS *Industry Wage Survey* data on individuals working in nine industries.	Standard deviation of log (wages) in union sector is on average 22 percent lower than in nonunion sector.
3. Hirsch (1982)	Cross-sectional analysis of 1970 census of population data on 3-digit industries.	Each percentage point of unionization lowered the variance of log earnings by .015 points.
4. Hyclak (1977)	Cross-sectional analysis of 1970 census data on earnings in SMSAs.	Each percentage point of unionization lowered the Gini coefficient .021 points.
5. Hyclak (1979)	Cross-sectional analysis of 1970 census data on male earnings in SMSAs.	Each percentage point of unionization lowered Gini coefficient for men by .038 points.
6. Hyclak (1980)	Cross-sectional analysis of 1950, 1960, and 1970 census data on family income in the 48 contiguous states.	Each 1 percent increase in the mean for unionization lowered the mean of the percent of families earning under $3,000 in 1970 by 3 percent. Similar findings for 1950 and 1960.

Table 3 (cont'd)

7. Plotnick (1982)	Time series analysis of current population survey data for men.	Each 1 percentage point of unionization lowered variance of log (earnings) by .065 points.
8. Freeman (1984)	Analysis of inequality of workers before and after unionization in 4 data sets	Workers who join unions have declines in standard deviation of earnings of .03 to .09 points compared to workers who leave unions.
9. Freeman and Medoff (1984)	Analysis of total impact of unions on earnings inequality using various data sets	Unionism reduces standard deviation of log of earnings by 3 percent.

Sources: (1) R. B. Freeman, "Unionism and the Dispersion of Wages," *Industrial and Labor Relations Review* 34 (October 1980), pp. 3–23. (2) R. B. Freeman, "Union Wage Practices and Wage Dispersion Within Establishments," *Industrial and Labor Relations Review* 36 (October 1982). (3) Barry Hirsch, "The Interindustry Structure of Unionism, Earnings and Earnings Dispersion," *Industrial Labor Review* 36 (October 1982). (4) Thomas Hyclak, "Unionization and Urban Differentials in Income Inequality," *The Journal of Economics* 3 (1977), pp. 205–7. (5) Thomas Hyclak, "The Effect of Unions on Earnings Inequality in Local Labor Markets," *Industrial and Labor Relations Review* 33 (October 1979), pp. 77–84. (6) Thomas Hyclack, "Unions and Income Inequality: Some Cross-State Evidence," *Industrial Relations* 19 (Spring 1980), pp. 212–15. (7) Robert D. Plotnick, "Trends in Male Earnings Inequality," *Southern Economic Journal* 48 (January 1982), pp. 724–32. (8) R. B. Freeman, "Longitudinal Analysis of the Effects of Trade Unions," *Journal of Labor Economics* 2 (1984), pp. 1–26. (9) R. B. Freeman and James L. Medoff, *What Do Unions Do?* (New York: Basic Books, 1984), p. 91.

Note: Some of these studies used the variance of log earnings; others used the Gini coefficient, a related measure of inequality; still others used the standard deviation of earnings. The different inequality measures should yield different reductions in inequality, as they do.

more closely mirror the competitive ideal of a single rate in the market than does the distribution of pay in the nonunion sector.

Finally, because unions tend to organize more blue-collar than white-collar workers and have a larger wage impact on blue-collar workers, they reduce white-collar/blue-collar pay differentials by approximately the same amount as they raise blue-collar wages. In the average nonunion establishment, the white-collar worker earns about one and a half times as much as the blue-collar worker. In the comparable union establishment, the white-collar worker earns about one-third more than the blue-collar worker, a considerably smaller premium.[11] The union monopoly wage effect that is usually cited as a contributor to blue-collar inequality is at the same time a contributor to equality between blue-collar and white-collar labor.

Adding up the three inequality-reducing effects on wages among blue-collar workers indicates that on net unions reduce inequality. The effect depends, of course, on the size of wage effects, exceptions given to standard-rate policies, and the size of the union sector. With the rise of two-tier contracts, concession bargaining, and declining union density, the inequality-reducing effect of unions is likely to become less important.

Fringe Benefits

Consider two workplaces where employers are equally skilled, one union, one nonunion. Which workplace is likely to have a pension plan, better health care plans, more fringe benefits of virtually every type?

The answer from modern empirical work is unequivocal. Unionism increases fringe benefits at workplaces. It increases fringes in part because it increases wages (which can be viewed as part of its monopoly wage impact). Also, however, it raises the fringe share of the pay of workers with the same total compensation, particularly toward pensions; life, accident, and health insurance; vacation and holiday pay (Table 4). In 1979, 76 percent of unionized private sector workers had pension plans compared to 35 percent of nonunion workers.

In addition to increasing the number of fringes available to workers, unions affect the nature of those plans. Consider first the difference between union and nonunion pension plans: union pension plans tend to be defined-benefit plans, which promise workers definite amounts of retirement pay, rather than defined-contribution plans, which invest moneys and pay workers the return on the investment. Defined-benefit plans are generally favored by senior workers who enjoy the rewards of increased defined benefits without incurring the full costs. In the 1970s all but 10 percent of union private pension plans were of the defined-benefit type, compared with a bare third of nonunion private pension plans. The union preference for defined-benefit plans also reflects the desire of unions and workers to avoid the risk of allowing retirement pay to depend on fluctuations in capital markets. In the life, accident, and health areas, union plants are more likely to include dental and eyeglass benefits, as well as to increase medical and life insurance expenditures.

The union effect on fringes is greater in smaller firms than in larger firms and is especially significant in industries where workers are more attached to occupations than to employers (construction, for example), or where firms are relatively small (such as trucking). This is primarily because fringe programs with sizable set-up costs and deferred compensation require a large and permanent market institution to administer and maintain them, and in the above situations unions are the sole such institutions. Multi-employer programs, of the type initiated by unions, make benefits portable across employers and provide the size to reduce average set-up costs. The vast majority of multi-employer pension plans are union run (68 percent in the pension plan file of the Office of Pension and Welfare Benefit Programs, Department of Labor), and while a few have attracted attention for illicit practices (the Teamsters Central States Pension Fund being the most infamous case), most such plans provide workers with benefits otherwise unavailable in their sector.

Is the impact of unions in raising fringe benefits a plus or a minus to the economy? In terms of the conventional "monopoly wage" criticism of unionism, the part of the union effect on fringes that raises labor costs is an additional social cost of union monopoly power. In terms of the representation or voice role of unions, the increased *share* of fringes in compensation is likely to be an economic plus as it reflects the ability of unions to provide

Table 4

Estimates of Percentage Impact of Unionism on Wage, Fringe Benefits and Total Compensation

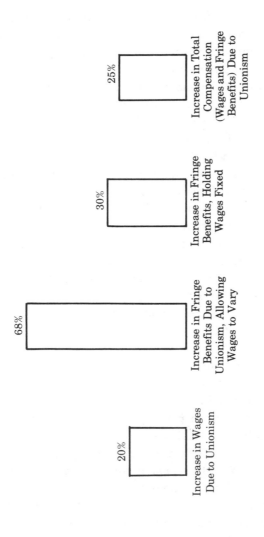

20%	Increase in Wages Due to Unionism
68%	Increase in Fringe Benefits Due to Unionism, Allowing Wages to Vary
30%	Increase in Fringe Benefits, Holding Wages Fixed
25%	Increase in Total Compensation (Wages and Fringe Benefits) Due to Unionism

Source: R. B. Freeman and J. L. Medoff, *What Do Unions Do?* (New York: Basic Books, 1984), p. 64.

management with better information about worker preferences (through bargaining) and likely cost savings due to group purchase. Whether the positive or negative effects on the overall economy are more important is unclear. What is clear is that unionism has greatly altered the ways in which workers are paid.

Exit-Voice: Turnover

The effect of unions on labor turnover and creating relatively permanent committed work forces is central to understanding what unions do to the economy. In theory, unionism can positively influence the functioning of individual enterprise and the overall economy by providing workers with a "voice" alternative to quitting when they are discontented with work conditions. In a nonunion setting the unhappy worker "votes with his feet" by quitting his job. In a union setting, he or she can negotiate changes in terms of work through collective bargaining and can obtain redress to individual grievances through the grievance-arbitration system. In addition, by serving as a mechanism for enforcing labor contracts, unions are likely to create greater opportunities for deferred compensation as part of labor contracts.

Because relatively permanent employees behave differently than short-term employees, the potential reduction in exit due to unionism has far-reaching implications for the operation of firms. How sizable is the union-caused reduction in exit and increase in permanency of work forces? To what extent are the effects of unions on turnover due to the potentially socially deleterious monopoly wage effects and to what extent are they due to the potentially beneficial "voice" effects?

Considerable research has been devoted to examining the relation between unionism and exit behavior. Some studies have compared the quit rates of workers with similar personal characteristics (age, sex, race, education), with similar wages, and in the same occupation and industry in the presence of unionism and in the absence of unionism. Other analyses compare the quit rates at establishments in industries that are heavily unionized with those in industries that are lightly unionized. Still others compare the number of years union and nonunion workers remain with the same firm. The most recent studies use work history files that follow people for as long as a decade to contrast the exit behavior of the same worker when he or she works union to when he or she works nonunion.

Regardless of their form the studies seek to control for the union wage effect by comparing workers paid the same wages. This is critical because union-induced monopoly wage increases which reduce quitting may be more harmful than beneficial to the economy, whereas reductions in quits due to better work conditions, grievance procedures, and the like are likely to be beneficial.

The evidence that unionism reduces quit behavior and creates a more permanent work force is compelling.[12] Every study finds that, independent of raising wages, unionism substantially reduces quits and increases the years a worker stays with his firm. Virtually every study finds, moreover, that the effects of unions on quits is far in excess of the impact of the union monopoly wage increase on quits. On average unionism reduces the probability that a worker quits by from 31 to 65 percent and correspondingly increases the number of years a worker stays with an employer from 23 to 32 percent.[13] Unionism is an important force in reducing turnover and creating permanent employment of the type that some believe contributes to the Japanese economic success.

Is the reduction in exit worth a lot to firms? To workers? How does the potential gain in social product from lower turnover compare with the monopoly cost of unionism?

For firms, a reasonable estimate is that the lower turnover due to unionism is equivalent to a one to two percent reduction in cost, or equivalently, to a one to two percent increase in productivity. While not negligible, these savings are dwarfed by the union wage effect, guaranteeing that firms will not invite organization to enjoy the benefits of lower turnover.

For workers, by contrast, the potential welfare gain from union work conditions is sizable. Our best estimate is that unionism is equivalent to a 40 percent wage increase: that is, one would have to pay nonunion workers 40 percent higher wages to reduce their quit rate to the union level. Translating this into an economists' "consumer surplus" yields a conservative estimate of the welfare gain of 0.2 to 0.3 percent of GNP, which is of comparable magnitude to the social cost of unionism estimated earlier. There is, however, one difference between these social losses and gains: the benefit of voice accrues to organized workers only, whereas the costs come out of everyone's pocket. Even so, it is striking that the voice benefits, traditionally ignored in quantitative evaluations of unionism, are as large as the monopoly costs.

Layoffs and Concessions

A firm faces a decline in demand for its product and must decide how to adjust its employment, wages, and hours. Should it lay off workers? Should it lower wages? Reduce work hours?

Trade unions are concentrated in highly cyclical parts of the economy—manufacturing and construction—so that union policies can greatly affect how the economy responds to the business cycle. In the United States, unions have generally opted for an adjustment pattern based largely on temporary layoffs rather than wage or hour reductions. Temporary layoffs typically last less than a month and generally end with the recall of the laid-off workers. Because workers are generally recalled or rehired, temporary layoffs are not as serious as permanent layoffs, which occur as a result of such permanent economic changes as the shutting down of an entire plant.

The difference between union and nonunion policies regarding temporary layoffs are substantial: layoff rates are two to four times higher in the union than in the nonunion sector, and union workers are 50 to 60 percent more likely to be on temporary-layoff unemployment as a result.[14]

Why do unionized workers and firms choose temporary layoffs rather than reductions in wages or hours? The most important reason is that temporary layoffs usually mean laying off junior workers, not the senior employees who have a greater influence on union policies than they would have on the policies of a nonunion firm. Faced with the choice of reduced earnings through fewer hours or lower wages or the unemployment of a junior worker, the senior worker will select the policy that is personally most beneficial. Except in cases where mass layoffs are threatened, this will lead him or her to prefer layoffs to the other forms of adjustment.

It is one thing to be laid off temporarily, knowing you will be recalled to your job in a few weeks. It is another matter entirely to

face the danger of extended joblessness because of an event such
as a plant closing or bankruptcy. In a temporary layoff, the senior
worker is protected by inverse seniority layoff rules; when a shutdown threatens, all workers' jobs are seriously endangered. As a
result, union policies with respect to shutdowns on prolonged economic distresses differ from their policies with respect to temporary layoffs.

Faced with the threat of shutdowns or related long term company problems, unions in the 1980s have proven to be much more
flexible in their wage-setting policies than most observers would
have expected on the basis of earlier experiences. Unions in industries undergoing serious long-term economic problems have
negotiated wage concessions. In some sectors they have agreed to
two-tier systems of pay, which reduce the pay for new workers
while maintaining the pay of incumbents. Profit-sharing schemes,
once considered anathema among unionists, have been negotiated
in several cases. The lesson is that when jobs of senior union
workers are threatened unions are highly flexible and willing to
adjust in order to save those jobs. The stereotype of the union as
an inflexible institution on the wage side has been proven false by
these developments.

Productivity

Few issues regarding the economic effects of unions have generated more controversy than what unions do to productivity. As
Bok and Dunlop wrote in 1970:

For more than a century and a half, economists have debated the effects
of 'combinations of workmen,' or collective bargaining, on the efficiency
of business enterprises. The literature is replete with conflicting ap-
praisals of the impact of work stoppages, work rules, regulation of
machinery, apprenticeship, and training on employee efficiency and
managerial decisions.[15]

Modern quantitative analysis of productivity in organized and
unorganized industries and plants suggest that, on average,
unionism is associated with higher productivity, by perhaps 6 to 10
percent on average with however wide variation across sectors,
plants, and time periods.

From one perspective the productivity findings are to be expected, at least in sectors where unionized firms compete with nonunion firms. Given that unionized firms pay higher wages, one should expect management to undertake activities that raise productivity; if they cannot do so, the firms will eventually be driven out of business. The surprise is that productivity seems to be higher in unionized settings not only because of traditional economic responses to higher wages, such as increased use of capital and less employment (which are socially undesirable) but also because of the reduction in quits and changes in labor practices which unions bring to workplaces (and which are generally socially desirable).

It should be stressed, however, that of all the findings of the modern empirical research the positive union effect on productivity (above and beyond monopoly-wage induced increases in capital per worker) is by far the most controversial. It is controversial in part because of the difficulty of comparing productivity across plants that often produce somewhat different outputs with somewhat different machines. It is also controversial because the routes by which unionized management and labor manage to raise productivity are difficult to specify. There is a modest gain from lower turnover already noted and a tendency for plants to bring in new management and supervisors and alter methods of management after unionization, but the quantitative impact of "productivity targeting," "more professional management," and so on have not been adequately measured.

Finally, the results are controversial because of evidence that the union effect on productivity is quite volatile, highly dependent on the nature of labor-management relations.

The changing pattern of productivity in bituminous coal provides a striking example of the volatile nature of the union productivity effect. During the period in which the United Mine Workers strongly pressed the John L. Lewis policies of mechanization, technological change, and rising wages, productivity in union mines was on the order of 33 to 38 percent higher than in nonunion mines (1965). Internal dissent in the union and labor-management conflict in succeeding years brought a major deterioration, with the result that in 1975 union mines were 17 to 20 percent *less* productive than nonunion mines.

Even within the same company unionization per se need not be a plus or minus to productivity. An analysis of productivity at eighteen General Motors plants found higher productivity where plant managers rated the industrial relations climate as good or where the rate of grievances filed by workers was low (suggesting that workers viewed the state of labor-management relations as good). A detailed study of paper mills yielded similar results: a plant with a low rate of grievances filed in a given period had notably better productivity than the same plant when it had a high rate of grievances filed. Consistent with this, a third study which examined productivity in nine plants over five years found that a cooperative union management program raised productivity in six of the eight plants for which productivity could be measured.[16]

Of equal or possibly greater importance than the union effect on productivity is the union effect on productivity growth. Here, it is difficult to reach a generalization. There is some evidence that unionism is associated with slower productivity growth but the extant results are in many cases statistically weak and show variation over time. As unionized industries tend to be older smokestack industries, slower productivity growth may reflect industry "lifecycle" patterns over which unions have little influence. In some industries productivity is advanced by explicit labor-management cooperative ventures. In the men's tailored clothing industry, for example, labor and management established a committee to develop and introduce automatic sewing machines to enable U.S. workers and firms to compete with low-wage foreign competitors, hiring Draper Laboratories, formerly a part of the Massachusetts Institute of Technology, to do the technical work. According to Dunlop:

The program has several distinct features. The Department of Commerce is contributing financially, although no more than the private-sector contributions from labor and management. The managements and the union in the clothing industry have been joined by two leading textile manufacturers and a leading synthetic yarn company to constitute a broad sectoral group to improve coordination and productivity. These joint responses of labor and management are beyond those that could be achieved at the workplace.[17]

While joint efforts are relatively uncommon, increased pressures from foreign competitors may induce other industries and unions to engage in similar cooperative activities in the future. Indeed, in the 1980s, as well as earlier, some unions have pressed management to modernize their plants with new investments, as they realize that failure to do so means ultimate loss of jobs.

In sum, a plausible reading of the productivity findings is that what matters is not unionism per se but how management and labor interact at the workplace. Higher productivity in union settings runs hand in hand with "good industrial relations" and tends to be spurred by competition in the product market while poor labor reactions and protected environments can produce the opposite.

Profitability

Companies which face organizing drives do not ask if unionism will benefit their workers or the overall economy. They ask what unions do to the corporate "bottom line." There is little doubt that unionism reduces company profitability. Indeed, it appears to be one of the major determinants of profitability, with the union effect on wages dominating any positive effect in productivity. Quantitatively, profitability appears to be roughly 20 percent lower under unionism.[18]

Is this socially good or bad? Persons favoring income redistribution may find it desirable that company profits are lower and worker wages higher. Persons who are concerned with investment and economic growth are likely to worry about what reductions in profits does to the operation of the overall economy.

In part, the answer to this debate depends on the locus of the union impact on profitability. If unions reduce profitability of industries in which firms have sufficient market power to obtain monopoly-level profits, one may place greater weight on the redistributive aspect of the union profit effect. If, on the other hand, unions reduce profits in competitive markets, driving firms out of business, one is likely to place greater weight on the negative effect of profit reductions.

Most studies of the union profit effect find that unions reduce profits largely in sectors where company market power is extensive and thus are more likely to constitute a redistribution of profits than a major force driving firms out of business. When market power changes greatly, however—as occurred in several U.S. industries in the 1980s—it takes considerable concession bargaining by labor and management to keep the firms afloat.

The union impact on profitability is, moreover, by no means always negative. There are two very different types of situations in which unionism is likely to raise rather than reduce profits: when union-induced cost increases in an industry lead the industry to charge monopoly-level prices and when union-induced cost decreases serve to rescue firms on the brink of collapse. In the former case, the union acts, indirectly, as the cartelizing agent in the sector, forcing all firms to act in such a way as to bring the industry closer to the price and output position of a pure product-market monopolist. Since monopoly price increases are socially harmful, the resultant increase in industry profits is socially undesirable. In the latter case, the union behavior, whether reflected in wage reductions or productivity-augmenting activities on the shop floor, is socially desirable.

As an example of an industry in which union wage increases have served to raise industry prices and profits, consider over-the-road trucking during the period of intense Interstate Commerce Commission regulation. When the policy of the commission was essentially to pass union-induced cost increases on to consumers by raising the regulated charges in the sector, profits seem to have been higher than they otherwise would have been. Indeed, profitability in trucking rose after the Teamsters negotiated the nationwide National Master Freight Agreement, which brought virtually all over-the-road drivers into one agreement. Initially, the industry feared such an agreement because of the potential increase in union monopoly power, which many thought could enable the Teamsters to close down trucking in the whole country. In fact, however, the industry as well as its workers benefited from the union's ability to determine all over-the-road wages in one package. In the decade after the agreement, the industry profit rate rose from below the average manufacturing-wide profit rate to a level exceeding the rate for manufacturing.

As an example of more socially desirable union efforts to improve profits in firms, consider the efforts to lower costs under the so-called Scanlon Plan and its close relatives. Under this plan, devised in the 1950s by a former union leader, unions and management work together sharing productivity gains, and in many instances manage to pull companies back from the edge of collapse.

That unions can raise profits by increasing or decreasing costs, with very different consequences for social well-being, demonstrates an important point about the impact of unions on profits: there is little normative content in the direction of the effect per se; rather, what matter are the market conditions and routes by which unionism alters profits.

An Overall Assessment

Is trade unionism good or bad for the economy? Because unionism has beneficial effects on some aspects of economic performance and harmful effects on others and shifts the distribution of income, there is no simple "benefit-cost" that can answer our question. What empirical analysis can do is quantify the magnitude of both the pluses and negatives of the institution. In capsule form, extant research suggests that:

1. Unions raise wages and the cost of labor to firms, with a modest misallocation of resources due to the consequent shrinkage of employment in the union sector.

2. Unions increase fringe benefits desired by workers.

3. Unions reduce inequality of wages in workplaces and across establishments and reduce white-collar/blue-collar pay differentials.

4. Unions reduce quits and increase job tenure, with a resultant modest increase in productivity to firms. The reduction in turnover reflects the extra welfare to workers from unionism.

5. Unions are associated with high productivity in many but not all cases.

6. Unions reduce company profits.

Would the economy function better if it were union free? The evidence does not support such a conclusion. Would the economy function better if it were dominated by unions? The U.S. experience rejects that view also, as unions—like other institutions—need competition to keep them doing their best.

Perhaps the most sensible conclusion to draw from the evidence is that the economy functions best when there are both union and nonunion sectors. Competition reduces the "monopoly wage" costs of unionism and encourages the positive aspects of unionism. Competition keeps nonunion firms from taking advantage of their workers and forces them to adopt union-initiated work practices and modes of pay favored by employees to maintain their nonunion status. In the world of perfect full employment and competitive markets, unions would be unnecessary. In the real world in which we live unions can and generally do perform valuable economic functions. An economy is likely to operate efficiently when there is a sufficient number of union and of nonunion firms to offer alternative work environments to workers, innovation in workplace rules and conditions, and competition in the market.

8

DANIEL K. BENJAMIN

Combinations of Workmen: Trade Unions in the American Economy

Trade unions have been controversial institutions since their inception hundreds of years ago.[1] Indisputably, they increase the incomes of their members, enhance employee influence in the workplace, and bargain for extensive compensation packages. Conversely, they reduce business profits, encourage economically inefficient patterns of consumption and production, and alter the distribution of income in ways that are arguably negative. What is one to make of these "combinations of workmen" who currently represent slightly under one-fifth of the American work force and once controlled twice that proportion?

Economists and other commentators have argued this question vigorously. Supporters of unions contend that they elevate workers' pay and fringe benefits, enhance the voice of employees in determining working conditions, promote economic equality, and improve workplace productivity. Critics of unions say that they raise wages to unrealistic levels, reduce economic equality, obstruct the normal operation of the workplace with restrictive work rules, and ignore the wishes of the rank and file.

The differences of opinion are sharp and strongly held. In reviewing their foundations I begin with a brief history of the American labor movement. Much of the chapter focuses on the impact of unions on the earnings of their members because the wage bargain is a central element of union activity. I then address the implications of recent research on the impact of unions on productivity and the distribution of income. The chapter concludes with an attempt to assess the overall effect of unions on the American economic system.

Historical Background

Membership in the early unions was confined to skilled workers— those who practiced a specific craft such as printing. These workers had the education needed to form and run a union, and they also had the commitment to their trade that came from years of training as apprentices. Unskilled workers tended to rely not on unions but on mobility—upward occupationally or outward to the frontier—to better their lot. From the outset, both employers and the courts looked upon unions with hostility. Indeed, in 1806 the courts found a strike for higher piece rates to be a criminal conspiracy, punishable by imprisonment. Although the attitude of the courts gradually softened over the rest of the nineteenth century, the tendency to regard union activities as restraints of trade proved to be a major impediment to union organizing activities.

The first local craft unions were wholly independent organizations, and it was not until the 1820s that city-wide federations of locals were formed. Although attempts were made over the next twenty years to establish national federations of unions, the efforts had only short-lived results. The spread of the railroad, however, intensified interest in national unions, and in the early 1850s the first national unions were formed—by printers, machinists, locomotive engineers, and others. Part of the impetus for the national unions came from the product competition that arose when goods were shipped from low-wage areas to markets where local unions had been able to obtain higher wages. The national unions also played a key role in establishing rules of admission for members who moved from city to city, often in response to wage differentials, and sought membership in the local of their new home.

Union membership rose rapidly during the Civil War, and there were efforts after the war to form a central federation of the various national unions. These federations proved short-lived, however, and it was not until 1886, with the formation of the American Federation of Labor (AFL), that a permanent national federation was established. Within a few years virtually all the important national unions had joined the AFL, and it soon became a dominant force in the American labor movement.

The next sustained surge in union membership came from 1897 to 1904, when it quadrupled to reach just over 2 million workers. After a brief hiatus, membership rose again sharply during World War I, reaching 5 million in 1920—some 20 percent of total nonagricultural employment. Much of this growth came in the membership of the new industrial unions, which organized all workers in an industry without regard to skill or occupation. The first of the industrial unions—the United Mine Workers—had not been formed until 1890.

Between 1920 and 1933 union membership declined steadily, and amounted to only about 11 percent of the work force by 1933. The adverse labor market conditions of the Great Depression brought renewed interest in the trade union movement, however, particularly in Congress. In 1932 the Norris-LaGuardia Act was passed, making it almost impossible for employers to oppose union organizing efforts with the aid of federal injunctions. In 1933 the National Industrial Recovery Act (NIRA) was enacted, including provisions giving workers the right to collective bargaining by representatives of their choice. Although the NIRA was ruled unconstitutional by the Supreme Court in 1935, Congress moved that same year to enact the Wagner Act, which went well beyond the labor provisions of the NIRA. In addition to reaffirming the right to collective bargaining, it delineated a series of unfair labor practices, including employer discrimination against union members, and established the National Labor Relations Board (NLRB) to ensure that the rights of employees to organize and bargain were enforced. The NIRA and the Wagner Act produced a burst of union organizing activity, and between 1933 and 1937 union membership doubled. The industrial unions, such as the United Auto Workers and the United Steelworkers, were particularly successful, and in 1938 they formed the Congress of Industrial Organizations (CIO). The CIO remained the AFL's chief rival within the labor movement until 1955, when the two organizations merged to form the AFL-CIO.

Union growth continued rapidly through World War II, and by 1945 union membership accounted for over 35 percent of the work force. With the continuing success of unions in organizing came a growing public perception that the Wagner Act had gone too far. Hence in 1947 the Taft-Hartley Act was passed, restoring a number of rights to both employers and individual workers. Among other things, unions as well as employers could now be charged with unfair labor practices, and elections could be held to decertify as well as certify unions as bargaining agents. The public's perception of unions continued to deteriorate in the 1950s as congressional hearings revealed numerous instances of corruption and misuse of union funds, as well as union governing policies that appeared far from democratic. In 1959 Congress passed the Landrum-Griffin Act, requiring among other things, public disclosure of union finances and regular union elections.

Although total union membership has continued to grow during the postwar years, it has done so more slowly than the work force as a whole. As a result the share of the private work force that is unionized has declined steadily. By 1970 fewer than 30 percent of private workers were unionized, and today less than one worker in five belongs to a union. This decline in unionization appears to be due to the conjunction of three factors: changing industrial and demographic structure, a decline in union organizing activities, and increased managerial opposition to unions.

Young people, women, and better educated individuals are generally less likely to join unions. The same is true of white-collar employees and workers living in the South. The relative economic importance of all of these groups has increased over the past three decades, suggesting a tendency toward reduced unionization. This cannot be the complete story, however, since, as noted elsewhere in this volume, similar industrial and demographic trends have been observed in other nations, such as Canada, where the union share of the work force has grown.

An important contributor to the decline of unionization in the United States has been the reduction in organizing activities by unions. From the early 1950s until the mid-1970s constant dollar union organizing expenditures per nonunion worker fell more than 30 percent. Although this decline has not yet been fully explained, an important factor is probably the merger of the AFL and CIO in 1955. Prior to that merger, competition between unions in the rival organizations produced organizing dollars and choices (for both workers and employers) that stimulated membership. Since then, union representation elections with more than one union on the ballot have fallen by roughly three-quarters. The associated decline in rivalry among organizing forces has certainly impeded union expansion.

The final factor, enhanced owner opposition to unions, has also retarded union growth over the past thirty years. Some of this opposition has been extra-legal, as charges of unfair labor practices against employers have risen more than 300 percent over the last thirty years. However, legal means of opposition have risen as well. A simple expedient is that of offering workers higher compensation or better working conditions if they remain nonunion, thereby preempting union blandishments. This is often accompanied by a vigorous management campaign encouraging workers to vote against certification of the union; delay the certifying election; or, when the union already has representation rights, decertify it as the authorized collective bargaining agent. Of the three causes of the decline in postwar unionization discussed here, managerial opposition and reduced union organizing efforts are probably the most important, with industrial and demographic trends a distant third.

The Current Scene

The stereotype of today's union member—a white, male, blue-collar worker who lives outside the South—turns out to be remarkably accurate. Men are more than twice as likely as women to be union members, and although the proportion of nonwhites who are union members is higher than that of whites, nonwhites remain a small minority of total membership. The unionization rate among blue-collar workers is roughly triple that of white-collar workers, while a worker in the South is only about half as likely to belong to a union as a worker living elsewhere. Finally, union members tend to be concentrated in the traditional goods producing sectors: workers in mining, construction, and manufacturing are three times more likely to be unionized than wholesale and retail employees, and four times more likely than service workers.

The backbone of the union organization consists of the locals, of which there are about 65,000. The locals supervise the administration of the collective bargaining agreement, operate the grievance process, and, to varying degrees, participate in the negotiation of the collective bargaining agreement. Almost all locals are members of one of the 170 or so national or international unions, which are generally organized along industry or craft lines. Although local unions take the lead in negotiating contracts in geographically narrow markets, such as in construction, the international union typically has principal responsibility for collective bargaining when product markets are national in scope. This can mean either negotiating an industry-wide master agreement or overseeing a process of "pattern bargaining" in which locals in one area follow the lead set by locals elsewhere. The internationals also provide financial and administrative support to local organizing efforts and represent the interests of their members in the legislative and regulatory processes. About 60 percent of the internationals, representing 70 percent of all union members, participate in the AFL-CIO, a voluntary association of unions. The AFL-CIO does not participate directly in the administration or negotiation of collective bargaining agreements. Rather, its principal role is political, and includes voter registration and lobbying, as well as fundraising for political candidates via its Committee on Political Education. Thus the impact of the AFL-CIO's activities on union member well-being is considerably less direct than the activities of either the internationals or the locals.

An Overview of the Wage Bargain

The activity for which unions are best known is the attempt to raise the wages of their members. Part and parcel of this process are union efforts to improve the fringe benefits of their members—fringes such as pensions, insurance, vacations, holidays, and overtime. Indeed, at least for the last thirty years, unions have placed more emphasis on—and had proportionately more success in—improving fringe benefits rather than wages.

The process by which unions raise their members' total compensation—wages plus fringe benefits—can be thought of in two equivalent ways. First, a union can restrict the number of workers available to firms in an industry and then simply allow firms to bid up the compensation offered to workers. For example, if the collective bargaining agreement stipulates that only union members may be hired, the union can simply restrict membership to the desired number of individuals. The second method is for the union to negotiate a compensation package more generous than would otherwise prevail and then simply allow firms to hire the desired number of union workers at that higher compensation level.

Whichever method of compensation is used, one impact will be immediate: fewer union members will be hired. This is readily apparent in the first case because the means by which the union elevates compensation is to reduce the number of union members who are available for work. The effect is the same in the second instance, however, because of the operation of the First Law of Demand: *the higher the price of any good, the lower will be the desired rate of purchase by buyers of that good.* A familiar example of the operation of this law is found in the efforts of consumers to reduce their use of petroleum products when oil prices skyrocketed: people installed more insulation in their homes, purchased cars that offered better gas mileage, and turned down their thermostats. The same Law of Demand holds for all goods, labor included. Intuitively, when the price of labor is raised, employers—the purchasers of that labor—seek new ways to use less of it. Equipment that uses less labor to get the job done will be installed. Arrival and departure times of workers will be monitored more closely, as will meal and rest breaks, so that there is less wastage of the now more expensive labor time. More intensive screening methods will be used in hiring because bad hires are now more expensive. And if there are differences in productivity among workers, only the best will be retained.

No matter how diligent are employers in attempting to conserve on the use of labor, they will find that their costs are higher. Their natural inclination will be to attempt to recoup these higher costs from consumers in the form of higher prices, but in this they will be only partially successful. Consumers will respond to higher prices by reducing their purchases of the good in question; as a result, some firms will be unable to sell enough output to cover costs and will go out of business, laying off their workers. Other firms, trying to capture a share of the smaller market, will shave their prices to avoid sales losses. The resulting squeeze between prices and costs will spur them on to find new ways of reducing their usage of labor. Along the way, of course, employers will find that, with costs having risen more than prices, and sales volume down, profits are now lower as well.

The loss of jobs caused by the more expensive compensation package will create tension within the union, for some members will find themselves without work. Indeed, it is the potential for this tension—and dissension—within the membership that serves as a brake on union demands at the bargaining table. Otherwise, the union could find itself with a very attractive "compensation package" being paid to none of its members. In addition to tempering wage demands, the prospect of job losses will induce unions to attempt to impose "work rules" that cut down on these losses. For example, the union may press for an agreement by firms that they not automate certain production processes. The new contract may contain provisions restricting the maximum speed at which assembly lines may be operated by the firm. And if there are multiple crafts in a plant or industry, when one of them wins an attractive new compensation agreement, it will almost certainly contain a proviso that work traditionally done by members of that craft must continue to be done by them—after all, one cannot tell how much damage might be done if a plumber rather than an electrician were allowed to change a light bulb.

Although such restrictive work rules will help to *mitigate* job losses (and hamper employer efforts to respond efficiently to the new compensation package), they can never eliminate those losses. Consumer unwillingness to buy the same amount at higher prices and producer unwillingness to operate at a loss forever will ensure that. The inevitable job losses can come in either of two forms: layoffs or attrition. The former are most likely among firms ceasing operations, since quits and retirements are unlikely to draw away all of their workers before shutdown occurs. Firms remaining in operation will generally use a mixture of techniques— refraining from replacing some workers who quit or retire and laying off others. Those who are laid off are most likely to be younger, less experienced, and least productive, for with the more expensive compensation package employers will find it profitable to retain only their most experienced, productive workers. Prominent among the losers in the process are those workers who are laid off; they will be forced into other activities that are certainly less desirable and probably lower paying than otherwise would have been the case. Less prominent but no less losers will be those workers who would have been hired in the absence of the more expensive collective bargaining agreement. They too will find themselves with job market alternatives that are less attractive and lower paid. Again, they are likely to be the less productive, lower paid workers, since employers will select only the most productive workers to replace those who quit or retire.

Of course for those workers who retain their jobs, the new compensation package will be quite attractive. For example, if the original package was worth $8 per hour and the new one is worth $10 per hour, compensation is now higher by about $4,000 per year. At a 10 percent rate of interest this has a present value of about $40,000 for a worker's lifetime career. This sum—compensation over and above what workers could earn in alternative employment—represents the "prize" that is attached to a union job. The workers will be aware of this potential prize, of course. If the firm was originally nonunion, many workers would be willing to devote resources and expend energies to achieve the union status needed to create the prize—lobbying fellow workers to vote for union representation, having flyers printed urging the same, and perhaps even bringing in consultants from the appropriate international union or the AFL-CIO to advise on the best organizing strategies. The owners of the firm also will be aware of the prize— one that they will lose if the union is successful. Hence they will devote resources and energies to stopping the drive to organize. Workers will be cajoled to rebuff the union, management consultants retained to advise on strategies, and, perhaps, leaders of the organizing drive will be threatened with demotion or dismissal if they do not cease and desist.

Both owners and workers are expending real resources—their time and effort and those of the outside consultants that are retained—in a dispute over a "transfer payment." The prize that exists because a union has the right to bargain collectively for employees will ultimately end up either in the hands of owners or workers; the total available to society as a whole—including both parties—cannot be increased. Yet both parties quite rationally use resources to determine ownership of the prize rather than to create consumable goods. The situation is much like that confronting two beachcombers on an otherwise deserted island who find a uniquely beautiful branch of coral. No matter which of them possesses the coral branch, there will still be just one for the entire island. It is rational for each to attempt to possess it solely for himself. Yet in their struggles for ownership, they may destroy the branch, thereby "dissipating" its value because that value is no longer available for residents of the island to enjoy.

Assuming that the workers are successful in their efforts to organize a union they must decide the best way to achieve the ultimate desired goal—higher compensation in one form or another. Their best weapons are the strike and the slowdown. The former is simply a stoppage of work, while the latter is continued production at a rate that is too low to maintain the profitability and hence viability of the firm. Owners, meanwhile, will need to consider tactics of their own while at the bargaining table. The lockout, in which workers are prevented from reporting to work, is a possibility. In reality, this is rarely necessary since an intransigent stance in bargaining by owners is often sufficient to provoke a strike or slowdown. Whatever the proximate cause—strike, slowdown, or lockout—the result of union efforts to obtain the prize is the same: production is reduced, to the ultimate loss of society as a whole.

Once the bargaining process is complete and the size of the prize determined, there will be further ramifications of its existence. Workers who originally would have been willing to take jobs paying more than the pre-union compensation rate now will leave only for jobs offering at the least their new higher compensation; hence their quit rate will fall. Workers who are temporarily laid off because of transitory decline in sales will be less likely to seek alternative employment while awaiting recall: they know that other employers will be reluctant to hire them for fear of losing them once the recall occurs. Individuals looking for work will tend to remain unemployed longer, searching for a job with the union compensation prize attached. This increased competition for union jobs will prompt existing members to seek ways of restricting entry to the union. Training and experience standards will be raised, and if there is a union apprenticeship program its requirements will be raised and made more rigorous. In a variety of ways, then, existing and potential union members will devote resources to maintaining or establishing ownership of the prize that has been created.

The Effects of the Wage Bargain

Before turning to a discussion of other aspects of union behavior, it is useful to summarize the implications of their wage setting behavior and provide some estimates of the magnitude of its impact. Historically, the ability of unions to obtain higher compensation has varied greatly. During the 1930s unions were relatively successful in resisting the deflationary pressures of the Great Depression. As a result the compensation earned by their members came to exceed that of nonunion workers by more than 40 percent. During the late 1930s and early 1940s labor market conditions improved and the union premium declined sharply. By the end of World War II union workers were earning only about 5 percent more than nonunion workers. After the war unions were able to reestablish a substantial premium, which averaged 15 to 20 percent over the next two decades. During the 1970s the premium widened to roughly 30 percent and, despite the "givebacks" of the early 1980s, still averages about 25 percent.

The most immediate effect of the higher compensation obtained by union workers is the reduction in the amount of labor used by unionized firms. The extent of this reduction depends on the size of the union compensation premium. At the current premium of about 25 percent the reduction in labor usage by union firms is probably 16 to 18 percent, although some estimates put it at higher than 20 percent. In general, people who are displaced from union jobs do not simply become unemployed; the vast majority manage to find work elsewhere. However, since there are now more people seeking nonunion jobs, wages in the nonunion sector will tend to decline. The size of this decline is greater (i) the larger is the union sector and (ii) the greater is the union compensation premium. Under present circumstances the displacement of workers from union firms probably reduces wages in nonunion jobs by about 3 to 5 percent. For an individual who would otherwise be making $20,000 per year this amounts to an annual loss of $600 to $1000.

Accompanying the reduction in the employment of labor by unionized firms are two additional effects. Unionized firms tend to use relatively more of other factors of production, such as capital, in an effort to avoid some of the higher costs implied by the union premium. As we have seen, not all of these costs can be avoided; thus output prices are higher, and consumers correspondingly reduce their purchases of the goods produced by unionized firms. The union compensation premium thus creates two types of inefficiencies: the mix of inputs used in production is distorted, and the mix of products chosen by consumers is distorted. On both counts society as a whole derives less benefit from its scarce resources than it would in the absence of unions. It is possible to estimate the size of this loss, which again depends on the size of the union premium and the share of the work force that is unionized. Currently this loss amounts to about 0.3 to 0.4 percent of GNP. Annually this is some $10 billion to $15 billion, or about $50 to $75 per person.

Although the conventional efficiency losses associated with unions are substantial, they pale in comparison with the potential loss created by competition for the prize associated with a job paying the union premium. The most obvious dissipation created by efforts to capture this prize comes in the form of strikes. In a typical year, strikes reduce GNP by about 0.2 percent—slightly over $7 billion in today's terms. Despite being obvious, the output lost from strikes is itself small compared to the premium-induced dissipation associated with unions. A rough estimate of the potential loss can be obtained by accounting for the size of the union premium, the proportion of the work force that is unionized and the importance of labor in the production process. Doing this calculation implies a potential loss of 3.5 percent of GNP—about $125 billion, or nearly $600 for each member of society. This potential loss, resulting from strikes, organizing efforts, time spent at the bargaining table, restrictions on union membership, and so forth will not necessarily be incurred in full each year. Indeed, both unions and owners will do their best to ensure that the rights to this disputed sum are settled at the lowest possible cost. Nevertheless, the magnitude of the prize at stake— $125 billion—is a good indicator of the resources that will be devoted to its capture.

The Fabled Givebacks

Thus far the discussion has centered on the compensation *gains* that unions have obtained for their members. Yet the last several years have witnessed *reductions* in the earnings of union members, often referred to as "givebacks." These concessions in wages and fringe benefits have been granted by roughly 2 million union members, ranging from automobile workers to airline pilots. Typically, the givebacks have represented reductions in compensation—wages and fringes—of 5 to 10 percent. Since most collective bargaining agreements are two to three years long, and since the inflation rate has been about 4 percent a year, the *real* impact of the givebacks on the compensation of the affected workers has been about 15 to 20 percent. Indeed, it is the concessions of the early 1980s that account for much of the erosion in the wage gains obtained by unions in the 1970s.

Initially, many commentators thought that the givebacks heralded a "new era" in labor negotiations, one in which unions would be severely hampered in their efforts to obtain compensation premiums for members. Hindsight suggests that this view is wrong: the fabled givebacks are better viewed as a product of three forces that are unlikely to coincide again.

First, there were back-to-back recessions, in 1980 and 1981–82, and the latter was one of the deeper on record, putting severe deflationary pressure on labor markets. This was particularly the case in durable goods markets, where unions tend to be concentrated. Second, beginning in 1981, high interest rates in America made the U.S. dollar attractive to foreigners. The resulting rise in the demand for dollars drove up their value. Equivalently, the value of foreign currencies fell, driving down the cost of foreign goods. As a result, Americans bought more foreign goods and foreigners bought fewer American goods. This increase in imports relative to exports and the resulting deficit in the balance of payments contributed to the deflationary pressure on labor markets. Finally, several important industries that were heavily unionized, including airlines and interstate trucking, were deregulated at the end of the 1970s. Entry into these industries by predominantly nonunion, low cost firms brought added competition that intensified downward pressure on union compensation. Together, these three factors—recession, heightened international competition, and deregulation—probably explain much of the givebacks of the last few years and suggest that the givebacks will not recur unless a similar set of circumstances arises in the future.

The New Learning: Freeman and Medoff Revisited

Thus far the discussion has centered on the efforts of unions to obtain higher compensation for their members. This is not the sole activity of unions, as has long been recognized by commentators. In recent years, however, increased attention has been paid to the other dimensions of unions in the workplace. Their impact on worker morale, employee relations, and managerial efficiency has been a prime area of study. The effect of unions on the distribution of income also has come under renewed scrutiny. Finally, the union role in determining the composition of the workplace compensation package, particularly as it reflects the preferences of older versus younger workers, has been studied more intensively than ever before.

Prominent in the reexamination of the role of unions in the marketplace has been the work of Richard Freeman and James Medoff. Conducted over the last decade, compiled in their book *What Do Unions Do?*, and summarized by Freeman in this volume, their work represents a major contribution to our understanding of union behavior. While acknowledging the deleterious effects of union wage setting behavior, they conclude that unions also have

(i) raised workplace productivity, (ii) improved the distribution of income and (iii) beneficially altered the components of worker compensation in favor of older, established employees. In this section, I discuss both the limitations and implications of these conclusions.

Productivity. The impact of unions on productivity has been debated by economists for at least two centuries. The literature is replete with examples of restrictive work rules imposed by unions in their efforts to mitigate the job losses caused by their demands for higher compensation. These work rules range from featherbedding to restrictions on the right of employers to interchange the tasks performed by workers. Productivity is reduced by such practices because workplace flexibility is impaired and labor usage is higher than is cost minimizing. Countering the negative effects of union work rules are union arbitration and grievance procedures that tend to improve worker morale and workplace communications. Similarly, seniority based promotion and pay systems, far more prevalent in unionized firms, are likely to reduce feelings of rivalry among workers and increase the amount of informal training that experienced workers offer to junior employees.

One generally recognized impact of unions on productivity arises from the fact that union workers are 30 to 50 percent less likely than nonunion workers to quit their jobs in any year. Lower quit rates for union workers mean lower recruiting and training costs and thus higher productivity. A portion of the lower quit rate is due simply to the union compensation premium, which reduces the chance that a union member can find a better paying job elsewhere. Nevertheless, much of the lower quit rate among union workers, perhaps two-thirds or more, appears to be due to grievance and arbitration procedures that improve labor-management communications and to seniority rules that encourage long-term employment relationships.

Freeman and Medoff estimate that the positive influence of lower union quit rates on productivity is equivalent to an increase in GNP of 0.2 to 0.3 percent, some 7 to 10 billion dollars. However, this estimate ignores the fact that quits do have a socially beneficial side to them: workers who quit typically do so to take higher paying and thus more productive jobs. The negative union impact on quits thus discourages the reallocation of resources to higher valued uses, implying an opportunity cost that must be deducted to estimate the net benefit of lower quits. Doing so reduces the Freeman and Medoff estimate by about two-thirds, leaving a positive but quite small net social gain from the union impact on quits.

In assessing any further impact of unions on productivity it is important to recognize the existence of what I shall term the "MPG effect." In response to the higher gasoline prices of the 1970s, car makers began producing autos that offered greatly improved gas mileage. These improvements were obtained only at great expense, including redesign, retooling, and consumer adjustment to "downsized" cars. Although these adaptations were desirable responses to higher gas prices, in that they "made the best of a bad lot," few people would argue that the OPEC oil cartel made Americans better off because its behavior stimulated higher MPG estimates. The same caution must be noted when assessing the impact of unions on productivity. The more expensive compensation package demanded by unions implies that unionized firms will (i) tend to hire only more productive workers, (ii) monitor their time more closely and (iii) substitute capital for labor in the production process. These adjustments will tend to raise the measured productivity of union labor in much the same way that adjustments to higher gas prices yielded improved gas mileage.

To get a measure of the net social value of unions in the production process it is necessary to correct observed differences in productivity for those that are due solely to the compensation demands of unions. Researchers investigating the productivity issue have recognized this problem and have attempted to account for it. For example, they have controlled for the age and education of employees, as a means of accounting for inherent differences in productivity among workers. They also have attempted to refine measures of the amount of capital used per worker. Despite these efforts, significant problems remain. Age and education are not the only worker attributes determining their productivity; since unionized firms deliberately select workers possessing high productivity attributes and since some of these attributes are omitted from the analysis, the productivity of unions as workplace institutions will be overstated. Moreover, the measurement of capital, done in dollar value terms to avoid comparisons of apples and oranges, is notoriously difficult in a world with gyrating inflation rates and depreciation schedules driven by tax codes. Finally, no one has yet devised an effective method of measuring differences in monitoring intensity across firms. On balance, these problems produce estimates that overstate the productivity of unions in the workplace.

A second defect in existing estimates of unions' impact on productivity is that "productivity" is typically measured by "value added"—the difference between the value of materials that firms buy and the value of the goods they sell. If unions enhance productivity, the work of their members will yield more output—and hence more value—from any given amount of raw materials. The problem with trying to measure this effect is that value added depends on both the quantity of output sold *and* the price at which the output is sold. Union firms that charge higher prices because they have higher labor costs will *appear* to be more productive, even though the higher costs are due simply to the greater compensation demanded by the union. Brown and Medoff have estimated that if union firms can recover 20 percent of the increase in union compensation in the form of higher prices, estimates of the union productivity gains are overstated by about 25 percent; if the recoupment rate is 80 percent, the degree of overstatement is more than 80 percent.

The final flaw with studies of the union impact on productivity is that they assume that the capital used by both union and nonunion firms is equally productive. Yet the substitution toward capital implied by the higher cost of union labor can be accomplished in either the quantity or quality dimension. Some aspects of quality can be accounted for in original purchase prices, which will be positively related to quality, just as Mercedes automobiles command higher prices than Volkswagens. However, no series adequately accounts for the maintenance and repair activities that enhance capital's productivity. Although there is no comprehensive estimate of the differential quality of the capital used by union and nonunion firms, Brown and Medoff have found indirect evidence that the capital in union firms is more productive, in the sense that a given amount of capital is responsible for a greater share of output in union than nonunion firms. Failing to account for this yields serious overestimates of the productivity of union workers.

Although estimates of the differential productivity of capital in union and nonunion firms are none too precise, the best of them suggest that capital is responsible for a share of output that is perhaps 6 to 7 percentage points higher in union firms. A differential of this size is sufficient to *reverse* the estimated impact of unions on productivity, implying that they *reduce* productivity by roughly 20 percent, presumably through excessive personnel requirements and restrictive work rules. Since about one-fifth of the work force is unionized, this estimate implies that unions reduce GNP by 4 percent—some $150 billion. Although this estimate is admittedly crude, it provides a striking contrast with arguments that unions enhance productivity.[2]

The compensation package. The second area of examination by recent work on unions has focused on the design of worker compensation packages. All firms generally compensate older, experienced workers more generously than younger, inexperienced workers. However, nonunion firms tend to offer a mix of compensation—more wages relative to fringes—that is geared more heavily toward the preferences of younger workers. They do this because younger workers are more mobile and hence more suitable for use in responding to changing economic circumstances. Unions press for compensation packages better suited for their median—and somewhat older—member, including a heavier emphasis on pensions, insurance, and vacations. Although this has the advantage of producing compensation that is more in accord with the tastes of the "typical" worker, it also has an important drawback. Union-backed compensation packages hamper the ability of unionized firms to compete for the younger, mobile workers who are best suited for responding to changing business conditions. This reduces the efficiency of unionized firms, and although the implied reduction in total output is probably quite small, it must be taken into account in judging the desirability of union compensation packages.

Economic equality. The last point argued by Freeman and Medoff is that unions tend to promote economic equality by (i) raising the earnings of blue-collar workers relative to higher paid white-collar workers and (ii) suppressing the dispersion of earnings within and across unionized firms. Several caveats need to be attached to these results. Union members typically earn much more than can be explained simply by unionization, largely because they tend to be older, more experienced, and have more skills than the average blue-collar worker. Thus the union compensation premium is earned by those blue-collar workers who would earn more than the average in any event, implying that unions reduce income equality among blue-collar employees. Moreover, one must consider the identities of the individuals most likely to suffer from the effects of union wage demands. In areas of the country that are more heavily unionized, women, non-whites, and the young are most likely to earn lower wages and face higher unemployment, implying an additional negative union impact on the equality of income distribution. Finally, the union-induced compression of earnings within and across firms is not without its own costs. Differential earnings are both a reward for superior performance and a penalty for inferior work. Reducing these differentials discourages excellence and rewards mediocrity. The result is reduced economic efficiency and lower income for society as a whole.

Conclusions

The controversy stirred by unions since their inception is unlikely to abate anytime soon. Partly this is because their most immediate impact is so clear. Few would dispute that unions raise the cost of labor and decrease business profits; nor would many argue that union members suffer as a result. But in part, the controversy will continue because some of their most important influences are so difficult to establish definitively. Although the size of the union compensation prize has been extensively documented, the extent to which it is actually dissipated is less clear. And while the impact of unions on productivity has been vigorously debated, the exact magnitude of its effect remains uncertain. Despite these unresolved issues, Adam Smith's admonition regarding businessmen is instructive: "People of the same trade seldom meet together, even for merriment and diversion, but the conversation ends in a conspiracy against the public. . . ." The same conclusion almost certainly applies to the "combinations of workmen" who are their employees.

9

MORGAN REYNOLDS

The Case for Ending the Legal Privileges and Immunities of Trade Unions

We live in an era of deregulation. In telecommunications, trucking, railroads, financial services, airlines, oil and gas, advertising in the professions and perhaps other industries to come, the strait-jacket of government regulation is being loosened. Price and service competition have progressively increased in the newly freed markets, much to the benefit of consumers. Long-distance air fares have fallen by 50 percent, the price of trading common stocks has fallen by 70 percent, and truckload rates are lower than they were in 1980. Perhaps less noticed has been the efficiency and employment gains in these industries. Airline productivity, for example, increased 20 percent between 1981 and 1983, while airline employment shot up 100,000 between 1983 and 1985, by far the largest two-year gain in airline history. Deregulated industries offer a growing array of new products and services.

If product markets can be deregulated, why not factor markets too? We have a propitious environment in which to rethink the fundamentals of regulation in all areas of the modern administrative state. Of the interventions wrought by the New Deal, none is a more promising candidate for reexamination than the National Labor Relations Act (NLRA) of 1935. This law, popularly known as the Wagner Act, is the centerpiece of a vast labor code that has grown up outside the common law. To appreciate the extent of the regulatory and bureaucratic rules that govern labor relations, we need only look at the *Decisions and Orders of the National Labor Relations Board*, a series occupying more than fifty feet of shelf space and over 400,000 pages. Has this legislation brought tranquility and order to labor markets? No. The NLRB's *Annual Report* for 1979 understated the situation by saying, "the uninterrupted growth of the NLRB case load underscores that the field of labor relations in the United States remains controversial and volatile, an area of national importance and concern, forty-four years after the labor relations statute was enacted and the Labor Board established."

Labor policy can move in three directions: retain the status quo, impose stronger federal controls, or move toward deregulating labor markets. The purpose of this chapter is to recommend deregulation: we should repeal the legal privileges and immunities that current statutes and rulings grant to unions. The argument may seem "radical" to some readers because the status quo exerts a powerful influence, because unions long ago identified themselves with the public interest, and because of the dominance of collectivist thought and social engineering throughout the twentieth century. Yet deregulation, on its merits, is superior to continuing down the path of the last fifty years or imposing more draconian control on labor relations. This proposition is true whether the criterion of choice is justice, liberty, equality of income, or general prosperity. Our object should be repeal of all the special interest legislation supporting unions and restoration of the rule of law in labor relations. The common law ("judge-made") has the crucial properties of generality, impartiality, and predictability that labor legislation does not. "A free field and no favor," as Woodrow Wilson summed it up in a phrase then common in the sporting world.

The Legal Privileges and Immunities of Trade Unions

Immunities relieve particular persons, special classes, or groups from the duties and obligations required by law of other people. Privileges grant special prerogatives (or "rights") as peculiar benefits, advantages, or favors to particular persons, classes, or groups. In other words, immunities exempt favored persons from legal obligations ("negative" privileges) while privileges are positive acts conferred by the state on behalf of favored groups. Legal privileges and immunities traditionally have been regarded as repugnant, but as the late Roscoe Pound, Dean of the Harvard Law School, observed, "because of a deep-seated feature of human nature they have been a fairly constant phenomenon in legal history."[1]

The unsavory character of privileges and immunities stems from their obvious violation of the principle of equality before the law, their partiality and their arbitrariness. The statue of Justice—with its blindfold, scales, and sword—peeks and plays favorites. Some observers would claim that *any* law that is not intended to apply impersonally to everyone cannot be a worthy law. Others would not be so uncompromising, while sharing the community's skepticism toward privilege or immunity.

The current privileges and immunities of labor unions are of such long standing that they have come to be taken for granted. Further, the privileges are so extensive that it is hard to sum them up with both economy and accuracy. In a characteristically blunt assessment, economist Ludwig Von Mises, a dozen years before the New Deal ushered in the modern era of labor law, said: "The long and short of trade union rights is in fact the right to proceed against the strikebreaker with primitive violence, and this right the workers have successfully maintained."[2] Mises, along with a handful of writers like W.H. Hutt, Henry C. Simons, and Sylvester Petro, have emphasized that threats and violence are essential in making strikes *effective*. In order to force buyers (that is, firms and ultimately consumers) to pay more than is necessary for labor services, trade unions must control the *entire* labor supply, forcing everybody to strike for the higher wage rates to be received by union members.

In 1958, two decades after the New Deal transformation of labor relations law, the late Roscoe Pound wrote that:

... the substantially general privileges and immunities of labor unions and their members and officials [are] to commit wrongs to person and property, to interfere with the use of highways, to break contracts, to deprive individuals of the means of earning a livelihood, to control the activities of the individual workers and their local organizations by national organizations centrally and arbitrarily administered beyond the reach of state laws, and to misuse trust funds—things which no one else can do with impunity.[3]

Senator Barry Goldwater summed up the privileges of unions in an address to the American Bar Association in 1962. What the list loses in complexity and subtlety, it gains in basic truth. Unions receive, he stated:

1. Almost total immunity under antitrust laws.
2. Immunity from taxation.
3. Ability to use union funds for purposes not directly related to collective bargaining, even if union dues are compulsory (a less clear "truth" today than in 1962).
4. Immunity from injunction by federal courts.
5. Power to compel employees to pay union dues as a condition of keeping their jobs.
6. Power to represent all employees in a bargaining unit, no matter how small the majority of those voting, including those compelled to join and those denied membership.
7. Power to compel employers to bargain "in good faith" with "certified" union officials.
8. Power to deny membership to employees in a bargaining unit.
9. Power to compel enterprises to make their private property available for use by union officials.
10. Comparative immunity from payment of damages for personal and property injury inflicted on anyone by union members engaged in strikes, picketing, and other tactics in disputes.
11. Power to strike for objectives not related to a collective bargaining dispute.
12. Power to examine an enterprise's books and records, including confidential data on costs, earnings, and prices.
13. Relative immunity from state labor law under the doctrine of federal preemption.[4]

While the summaries offered by Mises, Pound, and Goldwater suggest the nature of the privileges of unions, precision demands that we examine the details to confirm their analysis. Consider the Norris-LaGuardia Anti-Injunction Act, signed by President Hoover on March 23, 1932, after it had passed the House by a vote of 363 to 13 and the Senate by 75 to 5. It was the culmination of a fifty-year campaign against "government by injunction." The threefold purpose of the act was:

1. To declare nonunion oaths (so-called yellow-dog contracts) unenforceable in U.S. courts (Section 3);
2. To relieve labor organizations from liability for wrongful acts under antitrust law (Sections 4 and 5); and
3. To give unions immunity from private damage suits and nullify the equity powers of federal courts in labor disputes (Sections 7 through 12).

The overriding object of the act was to allow unions to be freer of the constraints that bind businessmen and everyone else, thereby allowing unions more latitude to use their aggressive tactics. An immediate result was that the number of strikes suddenly doubled between 1932 and 1933 to 1,695 and then continued to climb to a 1930s peak of 4,740 in 1937. This was during a period of deep depression and massive unemployment—conditions that normally would diminish strike activity.

The National Industrial Recovery Act(NIRA)—the New Deal system of industry codes (cartel agreements) intended to push up prices throughout the economy—was struck down by the Supreme Court in the Schecter Poultry Case of 1935 on the grounds that the act delegated virtually unlimited legislative power to the President. Congress then adopted almost identical labor regulations in the 1930s piecemeal, in surviving legislation like Walsh-Healey and Fair Labor Standards. The most famous and important example was the National Labor Relations Act, a rewrite of the NIRA's Section (7a). The act passed by a 63 to 12 vote in the Senate, an unrecorded voice vote in the House, and was signed by President Roosevelt on July 5, 1935.

The NLRA declares that the policy of the United States government is to encourage the practice and procedure of collective bargaining, as well as the protection of worker designation of representatives to negotiate terms and conditions of employment. All legislation announces high-minded goals, but this act basically uses federal power to make it easier (less expensive) to impose unionization on enterprises and employees in the private sector who otherwise would not participate in unionization and collective bargaining. The main regulatory features of the act were:

1. Creation of a political board—the National Labor Relations Board—to enforce the act.
2. Limiting buyer resistance to unionization by specifying "unfair labor practices" by employers.
3. NLRB enforcement of majority elections for union representation.
4. NLRB determination of eligible voters.
5. NLRB enforcement of exclusive (monopoly) bargaining rights for certified representatives.
6. NLRB enforcement of union pay scales for all represented employees, whether they are union members or not.

In April 1937 the Supreme Court declared the Wagner Act constitutional by a 5 to 4 vote in the famous "switch in time that saved nine." The Wagner decision marked the judiciary's general abandonment of constitutional protections of economic rights and economic due process, relinquishing constitutional constraints on federal intervention in economic matters.

Federal legislation modifying the NLRA—principally Taft-Hartley in 1947 and Landrum-Griffin in 1959—has not been so favorable to unions, but this can be exaggerated. Neither law tampered with the basic privileges supplied to labor organizations. As legal scholar Richard Epstein observes, Taft-Hartley was a partial union victory because it kept the original structure of the statutes, making it more difficult to return to common law rules.[5] Government regulation expanded to deal with some of the effects of union power, largely created by privileges and immunities. This is a familiar pattern in regulatory behavior because, once monopoly rents (i.e., transfers of income caused by intervention) are created and enforced by government (through tariffs, marketing orders, licensing, and a wide range of redistributions), the tendency is to dissipate rents in response to pressures by aggrieved groups. Ad hoc balancing of interests displaces protections of universal rights.

To illustrate the immunities of unions, consider Section 602a of the Landrum-Griffin Act:

It shall be unlawful to carry on picketing on or about the premises of any employer for the purpose of, or as part of any conspiracy or in furtherance of any plan or purpose for, the personal profit or enrichment of any individual (except bona fide increase in wages or other employee benefits) by taking or obtaining any money or other thing of value from such employer against his will or without his consent.

The parenthetical exclusion speaks loudly about the nature of the legal structure in the labor area.

The National Labor Relations Act declared five employer activities "unfair labor practices" (Taft-Hartley added a like number, though not equivalent, of unfair union activities). Among the unfair employer practices is "to dominate or interfere with the formation or administration of any labor organization or contribute financial or other support to it" [Section 8(a)(2)]. This restriction spelled the demise of most independent or so-called company unions, relieving unions of an effective competitor. During the 1920s and early 1930s there were nearly 1,000 employee representation plans and company unions with over 1.5 million members. As Taft wrote, "These organizations [company unions] were not always initiated by management, and frequently employees themselves took steps to prevent the forming of outside organizations."[6] Independent unions generally did not use force or take to the streets; Section 8(a)(2) eliminated an option for interested employees and companies.

The NLRA does not expressly compel employers to reach an agreement with a labor representative, but the right to refuse is attenuated by the fact that employers are obligated to "bargain in good faith" with union officials, a phrase interpreted by the political appointees of the board. To illustrate how the statute operates in practice, the Supreme Court ruled that in-plant food prices and services are mandatory subjects of bargaining, even if the food operation is operated by a third party (*Ford Motor v. NLRB*, 1979). Justice Byron White, writing for the Court, said that although "disputes over food prices are likely to be frequent and intense," national labor policy supported the conclusion that "more, not less, collective bargaining is the remedy."[7]

The ingenuity of legislators and jurists in preserving the facade of law but excluding unions from its bite is a fascinating chapter in human affairs. A prominent example is the treatment of labor union violence under the federal anti-extortion statutes. The Anti-Racketeering Act of 1934 proscribed the exaction of valuable consideration by force, violence, or coercion in matters of interstate commerce, "not including, however, the payment of wages by bona fide employer to a bona fide employee." Congress tried to exempt unions from the federal prohibitions on coercion because organized labor feared that the term "coercion" might be applied to its traditional tactics like strikes and picketing, which are intended to compel employers to recognize the union, compel payment of union wage rates, or cease hiring nonunion workers. In *Teamsters Local 807* (1942), however, the Supreme Court was called upon to clarify the boundaries of organized labor's immunity. The defendant unionists met trucks as they entered New York City and used threats and violence to obtain the equivalent of a day's wages for driving and unloading the trucks within the city. In some instances the defendant unionists performed partial work for full payment but in many instances did no work at all. In more tortured language than in the act itself, the court virtually emasculated the act as a check on union violence. To put it bluntly, the Court embraced the idea that the end justifies the means. The Court declared: "The history of labor disputes is studded with violence which unhappily is not yet obsolete; but, although the means employed may be the same as those here condemned, the end is always different, for it is to secure work on better terms."[8]

The congressional reaction to the Local 807 case was swift and negative, culminating in the Hobbs Act of 1945. Congress rewrote the law and took pains to eliminate the specific language on which the Supreme Court based its decision. Judicial reluctance to apply Hobbs to union violence continued to surface, however, culminating in *U.S. v. Enmons* (1973). The defendants were indicted for firing high-powered rifles at three utility company transformers, draining the oil from a company transformer, and blowing up a transformer substation owned by the company—all in the pursuit of higher wages and other benefits from the company. The district court dismissed the indictment on the grounds that the Hobbs Act did not prohibit the use of violence to obtain legitimate union objectives. On appeal, the Supreme Court upheld the ruling, saying "... the [Hobbs] Act does not apply to the use of force to achieve legitimate labor ends."[9] The decision distorted the legislative history of the Hobbs Act in order to justify the opinion, irritating Justice Douglas, who wrote in his dissent:

> At times, the legislative history of a measure is so clouded or obscure that we must perforce give some meaning to vague words. But where, as here, the consensus of the House is so clear, we should carry out its purpose no matter how distasteful or undesirable that policy may be to us.[10]

Why Unions Obtained Privileges and Immunities

Why did the political community adopt these labor policies? Friedrich von Hayek, the Nobel laureate in economics, argues that political opinion in the long run is determined by the active intellectuals. What made unionism successful was that the world began to receive its ideas sympathetically. Eventually, circumstances and politicians combined to support unionism and collective bargaining through the force of law. Ultimately, it is not strike threats, picket lines, boycotts, and unions' political spending that counts, but what people believe about unions and their impact that counts. Unions constantly appeal to our best instincts, arguing that unions help the "underdog," though rational analysis shows that unions harm the disadvantaged in our society, both as workers and consumers.

A combination of active self-interest, misguided idealism, and a belief in the erroneous purchasing power doctrine led to the labor legislation of the 1930s. Labor unions historically were difficult to organize and sustain in the United States because of the familiar obstacles to cartels: large numbers of demanders and suppliers, ease of entry and exit, high turnover, high mobility, geographic dispersion, active resistance among firms and workers, and differences of opinion about collectivism and the use of force. The courts also tended to restrict union tactics like threats, violence, and interference with voluntary trade; unionists, therefore, were prominent demanders of governmental privilege and mounted persistent political campaigns for favorable legislation.

Prior to World War I, unions had relatively little to show for their political activism. Organized labor had agitated for anti-injunction legislation and exemption from antitrust since 1880. The Democratic Party platform had a plank that denounced labor injunctions and supported restrictions on the courts as early as 1896. As Edwin Witte described it: "The virtual partnership of organized labor with the Democratic Party continued through the congressional elections of 1910 and the presidential elections of 1912 and led to the enactment of the Clayton Act in 1914."[11] The Clayton Act exempted worker cartels from the Sherman Antitrust Act, restricted the use of injunctions in labor disputes and provided that picketing and similar union activities were not unlawful. However, judicial rulings quickly neutralized the pro-union provisions.

World War I was pivotal for governmental policy toward unions. The national emergency provided much of the experience and precedent for subsequent labor legislation, as well as other cartel-like policies. To ensure "labor peace" in a period of labor scarcity, the government set up federal wage and labor boards to promote unions and collective bargaining and included union officials as board members. The government proclaimed its support of unions, ordered the establishment of work councils of employee representatives in nonunion plants, forbade interference with union activities, ordered companies to reinstate union members with back pay, seized defiant companies like Western Union and Smith and Wesson, and in one case even created a union, the Loyal Legion of Loggers and Lumbermen. Some of the federally-ordered organizations later became company unions.

The federal measures forcing industry to negotiate with unions ended after wartime orders were completed. The labor market was deregulated via the return to common law rules. Although unions had gained 2 million members during World War I and its immediate aftermath, membership plunged 1.5 million by 1923, nearly erasing the wartime gains. Union losses were concentrated in industries run by government during the war. In the mid- and late 1920s membership stabilized at 3.4 million, but by 1933 the depression had reduced membership to 2.8 million and unions were in a free fall until the massive federal intervention of the 1930s.

During the 1920s legislation favored by unionists and their academic supporters, such as anti-injunction bills, got nowhere in

Congress, state legislatures, or the courts, despite persistent effort. More ambitious peacetime interventions like the Wagner Act were politically unthinkable until the onset of the Great Depression and the National Industrial Recovery Act. Even in the midst of the depression, the Wagner Act faced significant opposition and was widely believed to be unconstitutional at the time it was passed, especially after the Court struck down NIRA. Some senators who voted for the Wagner bill wanted to avoid antagonizing the American Federation of Labor (AFL) at the polls and expected the Court to nullify the act. The special nature of political conditions in the 1930s is highlighted by the swing of the political pendulum against legislative benefits for unionism beginning in the late 1930s. State legislatures began to adopt restrictive measures to control union actions, Congress passed the Hobbs amendment to include labor violence in the Anti-Racketeering Act, and Congress passed Taft-Hartley over a presidential veto only twelve years after passing the Wagner Act.

The Case for Repeal

Once the privileges and immunities of labor unions are described, the case for repeal is almost self-evident. Nevertheless, we should explicitly consider the desirability of repealing the privileges of unions by four standards: justice, liberty, equality, and general prosperity.

Justice. There is no universally shared standard of what constitutes the just and the unjust, but a dictionary definition refers to "the assignment of merited rewards or punishment." Hayek, among others, argues that the true rules of justice are predominantly negative.[12] The rules forbid unjust conduct rather than specify what is to be considered just conduct. In the administration of criminal justice we perhaps come closest to a consensus: people guilty of serious violence and coercion against the rights of others should receive their just deserts. It is unfair (unjust) to allow users of private coercion to escape the costs of their aggression, while those with the moral character to restrain themselves from committing crimes suffer as victims. Injustice is the Darwinian jungle: the strong plunder the weak and the advantages of peaceful cooperation and personal security evaporate.

Current arrangements allow unions to violate justice as defined here. The *means*—the *tactics* that unions use to pursue their ends—are defective; their tactics cannot pass the Kantian universalization test. A preeminent tenet of liberal Western thought holds that means must be evaluated on their own; that they tend to determine ends; indeed, that the means are the ultimate ends. As Milton Friedman has written:

> To deny that the end justifies the means is indirectly to assert that the end in question is not the ultimate end, that the ultimate end is itself the use of proper means. . . . To the liberal the appropriate means are free discussion and voluntary cooperation.[13]

Founded largely on coercive techniques, unions tend to use coercion or the threat of coercion on a more or less regular basis. Nor is it confined to compulsory union dues. Consider the United Mine Workers (UMW), for example. Mining coal has always been dangerous, dirty work performed by generally strong and rough employees. The UMW still relies on dynamite and intimidation to coerce acceptance of the union's demands. Unionized mines do not try to operate during a strike, so most of the violence is directed at nonunion employees (many of whom are intensely anti-union), nonunion mines, and rival labor organizations. During the 1981 strike, for example, nonunion miners and mine operators armed themselves or shut down their operations for the duration of the strike. Truck convoys used lead trucks with five-foot long magnets to sweep up nails and spikes on the road. When UMW ambushes and gun battles broke out, Kentucky Governor John Y. Brown adopted a policy of what he termed strict neutrality, declaring that "We're not going to camp on one side or the other."[14] A nonunion operator protested, "The concept of neutrality toward breaking the law is not found in any statute or practice in our society."[15]

Many governmental officials do little to protect law-abiding citizens and their property from union coercion because of the belief that it helps "labor." A century of intellectual effort has promoted the idea that the noble purposes of unionists justify their means. If A threatens to strike B on the head with a baseball bat to take $20 from B's wallet, it is a crime. However, if A is an organized worker wielding the bat on the picket line to prevent B—legally hired to fill a position voluntarily abandoned by A—

from peacefully going to work, then the Board and the courts often declare it "picket line horseplay" or "exuberance short of coercion" despite the fact that access to unionized employment opportunities is worth thousands of dollars to B.

The shadowy privilege of unions to use violence is the only important instance of the state failing to guard jealously its monopoly on coercion. Union privileges and immunities violate the three ideals embodied symbolically in the statue of Justice— the blindfold, scales, and sword—because justice peeks, tips the scales in favor of unions, and allows them to use the sword to initiate violence.

Liberty. Freedom or liberty is another disputed concept. For present purposes, liberty is the state of being free of arbitrary or despotic controls imposed by men; it is the opposite of slavery; it is the right to do as we please, provided that we do not actively interfere with the equal rights of others to do as they wish. Liberty is not license because we must respect the equal rights of others, nor is it anarchy because the state is entitled to prevent the private use of aggressive violence and to enforce voluntarily arrived-at contracts. Common law rules are based on this intellectual orientation in favor of individual rights, limited government, and the maximization of private autonomy.

By this definition of liberty, federal labor regulations clearly harm liberty. Regulation, in fact, may be defined as a foreclosure of options imposed upon a market by political authorities. Restrictions on the liberty of employers are obvious, including infringements on their first amendment rights of free speech, their right to offer higher wage rates to their employees (e.g., during a union organization drive), their right to participate in a company-sponsored labor organization, and more generally, their human right to employ people on whatever terms the free marketplace may dictate. Similarly, employees are prevented from accepting voluntary private arrangements that would otherwise be available for the mutual benefit of both themselves and employers.

These consequences of labor legislation, under our working definition of liberty, are incontestable. Defenders of the status quo can argue, however, that the reductions in freedom are small and constitute a worthwhile trade-off because they yield sizable benefits, especially a purported gain in "equality of bargaining power" and worker dignity. Putting aside the validity of such claims for the moment, the argument must be recognized as a form of social engineering. The state deliberately steers labor relations into a form that would not have evolved through voluntary arrangements, in the belief that workers benefit. But have employees materially benefited by these forced arrangements? The answer is clearly no, as established below and in the preceding chapter.

Equality of income. Have labor unions succeeded in helping the underdog? No, because unions are out to help themselves. Although unions may give the impression that they are mostly made up of disadvantaged workers and hospital orderlies fighting for "social justice," unions have always been disproportionately composed of well-placed and highly paid workers in mining, construction, printing, manufacturing, trucking, and so on. Unions redistribute income toward their members, who are predominantly white, male, and well paid, at the expense of consumers as a whole, taxpayers, nonunion workers, the poor, and the unemployed—all groups with lower average incomes than union members. While the unions' policy of the "standard wage" for the job tends to marginally equalize earnings within unions (though harming incentives for individual productivity), this effect fails to offset the overall disequalizing tendency of union wage effects.

More competition and mobility in labor markets would allow workers to freely pursue their high-yielding alternatives without union constraint, thereby expanding total output and diminishing inequalities as well. As W. H. Hutt puts it, "The effect of competition among workers in different fields, if it had been unrestrained, would have led to far more people in the higher paid kinds of work and far fewer in the lower paid kinds of work."[16] This effect is increasingly visible in the deregulated industries like the airlines, where new firms have dramatically widened the employment opportunities for people who had been previously shut out of unionized labor markets.

General prosperity. We can be brief on this issue because few professional economists that I am aware of, past or present, contend that the actions of unions raise the standard of living for working people as a whole. Instead, the quarrel is over how much unions reduce national income. Unions reduce the real national income for the same reason that other cartels and monopolies do: they restrict supply, distort the structure of relative prices, and produce a misallocation of resources. Union pricing diverts labor from high productivity to lower productivity jobs. In addition, unions impede productivity on the job by limiting management flexibility; opposing new technology; featherbedding; restrictive work rules; and by disrupting production through strikes, strike threats, and other adversarial tactics.

The flow of output, by definition, can be divided into two components: (1) the output produced per unit of labor ("labor productivity") and (2) the amount of labor employed. Union actions reduce both output per person and total employment, especially over the business cycle, thus helping to spread poverty.

The consequences of repeal. An advocate believes that the "good" effects of a prescribed remedy outweigh the "bad" effects, and I am no different. Repeal is meritorious because there is no sound reason to grant privileges to labor unions. The present framework is defective beyond repair. It would be a mistake to build on the present structure in an attempt to outlaw unions or repress them in any special way. This would only reinforce their underdog image and sense of paranoia, would be contrary to the idea of a society of free and responsible individuals, and would be ineffective or counterproductive in practice, as demonstrated by the Taft-Hartley and Landrum-Griffin acts.

Deregulation is the answer, either piecemeal or wholesale. For example, I have proposed that Section 14b of the Labor Management Relations Act—which allows state governments to prohibit mandatory union membership as a condition of employment (so-called "right to work" laws)—be expanded to allow states to pass laws *permitting* employers and employees to cooperate in labor organizations. The ultimate aim, however, is to repeal and abolish all the labor legislation promoting bilateral monopolies in both private and public sectors. This recommendation applies to the Railway Labor Act, the Norris-LaGuardia Act, the National Labor Relations Act as amended, and their compulsory bargaining counterparts in the public sector. It would also include the dismantling of the relevant commissions and boards, and the repeal of preferential executive orders, state laws, rulings, administrative orders and regulations. Unions and their members would then be treated like everyone else under ordinary contract, tort, and criminal law.

Doubtless there would be a period of adjustment as participants learned to cope with the new opportunities. Labor disputes would be handled in the same manner as other disputes rather than having special arrangements. The number of labor disputes would decline because the strong unions would shrink without their special interest protections, further accelerating the deunionization of the U.S. economy. Direct access to the courts in labor disputes would reduce the use of strong-arm tactics and threats. Experience would gradually establish that threats and violence occur due to the incentives arranged by the exemptions accorded unionism rather than worker "alienation" from capitalism.

More generally, greater diversity would develop in employer-employee relations. The details are impossible to describe because we cannot know in advance exactly how a freer labor market will evolve. The marketplace is too rich and unpredictable to be typecast, although likelihoods can be suggested. Just as in the 1920s, unions and collective bargaining would not disappear but unions would be under greater pressure to respond to their constituencies. A different mix of union officials would gradually emerge, less wedded to the adversarial and aggressive schools of thought. Nonunion companies would be free to experiment with a richer menu of personnel policies, including the participatory forms of management demanded by a well educated work force.

In economic terms, repeal of the labor codes would undermine monopoly in labor markets and facilitate entry into these markets. Opening previously restricted markets tends to punish the guilty and reward the innocent by releasing pressures to equalize rewards. The supra-competitive wage rates of unions will be forced to adjust to competition due to new opportunities for nonunion workers and the unemployed. The flexibility of the price system, its efficiency in coordinating resource flows, the tendency of markets to fully employ our labor and capital, and our competitiveness in international markets would all improve. The eco-

nomic pie would expand and redistribution in favor of union officials and members would erode.

Conclusion

This chapter reconsiders the framework of labor legislation that
confers privileges and immunities on labor unions. Recent experience in deregulating product markets suggests that we can
successfully deregulate labor relations and replace the labor codes
with the common law. There is no merit to current arrangements,
which are based on the tenacious myth of "labor's disadvantage"
and assorted misconceptions from the 1930s. Whether the criterion is justice, liberty, equality of opportunity, or prosperity, our
contemporary labor rules fail to measure up.

The common law is not perfect, merely better than current
labor relations rules. Scholars in the burgeoning field of law and
economics argue that the common law process tends toward efficiency in the enforcement of rights and hence promotes efficiency
in the operation of markets. This proposition rests on various
arguments, including disinterested judges versus interested political bodies, the presence of evolutionary forces tending toward efficiency, and the more numerous opportunities for correcting
mistaken rulings.

Terminating the special labor legislation that protects unions
and the practices of collective bargaining may appear politically
unrealistic, yet political reality keeps changing in unpredictable
ways. A tiny but growing band of scholars, beginning with Heldman, Bennett, and Johnson in 1981, has been analyzing, as best
their tools allow, the impacts of governmental policies and the
possibilities for deregulation of labor law.[17] Further, there are
signs that the nation's labor laws are the subject of a growing national debate, especially in the wake of recent NLRB rulings tilt-
ing toward employers (consumers). As noted earlier in this book,
AFL-CIO President Lane Kirkland has suggested repeal and letting business and unions battle it out "mano a mano." Other union
officials have declared that, on balance, they would be better off
without the Wagner Act and the National Labor Relations Board.
Management lawyers have been cool to the idea, claiming "union
leaders would repeal only certain parts of the labor laws, the ones

that get in their way." A House subcommittee has issued a report declaring that "labor law has failed," a Reagan administration official has rejected the idea of repeal as "demagoguery," and a Senate subcommittee has reviewed the labor laws.[18]

Although the socially desirable policy is relatively easy to identify in this area, the politically attainable, as usual, is hard to forecast accurately. One thing is clear: the time is ripe for a reexamination of the purposes and policies of our labor laws. Age has conferred no virtue on the legislation and the debate has already begun. Congress had better prepare itself to think "the unthinkable" about our labor laws.

IV

The Public Sector

10

DAVID LEWIN

Public Employee Unionism in the 1980s: An Analysis of Transformation

In an article written ten years ago, this author observed that, "In the 'second generation' of [public sector] bargaining that is now evolving, the limits to union power are both more operative and visible as governmental decision makers respond in various ways to 'consumer' demands for reduced expenditures, stable—if not lower—tax rates, and improved management."[1] This statement was set against the facts of rapid growth of public employment, employee unionization, strikes, and state legislation supporting collective bargaining for public employees during the 1960–1975 period—the so-called "first generation" of public sector bargain-

Figure 1

Public Sector Union Membership

(Percentage of Work Force Organized, 1960–1982*)

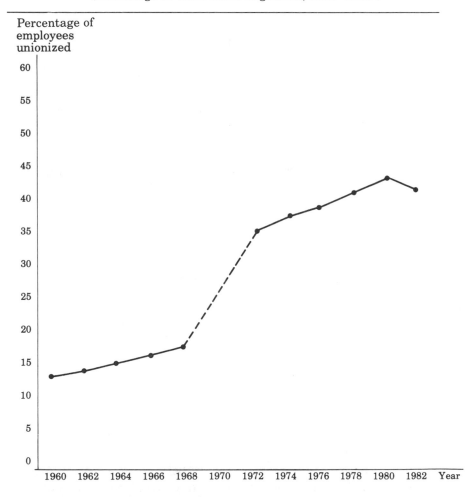

*Includes union and association membership (association membership tabulated only since 1968).

Sources: Leo Troy and Neil Sheflin, *Union Sourcebook: Membership, Structure, Finance, Directory, First Edition.* (West Orange, N.J.: Industrial Relations Data Information Service, 1985), various pages, and Richard B. Freeman, "Unionism Comes to the Public Sector," National Bureau of Economic Research, Working Paper No. 1452, September, 1984, p. 7.

ing in the United States. How has the second generation of public sector bargaining evolved in the mid-1980s, and how well does the observation about the portending second generation of public sector bargaining hold up after a decade or so of additional experience?

In addressing this question, the first section of the chapter briefly reviews recent trends in public employment, unionization, and strike activity. The second presents a model for examining the effects of environmental changes on the public sector collective bargaining process and bargaining outcomes. The third focuses on how changes in the economic-financial climate of government have affected "production," delivery, technology, and labor relations in one area of public service—public refuse collection. The fourth and concluding section then draws some broader lessons from the sanitation experience and offers some predictions about future developments in public sector labor relations.

Public Sector Employment, Unionism, and Strikes

Between 1960 and 1975, public employment in the U.S. grew at an annual average rate of about 5 percent, or more than twice the rate of private employment growth. In contrast, between 1975 and 1983, government employment rose by less than one percent annually, on average, while private employment grew at an annual average rate of almost 4 percent.[2] Indeed, during the early 1980s (specifically, 1980–83), public employment declined by some 400,000 persons or about one percent annually, on average. Put differently, it grew from 15.4 to 19.1 percent of total U.S. employment between 1960 and 1975, but by the mid-1980s it had declined to 16.7 percent. This decline was heavily concentrated in local government, which presently accounts for about 9.5 million of the nation's approximately 16 million public employees.

These data support the inference that the American citizenry has shifted its collective "preference function" with respect to investing in public services. Between 1960 and 1975, the citizenry by and large approved of tax increases to finance an enlarged public sector (relative to private industry). In the late 1970s, however, the citizenry "voted" to slow the rate of public sector growth. California's Proposition 13 and the Federal Civil Service Reform

Table 1

Number and Percentage of Full-Time Organized Employees, State and Local Government, 1975–82

Percent organized by function	Year							
	1975	1976	1977	1978	1979	1980	1981	1982
Total full-time employment (in 000's)	9,397	9,514	9,861	9,948	10,193	10,314	N/A	10,161
Membership in employee organizations (in 000s)	4,702	4,737	4,711	4,788	4,881	5,031	N/A	4,645
Percent organized	50.0	49.8	47.8	48.1	47.9	48.8	N/A	45.7
Education	58.2	58.3	56.2	55.8	N/A	55.4	N/A	52.6
Instructional Staff	68.9	68.6	64.3	65.4	N/A	64.9	N/A	61.1
Other	37.3	37.9	39.7	38.0	N/A	38.2	N/A	36.8
Highways	46.3	44.3	43.2	44.4	N/A	45.0	N/A	44.1
Public welfare	40.2	41.3	38.2	40.9	N/A	41.8	N/A	43.8
Hospitals	42.0	39.5	38.2	38.3	N/A	40.0	N/A	30.0
Police protection	54.0	54.3	53.2	54.4	N/A	52.7	N/A	51.2
Fire protection	72.4	71.6	72.9	72.2	N/A	70.6	N/A	66.5
Sanitation other than sewage	48.1	49.2	45.9	44.8	N/A	40.2	N/A	43.8
All Other	36.9	36.9	35.6	36.2	N/A	39.4	N/A	37.4

N/A Not Available

Sources: U.S. Bureau of the Census, *1982 Census of Governments, Volume 3, Public Employment, Number 2, Compendium of Public Employment* (Washington, D.C.: G.P.O., 1984), various pages; U.S. Bureau of Labor Statistics, *Labor-Management Relations in State and Local Government: 1980, 1978, 1976, and 1974.* Special Studies Nos. 102, 95, 88, and 75 (Washington, D.C.: G.P.O., 1981, 1980, 1978, and 1976), various pages.

Act, both of which came into being in 1978, provide only two examples of the public's new-found interest in limiting tax levies and improving the productivity of government services. By the early 1980s, these and numerous comparable measures in a wide variety of state and local governments combined to produce an absolute shrinkage in the size of the public work force.

Has the "new" economic-financial environment of the public sector also brought about a reduction in public employee unionization? The apparent answer to this question is a qualified "yes," as is suggested by Figure 1, which shows the changes in union and association membership for all public employees (full-time and part-time) in all levels of government (federal, state, and local) over the 1960–1983 period. The figure displays the well-known rapid growth—some might say explosion—of public employee unionism in the U.S. during the late 1960s and early 1970s. However, the growth rate slowed considerably in the late 1970s, and public employee unionization appears to have peaked in 1980 and turned down thereafter, at least until 1983 (the most recent year for which data are available).

The changing incidence of public employee unionization can perhaps be better and more precisely appreciated by focusing on full-time state and local government workers, who comprise approximately two-thirds of all public employees. As shown in Table 1, the unionization rate among this category of employees was at 50 percent in 1975, fell between one and two percentage points lower over the next several years to 1980, and then declined to 45.7 percent in 1982. Disaggregation of the data shows that, between 1980 and 1982, the incidence of unionization was reduced by 10 percent among hospital employees, by almost 4 percent among public schoolteachers and firefighters, and by one and one-half percent among police. Three of these groups are the most heavily organized employee groups in state and local government, with education alone accounting for slightly less than half of all full-time state and local government employees in the U.S. In absolute terms, unionization among full-time employees in state and local government declined by more than 380,000 between 1980 and 1982.[3]

The part-time work force of state and local government totals

about 3 million persons,[4] and for several reasons this often over-
looked group merits close attention in an analysis of public
employee unionization. First, the ratio of part-time to full-time
employment in state and local government has risen steadily in
recent years so that by 1982 part-timers constituted 22 percent of
all state and local government employees. Second, part-time
employees comprise an even larger portion of the public work
force in certain functional service categories. As examples, part-
timers account for fully 30 percent of all public education
employees (and 45 percent of all nonteaching personnel) and 25
percent of all firefighters in state and local government. Third,
and most important, the incidence of unionism among part-time
public employees is very small; it stood at 7.9 percent in 1982, and
this figure represented a slight decline from 1980. If full-time and
part-time employees of local government are combined, the total
unionization rate is well under 40 percent—specifically 37.5 percent in 1982.

None of this disputes that the incidence of unionization among
public employees has grown rapidly, indeed remarkably, over the
last quarter century or that today the public sector is much more
heavily organized than the private sector of the U.S. economy. A
relatively small, short-term decline in the incidence of public
employee unionism should neither be taken out of context nor
viewed as ineluctably presaging a long-term trend. Nevertheless,
the data present a picture of a public sector unionization rate that
peaked in the mid-to-late 1970s and that has declined, albeit
modestly and irregularly, since then. This pattern of unionization
parallels recent changes in the economic-financial environment of
and employment in the American public sector.

What has been the direction of public employee strike activity in
recent years? The relevant data are presented in Table 2, and they
reveal a strike record that is similar, but only somewhat similar,
to those of employment and unionization in the public sector. Observe that the volume of public employee strikes grew very rapidly
during the late 1960s, fell in the mid-1970s, fell and rose again in
the late 1970s, and fell still once more during the early 1980s. Two
rather different views of this strike record may be taken.

On the one hand, public employee strike activity did indeed
decline between 1979 and 1982, and this may mark the beginning

Table 2
Public Employee Work Stoppages by Level of Government, United States, 1960–1982

Year	Total			Federal Government			State Government			Local Government		
	No. of stoppages	Workers[a] involved	Days idle[a] during year	No. of stoppages	Workers[a] involved	Days idle[a] during year	No. of stoppages	Workers[a] involved	Days idle[a] during year	No. of stoppages	Workers[a] involved	Days idle[a] during year
1960	36	28.6	58.4	b	–	–	3	1.0	1.2	33	27.6	67.7
1961	28	6.6	15.3	–	–	–	–	–	–	28	6.6	15.3
1962	28	31.1	79.1	5	4.2	33.8	2	1.7	2.3	21	25.3	43.1
1963	29	4.8	15.4	–	–	–	2	.3	3.2	37	22.5	57.7
1964	41	22.7	70.8	–	–	–	4	.3	3.2	37	22.5	57.7
1965	42	11.9	146.0	–	–	–	–	–	1.3c	42	11.9	145.0
1966	142	105.0	455.0	–	–	–	9	3.1	6.0	133	102.0	449.0
1967	181	132.0	1,250.0	–	–	–	12	4.7	16.3	169	127.0	1,203.0
1968	254	201.8	2,434.2	3	1.7	9.6	16	9.3	42.8	235	190.9	2,492.8
1969	411	160.0	745.7	2	.6	1.1	37	20.5	152.4	372	139.0	592.2
1970	412	333.5	2,023.2	3	155.8	648.3	23	8.8	44.6	386	168.9	1,330.5
1971	329	152.6	901.4	2	1.0	8.1	23	14.5	81.8	304	137.1	811.6
1972	375	142.1	1,257.3	–	–	–	40	27.4	273.7	335	114.7	983.5
1973	387	196.4	2,303.9	1	.5	4.6	29	12.3	133.0	357	183.7	2,166.3
1974	384	160.7	1,404.2	2	.5	1.4	34	24.7	86.4	348	135.4	1,316.3
1975	478	318.5	2,204.4	1	–	–	32	66.6	300.5	446	252.0	1,903.9
1976	378	180.7	1,690.7	–	–	–	25	33.8	148.2	352	146.8	1,542.6
1977	413	170.2	1,765.7	2	.4	.5	44	33.7	181.9	367	136.2	1,583.3
1978	481	193.7	1,706.7	1	4.8	27.8	45	17.9	180.2	435	171.0	1,498.8
1979	593	254.1	2,982.5	–	–	–	57	48.6	515.5	536	205.5	2467.1
1980	502	233.1	2,406.7	–	–	–	22	16.0	89.7	480	217.1	2,317.0
1981	400c	200.0c	1,800.0c	N/A	N/A	N/A	N/A	N/A	N/A	N/A	N/A	N/A
1982	300c	150.0c	1,200.0c	N/A	N/A	N/A	N/A	N/A	N/A	N/A	N/A	N/A

[a] in 000's
[b] no strike activity reported
[c] estimated by the author
N/A Not Available

Sources: U.S. Bureau of Labor Statistics, *Work Stoppages in Government, 1980* (Washington, D.C.: G.P.O., 1981), various pages (and prior issues); U.S. Bureau of Labor Statistics, *Labor-Management Relations in State and Local Government: 1980*, Special Study No. 102 (Washington, D.C.: G.P.O., 1982), various pages (and prior issues); U.S. Bureau of the Census, *1982 Census of Governments, Volume 3, Public Employment Number 2, Compendium of Public Employment* (Washington, D.C.: G.P.O., 1984), various pages.

of a long-term decline in public sector union militancy generally. Moreover, the (estimated) volume of public employee strikes in 1982, namely, 300, and the (estimated) total days of strike-related idleness, namely, 1,200,000, were the lowest recorded since 1968 and 1971, respectively. On the other hand, in a relatively restrictive economic-financial climate, public employers are pushed to examine more closely the costs of "labor peace" and to consider the uses of alternative resources to "produce" public services when work stoppages occur.[5] The ill-fated 1981 strike and subsequent dissolution of the Professional Air Traffic Controllers Organization, while hardly providing a replicable "model" of public sector labor relations, demonstrated the ability of a governmental unit to produce services during a work stoppage.[6] Thus, some public employers may from time to time judge strikes to be worth calling and may not seek to settle them at "all costs." If this is even partly so, it may help to explain the recent public sector strike record of the U.S., and it suggests that future changes in the volume of public sector strikes will not necessarily be closely correlated with changes in public sector employment and unionization.

Environmental Changes and the Public Sector Bargaining Process

The slower growth and, in some cases, reduced levels of expenditures for public services that have developed since the mid-1970s have had important effects on the public sector collective bargaining process and bargaining outcomes. To better understand these effects, consider the model of the public sector labor relations process shown in Figure 2. This model, which is derived from research into public sector bargaining that has been conducted over the last fifteen years or so, underscores the role of certain environmental and organizational forces in determining the bargaining process and bargaining outcomes.[7]

For example, during the first generation of public sector bargaining in the U.S., the economic environment of government was almost universally an expansionary one and so, too, was the legal environment. Indeed, between 1960 and 1975, some thirty-eight states adopted legislation providing unionization and bargaining rights for public employees; only one such law existed in 1959.[8] Further, in 1962, a presidential executive order authorized unionism and collective bargaining for federal employees, and this order was eventually strengthened and incorporated into federal law.[9] Such legislation has been shown to spur public employee union growth.[10] Union organizations (Figure 2) thus emerged, grew, and their leaders began to negotiate written agreements with public employers (shown as employer organizations in Figure 2). In the process, various bargaining structures, typically decentralized ones, were created; the bargaining process evolved, usually along traditional adversarial lines; and wage, benefit, work rule, and other bargaining outcomes resulted from collective negotiations.

During the late 1970s and early 1980s, the environmental forces affecting public sector bargaining were of a very different order. Not only did a much more restrictive economic environment develop in the post- (compared to the pre-) 1975 period, but the legal environment shifted from one that emphasized public employee unionism and bargaining rights to one that emphasized the imposition of penalties for illegal strikes, the occasional removal of unionism and bargaining rights for supervisors and managers, and tighter restrictions on arbitrators' discretion in deciding the terms and conditions of public sector labor agreements. In the political arena, candidates for public office began to adopt tax and expenditure reduction platforms that inferentially or explicitly included union containment provisions. In the late 1970s and early 1980s, several elected officials who had once campaigned for expanded public employee unionism and bargaining rights were cast—or cast themselves—in opposition to public employee unions.[11]

This confluence of environmental forces has had notable effects on public sector bargaining structures, the bargaining process, and bargaining outcomes. As examples, under the pressure of fiscal crisis and imminent bankruptcy in the mid-1970s, the structure of bargaining in New York City municipal government was altered in such a way as to reduce some eighty separate bargaining units to a single union coalition that negotiated terms and conditions of employment for 200,000-plus city employees; several city and state governments entered into productivity-enhance-

Figure 2

A Model of the Public Sector Labor Relations Process

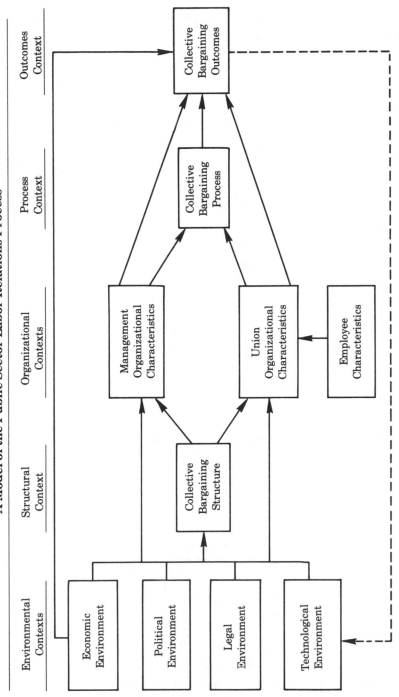

Source: Adapted from David Lewin, Peter Feuille, and Thomas A. Kochan, *Public Sector Labor Relations: Analysis and Readings*, Second Edition (Sun Lakes, Ariz.: Horton and Daughters, 1981), p. 3.

ment, joint study, and quality-of-working-life improvement arrangements with organized employees; and numerous concession bargaining agreements were reached with a variety of unions.[12] Concession bargaining, which some observers judge to have become the dominant type of bargaining in the private sector during the 1980s, has produced such public sector bargaining outcomes as pay freezes and reductions, fringe benefit givebacks, broadbanding (that is, the expansion of certain jobs to include several specialized tasks and classifications), more flexible work rules, the subcontracting of certain public services, the implementation of work force reductions by attrition, and a generalized increase in managerial authority and decision-making responsibility.

In the next section we will examine the specific case of municipal sanitation service to illustrate more fully how changes in environmental forces have affected the public sector bargaining process and bargaining outcomes in recent years.

Sanitation Labor Relations: The Public Sector in Microcosm[13]

Sanitation service in the U.S. is popularly thought to be provided by municipal governments to recipients, but most cities have two or more types of service providers. Further, the mix and proportional distribution of service providers vary by category of service recipient, as shown in Table 3. Municipal governments provide the bulk of sanitation service for streets and other open or public spaces, while private firms provide the largest share of sanitation service to institutional, commercial, and industrial recipients. In the case of residential recipients, the distribution of service providers varies by detailed category of recipient, but clearly, municipalities, private firms, and self-service all have important places in this "market." The use of special districts or authorities to provide sanitation service (which are the main components of the "other" column in Table 3) is substantial in the cases of streets, parks, and litter baskets and, to a lesser extent, for institutional recipients.

Employment in municipal sanitation departments is shown in Table 4. On average, there were forty-six full-time paid personnel per municipal sanitation department in the U.S. in 1983, or 0.70 per 1,000 population. More notable, however, are the data pertaining to changes in municipal sanitation employment, which are summarized in Figure 3. Between 1975 and 1983, proportional sanitation employment in U.S. cities declined by fully half, from 1.41 to 0.70 full-time paid employees per 1,000 population. Note that this was a far larger employment loss than occurred over the same period for police and firefighters who, along with sanitation personnel, comprise the major uniformed services of most municipalities.

Unionization among municipal employees has also declined notably in recent years. Full-time sanitation personnel were more than 50 percent organized in 1972, but by 1980 the unionization rate had fallen by fully ten percentage points. And, though municipal sanitation unionization grew slightly between 1980 and 1982, the incidence of unionization in this functional service category was still well below those prevailing in public education, police and fire protection, and highways (Table 1). Indeed, among all major categories of state and local government employees, only hospital employees have a lower incidence of unionization than sanitation employees.[14]

What elements can explain the recent decline of employment and unionization in public sanitation service? Two factors are of paramount importance, namely, private contracting and technological change. In the mid-1970s, evidence began to be produced that showed publicly provided sanitation service to be significantly more costly than privately provided sanitation service. For example, a 1975 study of 315 municipalities found that "the average city with a population of more than 50,000 [which was] served by a municipal [sanitation] agency had costs which are from 29 to 35 percent more than the costs of an average city of the same size served by a private [sanitation] firm with an exclusive territory."[15] Similar, if smaller, cost differentials between privately and publicly provided sanitation service were also found to exist in smaller cities.

What accounts for these cost differentials? Table 5, which compares municipal and contract collection arrangements, provides some clues. Private contractors use larger trucks and proportionally fewer rear-loading vehicles than municipal sanitation

Table 3
Sanitation Service by Category of Service Recipient and Service Provider, 1975[a]

Service recipient	Total number of municipalities reporting service (a)	Service Provider							
		Municipality		Private Firm		Self Service		Other	
		No.	% of (a)	No.	% of (a)	No.	% of (a)	No.	% of (a)
Streets	1,830	1,463	79.9	59	3.2	N/A	N/A	314	17.2
Parks	1,735	1,347	77.6	188	10.8	N/A	N/A	227	13.1
Litter baskets	1,663	1,146	68.9	188	11.3	N/A	N/A	332	20.0
Residential									
Bulk	1,848	926	50.1	750	40.6	436	23.6	66	3.6
Mixed	2,052	768	37.4	1,368	66.7	376	18.3	19	0.9
Multiple dwellings	1,744	646	37.0	1,242	71.2	18	1.0	17	1.0
Institutional	1,942	616	31.7	1,196	61.6	115	5.9	207	10.7
Commercial	2,010	628	31.2	1,698	84.5	85	4.2	39	1.9
Industrial	1,579	334	21.2	1,099	69.6	232	14.7	141	8.9

[a]This table presents the number and percentage of municipalities which reported the availability of refuse collection service by one or more service providers for each class of service recipient. For example, 768 (37.4%) of the 2,052 municipalities reporting mixed residential refuse collection indicated that the municipality provides at least some of this service. Percentages add to more than 100 because some municipalities reported the availability of several classes of service providers.

N/A not applicable

Source: E. S. Savas and Christopher Niemczewski, "Who Collects Solid Waste?" in *The Municipal Yearbook — 1976* (Washington, D.C.: International City Management Association, 1976), p. 168.

Figure 3

**Sanitation, Police, and Fire Department
Employment per 1,000 Population, 1975–83[a]**

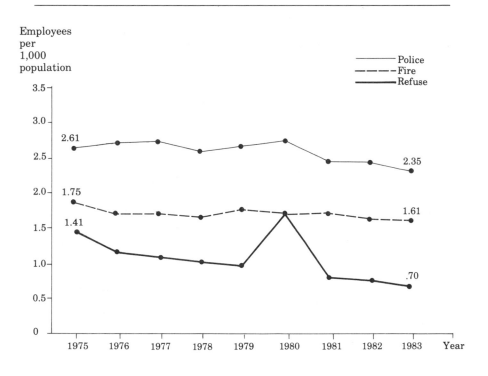

[a]Data for paid full-time personnel

Source: Gerard J. Hoetner, "Police, Fire, and Refuse Collection and Disposal Departments: Personnel, Compensation, and Expenditures," in *The Municipal Yearbook — 1984* (Washington, D.C.: International City Management Association, 1984), p. 145.

agencies, but the most significant differences have to do with labor utilization. Private contractors employ smaller crews, have less absenteeism, and operate under incentive systems more frequently than municipal sanitation agencies, and the differences are statistically significant in most cases. Hence, not only are operating costs significantly lower, productivity is significantly higher in contract than in municipal sanitation collection arrangements. This provides a clear incentive for financially pressed municipalities to adopt contracting arrangements, which is consistent with the observed proportional growth of private contracting and the decline of municipally provided sanitation service during the late 1970s and early 1980s.[16]

Another recent initiative undertaken by local government officials and managers has been to alter the technology of sanitation collection (and disposal). Among these changes, perhaps the most important has been the introduction and expanded use of semi-automated and fully automated collection systems.[17] Whereas conventional refuse collection featured a rear-loading vehicle with a three-person crew, modern refuse collection features semi-automated and fully automated vehicles that load from the side or front and that operate with two- and sometimes one-person crews. This form of automation means, in essence, that refuse is loaded onto a truck's waste bin by the truck's automated equipment rather than by manual labor. Recall that private sanitation collection differs from public sanitation collection primarily in terms of the types of vehicles used and in crew size. Thus, within the public sector, municipal sanitation agencies appear to be adopting "private-like" sanitation collection policies and practices.

Numerous other changes in the technology of publicly provided sanitation service have occurred in recent years, and they either accompany or complement the adoption of automated collection vehicles. These include the use of standardized carts, typically of 82–90 gallon capacity, which are issued to residents by a municipality; the conversion from metal cans to plastic bags for the containment of refuse; the substitution of curbside for backyard refuse collection and, in some cases, the reduced frequency of refuse pickups; the use of trucks with longer-life diesel-type engines, longer-life radial tires, and roll-off and tilt-type truck frame beds; more efficient and longer-life trash compactors; com-

Table 4

Full-Time Employment in
Municipal Sanitation Departments, 1983[a]

Classification	No. of cities reporting	Mean	Per 1,000 population
Total all cities	686	46	0.70
Population group			
Over 1,000,000	3	1,001	0.52
500,000–1,000,000	8	397	0.55
250,000–499,999	20	234	0.64
100,000–24,999	59	104	0.68
50,000–99,999	81	52	0.75
25,000–49,000	168	30	0.84
10,000–24,000	347	15	0.93
Geographic division			
New England	41	13	0.40
Mid-Atlantic	76	30	1.72
East North Central	127	38	0.57
West North Central	52	25	0.44
South Atlantic	147	52	1.15
East South Central	44	55	0.97
West South Central	111	68	0.82
Mountain	37	37	0.53
Pacific Coast	51	70	0.44
Form of government			
Mayor-council	251	57	0.69
Council-manager	398	41	0.72
Commission	23	37	0.59
Town meeting	13	10	0.64
Rep. town meeting	1	62	0.95

[a]Data for paid full-time personnel

Source: Gerard J. Hoetner, "Police, Fire, and Refuse Collection and Disposal Departments: Personnel, Compensation, and Expenditures," in *The Municipal Yearbook — 1984* (Washington, D.C.: International City Management Association, 1984), p. 146.

puter-controlled refuse collection and compaction equipment; two-way truck radio systems for crew assignment and response to refuse collection "problem" situations; three-wheel scooters for certain types of lighter trash collection; and supercarts for high density refuse generation and collection locations.

It is undisputed that private contracting and especially technological change have contributed greatly to the recent decline in public sanitation employment. Not only has this been confirmed statistically, a separate analysis of 135 incidents of technological change in municipal sanitation service that took place between 1971 and 1984 found that work force reductions occurred simultaneously or subsequently in 127 cases[18] (work force size was unchanged in eight other cases). Not a single instance of a sanitation employment increase following technological change was reported in the literature, and the average work force reduction in the first two years following technological change in the aforementioned 135 cities was 21 percent.

Technological change also appears to have a significant negative effect on municipal sanitation unionization. Such change is most widespread in older cities located in the Northeast and Midwest—cities that also tend to have the most heavily unionized and highest cost work forces. As these cities make changes in the technology of sanitation collection (and, in some cases, contract with private firms for a portion of sanitation collection), work force reductions translate into declines in union membership and, on a national basis, a lower overall incidence of sanitation unionization than previously existed.[19]

The negative effects of technological change on sanitation employment and union membership might plausibly be expected to be met by union opposition to change, especially when it is recognized that sanitation employees are the most strike-prone of all major employee groups in state and local government.[20] And, it is clear that this is what has occurred in some cities—for example, Tampa, Florida; Salt Lake City, Utah; Camden, New Jersey; Berwyn, Illinois; Covington, Kentucky; and Middletown, Ohio—where intended or adopted technological change resulted in strikes, picketing and other demonstrations, lawsuits, and occasional violence.[21]

In other cases, however—for example, Rochester, New York;

Table 5

**Management Practices in Sanitation Service,
by Collection Arrangement and City Size**

	Population				Cities having backyard collection location	
	50,000 and under		Over 50,000			
Management practice	Municipal	Contract	Municipal	Contract	Municipal	Contract
Mean crew size	3.08	2.06	3.26	2.15	3.04	1.98
Mean truck capacity (cubic yards)	19.04	22.21	20.63	27.14	19.90	23.50
Mean absentee rate	12%	6%	12%	6.5%	12%	4%
Mean % of vehicles loading at front and side	26%[a]	23%[a]	13%	44%	16%	30%
Mean % of cities with incentive system	57%	80%	80%[a]	86%[a]	73%	87%

[a]No significant difference at the .05% level

Source: Barbara J. Stevens and E. S. Savas, "The Cost of Residential Refuse Collection and the Effect on Service Arrangement," in *The Municipal Yearbook—1977* (Washington, D.C.: International City Management Association, 1977), p. 204.

Clinton, Oklahoma; Keysville, Texas; Atlanta, Georgia; Detroit, Michigan; Washington, D.C.; St. Louis, Missouri; and Chicago, Illinois, to name but a few—technological changes in sanitation service have occurred in the context of labor-management cooperation.[22] Specifically, labor and management have agreed on plans (or contractual provisions) for work force reductions via attrition; skill upgrading; programs of training, development, and communications; and joint labor-management productivity-improvement and technological change monitoring committees.

Perhaps the most notable example of union-management cooperation in municipal sanitation service under the impetus of technological change occurred in New York City during the early 1980s. There, city officials and the Sanitation Workers' Union (a Teamsters affiliate) engaged in productivity bargaining and, under the aegis of an arbitration award, agreed to replace smaller, less efficient refuse collection vehicles and three-person crews with larger, more efficient, semi-automated vehicles operated by two-person crews. The 1981 agreement, which covered selected rather than all routes, contained a no-layoff provision, and work force reductions were to be achieved (and, in fact, were achieved) through attrition. Additionally, each employee member of a two-person crew received an eleven dollar per shift bonus and an experiment in contracting out was postponed for two years. In light of the city's frustrating and ineffectual record of productivity bargaining with municipal employees during the 1970s, and the frequency of sanitation employee strikes and work slowdowns during the same period, the parties were probably correct in describing their agreement as "historic."[23]

The monetary incentives that were provided to New York City's municipal sanitation employees to help bring about the successful implementation of technological change are hardly unusual. Indeed, sanitation workers who remain employed following one or more technological changes typically receive a 5 to 15 percent pay increment, owing in large part to the combination of skill upgrading and productivity improvement that ensue in the wake of technological change. Ironically, this occurs whether sanitation labor relations are predominantly adversarial or predominantly cooperative. In fact, under both types of sanitation labor relations, technological change brings about reduced employment, higher pay and skills, fewer work injuries, and improved productivity—in other words, comparable bargaining outcomes (Figure 2).

Nevertheless, this section has emphasized the bargaining process, and why it is that some sanitation (and other public sector) labor relationships are largely adversarial and some are largely cooperative is not well understood. What can be said is that, in both (extreme) cases, the dominant response of sanitation unionists to technological change has been to attempt to cushion union members against the effects of change rather than to oppose the change, per se. This appears to be consistent with the larger record of union behavior in the public and private sectors of the U.S. economy.[24]

Lessons from the Sanitation Experience

The recent municipal sanitation labor relations experience provides some important lessons for understanding and assessing public sector labor relations more broadly. The first of these lessons is that changes in one or more environmental forces cause management and labor to rethink service "production" and delivery, technology, and labor relations. In sanitation and in virtually all public services, the most important environmental factor has been the financial-economic climate, which changed from one of expansion to one of slower growth and then contraction in the late 1970s and early 1980s, respectively. In response to growing demands of the citizenry for lower taxes and public expenditures, mayors, city councils, city managers, and town commissioners discussed and debated local government arrangements for sanitation service. In some cases, decisions were made to contract for sanitation service with relatively more efficient, lower cost private companies. While the opportunities for substituting privately produced for publicly produced service may be greater in sanitation than in other service categories, such substitution has occurred across a wide range of "public" services, and the potential for expanding the use of private contracting may be as important as the actual incidence of contracting.[25]

Second, a more restrictive economic-financial climate stimulates a rethinking and sometimes a realignment of the technology of public service production and delivery. In sanitation, the record of the last decade or so is one of major and multiple technological changes, which have resulted in the widespread substitution of capital for labor. Again, not all public services are as amenable to technological change as sanitation and not all technological change is as labor-saving as that in sanitation. Nevertheless, the lesson here is that public officials and managers need not be permanently saddled with a particular technology or an immutable capital-labor ratio in the production and delivery of public services.

Third and relatedly, decisions about the use of private contracting and changes in the technology of public services are fundamentally influenced by labor costs. In the first generation of public sector bargaining, roughly 1960–1975, organized public employees were able to make major pay and, especially, benefit gains. Indeed, recent research shows that during that period the average relative compensation (not just pay) effect of public employee unions was on the order of 20–25 percent, and the effects were even larger for unions of uniformed service employees (that is, police, fire, and sanitation employees).[26] In sanitation, this labor cost impact provided additional impetus for government officials and managers to pursue alternative refuse collection arrangements. As a result and as was shown above, public sanitation employment declined substantially during the initial phase of the second generation of public sector labor relations. Similar, if smaller, work force reductions have occurred in all major functional service categories, especially during the early 1980s, and this supports the generalizability of the union-influenced labor cost impact on public services and public employment.

Fourth, the nature of the labor-management relationship also influences the volume and technology of and organizational arrangements for public services. In sanitation, the relatively high incidence of public employee strikes has been a major factor in the decisions of some local governments to contract for sanitation service and (to a lesser extent) to change the technology of public sanitation service. Comparable decisions have been made in other public services in the wake of work stoppages, and this, in turn, seems to have brought about a diminution in the incidence (though hardly the elimination) of public employee strikes.

However, this should not be taken to mean that the parties to labor-management relations in the public sector always engage in adversarial bargaining or that a specific type of relationship, once established, will endure. The evolving second generation of bargaining in public sanitation service features some adversarial labor-management relationships, some cooperative ones, some that have changed from adversarial to cooperative, and vice versa. If market and technological forces are key variables affecting public sector labor-management relationships, as indeed they are, there is still room for organizational, institutional, and personal variables to influence the collective bargaining process and outcomes. To argue otherwise is to ignore the history of public and private sector labor-management relations and to take a very narrow view of human events.

To illustrate this point further, consider that, in recent years, concession bargaining has become commonplace.[27] Both in industry and government, pay freezes, fringe benefit givebacks, work force reductions, more flexible work rules, and altered work schedules have been agreed to by labor and management. Some of these agreements have been reached cooperatively, and often they include provisions for joint labor-management consultation and expanded worker participation in implementing new arrangements.[28] Other agreements have come about only after prolonged conflict and do not contain joint consultation and worker participation provisions. In both instances, for the most part, the parties have responded to new or enlarged competitive forces, yet their responses take on very different characteristics. Public sanitation service offers a prime example of this duality in the American labor relations character, a duality that is only imperfectly understood even after two decades of research on public sector bargaining.

What, then, can be said or prognosticated about the future of public sector labor relations in the U.S.? To this observer, the financial-economic pressures that have so fundamentally affected governments throughout the nation since the mid-1970s appear likely to continue and perhaps to become even sharper during the remainder of the 1980s. Increased domestic and international competition, additional tax reform and deregulation initiatives, the aging of the American population, and continued questioning of the absolute and relative performance of governments in producing and delivering public services, are among the contextual factors that give rise to this prediction.

Increased financial-economic stringency will produce even greater pressures on governments to engage in subcontracting, make technological changes, reduce the size of the public work force, and increase the proportion of part-time employees. These factors will, in turn, contribute to a further shrinkage in the incidence of public employee unionization. But this shrinkage is likely to be modest rather than of major proportions, at least through the remainder of the 1980s. To counter employment declines and a growing proportion of part-time government personnel, public sector unions will attempt to strengthen certain union security provisions, to obtain others (for example, the agency shop and the union shop, respectively), and to enroll part-time workers in separate but affiliated bargaining units. However, and in contrast to their private sector counterparts, public sector unionists are unlikely to undertake large-scale mergers over the next several years.[29]

As to the public sector collective bargaining process and bargaining outcomes, the remainder of the 1980s is likely to witness relatively modest increases in negotiated pay and benefits, expanded use of broadbanding and skill upgrading, a diminution of restrictive work rules and practices, more flexible work schedules, and increased managerial authority and autonomy. The last of these predicted outcomes will result, in part, from widened efforts (expected to be successful) to remove legally sanctioned unionism and bargaining rights for public sector supervisors and managers, and in part from the enhanced use of merit-based criteria to pay, promote, and otherwise reward public sector managers.

Finally, concerning union militancy and the characteristics of public sector labor-management relationships during the remainder of the 1980s, the frequency and duration of strikes are expected to decline, though not precipitously, and cooperative, problem-solving bargaining is expected to predominate over adversarial, win-lose bargaining. The basis of these expectations rests with the facts—and predicted continuance—of fiscal stringency, competition from the private sector, and public questioning of the value of government services.

When these constraining "environmental factors" first emerged in the mid-1970s, some public managers and unionists understandably had predicted that they would be short-lived. But as these forces continued into the early 1980s and as they develop further during the latter 1980s, public sector unionists will increasingly judge the costs of work stoppage to exceed the benefits, and public sector union and management officials will, in the main, subordinate their conflicts over particular terms and conditions of employment to the larger, joint issue of surviving in an increasingly "competitive" public sector world. If this seems to be an overly optimistic judgment, recall that it was but a short decade ago that public sector labor relations appeared to be in crisis. Since then, the American public sector generally, and public sector labor relations in particular, have undergone a major transformation. Who is to say that this transformation will not continue through the 1980s and perhaps even produce a "third generation" of public sector bargaining in which adversarial labor relations are expected to decline and labor-management cooperation is expected to make significant advances?

11

JOSEPH W. GARBARINO

Faculty Collective Bargaining: A Status Report

Collective bargaining by college and university faculty catapulted into the news in 1969 when the City University of New York (CUNY) and its faculty negotiated its first collective bargaining agreement. CUNY attracted notice because it represented a large (until 1982, the largest) faculty bargaining unit, located in the nation's media capital, and its agreement included a top professorial salary rate of more than $30,000, a munificent sum by the standards of the day. At about the same time several other less newsworthy public universities also negotiated agreements and the U.S. Supreme Court issued a decision that established that private institutions of higher education were under the jurisdiction of

Research assistance provided by Bruce Kieler

the National Labor Relations Act (NLRA). By the end of 1972 an estimated 285 institutions employing some 84,000 faculty members had recognized unions as exclusive representatives of their faculties, and it was clear that collective bargaining had penetrated a major new area of society.

In the mid-1980s in an atmosphere in which the American labor movement is regularly discussed in terms of at least temporary decline if not imminent demise, it is important to remember that the decades of the 1950s and 1960s were periods of a general expansion of unionism in absolute if not relative terms. In the private sector the labor movement reached its overall peak, measured in terms of proportion of workers organized, in 1955, but it continued to grow in absolute terms. Well into the decade of the 1970s, although the membership ratios of the private sector unions were declining persistently, their members were prospering and the relative wage and benefit advantages of union members over workers in general were substantial and growing. More important for faculty unionism were the developments in the public and nonprofit sectors of the economy.

Beginning in the late 1950s in large metropolitan areas of the East and Midwest, the movement to extend collective bargaining rights to public employees gained momentum. In 1959 Wisconsin became the first state to grant bargaining rights to most of its public sector workers. In 1963 what appears to have been the first instance of higher education faculty unionization occurred at Milwaukee Technical Institute, a two-year institution whose faculty was represented by an independent faculty association. Also in 1963 President Kennedy, who as a senator had supported the extension of bargaining rights to public employees, issued Executive Order 10988, which gave federal government employees a rudimentary version of bargaining rights. In 1966 the first four-year institution of higher education, the United States Merchant Marine Academy, was unionized by the American Federation of Teachers.

Throughout the 1960s other states were passing laws that gave their employees the right to organize, and union activity, particularly in elementary and secondary education, was burgeoning. The expansion of the scope of organization was not limited to the public sector but extended to nonprofit organizations. In the rapidly growing health care industry, employees were showing increasing interest in unionization and some of the states were bringing them within purview of their bargaining laws. In 1974 the nonprofit sector of health care institutions was included by Congress in the scope of the NLRA for the first time.

The year 1976 marked a major turning point for public sector unionism in general and for faculty unionism in particular. By the end of 1975, twenty-four states had enacted legislation permitting bargaining at some level of postsecondary education. Since 1975 only California, Illinois, and Ohio have enacted laws that expanded bargaining rights of higher education faculty; California, Ohio, and Illinois put them in effect in 1983.[1]

The loss of momentum in the expansion of the right of public sector employees to organize and bargain collectively more or less in the general pattern of the private sector was due to three major events that occurred within a short span in the mid-1970s. These were the New York City financial crisis, which was widely perceived as being at least partly due to the financial results of widespread unionization of municipal employees; a strike of San Francisco public employees resulting in a voter backlash aimed at making compensation less subject to bargaining and more to direct democracy; and a decision by the U.S. Supreme Court that limited the power of the federal government to regulate the personnel affairs of state and local government.[2] The *Usery* decision came at a time when there appeared to be a real chance that a federal law extending bargaining rights for state and local government employees might be enacted.

By 1980 the growth in faculty unionism had slowed to a crawl. In that year the Supreme Court dealt the always fragile private college sector of the movement a staggering blow when it ruled that the faculty members of Yeshiva University were managers under the terms of the National Labor Relations Act and that they therefore no longer enjoyed the protection of the NLRA in the conduct of union activities. Since that time a number of private college bargaining units have been disbanded on "Yeshiva" grounds.

Within the public sector, however, the actions of Illinois and Ohio in extending legal rights to their public four-year institutions has sparked a flurry of organizing activity in those states. The faculty of the California State Universities and Colleges (CSUC) established the largest faculty bargaining unit in the nation in 1982. And the Supreme Court has recently reversed its *Usery* decision.

This chapter assesses the changing fortunes of the faculty union movement in higher education fifteen years after the CUNY election touched off the first surge of organization.

The Extent of Organization

By the end of 1984, there were approximately 547 institutions of higher education formally recognizing and bargaining with their faculty members (Table 1).[3] Included in the bargaining units were about 168,000 persons, many of whom (perhaps most) were not actually members of the unions representing them. In 1982 there were about 3,200 institutions of higher education and about 695,000 instructional staff in the U.S., according to the National Center for Educational Statistics. This meant that about 17 percent of all institutions were unionized as were 24 percent of all full- and part-time faculty with the rank of instructor or above. Thanks to the organization of the 18,000 faculty of the California State Universities and Colleges in 1982, the percentage of all faculty represented by unions in that year was at an all time high.

Table 1, however, reveals that an absolute decline in represented faculty occurred in 1983 and in 1984, due primarily to a shrinkage in private college units.[4]

The number of represented faculty in four-year colleges surpassed the number in two-year colleges for the first time in 1971, and by 1982 more than three of five persons covered by bargaining were to be found in four-year institutions. The faculty union movement has always been predominantly a public sector phenomenon. This is partly because there are almost four times as many public two-year colleges as private two-year colleges and because the private sector institutions at all levels have very low levels of union organization. Only about 5 percent of all organized faculty in 1984 were in private institutions; about 7 percent of the organized faculty of four-year institutions were in private colleges.

The Yeshiva effect. The Supreme Court's decision that the Yeshiva University faculty's role in management of the institu-

Table 1
Institutions and Persons Represented, 1966–1983

	Total		Two Year		Four Year	
1966	23[a]	5,200[b]	22	5,000	1	200
1967	37	7,000	3	6,700	2	300
1968	70	14,300	60	11,000	10	3,300
1969	138	36,100	112	2,000	26	16,100
1970	17	47,300	137	23,900	40	23,400
1971	24	72,400	16	27,000	84	45,400
1972	285	84,300	183	29,700	102	54,600
1973	310	87,700	189	30,300	121	57,400
1974	337	92,800	206	32,100	131	60,700
1975	398	102,300	236	35,000	162	67,300
1976	450	117,000	261	38,030	189	78,970
1977	480	133,000	284	51,430	196	81,570
1978	506	140,610	295	55,520	211	85,090
1979	526	146,780	306	60,615	220	86,165
1980	534	148,856	312	62,002	222	86,854
1981	533	149,442	312	62,192	221	87,250
1982	550	169,117	316	64,113	234	105,004
1983	546	168,631	317	64,327	229	104,304
1984	547	168,171	320	64,947	227	103,224

Sources: Data through 1978 from author's files; Bill Aussieker and John Lawler provided research assistance. Data for 1979–84 calculated by using information on elections and decertifications for each year from the annual *Directories*, National Center for Educational Statistics.

[a] Number of "institutions" unionized. The definition of institutions corresponds in general to that of the *Education Directory: Colleges and Universities*.

[b] Numbers of persons in the units unionized. This figure differs from the 1984 totals given in the *Directory*, National Center, primarily because of the deletions noted in the footnote to Table 2 and because unit size is not stable and the data were collected in different years. Note that the figures for institutions are larger than the numbers of bargaining units reported by the National Center.

tion was so extensive that the faculty were "managers" within the meaning of the NLRA was a serious blow to the never very successful effort to organize private colleges and universities. In 1984 a further blow was delivered by the National Labor Relations Board when it ruled that the faculty of Boston University were not only managers but were also supervisors because of their role in personnel decisions. If this decision stands, it may further hamper private sector organizing and also further shrink the existing roster of organized institutions as administrators withdraw recognition from current agents.

Prior to 1980 only two small (less than 100 faculty) four-year colleges had decertified their bargaining agents and returned to nonunion status. By the end of 1984 the National Center reports that eighteen private institutions had lost or withdrawn their certifications as bargaining agents as a result of the Yeshiva decision. These institutions accounted for only about 1,700 faculty, but in 1983 the National Center reported that there were only about 9,000 unionized faculty in private institutions, and if the Boston University and Polytechnic Institute decisions remain in effect, they will reduce that number by an additional 1,080 persons. The faculty unions are attempting to secure legislation that would prevent the exclusion of faculty from the coverage of the NLRA by agency or court decision, but the prospects for passage are not bright.

It is at least theoretically possible that in some of the states, particularly those with comprehensive laws covering all public employees, an attempt might be made to exclude faculty in public four-year institutions from coverage on Yeshiva grounds. At least two unsuccessful attempts have been made (at the University of Alaska and Wichita State University) to advance this argument. In the public sector the more important result may be to raise the possibility that faculty in some four-year universities might be excluded from coverage in new collective bargaining laws.

If the Boston University and Polytechnic Institute decisions are sustained, at least one of four represented faculty in the private four-year colleges will have lost representation by a bargaining agent by the end of 1984 as a result of the Yeshiva decision. In view of the small numbers involved, however, these developments should be kept in perspective. The faculty union movement has always been a public sector phenomenon and for the foreseeable future its fortunes will be determined in that area.

The quality question. Since its inception, the faculty union movement has labored under the charge that unionism is limited to institutions not quite in the top rank in terms of quality or at least prestige. Although attempts to demonstrate an inverse correlation between some measure of quality and the propensity to unionize have been criticized, it is clear that if a collection of scholars of higher education were asked to name the top forty institutions in the nation, their lists might differ but few members of any of them would be found on the roster of organized institutions.

There is great interest in the rankings of universities, graduate departments, professional schools, and other academic units that are periodically published by a variety of sources, testifying to the high level of status consciousness among the faculties of at least the larger and more prominent institutions. Competition for status is keen and often expensive in terms of both energy and money. The belief that seems to exist among many faculties—that establishing a faculty union would have a negative effect on the image of the university in the councils of its peers—is probably a handicap to organization. Conversely, if one or two recognized leaders in the status competition were to vote in a union, further organization probably would be made easier.

One list of what are often described as "major research universities" is the membership of the Association of American Universities (AAU). The AAU includes fifty-seven universities (two of them Canadian), and while there undoubtedly are some arguable inclusions in and exclusions from the list, it is a convenient way of keeping score on the movement. As of 1985 the unions had been unable to organize any of the members although multiple attempts (as many as three) have been made in some instances.[5] In 1985 the University of Florida, which as part of a statewide system was organized in the 1970s, became a member of the AAU.

The closest a faculty union had previously come to winning an AAU university was in an election at the University of California, Los Angeles in 1981. In the first round of the election the combined vote for an independent Faculty Association and the American Federation of Teachers (AFT) actually was 55 percent of the vote cast. In the runoff between the Association and no agent, the latter choice won 51.4 percent of the total votes cast. It is interesting to speculate on what might have happened had the AFT not been on the first ballot, but the uncertainties of strategic voting make any serious analysis a dubious venture.

Over the years the unionized institutions seem to have acquired more self-confidence and to be less concerned with the quality question, but it is still true that a successful organizing drive at a prestigious university would be a morale booster for the movement.

The Faculty Organizations

As in education generally, there has been vigorous competition between the affiliates of the National Education Association (NEA) and the AFT for bargaining rights for faculty in higher education, with the American Association of University Professors (AAUP) as an additional competitor. Although all of the organizations have made some adaptation, the AAUP has been most affected by the decision to function as a collective bargaining agent, while the AFT has been least affected.

The AFT has been the traditional trade union entry in education at all levels since its beginnings before World War I. It is affiliated with the AFL-CIO and has always regarded itself as a trade union. During its early years it worked mainly through teachers' councils in a consultative style, but in the 1930s it formally adopted a policy of collective bargaining. With the great bulk of its prospective membership in the public sector, the AFT was ambivalent about the role of the strike in its activities, but in 1963, after it had been increasingly involved in strikes by teachers in the post-World War II period, it officially recognized the right of its locals to strike. Currently the AFT claims a membership of about 75,000 in its college department (not all in recognized bargaining units), which gives it the largest higher education membership of the three organizations. The AFT has a total membership of about 600,000 persons.

The NEA vies with the Teamsters Union for the title of the largest union in the United States with approximately 1.7 million members and, like the Teamsters, it is not affiliated with the AFL-

CIO. Its size and the geographical dispersion of its membership give it substantial political influence within the Democratic Party and in the political process generally. The NEA reports that some 62,000 of its members are in colleges and universities.

Until the 1960s the NEA functioned as a professional association. As public sector bargaining laws opened up the possibility of formal collective bargaining, the NEA was forced by the pressures of competition from the AFT in elementary and secondary education to convert itself into a professional union, including accepting the use of the strike as a bargaining weapon. This conversion required some internal organizational changes, the chief of which was the progressive reduction of the role of administrators in the organization.

The AAUP has long been recognized as the premier association of higher education faculty in the nation. It came to collective bargaining late and with considerable reluctance and, unlike the AFT and the NEA, it still has not been able to adjust completely to the new situation. In 1971 the AAUP declared that it had "...the unique potential, indeed the responsibility, to achieve through its chapters a mode of collective bargaining consistent with the best features of higher education."[6] In 1983 the AAUP reported about 52,000 active members, with almost two-thirds of them in collective bargaining chapters.[7] The remainder are individual members, some of whom are members of more or less active local chapters not involved in bargaining.

At the sub-national level, the relationship among the organizations has been a curious one. There are clear-cut differences among the three organizations that have kept them from carrying out any of the oft-rumored mergers between pairs of candidates. The NEA offers to potential affiliates in higher education a very large and politically influential, well-financed alliance with the rest of the educational sector. The AFT offers a link with the mainstream labor movement, politically vigorous at important levels of government and holding out the possibility of joint support in economic actions that might be undertaken. The AAUP's unique asset is its lack of ties to either elementary or secondary education or the traditional labor movement, combined with a long history of recognition as an effective and prestigious spokesman for higher education in its most attractive guise. Conversely,

in organizing campaigns, the NEA's local affiliates in higher
education are depicted in their opponents' literature as submerged
in an organization dominated by teachers in the lower strata of
education, the AFT affiliates as minions of blue-collar unions, and
the AAUP's chapters as relatively effete and ineffectual
newcomers to collective bargaining and political hardball. Both
the NEA and the AFT seem to be interested in merging with the
AAUP, but not with each other.

The results of the competition among the various contenders in
the bargaining elections are summarized in Table 2, which compares the affiliation record as of May 1974 with that at the end of
1984. As the table indicates, both the NEA and the AFT have
substantially increased their proportion of all faculty represented
by unions at the expense of each of the three other categories. It is
interesting that, in part, the shifts reflect not the acquisitions of
newly organized units but rather a transfer of affiliation from one
national organization to another.

Two examples of the instability of allegiances can be instructive. At CUNY the present faculty unit was originally two units,
one represented by an independent organization and the other by
the AFT. The independent association affiliated with the NEA and
then the two units merged into a single unit. Shortly afterward the
entire NEA and AFT state organizations united as well. After a

Table 2
Faculty in Bargaining Units by Affiliation

	AAUP	AFT	NEA	IND.	Coalitions	Total
1974[a]	15,100(17%)	17,400(19)	18,700(20)	4,800(5)	35,700(40)	91,700
1984[b]	22,305(13%)	50,293(30)	47,139(28)	3,208(2)	47,375(28)	170,320

[a]Data from J. W. Garbarino, *Faculty Bargaining, Change and Conflict* (McGraw
Hill, 1975), p. 87.

[b]Data from Table Seven, *Directory* National Center, with 11,542 persons deleted
because they were not "faculty", and 602 persons found in three "other" unions.
Major examples: 4400 University of California nurses (IND), 1,500 CSUC
academic support personnel, 1,600 Michigan and 1,600 Wisconsin teaching assistants (all AFT). But note that teaching assistants are included in some faculty
units, e.g., CUNY and Rutgers.

few years this merger was dissolved and the AFT retained control at CUNY. Recently the CUNY unit also affiliated with the AAUP so that, at the end of 1984, CUNY was represented by a coalition. When unionization became a legitimate possibility at the Florida State Universities, units of the NEA and AFT merged to form the United Faculty of Florida (UFF). As can be imagined, when the question of affiliation with a national organization came up, the UFF was divided. They affiliated with the NEA but became disenchanted after a few years and switched to the AFT. The situation repeated itself and the UFF recently joined the NEA.

The problem illustrated in these situations is one that goes back to the foundation of the modern American labor movement and the organization of the American Federation of Labor in the 1880s. The problem is described as "dual unionism," a situation in which more than one national union claims the right to represent the same group of employees. In the competition, the various local organizations compete with each other for representation rights. The winner then negotiates affiliation on the best available terms with the competing national organizations. With dual unionism, affiliation is constantly subject to organizational political maneuvering. The labor movement's current solution to this classic problem is the AFL-CIO's "no raiding" agreement of 1955, in which all affiliates of the AFL-CIO agree that any currently organized unit is the property of the national union holding the charter but that all unorganized workers are fair game for anyone. Unfortunately, of the three national faculty unions, only the AFT is a member of the AFL-CIO and thus a party to the no raiding agreement. The pertinence of this discussion is illustrated by the case of the largest faculty bargaining unit in the nation, the California State Universities and Colleges (CSUC).

After a long, bitter, and convoluted organizing campaign, the CSUC faculty in 1982 chose to be represented by the California Faculty Association (CFA), a coalition of the AAUP, the NEA affiliate, and the California State Employees Association (CSEA), originally an independent employee association. The CFA victory over its long standing opponent, the United Professors of California (UPC), the AFT affiliate, was a very close one, by thirty-nine votes of the 13,121 cast. After the election, for reasons only indirectly related to the situation in the CSUC, the state CSEA decided to merge with the Service Employees International Union, like the AFT an AFL-CIO affiliate. This merger appears to have blocked any future challenge to the CFA by the UPC, since the CFA through it member union CSEA has an affiliation with the AFL-CIO, bringing the no raiding pact into play.

In the early years of faculty unionism there was considerable theorizing that the collective bargaining agreements negotiated by the affiliates of the three national organizations would show basic differences that could be linked to the presumably disparate philosophies of the organizations. As the frequency of shifts of allegiance suggests, however, these studies have not demonstrated characteristic patterns in the content of agreements. When the parties get down to the bedrock of organizing and negotiating agreements at the local unit level, the pressures of competition force a convergence of policy and tactics on the parties. The AAUP, however, apparently has tried to maintain a more clear-cut position in favor of peer review of personnel matters and access of all faculty to governance machinery without reference to union membership. (But see the AAUP section below.)

The coalition phenomenon. As the faculty union movement grew during the 1970s, the role of coalitions of local units of the various national organizations grew in importance. On the face of it, the coalitions seem to represent a potential for a kind of "bottom up" merger movement. Coalitions are characteristic of the largest bargaining units. In 1983 there were eight bargaining units with more than 2,500 members among four-year university systems.[8] Of the eight units, four were represented by coalitions, two each by the AFT and the AAUP and one each by the AAUP and the NEA. The coalitions represent CUNY (AFT/AAUP), CSUC (NEA/AAUP/CSEA), the Pennsylvania State College System (AFT/AAUP), and the University of Hawaii (NEA/AAUP).

It is interesting to review the background of the coalitions. At CUNY the present coalition was formed when the sole bargaining agent, the AFT, decided to seek a link with the AAUP, which had not been a major player at CUNY. The Pennsylvania Colleges were originally affiliated with the NEA, switched to the AFT, and then joined with the AAUP. In the other two coalitions, Hawaii and the CSUC, the coalitions represent a pre-election response to a situation in which the AFT was the dominant single organization in the systems and their opponents established a coalition to successfully contest the election. Although the AAUP is everyone's favorite coalition partner as a member of all four coalitions, only at Hawaii would the AAUP have been a serious contender in the election in its own right.

The coalitions suffer from some serious internal organizational problems and are probably inherently unstable. In the CSUC, the umbrella organization, the California Faculty Association, became a direct membership organization before the election in 1982 and may gradually take over the membership of its affiliated groups. It is probably large enough to go it alone, at least if it could get an agency shop. Although the Hawaii AAUP chapter had a large faculty following at the time of the election won by the coalition, recently the coalition was reportedly close to severing its ties with the AAUP. The Pennsylvania State College unit was reported to be considering a similar move.[9]

The coalitions typically permit members of the affiliated groups to retain their separate memberships and then negotiate a split in dues between the local coalition and the various national organizations in a manner not unlike the so-called "per capita tax" used by traditional labor unions. The potential for invidious comparisons between the level of dues paid to and the type and quality of services received from the national units is obvious and creates difficulties for all the various parties involved, including the coalition members, the various national offices, and other locals of the national organizations.

Although it is possible that the coalitions will evolve toward a merged unit that could remain a free-standing, independent organization, past experience suggests that the advantages of affiliation with a national organization are decisive. Both CUNY and State University of New York (SUNY) were originally organized by independent faculty associations that found it desirable to affiliate with national organizations, although even today they each account for almost 10 percent of all unionized faculty. The more likely outcome is not a bottom up merger, but a direct affiliation by the present coalitions with the national teacher organization that possesses the best combination of political skill and money. As noted, the CSUC union has a *de facto* link with the Service Employees International Union, but this only serves to complicate the overall situation.

The AAUP at the crossroads (again). When the AAUP made its decision to enter the contest for collective bargaining representation in 1971, it was a difficult and divisive issue. Fourteen years later it still is. At the time when the controversy originated, the AAUP Bulletin, *Academe,* (March 1972) carried two statements, one supporting and one opposing the decision. The essence of the argument for adopting collective bargaining was that it was another form of participation in university governance and that the AAUP should extend its traditional concern for governance to this new version rather than run the risk of being excluded as the unions won exclusive bargaining rights. The opposition argued that the AAUP had acquired an enviable status as the spokesman for college and university faculty in a framework of cooperation and consensus and that it risked trading its unique professional role for that of a probably not very effective trade union representative.[10]

In 1971 the AAUP was a direct membership organization with a remarkable record of producing policy statements on significant issues of academic policy that were endorsed by the major associations of institutions of higher education (i.e., the employers). Its national office in Washington was located at One Dupont Circle, a building sometimes referred to as the Pentagon of higher education, along with the other college and university associations. By 1984 the membership had dropped from more than 91,000 to 52,000 active members; significantly, almost two-thirds of these were members of chapters engaged in collective bargaining. Moreover, the association had relocated to smaller and more modest quarters on 14th Street, and the leaders were engaged in a crucial debate about the structure and purpose of the organization.

Prior to 1971 the AAUP was a typical professional association led for the most part by faculty representatives from prestigious universities and benefiting from largely volunteer services from a talented group of faculty specialists in various areas of concern. Although some local chapters, e.g., Rutgers, were actively involved in local university affairs, it is generally true that local chapters, particularly those at major universities, were relatively small and inactive, and the AAUP presence and budget expenditures were minimal. Dues were low and membership was seen as a variety of professional obligation. Its 1971 membership was about 18 percent of all full-time instructional staff for that year, although some members were undoubtedly administrators.[11]

When local collective bargaining chapters were established, the level of required financial support for their activities rose dramatically. Direct members who were often opposed to collective bargaining themselves found their dues increasing (although to only just over five dollars a month in 1984) and the Association increasingly dominated by the concerns of the bargaining chapters. For their part the chapters involved in representation disputes and bargaining attracted members who often were only peripherally interested in the traditional AAUP programs, were skeptical of the value of AAUP affiliation, and were reluctant to see local dues diverted to the national organization. These particular attitudes are not limited to local affiliates of the AAUP, of course, but they are of particular importance because of the continuing dual nature of the organization. The direct member sees his dues go to the national office and, except in unusual circumstances, sees very little visible return coming back to the local chapters. The collective bargaining chapters contribute an amount to the national office that is negotiated, that reflects different circumstances, and that varies among local chapters.[12]

The AAUP has a goal of collecting at least two-thirds of the direct membership dues from each member of its collective bargaining chapter, but it is a long way from achieving that goal.[13] Meanwhile, direct membership has been declining steadily so that the political weight of the bargaining chapters has been increasing.

As the number of bargaining chapters increased in the 1970s, a Collective Bargaining Congress (CBC) was established within the AAUP structure. The result has been an informal bifurcation of the organization, reflecting conflict between the CBC and the traditional committee structure and leadership of the organization. The problem came to a head in the 1984 election for president of the Association when the nominating committee's two candidates for president were challenged by a third candidate backed by a group from the CBC and nominated by petition. One of the original candidates withdrew, setting up what was viewed as a contest between the traditionalists and the bargaining faction.[14]

The nominating committee's candidate won the presidency, a rotating two year position, but the new full time general secretary of the Association, Ernst Benjamin, is a faculty member from Wayne State University who was an active AFT supporter in the 1972 election campaign at Wayne State, which the AAUP won by a narrow margin. Benjamin proceeded to join the AAUP, became an officer of the chapter, and then a chairman of the CBC before being named general secretary in 1984. It remains to be seen whether this development will improve the relationship or simply change its character.

The AAUP is currently exploring the possibility of establishing a separate nonprofit foundation as the part of the organization that would conduct the traditional activities of the professional society separately from the collective bargaining activities. Collective bargaining has clearly had a great deal more of an impact on the AAUP than the AAUP has had on collective bargaining, and it will take a triumph of organizational politics to maintain the viability of the organization in its traditional role.

The Outcomes of Bargaining

In the early years of faculty bargaining, predictions that unions would bring large scale changes, mostly bad, to colleges and universities were the order of the day.[15] Some of the predicted changes have actually occurred, while others have turned out to be at least delayed if not forestalled indefinitely.

Administrative outcomes. The predicted change that has most clearly materialized is the increase in bureaucratization and formalization under collective bargaining. The conduct of elections, the negotiation of agreements and their day-to-day administration, have inevitably created additional positions for lawyers, labor relations specialists, and their support personnel. Collective bargaining creates legal obligations both in the areas of the procedures of due process and in the areas of agreement content and substance. In most of the literature on the subject, written largely for a market of administrators and nonunionists, pejorative words such as bureaucracy, inflexibility, cost, and delay tend to predominate. Of course, one man's delay and inflexibility is another man's due process.

A possibly more serious result of bargaining is a clear-cut tendency for power to shift toward central offices on the individual campuses and especially in multi-campus institutions and in multi-institutional systems. Presidents of unionized campuses not only reported that bargaining had increased the power of off-campus central agencies but that the effect had increased between 1974 and 1979.[16]

For sophisticated managers, centralized bargaining has provided a "management tool" that at least in some instances has permitted the achievement of goals that would have been more difficult to achieve in a looser, more consensual system of decision-making. A collective bargaining negotiation involves the joint consideration of multiple issues in an atmosphere conducive to an exchange of concessions. Ultimately, it produces a package settlement that must be approved by a simple majority of the union constituency in a ratification process in which the negotiators are active proponents of approval. The machinery of "collegiality," on the other hand, tends to operate on issues one at a time, without explicit packaging of concessions, without simple majority rule, and without the creation of explicit public ratification procedures. It was the fear of this effect that led to widely expressed concern that tenure might be bartered away for financial benefits (a concern that seems to have been unfounded).

Unions and senates. In contrast to the accuracy of the predictions about bureaucracy and centralization, most commentators went wrong in forecasting that unions would eliminate or take over academic senates. It is generally agreed that this has not happened in the typical situation.[17]

The reasons for the lack of conflict seem to be twofold. In many institutions, senates have traditionally exerted little power or perhaps did not exist at all, particularly in two-year institutions. In other instances the senates were not involved with the kinds of issues with which unions have been concerned, or did not deal with them effectively. Baldridge, Kemerer, and Associates (BK) report that both administrators and union representatives agreed that the principal impact of unions has been in the areas of wages and benefits and grievance procedures, with professional issues, presumably the principal domain of the senates, lagging behind.[18]

It appears that on balance unions have strengthened the senates as local governance institutions rather than contributing to their demise.

Personnel matters. Another of the underlying concerns found in the literature anticipating the consequences of faculty union-ism is the belief that the emphasis on egalitarianism and job security attributed to unions would undermine quality and merit as principles for personnel selection and reward. There is no ques-tion that unions have written formal procedures and safeguards into their contracts with increasing frequency. An analysis of con-tract provisions contained in a sample of contracts negotiated be-tween 1971 and 1979 found that for fourteen different elements of personnel policy thirteen had increased in frequency of occur-rence, and that by 1979 eight of the thirteen were found in 85 per-cent or more of the contracts. The lone element whose prevalence decreased, interestingly, was promotion policy.[19]

Few unions directly restrict the operation of the system at the time of initial appointment, although an indirect effect sometimes results from the practice of giving recall rights to recently sepa-rated faculty. Still, there is no question that unions have devoted much effort to protecting existing faculty against dismissal for any reason, including adverse judgments as to merit. How serious the effects of this defensive posture is for the average quality of faculty cannot be assessed in the absence of data. The unanswered question is: How effective would the promotion procedure have been in the absence of unionism? In brief, we do not know what proportions of faculty are turned down on merit grounds under nonunion conditions and if, when such decisions are made, the judgments are more valid than those made in unionized institu-tions.

Fragmentary data suggest that only in a minority of institutions are substantial percentages of faculty dropped on academic grounds, and there is no information available on the validity of the screening process employed.[20] There is no reason to doubt that unions have made it more difficult to take disciplinary action against faculty because of the protections, which include, *inter alia*, appeals to outside arbitrators, virtually unknown in non-union conditions. Against the presumed benefits of providing due process in at least some cases must be offset the possible loss in effectiveness resulting from a reduced ability to control and direct faculty personnel.

One of the areas where a clear-cut impact of unionism can be found is in the area of retrenchment, a topic of great concern since the early 1970s. The BK survey of contract provisions found that in 1971 only 15 percent of their sample had provisions pertaining to staff reduction, but that by 1979 this proportion had risen to 88 percent. Simply by delaying action and forcing the consideration of alternatives, contract provisions (and court actions in some nonunion institutions) have cut down the numbers of personnel eventually terminated. In addition, unions often include in their retrenchment procedures recall provisions for faculty that apply to a specific period of time after layoff.

Economic benefits. Perhaps the single question most often asked during campus organizing campaigns is whether unionization will raise faculty salaries. The most systematic attempt to measure the effects of unionization is that of Richard Freeman, which unfortunately only covers the period 1970–71 through 1976–77.[21] Freeman found that unionism improved total compensation, fringes somewhat more than salaries, and produced somewhat larger benefits for the higher ranks. His most interesting finding was that the magnitude of the gains was related to the date of organization, the earlier the date the larger the improvement. This could mean that gains accumulated as the period organized lengthened, or that the later years offered fewer opportunities for winning gains, or some combination of explanations. Later studies have found mixed results, but the question of how much each of the factors cited should be weighted by a faculty currently considering organization remains unanswered.[22]

Conclusion

As of the mid-1980s the faculty union movement appears to be a well-established element of the public sector labor movement in the approximately one-half of the states with supportive labor laws. Measured by numbers of faculty covered by agreements, it has never been a major factor in private higher education, and the effects of the Yeshiva decision have eroded that slender base. There is already a high level of penetration in the states with favorable laws, so that further expansion is dependent either on the organization of the "flagship" universities in states such as California, Michigan, Minnesota, and Pennsylvania, or on the passage of favorable laws in other states. Neither of these events is likely to occur in substantial numbers in the near future. With about 24 percent of all full- and part-time faculty represented by unions in 1984, the prospect is for continued slow growth over the next few years. Unionism has so far turned out to be virtually irreversible in the public sector—the first and only decertification was reported by the National Center in a two-year institution in 1980.

Both administrations and unions have settled into a more or less routinized pattern of relationships. Unions have contributed to an increase in bureaucratization and centralization of decision making (both trends underway for other reasons as well), have strengthened the academic senates on balance, have provided due process in personnel decisions at the expense of flexibility and lower costs, and have increased compensation a modest but not insignificant amount on the average. Effects on promotion and merit pay decisions have yet to be determined, but I suspect they are not likely to be favorable.

The overall picture is a mixed one with significant but limited benefits from the standpoint of the organized faculty. Given the difficult environment of the past decade and a half, this can be regarded as a substantial accomplishment with no identifiable serious costs to the institutions involved. Perhaps the key test of the significance of faculty unionism for higher education will come when and if a major "elite" institution is organized, but to date the verdict would be a mixed report, favorable on balance.

V

Outside and Inside

12

SEYMOUR MARTIN LIPSET

Labor Unions
in the Public Mind

The falloff in union membership and in support in Labor Board representation elections over the past decade, reported in other chapters in this volume, has been explained by various analysts as a consequence of changes in the structure of the American economy and/or an increase in corporate opposition to unions marked by use of sophisticated personnel relations backed by an increasingly unsympathetic federal government, which has administered existing legislation governing labor relations in ways which inhibit union organization drives. There can be little doubt that these factors have had some effect. The decline in numbers of workers in the traditional centers of unionism, such as steel, auto, printing, garments, leather, and others has occurred in tandem with the rise in employment in high tech and service industries that have been difficult to organize. And clearly, changes in labor legislation from Taft-Hartley on and in the composition and administration of the National Labor Relations Board have had

I am indebted to Rita Jalali for research assistance on this chapter.

some effect on the ability of unions to retain and secure collective bargaining rights.

Beyond the impact of these factors, it is important to evaluate the possible effects of public opinion, of the attitudes toward unions prevalent among unorganized workers and the public generally, in contributing to the weakness of American unions. The importance of this variable is implicit in the losses that unions have been suffering in representation elections conducted by the Labor Relations Board, as well as in defeats in decertification referenda, that is, in elections held among workers who have been represented by a union. As Derek Bok and John Dunlop point out, "public opinion will have an influence simply because a hostile climate can weaken the loyalty of the members, harm the union in its political activities, or prejudice its efforts to organize new groups of employees."[1]

Americans today show an ambivalence toward labor unions not unlike their contradictory feelings about a number of other institutions, particularly the federal government and large corporations.[2] They approve of their functions, but disapprove of much of what they perceive to be their actual behavior. Large majorities of those interviewed by pollsters state that without unions, workers would have to endure lower pay and worse employment conditions. But unions are also seen as powerful, self-interested bodies working for their own advantage. Beyond this, organized labor bears the special burden of a leadership widely believed to be autocratic, corrupt, and contemptuous of the public interest. Americans raise the same criticism of big business as they do of trade unions—too much power, too little morality. In the case of labor, however, the charge of unethical behavior seems to carry special weight.

This chapter concentrates on reporting the results of many opinion polls that have dealt with attitudes toward labor groups. Analyses of the relationship of these opinions to larger values and structural factors and of the ways the views of the public affect the positions of unions are given in Chapter 17.

Lack of Confidence in Unions and Their Leaders

Labor unions are close to being the least esteemed institutions in American life, while the repute of their leaders is even lower. In six national samplings taken between 1975 and 1985, the Opinion Research Corporation (ORC) inquired about confidence in fourteen institutions by asking respondents to rate "how much trust and confidence you have" in each one on a scale from 1 (no trust) to 7 (complete trust and confidence). Labor unions consistently placed thirteenth out of fourteen as judged by the mean difference between high (6–7) and low (1–2) confidence scores. An average of 19 percent placed them in the high confidence category, compared to 32 percent for the other thirteen institutions. Looking at the distributions at the low end of the scale, that is, the proportion indicating no or very little trust and confidence (1–2), labor unions ranked at the bottom. On the average, a larger percentage, 27, placed them at this end more than did the same for any other institution, including the stock market (22 percent), large companies (18.5), banks (6.5) and the legal profession (15). Those expressing complete trust in unions have declined gradually but steadily from 22 percent in 1975 to 15 percent in 1985, while the proportion expressing no trust has moved up and down irregularly reaching a high point of 31 percent in 1979 and a low of 22 percent in 1985.

Trade unions also have done badly in repeated Gallup polls. This survey organization has inquired as to "how much confidence" respondents have in a variety of institutions, presenting the options of "a great deal, quite a lot, some, or very little." It has included the same seven, "church or organized religion," "the military," "U.S. Supreme Court," "newspapers," "Congress," "big business," and "organized labor" in eight polls conducted between 1975 and 1985. Labor ranked sixth in the four taken between 1975 and 1980, and seventh, the bottom position, in three out of the four conducted between 1981 and 1985, judged by the percentage answering positively, "a great deal, [or] quite a lot." Unions have done significantly worse in surveys during the Reagan era, with an almost unchanging rating of 28 percent, than in the previous ones in which their trust scores ranged between 39 percent (1977) and 35 percent (1980). Labor organizations also placed at the bottom of a list of twelve institutions evaluated in a March 1985 Roper poll. Respondents were asked to state for each, "whether your opinion is highly favorable, moderately favorable, not too favorable or rather unfavorable?" Just under half, 49 percent, were favorable to unions, compared to 64 percent for Congress, 66 for the public school system and 86 for both business and industry and the police.

The public disdain for labor organizations appears to be linked to even harsher feelings about their leaders, who stand lower in public regard than their organizations. A poll conducted by the Proctor and Gamble market research section in 1975 found only 12 percent expressing "a great deal of confidence" in "union leaders," compared to 21 percent with the same judgment about "organized labor." A national survey conducted by Civic Service, Inc. in 1980 reported that 27 percent said they had a great deal or quite a lot of confidence in "organized labor" compared to 23 percent who replied they had the same high level of confidence in "the people running organized labor."

Labor leaders also are evaluated more negatively than the heads of most other institutions in many polls conducted by a variety of survey organizations. In the thirty evaluations of the leaders of ten American institutions conducted by the Harris and the National Opinion Research Center (NORC) polls taken between 1966 and 1985, the percentage expressing "a great deal of confidence," rather than "only some" or "hardly any," in the leadership of organized labor has almost invariably been less than those received by the heads of other institutions inquired about.[3] The executives of major companies have out-ranked labor leaders in all surveys but one, averaging 25 percent for the entire span. Over the nineteen-year period, the average voicing high esteem for the heads of unions, 14 percent, has been significantly lower than the mean for the leaders of eight other institutions, 31 percent. The results for the Harris and NORC surveys are presented in Table 1.

The results for the leaders of organized labor are similar in both sets of surveys, although in recent years, 1983 and 1984, union officials scored somewhat lower in the NORC polls than in Harris. In general, however, they agree that the public has little confidence in the heads of labor unions. The gap between executives of major companies and union leaders has been much greater in the NORC surveys than in Harris'. Still, both find that the public values the heads of big business more than those of organized labor. Finally, it may be noted that union leaders, like those of other institutions,

Table 1

Confidence in Leaders of Labor, Major Companies, and Eight Other Institutions

"As far as the people running [organized labor or other institutions] are concerned, would you say you have a great deal of confidence, only some confidence, or hardly any confidence at all in them?"

Percent Expressing a Great Deal of Confidence in Leaders

Harris Surveys

Date	Major Companies	Organized Labor	Average Eight Other Institutions
Feb. 1966	55	22	49
Jan. 1967	47	20	45
Aug. 1971	27	14	29
Oct. 1972	27	15	30
Sept. 1973	30	20	36
Dec. 1973	28	16	32
Aug. 1974	22	17	33
Sept. 1974	16	18	31
Apr. 1975	20	14	27
Aug. 1975	20	18	30
Jan. 1977	20	14	28
Nov. 1977	23	15	31
Aug. 1978	22	15	28
Feb. 1979	18	10	25
Nov. 1980	16	14	25
Sept. 1981	16	12	27
Nov. 1982	18	8	23
Nov. 1983	18	10	28
Nov. 1984	19	12	34
Nov. 1985	17	13	27
Average 20 polls	24	15	31

Table 1 (cont'd)

NORC Surveys

Date	Major Companies	Organized Labor	Average Eight Other Institutions
March 1973	29	16	33
March 1974	31	18	35
March 1975	19	10	28
March 1976	22	12	32
March 1977	27	15	35
March 1978	22	11	26
March 1980	27	15	27
March 1982	23	12	28
March 1983	24	8	25
March 1984	32	9	29
Average 10 polls	26	13	30

were less trusted in the 1970s than they were in the mid-1960s, and that their ratings in the 1980s have been on average even lower. The most recent surveys, those taken between 1983 and 1985, indicate a slight but basically insignificant improvement.

Further evidence that Americans hold labor leaders in low esteem may be found in different Roper studies. Four polls taken between 1975 and 1984 asked respondents for evaluations of the "ability" of the leaders in politics, business, and labor, "to make real contributions to our society." As noted in Table 2, labor leaders placed well below the other two.

The same pattern shows up in response to a different Roper question, which deals with opinions concerning people in eleven occupations and professions. The respondents were asked to state whether they had "a generally high opinion . . . , a fairly good opinion . . . , not too good an opinion, or a poor opinion of them." In four polls taken between January 1976 and October 1982, "labor leaders" placed behind nine other occupational groups in the percentage having a high or fairly good opinion of them. Doctors received an overwhelming positive vote, 85 percent on the average, as did businessmen, 78.5. Close to half, 47 percent, had a

Table 2

Confidence in Ability of Leaders to Contribute to Society
(Percent)

"So far as their ability to make real contributions to our society is concerned, would you say you have a great deal of confidence in this nation's leaders, a fair amount of confidence, or not much confidence in them?"

	Political Leaders				Business Leaders				Labor Leaders			
	1975	1977	1981	1984	1975	1977	1981	1984	1975	1977	1981	1984
Great Confidence	6	18	16	11	10	14	16	16	7	6	7	8
Fair Confidence	45	59	58	54	52	58	58	57	43	42	43	42
Not Much Confidence	45	19	24	33	32	23	22	22	42	42	40	42

Source: The Roper Poll

good opinion of advertising men, but only 37 percent were equally positive about labor leaders. The only group which was less well regarded than union officials was "politicians," with an average score of 26 percent with a high or fairly good opinion of them. In a similar vein, in April 1981, the *Los Angeles Times* poll asked a national cross section to give their impressions of "labor leaders" and of "businessmen or women." Labor leaders were judged negatively, 47 percent unfavorable to 41 percent favorable, while business people were approved of by 80 to 12.

The recurrent finding that the public esteems business leaders more than labor officials flows from the fact that Americans have a much better impression of the personal qualities of the former than of the latter. This judgment is suggested by the results of two groups of Roper surveys taken between 1975 and 1984. The first, conducted in 1975 and 1978, invited respondents to choose from a list the two "qualities you think would help get a person ahead fastest in . . . business and in the labor union movement." Those most often selected for labor leaders have a negative cast, while most of the qualities identified for business people are generally viewed as socially desirable ones. Thus, the four mentioned most often for labor leaders were "knowing the right people" (31 percent in 1975, 35 percent in 1978), "aggressiveness" (29 and 27 percent), "willingness to make deals and payoffs" (18 and 22 percent), and "playing the angles" (15 and 21 percent). For business, the requisite qualities were first, "intelligence" (33 percent in 1975, 40 percent in 1978), followed by "sheer hard work" (40 and 39 percent), "aggressiveness" (37 percent both years), and tied for fourth place, "knowing the right people" (28 and 29 percent) and "creative ability" (27 and 29 percent).

Roper secured similar results in response to a question posed in 1975, 1977, and 1984, inviting interviewees to check off from a list of twelve "words and phrases" those descriptive of a majority of the "country's top business leaders" and "top leaders in labor." As reported in Table 3, about the same proportions identified both as "self-seeking" (half) and as "fair in dealings with others" (one-seventh). But business leaders were more likely than the heads of labor to be seen as very intelligent, able and competent, forward looking, of high moral fiber, and not as behind the times or ruthless. Labor officials led on only one positive item, "sincerely in-

Table 3

Qualities Descriptive of Business and Labor Leaders
(Percent)

"Here is a list of words and phrases. Would you start at the top of the list and go down calling off all those you think are descriptive of a good majority of the country's top business leaders?" (Card shown to respondent). "Now would you call off all those you think are descriptive of a good majority of the country's top leaders in labor?"

	Top Business Leaders			Top Labor Leaders		
	1975 Feb.	1977 Feb.	1984 Feb.	1975 Feb.	1977 Feb.	1984 Feb.
Self-seeking	50	51	51	46	50	49
Very intelligent	44	39	42	27	17	16
Able and competent	39	35	44	23	17	21
Forward looking and progressive	41	40	45	26	21	22
Not sufficiently competent	11	9	9	20	21	23
Sincerely interested in solving social problems	13	10	10	18	12	16
Ruthless	30	24	24	35	38	32
Fair in dealings with others	12	11	14	15	11	14
Behind the times	9	6	9	13	12	23
High moral caliber	9	8	8	6	4	6
None or don't know	15	12	9	20	17	13

Source: The Roper Poll

terested in social problems," but only one-sixth or less gave either group a vote on this one.

The negative feelings about the behavior of unions and their leaders may also stem from the widely held beliefs that union officials are corrupt and autocratic, that they do not represent and do exploit their members, in addition to being "more unreliable, self-interested, and insensitive to the general welfare than other highly influential figures in the society."[4] Thus, in 1976 Harris found that almost two-thirds of respondents, 63 percent, agreed that "Many union leaders have known ties with racketeers and organized crime;" a smaller majority, 54 percent, felt the same way when the question was repeated in 1984. Other questions asked only in 1976 revealed a pattern of misgivings. Three-quarters, 76 percent, voiced agreement with the statement: "Many union leaders have used their union positions to benefit themselves financially." A sizable majority, 59 percent, saw union leaders as out of touch with their members and even cheating them. Close to three-fifths, 59 percent, agreed with the statements: "Most union leaders have become arrogant and no longer represent the workers in their unions" and "Many union leaders have abused union pension funds." In 1977, the Quality of Employment Survey, a national poll of employed persons, conducted by the Survey Research Center (SRC) of the University of Michigan, found that "Approximately two-thirds of the respondents agreed that ... [union] leaders are more interested in what benefits themselves than in what benefits union members," and 65 percent felt that "unions force members to go along with decisions they don't like."[5] In March 1985, ORC reported that three-fifths of a national cross section believed that union leaders express their own views rather than those of their members, when taking public stands, up from 54 percent who felt this way in 1977.

Consistent with these results are the findings of repeated Gallup, ORC, and Roper polls taken between 1976 and 1985 that labor leaders fall out near the bottom of the list of occupational groups on estimates of honesty and ethical standards (Gallup and Roper) and ethical and moral practices (ORC). In 1976, Gallup found that only 12 percent judged the ethical standards of labor leaders "high" or "very high," while 48 percent graded them "low" or "very low," and 38 percent saw them as having "average standards." A year later 13 percent rated them positively, while 47 percent were negative. In 1981, 14 percent put them in the two highest categories, and 48 percent placed them in the lowest ones. The 1985 findings were, if anything, more unfavorable, 13 percent positive, 52 percent negative.

The picture becomes worse from the union perspective when put in a comparative context. In 1976, each of the other nine occupational groups asked about, including business executives and building contractors, scored well above labor leaders. In 1977, labor leaders placed eighteenth on the list of twenty. The only groups receiving a lower ranking were car salesmen and advertising practitioners. All others—this time including insurance salesmen, realtors, undertakers, and local office holders—were judged by the public as having higher ethical standards than labor leaders. Business leaders did considerably better than them. Four years later, in 1981, when 24 occupations were evaluated, only car salesmen outranked union leaders in the proportion of the public who said their standards were "low" or "very low" (55 percent for car salesmen compared to 48 percent for union leaders). Less than a fifth, 19 percent, gave the same unfavorable rating to business executives.

In July 1985, labor leaders once more placed next to the bottom in evaluations of twenty-five occupations. Again, car salesmen constituted the only category to be judged as having worse standards of honesty and ethics. Stockbrokers, realtors, building contractors, insurance salesmen and advertising practitioners all did better. In the fall of the same year, the Roper Organization repeated the Gallup question, this time inquiring about 17 occupations, and obtained almost identical findings. Car salesmen once more were the one group regarded more negatively.

ORC also reports that labor leaders rank below almost all other occupational groups in judgments about their "ethical and moral practices." Thus in comparisons of assessments taken in 1981, 1983, and 1985, ORC found that on average a quarter of those polled evaluated the ethical practices of labor leaders as "poor," while only 3 percent said they were excellent. None of the eighteen other categories received equivalently adverse rankings, as indicated in Table 4.

In view of these results, it is hardly surprising that Americans

Table 4

Ratings of Occupational Groups on Ethical and Moral Practices
(Percent)

"How would you rate the ethical and moral practices of [specific category] (1) Excellent, (2) Good, (3) Only Fair, (4) Poor, (5) No Opinion?"

Categories	Excellent or Good			Only Fair or Poor		
	1981	1983	1985	1981	1983	1985
Labor Union Leaders	23	21	23	59	65	65
Average Workers	72	72	74	27	24	25
Small Business Proprietors	75	68	76	23	25	21
Corporate Executives	33	29	39	54	51	47
Corporate Board Members	28	27	35	58	54	51
Stockbrokers	31	34	34	45	41	43
Bankers	56	49	57	39	41	35
Advertising Executives	31	35	38	59	48	50
Lawyers	45	44	43	52	50	53
Physicians	75	70	76	24	25	23
College Professors	60	66	69	27	20	20
Scientists	69	64	75	20	19	14
Media News Reporters	57	58	51	41	38	47
The President	53	48	65	44	46	32
Supreme Court	56	49	57	39	41	35
Military Leaders	55	47	48	38	42	42
U.S. Senators & Reps.	36	33	42	60	52	52
Federal Govt. Officials	23	25	33	72	65	60
State & Local Govt. Officials	31	31	37	66	59	57
Average	48	46	51	45	42	41

Source: Opinion Research Corporation

have shown reluctance to endorse the idea of a labor leader as president. When Yankelovich, Skelly, and White asked in 1979, "Would it be good for the country or not good to have as president: a business executive, . . . a labor leader, . . .?", respondents approved of having "a business executive" in the White House by 59 to 25 percent, but rejected "a labor leader" by 53 to 30 percent. More surprisingly, blue-collar workers *opposed* a labor leader by 48 to 36 percent, while they *favored* a business leader by 55 to 29 percent. A year later, of course, a former union leader was elected, though not by unionists.

The Positive Social Role of Unions

Despite their lack of confidence in organized labor and its officials, and their strong criticisms of its operational practices, the majority of Americans believe that unions are essential and do more good than harm, that without unions employers would maltreat workers. General trust in labor unions is low, but a varying majority of the public has always answered "approve" to the question posed by Gallup in twenty-three surveys taken between 1936 and 1985: "Do you approve or disapprove of labor unions?" (Table 5).

Most Americans have repeatedly expressed approval of union functions by agreeing to statements such as, strong unions provide "the only way for employees to get a fair shake in the average big company today. . ." and "unions are in the best interests of working people."[6] In May 1977, a national cross section polled by Fingerhut/Granados agreed by a 50 to 34 percent margin that "most working people need labor unions to protect their rights." The same sample *disagreed*, by 54 to 35 percent, that "even if there weren't labor unions, big corporations would pay fair wages and give decent benefits to people who work for them." The 1977 Survey Research Center's survey of employed persons reported that over 80 percent felt that unions "protect workers against unfair practices," "improve job security" and "improve wages."[7]

In December 1976, Harris found that over four-fifths, 85 percent, of the public felt that "in many industries unions are needed so the legitimate complaints and grievances of workers can be heard and action taken on them." When he repeated the question in February 1984, the percentage agreeing, 82, was almost as overwhelming. In 1976 and 1984, a majority, 58 and 56 percent, approved the statement, "if there were no unions, most employers would quickly move to exploit their employees." More significantly, the public agreed in 1975 and 1984 that "Big unions serve as a good check on the power of big business" by 66 percent to 20 percent in the earlier poll and 61 to 29 almost a decade later.

As indicated above, the low level of trust in unions and their leaders is compatible with positive judgments about their functions, with the sentiment that unions are essential and do more good than harm, particularly for their members. Still, from the late 1950s, when unions reached a high point in membership strength, to the early 1980s, approval of the institution has been moving downward in Gallup polls, although 1985 showed a small improvement for the first time in two decades (Table 5). This gain, however, is out of the line with the judgments obtained by four other polling organizations and may, therefore, be a chance error.[8]

The responses to the Gallup question, the longest continuous series on attitudes to unions, display a series of peaks and declines. Approval was high during the New Deal 1930s, followed by a moderate decline during World War II and the early postwar years, possibly in reaction to wartime strikes and the subsequent high rates of inflation. The peak of union approval occurred during the "conservative" Eisenhower years, which were also a period of prosperity, low inflation, and generally high levels of confidence in all institutions. By 1979, approval of unions had fallen to an all-time low of 55 percent, while the proportion voicing disapproval continued to move up to a record high of 35 percent in the summer of 1981. These losses in approval ratings between the late 1950s and the early 1980s correspond to the steady falloff in the proportion of the nonagricultural labor force who belong to unions in these years.

Estimates of the underlying feelings of the public, as well as of trends, may vary with question wording. Three national polls taken by Cambridge Reports, Inc. (CRI) between 1983 and 1985 in the first quarter of each year indicate that Americans are less likely to endorse the worth of labor organizations when they are asked how *favorable* they are to "organized labor" than when they give an *approval* rating. The interviewers inquired "whether you have a very favorable, somewhat favorable, somewhat unfavor-

Table 5
Ratings of Labor Unions, 1936–1985
(Percent)

"In general, do you approve or disapprove of labor unions?"

Year	Approve	Disapprove
1936	72	20
1937	72	20
1939	68	24
1940	64	22
1941	61	30
1947	64	25
1949	62	22
1953	75	18
1957 (Feb.)	76	14
1957 (Sept.)	64	18
1959	68	19
1961 (Feb.)	70	18
1961 (May)	63	22
1962	64	24
1963	67	23
1965 (Feb.)	71	19
1965 (June)	70	19
1967	66	23
1973	59	26
1978 (April)	59	31
1979 (May)	55	33
1981 (Aug.)	55	35
1985	58	27

Source: Gallup polls

able, or very unfavorable opinion of organized labor." There was
no consistent trend across these three years, with the public dividing fairly evenly in its attitudes. In 1983, 43 percent were favorable, while 50 percent were negative; the comparable figures for
1984 were better for organized labor, 49 and 45 percent, but they
fell off again in 1985, reversing to 45 and 49 percent. By comparison, as with confidence surveys reported earlier, the respondents were much more positive in their evaluations of "business in
general" (Table 6).

Similarly, Roper reported no recent trend in three polls taken in
1977, 1981, and 1984 in the responses to a question inquiring,
"When you hear of a strike by a union against a large company,
and before you know any of the details, is your first reaction to
side with the union or to side with the company?" The plurality
supporting the company remained identical in all three, 32 percent, while the proportion backing the union moved up insignifi-
cantly from 28 percent in 1977 to 29 in 1981 and 30 in 1984.

The public clearly is conflicted in its view of trade unions. Majority approval of the functions of unions for their members does
not translate into willingness on the part of employed persons to
vote for them in representation elections or to approve of the AFL-
CIO. The Harris poll inquired in June 1985 of a national sample of

Table 6
Attitudes Toward Organized Labor and Business
(Percent)

"I'd like you to tell me whether you have a very favorable, somewhat
favorable, somewhat unfavorable, or very unfavorable opinion
of...business in general,...organized labor?"

	Organized Labor				Business in General			
	Very Fav.	Some-what Fav.	Some-what Unfav.	Very Unfav.	Very Fav.	Some-what Fav.	Some-what Unfav.	Very Unfav.
1983	11	32	27	23	17	59	17	4
1984	13	36	26	19	25	62	8	7
1985	12	33	27	22	24	61	10	2

Source: Cambridge Reports, Inc.

employed adults: "If an election were held tomorrow to decide whether your workplace should be unionized or not, do you think you would definitely vote for a union, probably vote for a union, probably vote against a union, or definitely vote against a union?" Only 34 percent said they would vote for the union, 12 percent definitely, 22 probably; 63 percent indicated a negative vote, 39 percent definitely, 24 percent probably. This estimate of overall potential support for unions in representation elections is close to those found earlier in national surveys of employed workers taken in 1977 (The Quality of Employment Survey) and of employed men aged 28 to 38 conducted in 1980 (The National Longitudinal Survey).[9] These findings are congruent with the results of a *Los Angeles Times* Poll which asked a national cross section in May 1983, "What is your impression of the AFL-CIO, the national federation of labor unions?" and found that only 39 percent expressed themselves positively, while the majority, 52 percent, had an unfavorable evaluation.

The unwillingness to vote for union representation undoubtedly reflects the ambivalence felt by the majority of the public and the workers among them toward the institution. Replies to various questions by the 1985 Harris sample of employed adults point up some of the conflicting ways in which many Americans continue to view labor organizations. Close to three-quarters, 73 percent, agreed that unions improve wages and working conditions, but a sizable majority, 58 percent, stated that "most employees today don't need unions to get fair treatment from their employers."

The AFL-CIO Committee on the Evolution of Work, which reviewed survey data, also noted that "American workers, and especially nonunion workers, are ambivalent in their attitudes toward unions." These contradictory attitudes are laid out in the Federation report:

Over 75 percent of all workers—and over 75 percent of nonunion workers—state that that they agree that unions in general improve the wages and working conditions of workers. Over 80 percent of all workers agree that unions are needed so that the legitimate complaints of workers can be heard. Yet when asked to assess the effect of organization on their present employer, 53 percent of non-union workers state that wages and fringe benefits would not improve and a much larger percentage, 74 percent, believe that job security would not increase.[10]

The Ambivalence of Union Members

As the authors of the AFL-CIO report acknowledge, union members, while much more favorable to labor organizations than nonmembers, also exhibit considerable ambivalence. The statistical analysis of the 1977 Survey Research Center study found that while union membership was one of the factors correlated with alternative images of labor organizations, the regression analysis only explained "a very small proportion of the variations in these responses (R^2 = .07) ... indicating that this ... image was generally shared by a majority of the workers in all the ... categories examined."[11] In other words, although members were more likely to endorse pro-union positions than nonunionists, the difference was small.

A similar pattern may be found in other studies which differentiate among American workers. Thus in expressing degree of confidence in organized labor to Gallup in May 1985, 39 percent of those part of labor union families voiced confidence in unions, 16 percent a great deal and 23 percent quite a lot, as compared to 26 percent, 6 a great deal and 20 quite a lot, among nonunion families. ORC's 1985 survey found comparable differences between those who are part of union households and those who are not, in response to the question: "How much trust and confidence do you have in labor unions?" Thirty-one percent of union household interviewees placed themselves at the high point "complete trust and confidence in them" (1–2), as contrasted to only 9 percent of others. But the majority, 54 percent, of those in union households interviewed by ORC refused to express any confidence, 31 percent giving the neutral response (4) and 23 percent a negative one (5–7). The same was true for the 1985 Gallup survey: most members of unions and their families would only express "some" (43 percent) or "very little" (16 percent) confidence in organized labor.

If persons with close ties to unions have been more favorable to them as institutions than those without such links, the same has been less true with regard to feelings about union leaders. Union members and their close relatives are almost as disposed as those without such attachments to labor organizations to view union leaders in the same light, usually negative. In general the heads of unions are seen by both groups as representing their own interests or views rather than those of their members. A 1978 CRI poll asked: "Do you think the average union leader represents the members of his union well . . .?" A plurality, 43 percent, replied "no," compared to 31 percent who answered "yes." Respondents from union households were evenly divided, 40 percent "yes" and 39 percent "no," while nonunion respondents were more likely to say "no," 45 to 27 percent. ORC found that 60 percent of the public and 59 percent of those affiliated with unions said in 1984 that union leaders express their own views, not those of their members, when taking stands on public issues, up from 54 percent of both in 1977. Only 5 percent of each group felt leadership positions reflect those of their rank and file in both years. In a more recent ORC survey, taken in the spring of 1985, there was a much smaller difference between the proportion of persons in union households and of others in judging "the ethical and moral practices of labor union leaders" as excellent or good, 26 percent to 22, as compared to variations between the two populations in ratings of confidence in labor unions. Almost one-third, 31 percent, of those in union households scored high on complete trust and confidence, while only 9 percent of the others did the same. A 1984 Harris poll found that only 16 percent of union members and those closely related to them had "a great deal" of confidence in union leaders, while 52 expressed "only some." Public reactions were lower, 8 percent "a great deal" and 47 percent "only some."

The ambivalent reactions of trade unionists to their organizations also showed up in two surveys taken in 1977 and 1980. The first, part of the Survey Research Center's study of the Quality of Employment, found that most unionists replied positively when asked : "How satisfied are you with your trade union?" A quarter, 25 percent, were very satisfied, 48 percent said they were satisfied, 17 percent indicated they were dissatisfied, and 10 percent answered they were very dissatisfied. But when these same workers were asked about their expectations for and evaluations of the performance of their unions, a pattern of criticism of the way the organizations were representing them came through the replies. As Thomas Kochan reports:

The greatest concern of the union members was for increasing the responsiveness of the union's internal administration. The highest priority rating was given to the concern for improving the handling of member grievances. The second highest was given to increasing the amount of feedback the union provides its members. In addition, the need to increase the influence the members have in running the union was rated as the fourth most important priority. Thus, three of the top four concerns of the union members reflected their interest in improving the governance of their union.[12]

The importance attached by unionists to the internal operation of their organizations, as contrasted to other issues, including their role on the job, may be seen in Table 7. It presents the differences between the percentage of "the respondents who indicated they would like to see their unions exerting a lot of effort on a dimension [and] the percentage of respondents who indicated their union was actually doing very well on that dimension."

The 1977 SRC Quality of Employment Survey and the 1980 National Survey of AFL-CIO members conducted for the labor federation by Opinion Research Surveys (ORS) used a similar method in asking unionists to evaluate how good a job their union was doing in different areas. Each invited respondents to evaluate on a four point scale, not good at all, not too good, somewhat good, and very good in the SRC study; and excellent, good, fair, or poor in the ORS one. However, there was minimal overlap in the issues in-

Table 7
Differences between Members' Expectations and
Judgments of Performance of Unions
(1977)

Issues	Percent Differences
Handling members' grievances	43.8
Providing more say in union	42.3
Providing more feedback from union	40.1
Getting better fringe benefits	35.2
Improving job security	30.0
Improving safety and health	26.3
Make jobs more interesting	25.2
Getting better wages	24.0
More say in how to do their jobs	21.9
More say in how business is run	18.9

Source: Survey Research Center; Thomas A. Kochan, "How American Workers View Labor Unions," *Monthly Labor Review* 102 (April 1979), p. 29.

quired about. As noted above, the first, sponsored by the U.S. Department of Labor, included items on workers' influence or "say" both in the union and the company they worked for, and their opinions of the quality of the job, as well as on economic issues. The union-supported study, whose designers repeated questions from the earlier one, dropped those dealing with the internal governance of unions, as well as with desire to affect company policy or feelings about the quality of work, and replaced them with more concrete specifications of economic and fringe issues and union participation in politics (Table 8). With a score of four being the highest and one the lowest in both surveys, the average for the eleven items in the Labor Department study, 2.69, was higher than the mean for ten items in the AFL-CIO one, 2.31. These translate to between "somewhat good" and "not too good" in the language of the former, and between "good" and "fair" in that of the latter.

Table 8

Evaluations by AFL-CIO Members of Union Services
(1980)

"I am going to read a list of services unions provide for their members, and for each one, I'd like you to tell me whether you think your union is doing an *excellent* job, a *good* job, only a *fair* job, or a *poor* job?"

	Mean Scores*
Increasing medical benefits	2.58
Improving health and safety on the job	2.56
Increasing wages	2.53
Representing member grievances	2.48
Improving working conditions	2.41
Supporting legislation in Congress for workers	2.33
Informing about voting records of Senators and Representatives	2.17
Increasing pensions	2.16
Increasing workers' compensation benefits	2.09
Supporting congressional candidates	2.04
Protecting jobs against plant closings	2.01
Average score	2.31

*Key: 4 = excellent, 3 = good, 2 = fair, 1 = poor

Source: Opinion Research Survey

It is impossible to compare these results or to draw any conclusions about trends given the variation in question wording, items used, and sample design. Both, however, suggest much less than complete membership satisfaction with the way American unions operate. The SRC survey indicates that the average unionist would like to see his organization more responsive to rank-and-file concerns, that his interest in having a greater impact on his union is greater than his desire to influence the company he works for or to affect the quality of his job. Those who determined the content of the labor financed survey did not try to produce further findings on these matters. Both polls gave unions a better than average score in dealing with wages, safety and health, and various other fringe benefits and grievances, although the AFL-CIO sponsored one found considerable discontent with the handling of pensions and workmen's compensation. The latter survey also reported unhappiness with union political activity, an area not dealt with in the Labor Department supported study. In sum, unions received a moderate vote of endorsement from their members for improving wages, fringe benefits, and job conditions, but a considerable amount of criticism of their internal governance and their activities in the larger political arena.

Comparing the findings of these two national surveys of union members with two studies of the attitudes of union leaders conducted by questionnaires in 1963 and 1983 points up some interesting variations between the views of officials and those of the rank and file. While, as indicated, union members asked for more "say" in determining union policy and wanted more feedback from their officers, 63 percent of the latter who sent in questionnaires in 1983 complained that their members do not understand what their union does for them, up from 54 percent in 1963. Only a minority of the leaders, 28 percent in 1983 and 27 percent in 1963, felt that "internal problems are weakening...labor union growth"; 59.5 percent disagreed in 1983, down a bit from 65 percent in 1963. But the same officers reacted more positively to the statement that the leaders hold "values of self-sacrifice, idealism, and dedication." The ratio of agreement to disagreement was much greater in 1983, 48 percent to 37, than in 1963, 43 to 44.

The answers do not mean that union leaders are satisfied with their situation, particularly in the 1980s. Close to three-quarters,

71 percent, believed in 1983 that "labor's collective bargaining power is weaker today" than in the past, an increase from 51 percent in 1963. Similarly, large majorities, 73 percent in 1983 and 64 percent in 1963, said there is a "lack of vitality in the labor movement." Surprisingly, only 51 percent in 1983 thought there is a "crisis in the labor movement." Those who felt that there is a crisis were then asked "What are the problems causing the crisis?" "The most frequently identified problems ... were union policies and structure, 'antilabor' government policies, and labor's public image."[13] Few mentioned the economy, union leadership, or the policies or activities of employers.

Union Power: A Source of Concern

Although the union leader respondents in the 1983 survey were convinced that the negotiating power of unions to affect wages and benefits had declined considerably, the opinion polls indicate that a major source of the public distrust of labor is the view that they are overly powerful and that they abuse their strength. Consistently the most common response in polls that ask whether particular groups have too much or too little power has been that unions are too powerful, even among those who approve of them. In a 1965 Gallup survey, for example, in which 70 percent of the respondents affirmed that they approved of labor unions "in general," 57 percent of the respondents agreed that "unions have too much power in this country." In 1974, Harris found that 63 percent of those surveyed believed that unions had too much power, 22 percent replied that they had just the right amount of power, and 6 percent said too little. Even union members felt that unions were too powerful, by 48 to 11 percent.

Two years later, in 1976, the Center for Political Studies (CPS) asked whether "labor unions have too much influence, too little influence, or about the right amount of influence on American life and politics today?" They reported that 64 percent answered "too much," 25 percent said "the right amount," and only 5 percent responded "too little." In September 1981, the CBS News/*New York Times* poll repeated the CPS question and found that hostility to unions had declined slightly, although the great majority, 60 percent, still felt they had too much influence, compared to 22 percent who said "the right amount," and 11 percent who answered "too little." Even among respondents who belonged to union members' families, 51 percent thought unions had too much influence.

A majority of the public, 53 percent, told CRI interviewers in 1978 that "labor unions have too much political power," compared to 7 percent replying "too little" and 25 percent, "about the right amount." When asked in the same survey, "In general, which side do you think has more power—business or labor unions?" 50 percent answered labor unions compared to 33 percent for business. The CRI respondents also said, by 44 to 31 percent, that "the present labor laws ... tend to favor labor unions [rather than business] in a dispute." In an analysis of the 1977 SRC study limited to employed persons, Kochan reported that two-thirds believed unions are more powerful than employers.[14] In four polls conducted between 1977 and 1980, Yankelovich, Skelly, & White found that about 70 percent consistently agreed with the statement, "Unions are too powerful in our economy." In 1980, in a national survey focusing on the problems of the American economy, Penn and Schoen reported that only 18 percent stated that "too much union power" was "not really a problem." Close to half the respondents thought it was a major problem, while 32 percent said it was a minor problem. Among the same national cross section, a majority, 53 percent, said they "would be more likely to vote for a political candidate who favored ... reducing union power," compared to 35 percent who said they would be less likely to support someone who took such a position. Not surprisingly, union members backed the minority view: 53 percent of them said they would oppose an anti-union candidate; but still over a third, 36 percent, would back one who favored weakening unions. In 1984, a Harris poll found that 57 percent agreed with the statement, "unions have become too powerful and should be restricted in the abuse of their power by law," while 34 percent disagreed.

One of the most extensive comparisons of the public's assessment of institutional power was carried out by the Roper poll in December 1978. Roper inquired "whether you think the country would be better or worse off if certain groups had more influence and freedom to do what they think best." Labor unions obtained the most negative evaluation of the seven groups tested; over six times as many people said the country would be worse off rather than better off if labor had more influence (64 percent worse off, 10 percent better off). The public also disapproved of more influence and freedom for business and government, but by smaller margins, by two to one, people felt that the country would be worse off rather than better off if business had more influence, while majorities of three to one felt that more authority for Congress and the administration would be bad for the country. The public was only slightly negative toward the press (five to four), while it approved greater influence for scientists and "educators in the public schools" by roughly two to one.

In November 1981 and again in January 1985, Roper returned to the topic with somewhat different wording, asking whether various groups and organizations had "too much influence, too little influence, or about the right amount of influence." Labor unions headed the list of excessively influential special interest groups, with 46 percent in 1981 and 57 percent in 1985 identifying them as such. Business and industry organizations (corporations) were second with 32 percent in the earlier survey and 51 percent in the latter crediting them with undue influence.

The best indicator of trends in public feelings about union power is to be found in eight ORC polls taken between 1971 and 1985, which asked respondents to react to three statements about union power. In each survey, the most favored response, given by from two-fifths to a majority, has been that unions are too strong, while a fifth or less have said that unions are not strong enough (Table 9).

The ORC polls indicate some increase in the size of the minority who feel that unions are too weak, from 8 percent in 1975 to 18 in 1977, and a further slight change to 20 percent in 1982 and 1985. But there has been no consistent decline in the proportion who see unions as overly powerful. The 1985 figure, 46 percent, is the same as that reported for 1972 and not much below that of the mid-1970s.

ORC found similar results when comparing judgments about relative union and employer power in December 1977 and March 1985. Unions were perceived to have the edge over employers in both polls, 60 percent to 14 in 1977 and 45 percent to 24 in 1985. Congruent with the findings in Table 9, the numbers believing

Table 9
Attitudes Toward Power of Labor Unions
(Percent)

"Please tell me which one statement best describes the way you feel about labor unions in this country: (1) Labor unions today are not strong enough. I would like to see them grow in power. (2) Labor unions today have grown too powerful. I would like to see their power reduced. (3) The power that labor unions have today is about right. I would like to see it stay the way it is."

	Too Powerful	Power About Right	Not Powerful Enough
1971	55	24	14
1972	46	31	10
1974	42	33	10
1975	50	29	8
1976	52	28	9
1977	51	26	18
1982	48	25	20
1985	46	31	20

Source: Opinion Research Corporation

that unions are more powerful had fallen over the eight year period. But still in 1985, respondents seeing organized labor as stronger outnumbered those viewing employers as advantaged by almost two to one.

Though most Americans seem to view unions as more powerful than business when queried about the two, people are less consistent in their views when asked to evaluate the power of unions compared with *big* business or *large* corporations. When faced with the latter choice, the public often, though not always, is more likely to see big business as the stronger. In Roper polls taken in 1973, 1974, 1977, and 1983, slightly larger proportions said "big business corporations" had too much power than felt the same way about labor unions in three of the four surveys. These polls asked about the power of thirteen different groups and organizations, including the press, various government agencies, and interest groups, and found that labor unions and big business corporations were the only ones consistently judged by substantial majorities as being overly powerful. The percent feeling this way about unions rose from 55 in 1973 to 65 in 1977 and then fell back to 56 in 1983, while concern about big business corporations declined from 66 percent in 1973 to 65 in 1977 and to 56 in 1983.

Gallup found a similar pattern of varying reactions in the responses to questions inquiring about potential threat rather than power. When he asked "Which of the following will be the biggest threat to the country in the future —big business, big labor, or big government?" in polls taken from the 1960s to the 1980s, there was no consistent pattern as between "big business" and "big labor." "Big government," however, was always seen as the greatest danger, by proportions ranging from 39 to 51 percent. Larger percentages cited "big labor" (21–26) than "big business" (12–23) in surveys taken in 1967, 1968, and 1977. In 1979, however, 28 percent viewed "big business" as a greater potential threat than "big labor," 17 percent. In 1981 and 1983 the two institutions were tied, with 23 percent naming each in the former and 19 or 18 percent in the latter. There was a small change in the most recent poll, taken in 1985, with slightly more, 22 percent, mentioning big business compared to 19 percent for big labor.

The cue that affects the variation in response to large corporations or big business as compared to business is clearly the indication of size. When Americans are asked to react to the power of unions and business, they seemingly see unions as a large monolithic organization or movement, while business is perceived as a more diversified group composed of assorted companies, big and small. Hence, they express greater concern about union power. But when the contrast is with big business, both institutions are perceived as overly powerful, with big business seen as slightly more powerful, and, therefore, more threatening to the public welfare. "Small business" is thought to be weak and deserving of more influence and power. It is clear that in the case of business, as with labor unions, the public sees large units in much more negative terms than smaller ones. Americans, therefore, would like to see large corporations broken up, as the abundant poll data reported in *The Confidence Gap* document.[15] Thus, when CRI inquired in 1976, "Can you tell me whether you favor or oppose breaking up national labor unions into smaller, less powerful groups?" 50 percent favored the suggestion, while 25 percent were opposed.

Unions and Workers

The fear of union power does not imply distrust of the unions' constituency, namely workers. In 1972 and 1976, CPS asked respondents to its national elections surveys whether various groups have too much, too little, or about the right amount of "influence in American life and politics." Among the groups inquired about were "labor unions" and "workingmen." The results for these two groups are presented in Table 10.

Clearly, Americans perceive labor unions as being too powerful, while "workingmen" are seen in opposite terms. Between 1972 and 1976, the percentage who said that unions have *too much* influence went up. The public apparently differentiates between union power and workers' power. A comparable difference is evident in feelings about "workingmen" and "labor unions" as gauged by the CPS feeling thermometers. An extremely high proportion, 88 percent, expressed positive feelings about workers in the 1976 poll, compared to only 32 percent for labor unions. CPS repeated the feeling thermometer question in 1980 and found 93

Table 10
Evaluation of the Influence of Unions and Workers in American Life and Politics
(Percent)

"Some people think that certain groups have too much influence in American life and politics, while other people feel that certain groups don't have as much influence as they deserve. Here are three statements about how much influence a group might have. For each group I read to you, just tell me the number of the statement that best says how you feel: (1) Too much influence; (2) Just about the right amount of influence; (3) Too little influence."

	Too Much Influence	About Right	Too Little Influence
1972			
Labor Unions	56	33	4
Workingmen	3	49	44
1976			
Labor Unions	64	25	5
Workingmen	4	38	53

Source: Center for Political Studies, University of Michigan

percent favorable toward "working men and working women" compared to 50 percent for labor unions.

A similar variation between the way the two are viewed by most Americans is reported by ORC in three surveys conducted between 1981 and 1985 cited earlier, inquiring into ratings of the "ethical and moral practices of different groups and institutions." In each poll, over 70 percent judged the behavior of "average workers" as good or excellent, compared to less than 25 percent with comparable evaluations of organized labor.

The apparent tension between unions and workers in the public's view may be seen in the opposition of Americans to the idea of a union shop (i.e., the requirement that all workers must join a union in companies which have a contract). Gallup and ORC have repeated relevant questions a number of times since 1965. Gallup asked, "Do you think a person should or should not be required to join a union if he or she works in a unionized factory or business?" In 1965, 44 percent said they should be so required, while 49 percent disagreed. By the spring of 1977, the percentage approving of a union shop had fallen to 31, while 63 percent were opposed to it.

A similar trend is evident in seven surveys taken by ORC between 1965 and 1980 that inquired:

Which among these [three] arrangements do you favor for workers in industry?
(a) A man can hold a job whether or not he belongs to a union [open shop]; (b) A man can get a job if he doesn't already belong but has to join after he is hired [union shop]; (c) A man can get a job only if he already belongs to a union [closed shop].

Put this way, the proportion favoring the first alternative, the open shop, increased from 60 percent in 1965 to 68 percent in 1974 and 75 percent in 1976, and then held constant at 73 to 74 percent in 1977 and 1980. Very few, 4 percent or less, supported a closed shop while sentiment for the union shop declined from 32 percent in 1965 to 20 percent in 1980.

In 1978, Cambridge Reports, Inc. presented respondents with a statement that explained the case for the union shop: "Some people say that if a majority of employees of a firm or factory want to have a labor union, then every employee should have to pay dues to the union since the union will be representing them. Do you agree with this idea or not?" Given this argument, 39 percent endorsed the union shop, but 46 percent still opposed the policy. Clearly, most Americans do not approve of workers being required to join or pay dues to unions as a condition for employment, and the proportion opposed has been steadily increasing.

It may be noted that one poll which sought to evaluate the public concern with the ways in which business and labor organizations use their power to inhibit the democratic rights of workers found much more concern about labor. In 1978, Public Interest Opinion Research asked: "Which do you think is a bigger problem — companies that unfairly deny their workers a chance to join a union? Or unions that do not fairly represent their members?" Only 17 percent replied companies; 68 percent said unions.

The Effects of Unions on Inflation

Although the rate of inflation has declined greatly during the Reagan years, fear of increasing prices which undermine real income and form a particular threat to pensions and savings remains a major source of concern to many Americans. That fear may help explain much of the continued disdain for organized labor, since in the public mind, unions have borne much of the responsibility for higher prices, even though they have made major concessions in wages and working conditions during the eighties. During past inflationary periods, Americans have seen them as more culpable than business, although considerably less to blame than government. Both Gallup and ORC found this pattern in ten surveys taken between 1968 and 1979. These polls asked respondents to choose business, labor, or the government as the "most responsible for inflation." In a 1968 Gallup poll, for example, 46 percent blamed the government, 26 percent chose labor, and 12 percent business. By 1978, ORC found 57 percent blaming the government, 29 labor, and 15 business. The results changed slightly in a mid-summer 1979 ORC survey, which showed 54 percent holding the government primarily responsible, with labor and business each blamed by 22 percent. The government was held responsible by the largest proportion in all ten polls, always followed (at a significant distance) by labor. Business was consistently in last place, except in the 1979 ORC poll.

The propensity of the public to hold labor more responsible for inflation than business was brought out even more strikingly in two polls conducted for *U.S. News and World Report* in 1975 and 1977. These surveys did not require respondents to select just one culprit, but rather asked for separate evaluations of several possible causes of inflation. Respondents were asked to agree or disagree with each of four statements: that "business is *mostly* to blame for inflation," "government is *mostly* to blame for inflation," "labor unions are *mostly* to blame for inflation," and "the general public is *mostly* to blame for inflation" (emphasis in questionnaire). While four separate responses were solicited, the context of the question was clearly comparative, given the emphasis on the word "mostly" each time.

In the results of these polls, the four attributions grouped quite clearly into two pairs. Government and labor were blamed by most people; the general public and business were not. Given the statement, "government is *mostly* to blame for inflation," 67 percent agreed and 22 percent disagreed in 1977. In the case of labor unions, agreement (blame) outweighed disagreement by 64 to 24 percent. The sample disagreed, however, 52 to 33 percent, that "the general public is *mostly* to blame for inflation." And when asked whether business was "*mostly* to blame," disagreement here too outnumbered agreement by 57 to 30 percent. Overall, then, about two-thirds blamed government and labor, while only one-third held either the general public or business responsible.

Polls taken in the early 1980s by NBC News and the *Los Angeles Times* suggested the public might be in the process of changing its mind about the culpability of unions for inflation. The proportion holding government responsible increased sharply, while organized labor fell below business, particularly when the question mentioned big business. And in 1984, Harris reported that when offered different evaluations of union wage demands, only 37 percent cited them as a "major reason" for inflation, while 28 percent said they "have not been a greater cause" than other factors, and 22 percent felt that they "have been remarkably restrained and moderate in order to save the jobs of their members." These changes in attitudes toward union culpability are undoubtedly related to the decline in the rate of price and wage increases from 1981 to 1983, and the maintenance of a steady low level since.

Still, many have not given up their concern that union wage pressure has a negative effect on the economy. When asked in the 1984 Harris poll cited above: "How responsible have the auto ... [steel] unions been for the competitive trouble of these industries in recent years?" close to half, 49 percent for autos and 45 percent for steel, said unions bear "a great deal" of the responsibility. Almost a third, 30 percent, answered "some but not a lot" for each, and one out of seven, 14–15 percent, replied "little or none."

Perhaps the most surprising finding indicating the public's continued concern is contained in the results of six Roper surveys taken between 1975 and 1984, which invited respondents to choose among four statements bearing on union wage policy. Although there was a slight increase in the proportion supporting statements that approve of wage increases between 1982 and 1984, from 6 to 9 percent for getting the largest increase possible and from 30 to 35 percent for "cost of living adjustments," a majority, 52 percent, down from 59 percent, chose the two statements that called on labor union leaders to forget about wage increases or to "hold the line" (Table 11).

The same six Roper surveys included the question: "In today's times, do you feel that most union leaders are being reasonable and responsible, that some of them are, or that very few of them are?" Not surprisingly, given the judgments about union wage policy reported in Table 11, very few in any poll said that "most" labor leaders are being reasonable. The percentage giving this response has varied over the years between 10 and 13 percent; it was 12 percent in 1982 and 1984. Conversely, those replying that "few" union officials have been responsible has ranged between 36 and 46 percent. The figure has been around 40 percent from 1980 to 1984.

Conclusion

The studies and data reported here add up to a dismal picture for organized labor. Clearly, most Americans, including a majority of the employed labor force, view trade unions in negative terms, as overly self-interested, overly powerful within the larger polity, unrepresentative of their membership, and led by officers, many of whom are corrupt and autocratic, disdainful of the needs of the

Table 11

Attitude to Union Negotiating Policies
(Percent)

"Which of these 4 statements comes closest to expressing the position you think should be taken by labor union leaders in negotiations coming up during the next year or so with the country's large industrial companies?"

	1975 May	1977 May	1978 May	1980 April/ May	1982 April	1984 April
A. They should try to get the largest possible wage increase for their members because that is what everyone else is trying to do.	6	9	7	8	6	9
B. They should hold down trying to get wage increases except for cost of living adjustments	31	40	34	38	30	35
C. They should forget about any wage increases for the time being, and only work for needed improvements in working conditions and benefits	15	14	14	14	20	19
D. They should hold the line on both wages and benefits in order to check inflation and protect jobs	38	31	37	34	39	33
E. Don't know	10	6	7	6	5	5

Source: The Roper Poll

country. At the same time, however, they see unions as needed to protect workers against corporations who would take advantage of them economically and in terms of working conditions.

Both the Gallup series of questions on approval of labor unions, which goes back to 1936, and the Harris estimates of degree of confidence in the leaders, which have been taken since 1966, suggest that faith in unions is still at a nadir, lower than that of big business or major companies. These findings are reinforced by many other surveys which, while not of the same duration with respect to repeating questions, do not indicate an improvement in the feelings about labor organizations.

These results do not bode well for the efforts of the labor movement to reverse the decline in membership and losses in representation elections. Richard Freeman, a sympathetic close student of trade unions, estimates that unless current trends are reversed, by "the year 2,000 unions will represent only 13 percent of all nonfarm workers,"[16] back to their position in 1930 before the gains made under the New Deal and during World War II. I try to account for the decline in some detail in Chapter 17.

Such pessimistic conclusions have been challenged by some who see a large group available for recruitment in the findings that between a quarter and a third of all employees who do not belong to labor organizations say they would vote for union representation.[17] But as Stephen Hills reports, the most important factor, by far, differentiating supporters from opponents of unions within the American employed labor force is whether or not they are currently involved in unions.[18] The large majority of nonunion workers in every industry except public administration state that they will not vote for union representation. Reporting on data collected in the National Longitudinal Surveys of younger male workers, Hills notes that "neither the differences in the characteristics of men employed in the union and nonunion sectors nor differences in the nature of their jobs explain the widely differing attitudes."[19] And he concludes that these "data imply that sharp limits may exist for the expansion of U.S. unionism unless dramatic changes take place in either the social or economic climate of the country." Meanwhile, according to Freeman, the union "share of the nonfarm, private work force is shrinking annually by 3 percent per year as members retire or lose their jobs in the smoke stack industries." But unions are winning only 0.3 percent of the work force every year in representation elections.[20] And nothing in this review of public and worker attitudes suggests that the negative feelings about organized labor are changing.

The contracts labor unions have signed in recent years involving givebacks of past gains, including wage increases which on the average are below the rise in the cost of living index, have not, as yet at least, resulted in an improvement in the image of the institution or of the responsibility of its leaders. A national survey conducted by ORC in February 1986 found that 57 percent felt that employers should "start taking a harder line" with unions than in the past. Conversely, only 39 percent said that "it's time unions took a tougher stand with management and not make more concessions." And the percentage replying that unions are necessary to "protect the interests and well-being of the average worker," while still a slight majority, fell to an all-time low for this poll, 53.

To sum up, the evidence is quite clear from a large number of surveys that the public views labor in contrasting lights. First, significant majorities see unions as legitimate forces in a democratic society, important in preventing the exploitation of their members and in serving the interests of the less privileged. Although the proportions voicing approval of and confidence in trade unions have declined greatly since the mid-1960s, unions are still regarded as necessary group defense mechanisms by majorities in the most recent poll on the subject. Most Americans who are normally sympathetic to the needs of the weak and the underprivileged do not classify labor organizations among the oppressed. Rather, like big business, they are seen as powerful and essentially self-serving. But corporations have an advantage in that the public also thinks they inherently contribute to the community in the form of jobs, goods, and services. Unions are perceived as worse than business in two respects; first, they are viewed as giving low priority to the public interest and as working against the good of the whole society, and second, their leaders are believed to be exceptionally corrupt and unethical. In short, the principal virtue of unions is that they serve the interests of their members. Their principal defect is that, by doing exactly that, unions seem to do little to benefit the public interest.

13

HERMAN BENSON

The Fight for Union Democracy

If you studied American government in a civics class using only the text of the Constitution, you might learn what the rights of citizens and the separation of powers are supposed to be, but the subject would remain a lifeless husk. Where would you find the struggles of parties and factions and interests? Any study of union government that relied mainly upon formal constitutions supplemented by printed convention proceedings and massive official files would remain just as limited, that is, false. A significant part of the street-life record of union government was originally available on flimsy newsprint and cheap mimeograph sheets, as handbills passed out by protesters and oppositionists outside union halls and at factory gates. At a time when labor historians and sociologists were not aware or interested, these papers yellowed and crumbled away. In the past fifteen years, especially since events in the United Mine Workers (UMW) focused attention on oppositional currents, there has been a change. Nevertheless, in all that is read and written on the subject of union government, we are inescapably dependent upon a selective and one-sided record. This preliminary caution is necessary because the nature of union government is shaped not only by the action of official bodies—which are amply documented—but also by movements in the rank and file below, where records are missing or scanty.

Organization and Oligarchy

The American labor movement is an assemblage of sovereign powers, 200-odd individual national unions (usually called "internationals" because they include some Canadian local affiliates) that represent employees in collective bargaining. About half the unions, with some three-quarters of the total membership, are affiliated with the "House of Labor," the American Federation of Labor-Congress of Industrial Organizations (AFL-CIO), a connection that leaves them as free and autonomous as any government represented in the United Nations. However, in the AFL-CIO, unlike the UN, a gentlemen's agreement restrains affiliates from criticizing one another's blemishes so that the officialdom of one union may conduct its affairs as it sees fit, corruptly and dictatorially, even honestly and democratically, without fearing public repudiation from the officials of another.

AFL-CIO influence over affiliates is essentially moral; the only substantive authority it exercises is the power to suspend or expel, a power used only rarely and under the most extraordinary conditions.

In theory, unions are constitutional democracies ruled from the bottom up; in reality they are oligarchies, some more absolute, some more limited, ruled from the top down by an administrative team dominated by national officers.

Levels of Union Government

Every union constitution provides for some form of representative government. When the Labor Management Reporting and Disclosure Act (LMRDA) commonly known as the Landrum-Griffin

Act, went into effect in 1959, many unions were compelled to amend their constitutions to strengthen the rights of members to elect officers by secret ballot, directly in membership referendums or indirectly through delegates to conventions. But even before 1959, union constitutions prescribed, at least on paper, some method of election from below.

The basic unit of national (or "international") unions is the local. Local unions in manufacturing may be limited to the organization of workers in a single large plant or, in the case of so-called "amalgamated" locals, of workers in a group of small plants in a contiguous area. Construction trades locals will enroll all workers in a single craft in a specific geographical zone: a city, metropolitan area, a state, several states. Trucking locals can be based upon a specific branch of the industry in a given locality: milk truck drivers, local delivery drivers, United Parcel drivers, and warehouse workers. Government employees' locals may be constituted by county, city, or state; there are some statewide locals so large that they are subdivided by city or department: labor, finance, social services, etc. A few unions maintain a single national structure without any formal locals, e.g., seafaring unions (based on branches but with union-wide, individual membership); but these are exceptions and even they provide some form of representation by subdivisions in the election of national convention delegates.

Some unions group locals into various intermediate bodies by locality, industry, or company, e.g., Painters' district council for all New York locals, Machinist lodges of employees of the same airline, auto locals of Chrysler employees. These intermediary groups exercise limited authority over locals and are, in turn, subject to the authority of the national organizations.

Outside the organizational structure of the individual, independent, sovereign national unions are the various AFL-CIO city and state central bodies, which are directly controlled by the federation in Washington and exercise no authority over their local affiliates. They conduct public relations, promote union labels, endorse local political candidates, and occasionally coordinate local activities around some general social issue, e.g., right-to-work legislation or support for some major strike in their locality.

Closest to the average rank-and-file member is the local union.

It is here that the dues-payers can assess their leadership with reasonable accuracy, watching how grievances are processed, how local meetings are conducted. Since by federal law local officers are elected at least every three years by secret ballot membership referendum, union members can have direct control over their local leaders, assuming an honest count—which is not always guaranteed.

It is here in the locals, and only here, that frequent turnover of leadership occurs. Where discontent with the national union mounts but members are frustrated by an inability to reach the national structure, they express their dissatisfaction, from time to time, by defeating local incumbents and electing oppositionists.

That said, it must be qualified. Although life in the locals offers the maximum potential for direct membership control, the actual government can range from town hall democracy to a miniature version of totalitarian dictatorship, and anything in between, depending upon the character of the industry and the quality of democracy in the national organization. In a local composed of a few thousand workers in a single plant, where they enjoy seniority protection and where the national union (for example, the United Auto Workers) will protect fair elections, due process, and internal civil liberties, it is easy for critics, dissenters, and opposition caucuses to reach the whole membership at the plant gates. But in a large amalgamated local whose members are scattered over many small plants, it is difficult for insurgents to get their message out, and nearly impossible if the location of plants under contract is treated like a classified national security secret by the incumbents. However, every three years at election time, an opposition can get a shot at the membership if it can afford the costs. Federal law requires the union, at a candidate's request, to mail his or her literature to the membership, but at the candidate's own expense.

In public employee locals with a sprawling statewide membership, it is a formidable task for an opposition to reach the union electorate. On the other hand, employee job rights are protected by civil service rules; the membership often includes highly educated individuals accustomed to formulating proposals and exercising administrative responsibility. That kind of membership can overcome obstacles and present a serious challenge to entrenched local leadership.

In quite a different world are the locals of workers in the construction industry where jobs are temporary, work is seasonal and without effective seniority protection, and workers with jobs on one construction project are already wondering where the next will come from. Job distribution is often controlled by business agents (BAs) who cultivate amicable relations with employing contractors and make side deals so that the agent's own supporters get the most lucrative jobs. Dissenters and troublemakers who file grievances on the job or in the union can find it hard to get any work. In an average local of, say, 1,000 members where perhaps thirty attend meetings regularly, any shrewd BA can dominate the local with a tiny band of favored supporters whose loyalty is sealed by the selective administration of job patronage. They vote properly at meetings to assure that malleable committees will be selected to supervise referendums and elections. In the worst case, exceptional but unfortunately not rare, a local can be taken over by organized criminals and the membership rendered helpless by threats, beatings, even murder.

These are the locals, in all their diversity, which constitute the base upon which the constitutional structure of national unions is erected. They elect delegates to national union conventions, which are theoretically the supreme authority in union government. Conventions may adopt or amend constitutions, act as the final court of appeals in internal union disputes, set policy. In a minority of unions, the national leadership is still elected by membership referendum, e.g., Steelworkers, Machinists, Miners; but in most unions, convention delegates, presumably elected in locals by secret ballot, elect national officers and executive board members, whose maximum term of office, by federal law, is five years. These officers and these boards run the national union between conventions and enjoy an almost unlimited authority to conduct its affairs.

Since the formal structure requires election from below, direct or indirect, the labor movement is composed of constitutional democracies. Actually, however, the constitutional prescriptions are not enough to assure democracy, because the whole process of union government, including the election of officers is closely controlled from above.

The "Official Family"

In the Steelworkers, former president I. W. Abel described the union administration collectively as the "official family." It is not only official, it is permanently organized, disciplined, and solidified by the common interests of its adherents in holding power. There is nothing inherently improper or undemocratic in the maintenance of a separate caucus, formal or informal, to support an administration. In any democratic system, incumbents surely deserve the same right to organize for holding onto power as does any opposition to remove them.

The problem of democracy in union government resides in the vast discrepancy in power, organization, and resources between the administration and any possible opposition, whether that opposition arises out of the rank and file or the secondary leadership. Union administration is power permanently mobilized, not merely to deal with employers but also to guarantee the continued dominance of the incumbent officialdom. Oppositions, on the other hand, are usually temporary movements thrown together from time to time in response to some specific events or grievances; they find no permanent base in the union structure, except sometimes in the locals where their position is invariably tenuous.

Any local leadership is subject to the ordinary unpredictable vagaries of democracy. But an *insurgent* local leadership faces the added danger that the national administration, which it opposes, will encourage and support local rivals. Hanging over any stubbornly recalcitrant local is the threat of trusteeship or even dissolution.

Unlike any opposition, the national administration has stability and continuity. There is no power above it; and, barring a split in the official family, which is rare, an international leadership is guaranteed reelection year after year, decade after decade. Rival groups do not alternate in office; power is not peaceably transferred from one party to another. When some wracking crisis forces a shift in power, the process is closer to a convulsive revolution than democratic change.

Since the union structure provides no separation of powers, the regime concentrates in its own hands full legislative, executive, and judicial authority, subject only to the putative check of the national convention, a ponderous body that meets infrequently and is incapable of controlling the officialdom because it is itself a political body controlled by that officialdom. It is upon this solid wall of organized bureaucracy that the occasional wave of insurgency breaks.

In conception, there is nothing new here. Back in 1915, the sociologist Robert Michels described these relationships as the inevitable outcome of an iron law of oligarchy. Some forty years later, in their study of the International Typographical Union (ITU), Lipset, Trow, and Coleman tested Michels' analysis and arrived at gloomy conclusions on the fate of union democracy. Despite the "deviant" two-party system in the ITU, union government seemed doomed to be governed by Michels' iron law.

In 1956, in his foreword to the ITU study, Clark Kerr wrote:

This study raises many fundamental questions on which scholars will disagree, for the facts are as yet far from fully known, the definitions still open to question, and the value judgments and the prescriptions for action hotly contested.[1]

Since those words were written, almost thirty years have passed; and, while the facts can never be *fully* known, new experience requires a new look at the issues.

The conclusions reached by this writer, after more than forty years as a union member, labor editor, and executive director of the Association for Union Democracy, may seem contradictory at first: Everything that reinforces oligarchical tendencies has been evident in the American labor movement, sometimes in intense fashion; and in this sense, the iron law has been vindicated. Nevertheless, although the basis for oligarchy has been strengthened, the state of democracy inside the labor movement is healthier and more encouraging today than at any time in the forty years since the end of World War II.

The explanation for this paradox lies in the power of countervailing forces. National trade union regimes have been aptly described as "one-party states"—but not one-party *dictatorships*—because official power is limited by variously effective checks, not only from within by members and secondary leaders, but from without. The moral support of the nation, embodied in federal law, has shifted to the side of union democracy. As a consequence,

union reform movements have proliferated; and they have
rallied support from democratic-minded allies outside the labor
movement.

Self-Image of the Bureaucratic Caste

I. W. Abel expressed the self-image of labor leaders as a special
reigning caste in connection with Edward Sadlowski's challenge of
the 1973 election for director of the union's District 31 in Chicago.
It was in reply to a question posed by attorney Joseph Rauh that
Abel defined the union administration as the "official family."
The phrase implies more than a mere leadership faction, more the
flavor of royal family, entitled to certain transcendental rights.
The "family" had been accused of stealing the election, and
Sadlowski, the insurgent who had been counted out, had complained to the Labor Department. "And you feel," asked Rauh,
"that Mr. Sadlowski shouldn't have gone to the government
even though there was ballot stuffing?" Abel replied, "Correct,
correct."

From one of the official family who actually did some of the
stuffing came the self-justifying rationale that motivates any ruling group which imagines itself indispensable to the welfare of
humanity and hence relieved of the obligation of conforming to
the ordinary rules of democracy:

I took an oath to uphold the tenets and doctrines which our Constitution
sets forth; which calls upon all of us to preserve, protect, unify, and
solidify our International union. In the heat of a bitter election, to
preserve the principles I took an oath to uphold, I did what I thought was
right. I dedicated myself to prevent the destruction of our organization by
individuals whom I personally assessed to be extreme radicals; seeking
only to infiltrate into positions of leadership in our union to cause dissolution in the labor movement with their subversive propensities. . . .[2]

From time to time labor leaders reveal a predisposition for the
succession principles of hereditary monarchies. S. Frank Raftery
inherited the presidency of the Painters Union from his father
Lawrence. Angelo succeeded his father, Peter Fosco, as president
of the Laborers. Tommy Van Arsdale took over the giant Brotherhood of Electrical Workers Local 3 in New York from his father
Harry; Maurice Hutcheson, the Carpenters from father William.

Edward F. Carlough handed down the Sheet Metal Workers' union to Edward J., his son. William Presser didn't have the presidency to pass on, but he did give his son Jackie his start in the Teamster family.

Apart from bloodline inheritance, the officials learn how to become painlessly self-perpetuating. Before LMRDA mandated periodic union elections, a union could go for decades without elections, so that the transfer of office from one individual to another more closely resembled the transfer of power under a totalitarian regime than in a democracy. Between 1920 and 1941, for example, the Laborers union went without conventions or elections; the international executive board became a self-perpetuating bureaucracy that filled vacancies as they occurred, by death or jail sentence, at their own whim. Between 1928 and 1948 the Printing Pressmen held only one convention; its board of directors met not once between 1941 and 1947.

Now that periodic elections are a strict requirement of the law, it is common practice to minimize even the remote possibility of a serious challenge, or even an upset, by prudent preparations. For example, an international president who faces the looming age of retirement may accept reelection and then promptly resign to allow the international executive board, and not the membership or convention delegates, to fill the vacant spot. By the time the next election rolls around the official family choice is fully groomed as the incumbent, the electorate having been inured to his or her final ascension to power by an inner union public relations campaign, including the customary puffery in the official publications.

The Organizing Staff

At hearings before the Senate Labor Subcommittee in 1958, A.J. Hayes, then president of the International Association of Machinists and chairman of the AFL-CIO Ethical Practices Committee, estimated that there were 435,000 unionists "in positions of responsibility" in the trade union movement.[3] Sixty percent of those, he said, are unpaid. They are the foot-soldiers of the labor movement: the stewards, grievance chairpersons, local officers, executive board members, and all the other rank and file leaders who constitute the democratic base of trade union organization. Their voluntary activity is remarkable evidence of a degree of peoples' participation, more extensive than in any other private organization with the possible exception of the church.

Hayes reported too that there were "16,000 full-time paid national and international officials." These, the elected officers and the appointed staff of organizers and international representatives, are the cement that binds the national union together in the world of collective bargaining and politics; the staff has another function, at times more urgent than its outside public function. It is the machine, the elite corps, the shock troops charged with the duty of keeping the national regime in power.

The staff rides herd through the union to drum up support for the administration's position on any issue: dues increases, calling strikes on or off, adopting contracts, rallying support for constitutional amendments. They often serve as convention delegates, representing small locals too poor to send their own. John Herling computed that 40 percent of the locals were represented at the Steelworkers convention in 1968 by international officers and staff employees; of the union's 695 field staff employees, 562 were delegates. In a roll call when individual ballots are weighted by the local membership, they would have cast 13 percent of the total votes. But, he writes, "In the history of the Steelworkers, a roll call had never been held."[4] In 1968, it required the vote of 30 percent of all individual delegates to get a roll call; and in that calculation the vote of each staff delegate, regardless of how small the local, was equal to the vote of any other delegate, regardless of how large the local.

At conventions, the staff is free to roam the halls and hotels to convince wavering delegates—either by arguments, promises, or threats. When the Auto Workers was in its early rank and file stage, and hotly disputed issues were about to hit the convention floor, a chant would be taken up by the delegates: "Reps off the floor!" The chair would go through the ritual of instructing the union's employees to leave the convention. After Reuther had finally won firm control, when other delegates began the familiar litany, Reuther waived it aside and announced that staff members were entitled to remain. The change did not affect the situation in the union or the mood at convention; but the incident did demonstrate that the active membership understood the staff's duty to serve as the administration caucus's persuaders.

A key staff responsibility is to campaign for the administration in the election of union officers. When Ed Sadlowski ran for president as an insurgent in the Steelworkers in 1976–1977, he was backed by hardly half a dozen staff representatives. (The union votes by membership referendum.) In 1981 the union reported that there were 1,500 staff employees on its national payroll, but that figure included office clerks of all kinds. Of these 1,500, five hundred donated money to support the administration slate in the previous election and most were part of the union's basic field organizing and service staff. Their contributions swiftly filled the administration campaign coffer. Their watchful eyes guaranteed that the interests of the administration candidates would be amply protected at the 5,000 or more polling places.

At one point, it seemed that union officers might be compelled to curb the zeal of the staff members during elections and to force them to act more circumspectly. Sections 401(g) of the LMRDA provides that union resources cannot be employed to support any candidate for union office. Paid staff members campaigning on union time would appear to be a clear violation. But the U.S. Department of Labor, which has exclusive authority to enforce most of the law's election provisions, has interpreted that provision into oblivion. In 1977, when Sadlowski complained that the staff had blatantly campaigned for administration candidates on union time, the Department rejected his arguments, noting that staff reps had no set working hours, so that it was almost impossible to separate union time from their own personal time. The staff was therefore free to campaign any time during the day. Moreover, the Department held, even while on official union business, the staff could campaign if it was "incidental" to their assigned responsibility.[5] Under the best of circumstances, it is difficult for any opposition to police staff activities. After the Department's rulings, it is impossible.

Since the staff is hired and fired by the administration, usually by the international president, its own personal interests lie with that administration. Moreover, it is foolhardy for any recalcitrant to give open support to any opposition. But some might try to remain neutral or passive. When the LMRDA was first adopted, it

334   HERMAN BENSON

seemed as though its Bill of Rights, which established basic civil
liberties in unions, would offer some protection for the free speech
of staffers, especially those who held union cards. But in *Finnegan
v. Leu*, the U.S. Supreme Court held that the law's provisions
which protect unionists as *members* do not necessarily apply to appointed staff employees, who were therefore reduced at one stroke
to the status of patronage appointees at the mercy of the top officials. (At this writing, it is not clear whether the courts will protect even *elected* officers in the lower ranks of the hierarchy if
they criticize the official line. Future litigation will clarify that
issue.)

In 1976–1977, a public spotlight was focused on the Steelworkers national election. A memo circulated to the whole staff by
President Abel assured employees that they could support any
candidate without fear of reprisals, a policy that was repeated by
his successor, Lloyd McBride. After McBride died, the official
family fell out over the choice of his successor. Lynn Williams, who
defeated Frank McKee, soon demoted four unfortunate top staff
employees who had supported the wrong man. No staff employee
could possibly misunderstand the message.

Despite federal law designed to protect union democracy, the
field staff remains a disciplined cadre at the service of the national union administration in union elections.

The Professional Staff

Apart from its organizational staff, every national union of any
substance employs a versatile professional staff of editors, writers,
lawyers, public relations specialists, researchers, educational
directors, political affairs experts, historians, and others. Most are
directly on the union payroll; some are retained as independent
entrepreneurs. In normal times they serve the union in its dealings with employers and public. But if the administration is
threatened by opposition at election time, the professional staff,
no less than the organizational staff, is quickly converted into a
campaign apparatus.

It is simple enough to get around the provisions of the LMRDA
that bar the use of union resources to back candidates. Staffers
campaign, presumably on their own time, but who can watch

where and when they write those pieces extolling the officers' virtues? If they find it a nuisance to sidle about and differentiate between paid union time and private time and decide to go all out for the administration, employees may be granted vacations and engage in full-time campaigning for the incumbents. When the election is over, they regroup into their normal spots, a reserve army ready to close ranks and answer the call during the next election emergency.

In contrast, any opposition outside the official family power structure must hasten to improvise a makeshift amateur campaign staff, usually on the eve of an election. As if the balance were not one-sided enough, three major unions have recently adopted constitutional amendments that bar candidates from accepting contributions in cash or kind from anyone not a union member. The Steelworkers ban applies to candidates for national office. The IBEW electrical union goes further, applying to local and national elections; it even forbids a member of one IBEW local from donating to candidates in another IBEW local. The Service Employees rule, widest in scope, forbids candidates from accepting any assistance "direct or indirect" from a nonmember.

Barred from receiving donations or even non-interest loans from family and close friends, opposition candidates are compelled to squander valuable time soliciting dimes and dollars to get their effort airborne. Meanwhile, election day's winged chariot draws near.

The union press and legal staff are valuable political bodyguards for any officialdom. Major national unions mail an official publication to the home of every member. A few are interesting and well done. But many are dreary mixtures of propaganda for the official line on every subject, with house-organ stories on local activities. Family photos accompany stories on the sayings, writings, and doings of the officials, sometimes appropriately with reports on newsworthy events, more often highlighting their trivial comings and goings: President Smith receives plaque; Secretary Brown awards plaque; Vice-president Jones observes while Smith and Brown exchange plaques. With a few notable exceptions, the officialdom monopolizes the press; no oppositions exist in its pages, except from time to time when they are denounced as union wreckers and bosses' agents.

It is hard to know how widely the union press is read by the membership, probably not much, surely not avidly; most publications are too drab. The problem, therefore, is not that members are brainwashed by official propaganda. The effect of the monopolization of the press by the officialdom is not that it convinces the membership but that it creates an aura of leadership omnipotence, obliterates the notion that some alternative leadership might be possible, and demoralizes potential opposition among the active union cadres.

Union attorneys are hired to represent the union and its membership, which they do in "normal" periods when the union needs legal assistance in dealing with the outside world: the courts, the government, the employers. But when the leaders are in conflict with rank and filers or critics, dissidents, and insurgents, the attorneys invariably serve the incumbents. Lawyers become a main bulwark of the internal union power structure.

When a member faces trial inside the union, the attorneys advise the trial body, not the member. If the defendant is found guilty, fined, suspended, expelled, the attorney defends the discipline in court if necessary while union members must shift for themselves. If an opposition challenges election procedures, the union attorney is prompt to justify the official position.

The role of the union attorney in internal union affairs can be described, almost in parody, by the story told by many a dissenter: The union president, challenged from the floor by a critic, seeks support from celestial authority and turns to the attorney seated magisterially on the platform. Attorney pontificates before announcing that the full weight of judicial authority backs the precise ruling of the chair.

The International Brotherhood of Electrical Workers (IBEW) maintains a $5,000,000 legal defense fund that is deployed not merely to defend the union from legal attack from employers but also to protect the officialdom against the membership. If a member, expelled, goes to court, he or she must hire an attorney out of his or her own money. Union officials dip into the union fund. One U.S. Appeals Court noted that an IBEW member "believes the IBEW litigates union democracy lawsuits without regard to the costs or to the best interests of the members, simply to discourage members from bringing such lawsuits."

Legal aid is so crucial in internal union affairs that a national leadership will sometimes take extreme measures to deprive critics of such a resource. In 1967, the 22,000-member Lodge 837 of the International Association of Machinists at the McDonnell plant in St. Louis elected an insurgent local administration that sought autonomous rights in the district by a large majority. One day, the local lodge voted to retain an attorney to defend its interests; the very next day, the international imposed a trusteeship over the local, removed its officers, and took control of the substantial local treasury.[6]

After a lifetime as counsel for unions, unions leaders, and union insurgents, Joseph Rauh reached this conclusion:

> Union lawyers ought not to represent the union during contested elections because they always represent the incumbents. . . . Sadlowski [insurgent] was in the Steelworkers fight for more than a decade and never once did the Steelworkers lawyers take any position that differed from that taken by the incumbent Official Family. Not once! There must have been fifty opportunities to do otherwise. The only fair arrangement would be to have the union lawyers in an election situation become the lawyers for the incumbents, paid by them, and have some neutral agency—a court, or an arbitration association, or the bar—appoint a lawyer to represent the union. The union's interest and the interest of the members are separate and distinct from the interest of the incumbents. The interest of the incumbents is reelection, the interest of the membership is in a fair election.[7]

However, even if Rauh's suggestion were implemented, the balance in favor of the incumbents would not be eliminated but only mitigated. The incumbents would still be represented by attorneys whose expertise in the affairs of the union, in union democracy law, and in the industry had been acquired at the expense of the union and its members.

Trials, Appeals, Conventions

At hearings on trials and appeals, unions may provide a *lengthy* process, but, when dissidents are involved, seldom *due* process. There are usually written charges, hearings before committees, witnesses, and other trappings of due process but not necessarily the substance. The procedure is not judicial but political, it is inseparably intertwined with the union power structure. It is in this aspect of union government that the centralization of legislative, executive, and judicial functions proves most deadly to union democracy.

In the locals, an executive board may serve as the trials/appeals body, or a special committee may be chosen at union meetings. Decisions of the board may be subject to approval at membership meetings, so that an alert opposition occasionally can beat the system by mobilizing enough supporters to outvote the administration at a meeting or two. If the charges or appeals relate to union rules with no factional connotations, there is a reasonable chance for an impartial decision; but in cases wrapped up in the union's politics, the outcome depends less upon justice and fair play than upon who controls the board or the meetings.

In some unions, the national office can assert "original jurisdiction," remove a trial out of the local's jurisdiction, and appoint a "Special Trial Committee" to supersede the local body. Where the national officialdom decides that its own interests are at stake, it need not depend upon the unpredictable outcome of local membership opinion. The national officialdom easily rises above the membership in trials and appeals.

Dissatisfied members can appeal a local decision to higher union bodies. Once a case leaves the local upon appeal, the national administration is omnipotent. Appeals may go first to an international officer, then to the international president, to the international executive board, and finally to the convention. Appeals procedures lack even the appearance of due process for dissidents, who face a court composed of their political opponents.

Joseph Addison was subjected to a classic union trial in the California district of the International Association of Machinists (IAM) in 1961. An official IAM auditor had accused two top district union officers of misappropriating nearly $90,000 from the District 727 treasury. Addison filed charges against the two officials; they filed countercharges against him for slander. The international president appointed a special trial committee, which voted to expel Addison and to exonerate the two accused officials—both of whom happened to be political supporters of the national administration.

Only two unions provide a genuinely impartial agency, a public review board, as a kind of supreme court to consider appeals against the union's ruling bodies. One is the small, independent Association of Western Pulp and Paper Workers (AWPPW). The other is the United Auto Workers (UAW). Review board members are distinguished in their own professions, i.e., education, law, religion, are pro-labor civil libertarians, and have no organizational obligation to the union officialdom.

In the UAW, an aggrieved member has the alternative choices of taking an appeal either to the review board or to the convention. The board is empowered to overturn the decisions of the union's highest officers and its international executive board; and it has done so in highly controversial cases. It is prohibited only from intervening in matters concerning normal collective bargaining policy. Except for that limitation, its authority is wide-ranging. In adopting the public review principle, the UAW leadership surrendered a measure of its power. Apart from the small AWPPW, no other union officialdom is willing to take the risk of strengthening the rights of members in their own unions.

The supreme constitutional authority in union government is the convention. It sets policy; it is the final and highest step in appeals procedure; its delegates often elect the national officers. In theory, it disposes of powers like those of a combined U.S. Supreme Court and Congress, except that nothing is subject to presidential veto. And, since delegates are elected down below, by members in their locals, the convention is touted as the embodiment of democracy. The truth is quite different: the convention is the most perfect expression of the glaring gap between myth and reality. Except in a few unions or under unusual circumstances, the convention is normally a politically manipulated body easily controlled by the national officialdom.

One study of 1,725 convention appeals between 1945 and 1964 in 100 large unions found that the position of the international was reversed in only fifteen instances, and most of these were local autonomy cases. The national officers lost in only two cases of political significance; and in these,the result derived not from concern for justice but only because the appellants rallied their own political support.[8]

In major unions, conventions are large and cumbersome; thousands of delegates crowd into mass arenas where proceedings are—in fact, must be —carefully orchestrated by the national office. To prepare in advance policy resolutions and constitutional amendments, to devise convention rules, to hear appeals, special committees are appointed by the top officialdom. It is exceptionally difficult to initiate anything from the floor.

All proposals must be submitted to the delegates at some point for a vote, and in that requirement lies the potential, however remote, for an upset. But with the powers of the presiding chairperson, the national president can reduce that annoying possibility to the barest minimum. Voting is routinely by voice or by show of hands, judged by the chair. From time to time, after some ferociously disputed issue—dues, local autonomy, retirement age of officers—the shouted votes or raised arms may seem evenly divided to any impartial observer, or even to be running against the administration.

On such occasions, at UAW conventions, Walter Reuther would ask the delegates for each position to stand and move to separate sides of the hall where they could be accurately counted. But that is an unusually democratic union. Ordinarily it requires a thunderously one-sided roar of voices or a thick forest of arms to convince the chair that the administration has suffered one of its rare defeats.

When national officers are elected at conventions, and there is a contest, voting is usually by open roll call in which the choice of each delegate is publicly recorded. In unions where delegates can vote their choice without fear of retaliation an openly listed vote keeps delegates accountable to the members who elect them. But where opposition is treated as treason and those in power can punish their enemies, the lack of a secret ballot frightens off all but the most courageous or foolhardy.

The institution of conventions does not by itself democratize a union; rather, the union must be democratized before the convention can fulfill its theoretical role as a check on the officialdom. Precisely because the international officers begin with a near-monopoly of power and opposition seems hopeless, local leaders are reluctant to take a public stand in opposition to an establishment which has effective means of disciplining dissidents. In that atmosphere, the convention is deprived of fire and domesticated.

At rare moments, when the officialdom splits and there is a genuine contest between two more or less equal camps, the convention can come into its own as the final arbiter. That kind of event, however, occurs only at critical moments in the union's history.

In the constitutional requirement for a convention lies the sleeping spirit of membership control, but it needs the magic touch of democracy to awaken it to life. If challengers could reach the membership, could criticize without fear of retaliation, could get an honest count in elections, then the convention could be, as it already is in some unions, a genuinely democratic institution. Without these qualities, conventions remain only a simulacrum of democracy.

Normal and Abnormal Advantages of Incumbency

Superimposed upon the "normal" advantages of incumbency in one-party governments are certain extraordinary factors: a massive growth of insurance and welfare funds, racketeering, trends toward union conglomeration, dispersion of industry from concentrated metropolitan centers, and crude but widespread stealing of union elections.

All the traditional privileges of union power—high salaries, control over jobs, lavish expense accounts, possible payoffs from grateful employers or suppliers—are dwarfed by the perquisites available from insurance-type funds. A 5 percent "commission" for arranging a single $2,000,000 loan from a fund nets a fast $100,000. That explains how, according to one writer, the Central States Teamster fund, with 1.4 billion dollars in resources in 1976 could become a source of "venture capital for organized crime." Middle-level officials of the Laborers union in 1982 were convicted of collusion in tapping union benefit funds. In 1966, Dow Wilson and Lloyd Green, reform leaders in the San Francisco Bay Area Painters union, were murdered by two employers and a high union official when the two threatened to expose fraud in the union's insurance funds. In one 200,000-member local of state government employees in New York, the key issue that prompted the formation of an oppositional movement was the charge that the union's benefit fund, which paid out more than $35,000,000 in a single year for dentists, eye-care, and drugs, was being mishandled. In that same union, 6,800 county workers disaffiliated when their state union office tried to take control of the $3,500,000 benefit fund.

It is not likely that those who control such vast sums will passively let them dribble away merely because union members decide to cast little pieces of paper into ballot boxes.

These lucrative opportunities explain, in part, the persistence of high level corruption in the labor movement and its continued penetration by organized crime. Where racketeers take over a union, its membership is no longer confronted with the sociological phenomenon of one-party government but something more like criminal totalitarianism. A classic example is the domination of Teamsters Local 560 in New Jersey by the Provenzano family. The daughter of "Tony Pro" took over the local after he and then his brother went to prison. (Asked what her qualifications for office were, she replied, "I am a Provenzano.")

How widespread is racketeering in the labor movement? (I refer not to pilfering but to plunder.) This question is frequently posed but never resolved, not only because facts are elusive but because no one interested in the labor movement seems ready to face up to them. In any event, it is surely not simply a matter of "pockets" of corruption but of a deep-rooted malaise, an evil which permeates whole sections of the labor movement. The eradication of corruption is one of the great unfinished tasks of labor.

After the first revelations hit the McClellan Committee in 1957, George Meany, AFL-CIO president, commented, "We thought we knew a few things about trade union corruption, but we didn't know the half of it, one tenth of it, or the hundredth part of it."[9] When the CIO Executive Board met on February 24, 1955, Walter Reuther faced the problem in connection with the looming unity with the AFL and told his board,

> . . .it will clearly require bold courage to cleanse the labor movement of corruption, and it will require eternal vigilance to keep it clean. It is not an easy job, and if you think a united labor movement is going to mean we can sit back and say we have the declaration, we have the machinery, the job is won, you are deluding yourself . . . I think I know something about the forces we will have to meet, but I think the job can be done. . . . There are a lot of honorable people in the AFL leadership . . . we are equal to that challenge.[10]

But Reuther was sadly mistaken. The honorable people proved unequal to the challenge. After thirty years, the corrupt forces are as deeply rooted as ever, perhaps more so.

In 1958, Neil Chamberlain wrote, "No one knows how much labor racketeering goes on in the United States. It seems probable, however, that it represents a rather small fraction of total union activity."[11] The comment was prudent enough, but misleading. Of course racketeering is only a small fraction of "union activity." After all, unions are labor unions, not mere rackets! Lynching, for that matter, was only a small part of total activity in the old South. Crime is a small part of total activity in our cities. Even in a union badly infiltrated, like the Teamsters, racketeering is only a small part of the total activity of the hundreds of its locals. The point is that the rackets have penetrated so deeply that corruption has become a major problem. It poisons the labor movement just as surely as a few parts of a deadly chemical can pollute a whole water supply.

In 1959, after the abortive AFL-CIO campaign to eradicate corruption, Walter Galenson wrote, "The problem of corruption remained an unsolved one... in 1941.... [I]t was not until there occurred a drastic shift in internal power, occasioned by the merger between the AFL and CIO, that the American labor movement fully assumed its responsibility for eradicating the stain of corruption that had so long afflicted it."[12] Galenson, too, was mistaken. The shift in power went quite the other way.

How widespread? In recent years there have been major disclosures of widespread corruption in the construction trades, in the Teamsters, in the Laborers, in the Hotel and Restaurant union, in the Carpenters, Painters, east coast Longshoremen, Boilermakers. No one should indict an entire international union simply because locals are preyed upon by crooked officials. But, when there are repeated reports of corruption in one local and then another, and where the international turns its eyes away, then either the top national officials are unconcerned, or involved, or helpless. The inability of the labor movement to deal with massive corruption and racketeering is proof of how deeply they have corroded union government.

Union conglomerates. Labor history texts teach us that the old American Federation of Labor derived strength by organizing workers mainly by trades and sometimes by industry; and the CIO united mass production workers into cohesive industrial unions.

The great debate over craft v. industrial unionism is forgotten, both principles are obsolete. The labor movement today is becoming a motley combination of "one big unions" as every large union reaches out to organize anything anywhere; and jurisdictional lines crisscross and crumble. The trend seems slowest in the building trades, but is evident even there. When the Brotherhood of Painters, Decorators, and Paperhangers became the Brotherhood of Painters and Allied Trades, it was moving with the times. The Operating Engineers takes in coal miners. The Building Service Employees union drops the "Building" from its title and recruits everything under the sun and in the shadows: off-track betting employees and those at the tracks, nurses, public employees, university employees. Oil refinery workers become Seafarers; university professionals sign up as Auto Workers, or Hotel Workers, or whatnot. The Teamsters union was once restricted to drivers and warehousemen. No more. Free from the restraints of the AFL-CIO no-raiding pact, it reaches out into the whole universe of public and private employees. As jurisdictional boundaries vanish, unions disappear into one another. In the last six years, there have been twenty-nine mergers. The Packinghouse workers enter the Meat Cutters where they join together with the Furriers and the Retail Clerks and end up in the single conglomerated United Food and Commercial Workers. The historically ultra-democratic typographers will probably merge with an oligarchic union. Declining labor organizations all scramble to win over government workers so that public employees are mixed together with private employees in a medley of competing conglomerates. AFSCME woos telephone workers while the Communication Workers enrolls state government employees.

Meanwhile, industries disperse from their centers, and unions lose their cores of concentrated power. During World War II, three or four large Akron rubber locals wielded decisive influence in the union and could shut down the whole industry in an unauthorized "wildcat" strike. But Akron, as the rubber manufacturing center, is no more; the industry has departed, leaving behind only corporate offices. Birmingham, once a major steel center, is a university white collar and office machine concentration point.

As unions recruit a disparate membership, and steel, auto, and rubber plants scatter throughout the nation, the homogeneity of the union membership and its concentrated social power is drastically attenuated. The social weight of the rank and file falls, the power of the officialdom rises. The oligarchy remains the only centralized, organized, homogeneous force with clear common interests confronted by an atomized membership. Such is the modern tendency. Two unions that exemplify the trend in extreme fashion are the Teamsters and the Service Employees, each the equivalent of its own separate federation of labor. Unlike the AFL-CIO, however, their national officialdoms exercise central administrative authority over their affiliates below. In this odd fashion, the AFL-CIO principle of autonomy is yielding to centralization and increased power of the national officialdom over its membership.

Stolen elections. Election fraud is commonly viewed as a regrettable aberration not worthy of the attention of serious analysts; its long-term significance in suppressing opposition and solidifying the officialdom has been ignored. It is, however, a chronic danger when elections are hotly contested in big unions.

With some 75,000 locals electing officers at least every three years, and some more often, it would be impossible for any impartial private agency to police them all and impractical to depend upon any governmental bodies. For honest elections, most unionists will have to look to themselves; and in most locals, most of the time, that will be good enough. Where officers are unpaid or only minimally reimbursed for lost time, the motive for stealing elections is weak; and where voting takes place under the watchful eye of the membership, the opportunity is diminished. In some unions, by long habit and tradition, elections are honest; and members are assured of a valid count, short of some unusual crisis.

But in international unions (and some large locals) where immense power, big money, jobs, and prestige are at stake, the task of policing elections can be overwhelming. Here, where there is a substantial material motive for fraud the officialdom dominates the election process and can shape its course by control over the appeals procedures. Where national officers are elected at conventions by open roll call, it is almost impossible to falsify the count and hardly necessary so long as the officialdom continues to control the delegates. But where elections are by popular referendum in sprawling units, it is impossible for challengers to monitor the count. Ironically, voting by delegates makes it easy to get an honest count, but hard for any opposition to break through the bureaucracy to the membership; while in voting by referendum, it is easier to appeal to the membership but extremely difficult to assure an honest count. No opposition can marshal enough observers to watch the casting and counting of ballots in a big union. In the contested Steelworkers national election of 1976–77, even though the insurgents were well organized, they could muster observers in only some 800 out of 5,000 locals.

In 1965, the election for president of the International Union of Electrical Workers (IUE) was stolen by supporters of the incumbent, and the successful insurgent was installed in office only after a federal court impounded the ballots. The Miners election of international officers in 1969 was voided as fraudulent by a federal judge who ordered a recount, won by the insurgents. The United Steelworkers has had a long record of suspect elections, beginning with the contested election for vice president in 1955. In 1974 the U.S. Department of Labor upheld a complaint that the election for Steelworkers District 31 director had been stolen. Elections and referendums in Painters District Council 9, New York, were routinely stolen for years. In 1984 one of the officers of the 70,000-member Hospital Local 1199 in New York City admitted that he had participated in destroying thousands of ballots cast for opposition candidates and replacing them with fraudulent ballots marked for the incumbents. In every case, voting was by membership referendum.

A fraudulent count has an impact far beyond the outcome of a specific election. A fabricated tally falsifies membership opinion, and that fact remains even if the incumbents would have been easily reelected honestly. An opposition that actually garnered, say, 40 percent of the votes has no way of gauging the impact of its campaign if it is credited with only 10 percent. It is onerous enough for an opposition to mount a campaign in any big union. If on top of that normal disability it discovers that it cannot even get its vote recorded, that double burden is enough to demoralize its active supporters. Why go to all that trouble? There seems no point to running again. By stealing votes, an officialdom wins more than another term; it can discourage opposition and entrench itself permanently.

To sum up: the power structure in the contemporary labor movement appears overwhelmingly to confirm Michel's gloomy forebodings over the future of democracy in mass organizations and to vindicate the Lipset-Trow-Coleman misgivings about the possibilities for union democracy in the absence of a two-party system. But there is another side.

The Law

If the tendency toward oligarchy is inherent in the very nature of mass organization, it is possible to find opposition *in unions,* if nowhere else, in the form of counter-movements from below. Under certain conditions rivals can flourish even in the hostile environment of entrenched bureaucracy. Understanding all the obstacles, we can begin to examine the conditions that make for union democracy, beginning with the law.

To strengthen union democracy, Congress adopted the Labor Management Reporting and Disclosure Act of 1959. Passage of the act culminated a decade of public discussion in which corruption and democracy in unions emerged as a great national issue.

The transcript of six days of hearings before a House subcommittee was published in 1950 under the title "Union Democracy." By the mid-1950s a public investigation of corruption and suppression of union members' rights on the New York waterfront led to the expulsion of the International Longshoremen's Association from the AFL. Soon the television cameras were focused on hearings before the Senate McClellan Committee hearings that accumulated 20,000 pages of testimony in some forty volumes over a three-year period. Simultaneously, House and Senate labor subcommittees ran through their own extensive hearings. After so intense a scrutiny, the adoption of the LMRDA finally established a new moral atmosphere. The long debate over whether unions should be or could be democratic was finally resolved: the public interest demanded that unions had to be democratic.

In early 1959 Max Ascoli, editor-publisher of *The Reporter,* could editorialize about the "limited amount of democracy

organized labor can bear," adding, "[t]he institutions and principles of democracy can no more be transferred wholesale to the
realm of labor than to the realm of business. Indeed, democracy is
weakened and defiled whenever the attempt is made to extend it
beyond the range of public government."[13]

In 1958, at a conference on "Labor in a Free Society" Arthur
Goldberg, then counsel for the Steelworkers and the AFL-CIO
Ethical Practices Committee but not yet Secretary of Labor, enunciated his own rather crabbed conception of the nature of union
government:

> In discussion of union democracy, it is often assumed that the ideal
> would correspond to democracy as practiced in our political institutions.
> . . . The absence of competitive politics at the international union level, at
> least in most American unions, is regarded as a symptom of a lack of de-
> mocracy. . . . But is it true that we can uncritically transfer to unions the
> standards and criteria which we apply to governmental politics? I think
> a moment's examination will show that we cannot.
>
> If there is analogy to political government, the analogy is to a political
> government which may simultaneously face a revolution, and which is
> periodically at war. The constraints which by common consent we accept
> temporarily in the political arena when such conditions exist may
> perhaps explain and justify the existence of similar, although perma-
> nent, restraints in the practice of union democracy.[14]

The LMRDA brought that chapter in the debate to an end. In
the *Hotel Local 6* decision (1968), almost as though in direct
refutation of Mr. Goldberg, the U.S. Supreme Court noted:
". . .Congress' model of democratic [union] elections was political
elections in this country."

Could democracy survive in unions? That was the aim of the
law, and it created its own evidence to answer the question, for the
law stimulated a resurgence of union reform movements and led
to permanent changes in the nature of union government.

Looking back twenty-five years Clyde Summers, who wrote the
ACLU statement on democracy in labor unions in 1952 and whose
early writings on union democracy helped shape the character of
the law, concluded that the adoption of the LMRDA seemed like a
"political miracle." There was no organized lobby behind it, no politically powerful interests pressing for the defense of internal
union democracy. In the end, with rare and notable exceptions like
the Auto Workers, the labor movement opposed it. ". . . [T]here

was no organized group supporting legislation for union democracy," said Summers, "other than one of the less politically influential groups in this country, the American Civil Liberties Union."
He asked:

How did it come about? The most encouraging explanation is that there was deep down in the conscience of the American people, the belief that unions ought to be democratic. . . . There are times when values . . . are of such a nature that they have a political life and force of their own. . . . The statute was passed because it expressed the basic values of our society.

With or without an organized political constituency, the conception that union democracy merited public support had been germinating for decades. Repeated exposures of racketeering highlighted the need to protect members' rights in their unions, although union democracy is more than an antidote to corruption. However, it often requires extreme symptoms to expose some deep underlying disorder. Racketeering and corruption are such extreme symptoms in the labor movement.

As early as 1937, a Subcommittee on Labor Unions of the City Club of New York in addressing the issue of racketeering reported:

Experience has shown that *eradication of racketeering from a union can come only from an aroused and determined membership.* Sporadic prosecution is of little avail; one or two dishonest leaders are removed and others come to take their place. . . . the elimination of racketeering within a union must be primarily the concern of the membership, which is most directly affected by the racket. The problem is fundamentally one of promoting democratic control. (emphasis in original) [16]

In 1949, the House Labor Committee appointed a "Special Subcommittee on Union Democracy"; one of its five members was Representative John F. Kennedy. Although it consumed most of its limited time and meager budget on hearings on the Pressmen's union, its proceedings demonstrated a growing interest in what the committee referred to as ". . . the existence, nonexistence, or extent of undemocratic processes in labor organizations. . . ."

To a certain extent, the early concern for workers' rights inside unions was based upon a misunderstanding. As one researcher put it:

The notion that trade union members are the helpless captives of their

organizations and leaders is rather widely held. Particularly since the
development in the United States of large scale labor organizations, and
the concomitant bureaucratization of trade union government, there has
been a growing feeling in some quarters that rank and file members require protection from their leaders.[17]

The Smith-Connally Act of 1944 required a government-spon-
sored referendum before a strike. The Taft-Hartley Act of 1947 required a government-supervised vote of the membership before
unions could demand a union shop. Both these provisions were
dropped when the Smith-Connally referenda went 83 percent for
the official union position and the T-H ones, 91 percent. The
requirements were based upon the misconception that demagogic
union leaders were dragooning the mass of American workers into
extremist demands and irresponsible acts; and that if good, sober,
patriotic workers had a chance to express their true feelings, they
would take the prudent path of conciliation. Insofar as they dealt
with the relations between members and officers, these laws
sought to protect workers' rights *as against their unions*; and for
that reason they fell flat when workers displayed no enthusiasm
for being "liberated" from their unions.

In contradistinction, the Landrum-Griffin Act(LMRDA) of 1959
sought to protect *the rights of members inside their unions* and to
provide the democratic tools for reforming them from within.
Unlike the rank and file repudiation of the Smith-Connally and
Taft-Hartley acts, the response to the proposed LMRDA was evidence of a rising mood inside unions. "We received 150,000 complaints during the [McClellan] Committee's life," wrote Robert
Kennedy. "Seventy-five percent of them came from representatives of organized labor, mostly rank and filers."[18] Once the law was
adopted, demands for democracy and reform flooded one union
after another.

How effective can any law be as a means of strengthening the
position of union members vis à vis their officials? A quarter century of experience with the LMRDA provides the basis for a reply,
especially if we bear in mind that *this law* is ambiguous,poorly formulated in decisive aspects, that enforcement of its election provisions has been ineffective in the hands of a politically oriented
Secretary of Labor and that federal courts, which have sustained
some of its vital aspects, have erratically vitiated it in other

respects. Such judgments, at any rate, are held by those who have been most active in implementing the law to advance the cause of union democracy—people such as Joe Rauh, Clyde Summers, Chip Yablonski, Arthur Fox, Paul Alan Levy, Ed James, and Burton H. Hall.

Nevertheless, despite the law's built-in weaknesses, despite feeble enforcement, despite the erratic quality of court decisions, the law has made a decisive difference. One key to the future of democracy in American union government is the strengthening of law to protect it. Summarizing his own experience in a lecture on "Twenty-five Years of Landrum-Griffin," Joseph Rauh, one of the nation's eminent labor, civil liberties, civil rights attorneys, has said:

> ...when it (LMRDA) was first adopted in 1959 ... the law seemed to put an unnecessary and unseemly burden on labor unions. And I opposed it. ... I have always believed deeply that the labor movement is the strongest force for progressive social change in America. I still believe that. But...I also believe in Landrum-Griffin and I believe it's got to be strengthened if the labor movement is going to continue in that role.[19]

The law has established basic civil liberties inside unions and made sanctions against members on vague charges like "slander" or "causing dissension" illegal; it requires clearly formulated charges, presented enough in advance to permit charged members to prepare a defense.

Between 1960 and 1967 about two dozen insurgents were brought to trial on such charges in the Painters union in New York, and others in the same union in California and Minnesota. In every instance when the near-victims got into federal court, the judges voided the penalties and reinstated the reformers— some of whom, with their rights intact, went on to win victories in their local elections.

The law makes it possible to get into court promptly in union civil liberties cases without fear of retaliation, nullifying the standard, onerous clauses in pre-LMRDA union constitutions that threatened members with expulsion if they failed to exhaust their internal remedies before going to court, a process that could take years. In the course of election campaigns in the National Maritime Union (NMU), since the adoption of the LMRDA, opposition candidates were suspended from the union, only to be reinstated by federal courts; the NMU administration remains in power, but the potential for dissent has survived.

One smaller miracle within the larger "political miracle" of LMRDA is evident in the Teamsters union where a reform opposition has thrived, won posts in locals, and affected the course of two national trucker referenda.

Constitutional clauses that effectively barred oppositions from the ballot have been voided. Elections are still stolen, but with care and with legal help, insurgents are sometimes able to get an honest count where, without the law, they would have been helpless, as in the Steelworkers, the Painters, the Miners, the International Union of Electrical Workers, to mention only some major examples. The law guaranteed an honest count and enabled insurgents to win elections whereas in earlier years they would almost certainly have been compelled to submit to election fraud as an officialdom was imposed upon members. The law has made a dramatic difference in two unions: the Mine Workers and the International Brotherhood of Electrical Workers.

Miners. No one will ever know who would have won an honest election for top officers of the United Mine Workers in 1926. But we do know that John L. Lewis was designated the winner in an election riddled with fraud. John Brophy, who ran against Lewis, with left-wing support, was faced with an amazing recorded vote in District 20 Eastern Kentucky, where per capita tax had been paid on only one member in 1926. Yet the district managed miraculously to cast a unanimous vote of 2,686.5 votes for the entire Lewis slate and not a single vote for Brophy's. District 7 supposedly came across with 3,704 votes for Lewis and only nine for Brophy. When the international board refused to act on Brophy's protest, he had no effective recourse. "There was no Honest Ballot Association or anything of the sort that could have been called in," he wrote in his autobiography, "and it was contrary to union custom to take such a matter into courts, which I could not have afforded to do anyway."[20]

As a delegate to the union's 1927 convention, he protested unsuccessfully. His supporter, Powers Hapgood, "was set upon on the convention floor, and later brutally beaten in his hotel room by administration strongarm men." In May 1928, he was expelled by order of the international executive board on charges of dual unionism when he helped to organize an opposition group, the Save the Union movement.

By 1944, twenty-one of the union's thirty-one districts were in trusteeship, their officers appointed by Lewis. On the international executive board, sixteen members had been appointed from above, with 287.5 votes and only ten with only 72.5 votes, were elected.[21] The union officialdom had evolved into a self-perpetuating clique, an oligarchy par excellence, or a monarchy.

LMRDA had been in effect for ten years when Joseph (Jock) Yablonski ran for UMW president against W.A. (Tony) Boyle in 1969. Like the 1926 election, the 1969 election was suspect, the same miraculous lopsided votes, opposition meetings disrupted, violence against Yablonski, the union journal used as a campaign organ for the administration. And the aftermath was far more grisly. Boyle hired murderers who killed Yablonski, his wife, and his daughter. But this time, there was also federal law and effective recourse for the insurgents.

After Yablonski's death, the opposition, reconstituted as the Miners for Democracy appealed to the U.S. Labor Department, which, under enormous pressure from Congress and under the shadow of the triple assassination, filed suit in federal court to void the election. The Miners for Democracy won the right to intervene in the suit; it presented massive evidence of election fraud.

Meanwhile various suits filed under the LMRDA reestablished autonomy in the districts, some of which had been under trusteeship for a whole generation or more. Upholding the challenge, the judge set the election aside, ordered a rerun under government supervision, and established a dual editorship for the union's newspaper under which the opposition controlled half the contents all through the election period. In the rerun, Boyle was defeated (he later was jailed for murder); and the opposition took over.

The UMW constitution was completely rewritten. A union which had been the archetype of oligarchy was turned into a model of union democracy. That transformation was made possible by federal law.

Electrical Workers. In 1956, before the adoption of the LMRDA, the constitution of the International Brotherhood of Electrical Workers contained the following provision that subjected members to expulsion for

> . . . mailing, handing out, or posting cards, handbills, letters, marked ballots, or political literature of any kind, or displaying streamers, banners, signs, or anything else of a political nature, or being a party in any way to such being done in an effort to induce members to vote for or against any candidate for L.U. (local union) office, or candidates to conventions.[22]

This and seven other similarly repressive rules, in combination, made it illegal to organize any opposition. The constitution also strictly limited members' access to the courts:

> Any member resorting to a court of law for redress for any injustice he may believe has been done him by the IBEW, or any of its LU's, until he has first exhausted all his remedies through all the courts within the IBEW, shall stand automatically expelled and without rights of any kind.[23]

After the adoption of LMRDA, these clauses were slightly rephrased but still left essentially intact and were enforced as before as though nothing had happened. A partial and inadequate inspection of records in ten of the union's twelve districts, authorized by federal court order in an LMRDA suit, revealed that between 1970 and 1980 there had been 705 cases in which IBEW members had been convicted under only four of the seven clauses that were already illegal under the law. An analysis of these partial results, extrapolating the figures for all seven clauses in all districts, suggests that thousands, literally thousands of IBEW electricians had been suspended, fined, or expelled under these provisions. Those who ran for office and criticized incumbents were routinely disciplined for "slander."

Enter LMRDA. In 1978, Dan Boswell won election as an insurgent to the executive board of IBEW Local 164 in New Jersey where he asked annoying questions about finances and hiring practices. In the customary course of events, he was brought to trial on familiar charges, removed from the board, barred from running for office for six years, and fined $1,500, not an unusual case. But when Boswell managed to get into court under LMRDA Title I, the judge did more than order the victim reinstated: the union was compelled to eliminate or revise the seven repressive clauses and bring them in line with federal law. The outcome in New Jersey had immediate repercussions as far off as British Columbia where other IBEW members had appeals against similar penalties pending. They were also reinstated on the basis of the decision in *Boswell*. Since then, insurgents have campaigned for office in other locals, distributed handbills, and published newsletters without the pre-LMRDA retaliation.

At the 1982 IBEW convention, Charles Delgado, business manager of Local 527 in Texas, ran for international president against Charles Pillard, the incumbent. Delgado lost, but he mounted an impressive campaign. Before the convention, he got the endorsement of over 170 locals on a petition to amend the constitution to provide for the election of the union president by secret ballot vote of the delegates at the convention; but the international office simply waived it aside.

LMRDA enabled him to mail his literature to the delegates; and in an open roll call, he polled 11 percent of the votes, an excellent showing in a union whose international office has potent means of punishing critics. The last time an opposition candidate had run for president was in 1974 when A.J. White got only one percent.

The IBEW experience hardly equals the Miners' as a success story. But for that very reason it illustrates the more routine effect of law on union democracy. The IBEW administration, only slightly shaken, remains firmly in power, always ready to express its outrage against those who would question its omnipotent right to deal with oppositions. Nevertheless, here in this construction union, with a long record of suppressing membership rights, insurgents with the help of law have carved out a foothold for union democracy.

Summing up twenty-five years of LMRDA, Clyde Summers has said, "It has made a crucial difference." The record supports that conclusion.

The Roots of Insurgency

When a small group of officials holds a tight rein and a dead calm has settled over a union, the result is widely interpreted as membership apathy. But that apparent passivity is not necessarily organic; it is frequently implanted. What may strike the outsider as apathy is often not the cause of a bureaucracy's triumph but its result. Such a surrender is no more widespread in union government than in public government, probably far less so. If we add the number of unionists regularly active to one degree or another in committees, as stewards, etc., the total might range between 5 and 10 percent of the membership.

Even if moved by some overwhelming impulse, it would be impossible for the mass of any large electorate to involve itself in the affairs of government. Individuals would simply fall all over one another, which is precisely what creates the need for *representative* government.

The tone of union government, like all representative government, is set by three interacting forces: (1) the power structure, (2) the great bulk of the electorate, and (3) an active cadre outside the power structure including critics, oppositionists, and assorted dissenters. The electorate is called upon from time to time to take some minimal action, at which point it is coaxed, stimulated, provoked, sometimes by those in power and sometimes by an independent active minority.

In public life, the rights and the existence of that active cadre, that leavening minority, are protected by a democratic society, whether it appears as permanent opposition parties, ad hoc groups, or vociferously dissenting individuals. That protection is a quintessential element of democracy. The crucial difference in this respect between public government and union government is that oppositional currents in unions, rather than finding their right to exist guaranteed, are eternally in danger. The difficulty is not so much that alternative leadership fails to take the form of permanent parties, but that once it has arisen, in whatever form, it is more often driven out of existence than tolerated.

On the other hand, a combination of forces inside unions and outside in the larger democratic society have stimulated insurgency and buttressed its position in the labor movement, counteracting the powerful tendencies toward bureaucratism. An evaluation of those forces is a key to understanding the possibilities of democracy in union government.

If we consider bureaucracy as the tendency of the officialdom to rise above the electorate, insurgency is the effort to bring it back under control; resistance may not always be as powerful as the tendency toward oligarchy, but it is just as "permanent." In *Rebellion in Labor Unions* (1924), Sylvia Kopald described a wave of rebellion that took the form of strikes unauthorized by top officials in the early 1920s:

> In discussing the general question of leadership. . .we pointed out the conflict between efficiency and democracy, the power in the hands of machine leaders in their dealings with members, and their unity in dealing with rebellious members. . . .
> Only one thing is certain, the fight within the unions is on—whether in the name of amalgamation, industrial unionism, or what not. Behind the conservative officials is the power of the official machine. Behind the radicals is the trend of the times. The outcome remains to be written.[24]

Fourteen years later, Harold Seidman wrote in *Labor Czars* (1938):

> If any hero has emerged in our sordid narrative of union corruption, that hero is the rank and file. Though the odds against them are overwhelming, valiant men are still struggling to free unions from parasites who have all but wrecked the American labor movement. The rank and file can be counted on to continue its gallant fight, but unless drastic changes are made, its chances for success are remote indeed.[25]

As though unionists had been awaiting the trumpet call, a surge of democratic activity responded to the McClellan hearings in 1957 and to the adoption of LMRDA in 1959. George Meany, AFL-CIO president, and William Schnitzler, secretary treasurer, called upon the rank and file to "complete the rout of corruption from the labor movement." Senator John F. Kennedy told unionists that the "scourge of racketeering" could not be eliminated from the labor movement "without the courage and initiative of the rank and file. . . ." Provoked by scandals that had been on the public record for decades, encouraged by actions of the AFL-CIO and by its Ethical Practices Codes, and finally, under the illusion that they would be amply protected by federal law, many unionists came forward to do precisely what Kennedy had called for: they "rose up" against crooks in their unions and against those who were stamping on democracy. Movements for democracy and reform arose not only in the old AFL unions but in some of the CIO unions where bureaucracies were solidifying.

In the International Organization of Masters, Mates, and Pilots, a reform group that had been battling for five years won office in the union's largest local, in New York, after the international president was convicted of selling jobs; democracy was restored in the international in short order after the victory in New York. In the old AFL-CIO Papermakers, part of the leadership called for democratizing the union and for a public review board like the UAW's; they won half the seats on the international executive board before going down to defeat. After a Rank and File Movement for Democratic Action lost at the Pulp, Sulphite, and Paper Mill Workers convention in 1962, dissidents seceded in 1964; and, together with insurgent west coast Papermakers locals, they established a new, independent, democratic union on the west coast and won bargaining rights for more than 20,000 workers away from the two AFL-CIO unions.

In the next five years, there were notable insurgent groups in the Teamsters, Operating Engineers, Machinists, National Maritime, Marine Engineers, Musicians, Steelworkers, Electric Workers, Hotel and Restaurant Workers, Painters, and, finally in 1969–72, the most successful of all, in the Mine Workers.

The Musicians union accommodated itself to its own reform movements and emerged as one of the nation's more democratic unions. In the Teamsters, still infiltrated by organized crime, a vigorous reform group has been active for some fourteen years. In the National Maritime Union where the heirs of Joe Curran remain ensconced, successive opposition groups have warded off expulsion attempts and have conducted vigorous campaigns for national office. Edward Sadlowski, who led an opposition in the Steelworkers for about ten years, failed in his bid for the presidency; but he describes the lasting accomplishments of the opposition in these words:

> Years ago if you stood up and opposed someone, you were charged with slander. In my local, I can recall, some guys were thrown down the stairs. That doesn't exist any more. I'd like to think that it doesn't exist because people have stood up and changed and now have the right to say what they want to say. We do have the right to a lot of things that did not exist twenty years ago, ten years ago, five years ago. And those rights came about by people standing up, demanding what they thought was their just due and were willing to fight for. . . .[26]

This activity of organized groups inside unions, independent of the power structure or in opposition to it, covers a period of some thirty years, long enough to suggest a basic trend rather than a momentary aberration. Most group members were courageous; they had to be. Some were blacklisted, some expelled. A few were murdered. A few were successful. No single caucus endured for the whole period, although the Teamster opposition movement has lasted for fourteen years. There have been no permanently organized parties like those in the ITU but rather a persisting tendency that, when it disappears or is repressed in one union, reappears in another. Democracy in unions, which at first glance seems so fragile a flower, is actually a hardy perennial.

Union Democracy: The Phoenix

In the face of all the obstacles, how may one account for the resilience of union democracy?

Above all is the impulse that is generated from within the labor movement itself and marks unions as distinct from other private organizations. Unionism begins by serving the immediate needs of wage earners, but it pursues that end by its own methods. By depending upon democracy to mobilize the power of numbers against the power of accumulated wealth, it stimulates the aspirations of workers for dignity and self-respect even while it strives to achieve the most down-to-earth demands.

On one hand, the labor movement builds on the workers' sense of fair play, and personal worth—and all the ideals that emerge in a democratic society. On the other hand, in search of its own security, a union oligarchy is driven to repress in its membership those very ideals that the labor movement stimulates. Stand up and be strong—against the employer when it is time to organize. But sit down and shut up inside the union when it is time to look at the books. When so glaring a gap opens between promise and performance, noble ideals and sordid reality, there will be men and women who demand that the best prevail.

If we could conceive of the labor movement as an isolated society, which of course is not possible, the complete dominance of oligarchy would be its inevitable destiny. But the labor movement, with its officialdom, lives in the larger society. It can prosper and survive only if it can count on the active support of its membership—especially at critical moments. The Achilles heel of the bureaucracy is the impossibility of extinguishing the spirit of human dignity within the unions, precisely because the labor movement cannot live without it.

The clash between democracy and oligarchy arises in the labor movement not simply because the officialdom seeks to perpetuate itself in office and enjoy the perquisites of power. But as the officialdom rises above the membership and becomes independent of membership control, it begins to take care of its own interests *at the expense of the rank and file.*

It solidifies its position by accommodating to employers, neglecting grievances, mishandling pension and welfare funds, overlooking safety violations. Opposition to bureaucracy becomes not an empty fight over power but is linked to the opposing social interests that separate the officialdom from the membership. This is what gives the conflict its intensity.

Insurgent movements are touched off by the most disparate of immediate causes: suspicion that the treasury is being looted, mismanagement of insurance funds, failure to process grievances, denial of the right to run for office, discipline of critics, favoritism and blacklisting on the job, ignoring contract violations—the list is long and, to the outsider, sometimes tedious. Each group reacts to some immediate irritant, one thing leads to another, and they all acquire a similar quality. They begin by demanding, say, what happened to the money? And they end by protesting against what happened to their rights as union members.

Analogously, the quest for racial equality in America could be reduced to a long list of specific demands: use of toilets, drinking fountains, swimming pools, libraries; rights in jobs, schools, voting. But the battle for service at lunch counters derives its intensity from the demand for human dignity. If we focused only on the limited aims, we would lose sight of the greater goals. That quality belongs to the movements for union reform.

In my own dealings with thousands of unionists in reform groups all over the nation, a single small incident will remain unforgettable. It involved a little old man named Solomon Salzhandler, a retired New York City housepainter who was elected financial secretary of his Local 442 and then had a falling out with his local business agent. The BA began to kick Solomon out of the union office whenever he tried to use his desk and abused the old man verbally whenever and wherever they met. Solomon complained to a friend who advised him to give the BA a fifth of scotch every week.

Solomon took the advice and all began to go smoothly. He got his desk back; he performed his union duties without interference; life in the local became tolerable again. But every week there was that bottle. One day, as he told me, Salzhandler asked himself, "Why? A union is not some kind of racket; it's for the working-man." And so he cut off the weekly whiskey supply and the battle resumed.

Such was the origin of what became the landmark case in union democracy law, *Salzhandler v. Caputo*, which established basic civil liberties in unions.[27]

Events in the larger society had their inevitable impact inside unions, sharpening the edge of insurgency. In the 1950s veterans of World War II, taking up jobs in the construction trades, found racketeering and job favoritism intolerable, especially when measured against the ringing calls to bring freedom to the world. In the 1960s among the hard hats demonstrating in the streets of New York in support of the Vietnam War were young tradesmen with long hair, drafted for the parade by their business agents. The radical movements of the sixties left an imprint on younger workers, some of whom had taken jobs in construction during the summer and returned to the trade after graduating from college. In the 1970s a few thousand of these new, young, socially aware unionists made their appearance at unofficial conferences that attracted rank and filers looking for fresh policies in the labor movement.[28]

Meeting with young unionists who are active in independent rank and file groups and insurgent caucuses, one is struck by their level of education; command of language; ease of reading, writing, and speaking about union affairs. This impression is confirmed by statistics. The percentage of those in the civilian work force with no more than eight years of elementary schooling declined from 34.5 percent in 1957–59 to 19 percent in 1970–72, and is projected to go down to 6.1 percent by 1990. Those who completed four years of high school rose from 27.9 percent to 37.5 percent and to a projected 41.2 percent by 1990. Those with at least one whole year of college rose from 18.6 percent in 1957—59 to 26.6 percent in 1970—72 and is projected to rise to 40.2 percent by 1990.[29]

A rising level of education by itself is no guarantee of a corresponding rise in the level of democratic activity inside unions. If union work seemed pointless and boring, a more educated work force might seek more satisfying outlets for its abilities and energy. But once an insurgent movement has been spurred into action, trained leaders can utilize their talents to turn it into a formidable force. One of the most impressive reform movements arose in the Public Employees Federation, a union of 50,000 professional, scientific, and technical employees of New York state government. It calls itself the State Coalition for a Democratic Union (SCDU). Most of the members, and virtually all the SCDU leaders, have at least a bachelor's degree and together possess all the skills required to keep any movement going well.

The key to democracy in the labor movement is in the potential for insurgency. The weakness of the Lipset-Trow-Coleman analysis of the ITU lay in equating union democracy with a two-party system; then, not seeing the possibility of a replica of that system in other unions, they foresaw dismal prospects in the rest of the labor movement. Their strength, and their contribution, was in seeking the sources of a robust democracy not only inside the union but outside. For one thing, outside the labor movement today there is federal law which puts the power of government behind union democracy and gives moral support to it. But the law is not self-enforcing. Making the statute more than a hope-chest of good intentions and transforming it into a tool of democracy has required that a section of the democratic-minded public ally itself with the aspirations of union reformers.

The Allies

In the mid-1880s, the moral status of the labor movement in the nation rose when a group of economists and historians, led by Richard T. Ely, inspirer of the Wisconsin school, argued that unions were a constructive, stabilizing, and necessary force in America. Independently minded intellectuals had become sympathizers of the organized working class. That kind of moral support, in recent times, goes to union democracy.

In 1943, Selig Perlman and Philip Taft, both prominent labor historians of the Wisconsin school, and John Fitch, a disciple, signed a report of the American Civil Liberties Union on "Democracy in Trade Unions" along with twenty-three other notables, stating gently, "It is essential . . . that trade unions which now receive governmental recognition and protection should respond by freeing themselves from any remnants of the autocratic practices which accompanied the era of industrial warfare." (One of the signers was Lewis Mayers, a lawyer and law professor who later became a founding director of the Association for Union Democracy.) While they obviously were convinced—erroneously—that traces of "autocracy" were a relic of the past, and they were careful to insist that "American trade unionism is on the whole democratic," they did endorse legislation to assure "that the democratic rights of union members under union constitutions shall be protected." The interest of the ACLU was a harbinger of a growing concern among pro-labor intellectuals and civil libertarians for union democracy.

In the early 1950s, William Leiserson, a prominent second generation Wisconsinite, expressed much stronger misgivings about the effects of the rise of centralized authority in the labor movement. In 1957 he wrote:

> May it not be, then, that the autocratic practices which have been considered exceptional—the denial of the right to oppose the union's administration, the expulsion of members for criticizing union officials, the granting of arbitrary authority to executives, and the tendency to govern by decree—are indications of a trend toward one-party union government in conformity with the single-party concept of industrial democracy? Is there any reason to believe that the one-party system of industrial government or union government is likely to be any less disastrous in its effects on individual freedom than such systems have been under political government?[30]

In 1958, declaring that "A free society needs the practice of civil liberties, not only by government, but by all of its other great institutions," the ACLU drafted a forthright "Bill of Rights" to advance civil liberties in unions. That kind of concern, expressed in books, articles, and statements, led some to become partisans of a cause. Professor Clyde Summers wrote the ACLU statement on "Democracy in Labor Unions" in 1952; in 1958, he joined Norman

Thomas and John Lapp, a prominent labor arbitrator and Catholic lay leader, in a three-person committee that sought (unsuccessfully) to win reinstatement of two machinists expelled from the International Association of Machinists by order of its president, A.J. Hayes.

In the mid-1950s a group of young activists in the New York branch of the Association of Catholic Trade Unionists became champions of movements for reform in various unions. One of their leading attorneys, John Harold, represented expelled insurgents in Local 88 of the Masters, Mates, and Pilots. With his help in New York State court in *Madden v. Atkins* [4 App. 2s1, 162 NYS 2d 576 2nd Dep't 1957], a case that established basic civil liberties in New York unions in advance of the LMRDA, they won reinstatement; and with their rights protected, they won their union battle.

In the mid-1960s, Frank Schonfeld, reform leader in the New York City Painters union, gained the support of Norman Thomas and of Burton Hall, a pioneering union democracy attorney, and other lawyers. When the two painter reformers, Dow Wilson and Lloyd Green, were murdered in San Francisco in 1966, a citizens committee of some twenty-six pro-labor civil libertarians, with Norman Thomas prominent among them, called for a federal investigation of racketeering in the painting industry. Later in 1972, many of the committee members joined with others in the Association for Union Democracy, which described itself as "the first attempt by private agencies to sustain a continuing effort on behalf of union democracy."

The same kind of intervention by civil libertarians and reformers outside the labor movement made 1969 a momentous year in the history of union democracy, for that was the year when Jock Yablonski, in his insurgent campaign for president of the United Mine Workers, announced that "Union democracy is the main issue." His campaign, vigorous and effective, was turned back by election fraud, violence, and finally by the murder of Yablonski himself, his wife, and daughter.

Yablonski was able to mount an impressive challenge. His discouraged followers were able to rally their forces after his death because they were spurred on by sympathizers and active collaborators outside the union: attorneys, political leaders, and professionals. They included Ralph Nader, concerned with mine safety, and Ken Hechler, House of Representatives member from West Virginia who was drawn in by appeals for help from his miner-constituents. Their interest encouraged Yablonski to raise the flag of revolt.

Joseph Rauh, famous as a union attorney, early New Dealer, civil rights leader, civil libertarian, founder and former president of the Americans for Democratic Action, became Yablonski's attorney. After the murders, Rauh enlisted a team of volunteer lawyers and raised money from liberal foundations to keep the movement going. They successfully challenged the legality of the 1969 miners election, first in an appeal to the U.S. Department of Labor and then in federal court where they won equal space in the *United Mine Workers Journal* during the government-supervised election of 1972. They sued successfully to lift trusteeships from several UMW districts and pressured the Labor Department to move forward with its own stalled suit against other district trusteeships. Don Stillman quit his job as a university teacher, and Ed James interrupted his studies at Harvard Law School, to become public relations directors for the Miners for Democracy in its campaign to elect Arnold Miller against Tony Boyle as UMW president. After the spectacular reform victory, Clyde Summers helped write a new democratic union constitution.

Without federal law, the miners opposition would surely have been crushed and would have left no trace like all the others in the past. An officialdom ready for murder would hardly shrink from expulsions. But without their allies outside the union, the Miners for Democracy could never have won the drawn-out legal battle, and their cause would probably have been hopeless; and the Boyle faction would still have the UMW in its grip today.

The miners battle brought together union reformers and intellectuals and professionals. If the intervention of liberal reformers gave the Miners for Democracy that last final push to victory, the crusade for miners democracy, in turn, inspired a band of young attorneys to take up the cause of workers' rights, independent of unions or within them. As a single illustration, the Public Citizen Litigation Group, one unit in the constellation of Nader public interest associations, created its own labor section that focuses on union democracy, having already taken up the cause of

Teamsters, electricians, rural lettercarriers, and others with the aim of strengthening union democracy law.

In *As Unions Mature*, Richard A. Lester postulated a long range evolution of unions toward bureaucratic centralized control, a tendency that he found so fundamental that "a permanent alteration of direction in long-run trends seems exceedingly doubtful—at least in the foreseeable future." He illustrated his thesis by pointing to John L. Lewis' iron grip over the United Mine Workers. Since then, the officialdom that was part of the Lewis heritage has been overthrown by rank and file insurgency. If the tendency toward bureaucratic control is "fundamental" so is resistance to it. In the seesaw confrontation between the two, the miners battle displayed all the elements that strengthen the viability of union democracy.

Conclusions

1. The tendencies toward the rise of bureaucracy and the dominance of oligarchy in mass organizations that were disclosed by Robert Michels in his pioneering study, *Political Parties*, are confirmed by the inner life of the American labor movement in even more striking fashion than in the German Social Democratic Party that served as his model. Strengthening all the "normal" sociological factors he described, are the extraordinary, illicit, even illegal aspects that are familiar in some American unions: collusion between corrupt officials and employers, racketeering, deliberate suppression of members' rights, etc.

2. Michels sought to correct the prevailing illusions of his day about the nature of the labor movement, illusions which anticipated an easy triumphal sway of democracy with the assumption of political power by organizations of the working class. As he put it, one aim of his work was:

...the demolition of some of the facile and superficial democratic illusions which trouble science and lead the masses astray. Finally, the author desired to throw light upon certain sociological tendencies which oppose the reign of democracy and, to a still greater extent, oppose the reign of socialism.[31]

However, the experience of seventy-five years since the publication of his work has so thoroughly "demolished" those illusions, and the acceptance of his thesis has been so complete, that a different kind of illusion threatens to lead us astray. Michels' own pessimistic view was not one of unrelieved gloom:

> The writer does not wish to deny that every . . . movement inspired by the democratic spirit may have a certain value as contributing to the enfeeblement of oligarchic tendencies. . .it is true that the labor movement, in virtue of the theoretical postulates it proclaims, is apt to bring into existence (in opposition to the will of the leaders) a certain number of free spirits who, moved by principle, by instinct, or by both, desire to revise the base upon which authority is established.[32]

At a time of widespread democratic illusion, the iron law of oligarchy turned the rudder hard the other way. To avoid misconceptions now, it needs a corrective push in the opposite direction; and for that, it is essential to examine those factors which have strengthened democracy in the American labor movement.

3. In searching for countervailing forces that might offset oligarchy, Lipset, Trow, and Coleman examined the "deviant" case of the two-party system in the International Typographical Union (ITU). When they concluded that the system's strength seemed to lie in a special position of typographers in their union, in the industry, and in society, not likely to be duplicated elsewhere, their findings cast a shadow over the very possibilities of internal union democracy. It seems to this writer that, in their preoccupation with permanent parties as the essential bulwark of democracy, they were distracted from the actual sources of union democracy as they appear in the life of unions.

A system of competing parties implies the possible transfer of power and back again, peaceably and without crisis, among two or more permanent political organizations. Outside the ITU such a mechanism exists nowhere in the labor movement, and there is no indication that it ever will. Moreover, even in the ITU the two-party system failed as a buttress for democracy in the course of the recent bitter dispute in the ITU over merger with some other union.

In two other unions recently, other "deviant" cases have appeared. The Teamsters for a Democratic Union was formed out of a reform movement that has been active in the union for some fourteen years. In the Public Employees Federation in New York State, a remarkably well-organized democratic caucus of professional employees has functioned in the union for six years. Neither the Teamster nor the PEF group are "parties" that expect to alternate in power with incumbents; they are not exactly "permanent," but they are continuing.

In Local 134 of the IBEW in Chicago, rank and file electricians have maintained an "Oracle Social Club" for about 20 years; it runs opposition candidates from time to time under the rubric of the Progress Party. It never wins elections but it claims successes as a pressure group.

In general, however, democracy is kept alive in the labor movement not by permanent political parties but by temporary caucuses, oppositional currents, and dissident slates of candidates that come forward from time to time in response to some immediate needs. The health of union democracy requires the creation and defense of those conditions within unions which permit such leavening minority groups to arise when necessary, to continue to function, and even to disappear without a forced suppression.

4. If power in unions is so heavily weighted on the side of the officialdom, i.e., the oligarchy, what possibilities are there, really, for union democracy? The Lipset-Trow-Coleman study suggested an answer to that question when the authors looked for the roots of ITU democracy, not only inside the union, but outside in the larger society. In that approach lies the key to democracy in the labor movement. Printers may have shared experiences and a way of life peculiar to printers, but the ITU as a labor union shares with other unions certain common relations to the democratic society in which they all function.

The labor movement is the arena for a contest between two unequal contestants. The force of bureaucracy, buttressed by overwhelming reserves of power and revenues, is counterposed by comparatively weaker forces from below. If we could view unions as a closed social system, democracy would remain a remote possibility within it. But unions exist within a democratic society; and from that society the strength of union democracy is nourished.

5. The impulse toward authoritarianism in union government arises out of the ruling group's drive to retain power and protect its own interests whenever they conflict with the interests of its own constituency. In this respect, oligarchy, existing at the ex-

pense of the membership, has an exploitive and parasitical quality. It is the intensity of this counterposing of interests that gives to internal union democracy a stimulus that democracy may not have in other private organizations. Democracy *in unions* is a necessary weapon in the defense of the interests of members vis à vis their own representatives.

6. In the quest for institutional devices and arrangements that can serve to strengthen democracy in unions, one may look inward for proposals like the direct election of officers, regional election of executive board members, right to vote on contracts, election of stewards, local autonomy, etc. It is no derogation of such proposals to stress another side: In the U.S. labor movement today, the most promising source of strength of union democracy lies outside unions in the law and among public citizen allies of union reformers.

7. Even when unions appear thoroughly bureaucratized and the membership inert, the labor movement itself tends to regenerate the democratic spirit. When unions call for justice, equality, fair play, and human dignity in society, these stirring ideals are echoed in the ranks and demanded inside the unions.

The demand for democracy inside the labor movement is stimulated, too, by the workings of democracy on the outside. The level of education of workers has been rising; the proportion of trained professionals and white collar workers in unions goes up; demands on the outside for democratization of unions inevitably moves workers who are citizens not only of unions but of a democratic society.

8. Federal law to protect union democracy is the intervention of democratic society on the side of union members in their relations with their officials. The law has stimulated activism inside unions, which, in turn, has encouraged sympathizers in the general public to come forward in support of union democracy.

To sum up, power of internal union democracy as a counterweight to oligarchy in unions derives from three forces: (1) the activity of unionists themselves, without which nothing would be possible; (2) the power of federal law; and (3) allies of union reformers in the general public to assure the implementation of the law.

It is that combination of union rank and filers, backed by federal law, and assisted by pro-labor allies which explains the paradox, namely, that the trend toward increasing bureaucracy in unions is offset by an even stronger trend toward democracy, so that the state of union democracy today is healthier than at any time in the last two generations.

VI

Participants' Observations

14

GUS TYLER

Labor at the Crossroads

Without fanfare, in the recession summer of 1982, the Executive Council of the AFL-CIO appointed a special committee to "review and evaluate changes that are taking place in America in the labor force, occupations, industries, and technology." Who would have suspected that this posse, with the academic-sounding name of The Committee on the Evolution of Work, would be the beginning of American labor's Vatican II? But it was, and the potential impact on U.S. unionism is as profound as that of Vatican II on the Catholic Church.

It took two and a half years for the public—and for the unions— to find out where this committee was headed. It may take several more years to judge how valuable the initiative of the committee really was. But of this there can be no doubt: American unions are desperately in search of new goals and new methods.

Troubled Times

Apparently, there is some law of nature that causes troubled times to spawn introspection and insight. Decaying empires inspire great philosophy; anxious souls seek understanding. When all is going well, there is little need to look around or to look within. But when the present gets shaky and the future threatening, it becomes necessary to ask what is wrong. Easy answers give way to hard questions.

Individuals engage in this sort of reorientation all the time; institutions do it rarely. The former are less rigidified—especially if they are younger persons. The latter are corsetted in organizational imperatives with the top indulging in bureaucratic optimism, the middle toadying to the top, the bottom brainwashed and bewildered. When large hierarchical establishments do change, they generally have been hammered from the outside or exploded from the inside. Rarely does an existing elite publicly proclaim the need to explore the surround to discover what is really there and then to delve within to change oneself for a world in the remaking.

August 1982 was a troubled time. The economy was in bad shape: the jobless rate was double digit, real wages for workers were falling, the land was strewn with bankruptcies. The political atmosphere—for unions—was hostile: the first union president ever to become President of the United States was making a religion of his apostasy by appointing people to the Labor Department, the National Labor Relations Board, and the federal courts, who would reverse the labor-management trends of half a century. The unions were in retreat. Numerically they had fallen from representing 45 percent of the eligibles in 1954 to about 30 percent in 1982. Givebacks were the order of the day. Organizing efforts were increasingly fruitless. The public image of unions was unflattering. In these disquieting days, labor turned to reflection, establishing a committee to do what ceremonial committees usually do not do—to think painfully.

Nineteen eighty-two was, of course, not the first time that the American labor movement found itself on the decline. There were several such previous moments. And even a cursory look at past times of adversity would reveal a pattern, the circumstances when unions traditionally have lost ground:

1. When the business cycle turns down, labor is weakened. Unorganized workers fear joining a union when unemployment is widespread; unions hesitate to press their demands when firms

are infirm; hungry scabs walk through picket lines. Bad times for business have historically been bad times for unions. Graphs of the economy and of union power are almost parallel lines. In the slow growth years of the 1970s and in the real recession years of the early 1980s, unions could expect to suffer.

2. Unions find life difficult when a national administration is hostile. Increasingly, the National Labor Relations Act, under malevolent administration and retrogressive reinterpretation of board and courts, has become—in the eyes of labor—a National Anti-Labor Act. From his "bully pulpit" an unfriendly president can poison the atmosphere for unions in the same way that Roosevelt breathed new life into organized labor.

3. Unions are in trouble when the national economic mix changes, as unionized sectors wane and as unorganized sectors wax. The most dramatic such change has been the shift from a predominantly goods-producing economy (where unions were strong) to a predominantly service economy (where unions traditionally were weak). By the early 1980s, workers in the service economy made up 70 percent of the work force.

4. Unions are likewise shaken when economic centers move from one part of the country (with a union heritage) to another part (without such a tradition). A textbook example is the shift from the Snow Belt to the Sun Belt.

5. Finally, unions are discomfitted by any heavy influx of immigrants. The newcomers are fearful; they have lower expectations; they are pleased to have any job; they are viewed with suspicion if not distaste, and they view others with diffidence and distrust; they are outside the mainstream.

In the 1980s, American unions were hit simultaneously by five damaging conditions: recession, governmental animus, the shifts from North to South and from goods to services, the influx of about a million newcomers (legal and illegal) per year. A second reading of history might have eased labor's anxieties, for each of these traditional causes of union enervation seemed to contain a self-correcting potential, the seeds of its own resurrection. If unions go down when the "cycle" goes down, then unions will go up when the "cycle" turns up. So the thing to do is to wait for "recovery," or better, to work for national policies to stimulate recovery. If an administration is hostile, the thing to do is get out the vote, to reward friends and punish enemies. If the economy moves from goods to services, the unions merely have to move—as they have done quite impressively—from goods to services. If jobs go South, the unions go South. If new breeds of immigrants enter the labor force, give them time (and some help) and they will ultimately organize—as did the Irish, Jews, Italians, Blacks, Hispanics. History's prescription for the traditional infirmities is to apply the tincture of time—with patience, persistence, and prayer.

Turning to this well-established household remedy would have been the natural thing to do. Instead the AFL-CIO chose the painful path, really two paths—one leading outward and the other inward. They chose the hard way—and with reason.

Changing Problems

The 1980s are not the 1930s. Solutions that were valid fifty years ago are not valid—or equally valid—today because, in no small measure, the problems have changed. The differences that have developed over a half century are not quantitative alone, they are qualitative; they are not incremental, they are gross. On a global scale, there are changes under way that are profound, puzzling, and—in some cases at the moment—imponderable. Within the unions, changes are also under way—sly, subtle, unintentional, and insinuating changes—that are making unions much different from what they set out to be or what they presently believe themselves to be. To cope with the new realities, unions must look afresh at the world about and the condition within.

The 1980s are not the 1930s in at least three crucial ways. First, the robot is here; second, the economy is global; third, the labor force is elusive. Put otherwise, the economy has undergone profound changes technologically, geographically, and spiritually. For unions, this means that their potential membership will be dispossessed by electronic gadgets, that governments will be less effective instruments for taming corporate power, and that those who are the working force will be more difficult to compose into an effective social force. The old premises of unionism—people with jobs, governments with power to regulate their domestic economies, and individuals with definable "careers"—will be shaken, if not shattered.

The essence of the committee's first report in August 1983, entitled "The Future of Work," was the newly developing role of the robot—although it was not stated that way. The opening sentence stated plainly: "Massive changes in the structure of the U.S. economy are under way." The key word to remember is "structure."

Unemployment in the future will be increasingly *structural*, not arising simply from an imbalance between production and consumption but from the displacement of persons by robots. "Technology is displacing workers and overturning traditional work patterns," says the report. "Industries and occupations are changing." By "technology" is meant:

the new microtechnology with its information communications potential [that] is bringing change which is perhaps more revolutionary than the industrial revolution brought by the steam engine in the nineteenth century and the transportation revolution brought by the internal combustion engine earlier in the twentieth century.

Labor's fear is real despite its experience with automation that, contrary to many expectations, did not cause massive unemployment during the 1950s and 1960s. The reason for the fear is that the robot and the automaton may be kin but they are not the same. Automation provided muscle but not brain; it could handle big lots but not small ones; it worked well for some standardized operations on farms and in factories but was not particularly adept in stores, offices, banks, information processing, or designing. Because workers displaced by automation from farm and factory could find employment in the service sector, the percentage of unemployment in the total society did not rise.

But when the "chip" invades the service sector, then where shall the displaced go? "Robots in the factory, word processors in the office, scanners at the check-out counter, push-button banking, computers in the home, satellites in the sky," the report notes, "remind the nation of the pervasive impact of advancing technology."

Even public employment—about one-third of the service sector—is not likely to rush to the rescue. Budget-badgered governments at all levels are more likely to fire than to hire more employees.

A "Labor Surplus Society"

Labor fears what the report calls a "labor surplus society," a fear
that seems to be confirmed by trends in unemployment since
1969. Since then, every "recovery" has been less of a recovery.
When Lyndon Johnson left office (1969) the unemployment rate
was 3.4 percent. After two years of Nixon, the jobless rate had
risen to 5.8. By 1973, after the application of a few stimulants, the
jobless rate was cut back—not to the original 3.4, but to 4.8
(unemployment was rising in good times). By 1975, we were in
deep recession with a jobless rate of 8.3. In the following "recovery" (1979) the jobless rate was not back to the original 3.4 or
even the subsequent 4.8 but stood at 5.8. By 1983, we were in
recession again with a jobless rate of 9.7. In the recovery of
1984–86, the lowest unemployment fell to was 6.8. Because the
hard core unemployment rate has been rising steadily for a decade
and a half, what would have been called a deep recession (almost a
depression) in the early 1970s is now called "recovery."

   In the ingenious ways of some more imaginative economists,
this frightening trend, an ever larger portion of the population
without jobs, has been rationalized into a virtue—or at least a
necessary evil. The rationale goes by the name of NAIRU, an
acronym for Non-Accelerating Inflation Rate of Unemployment.
This bit of arcanity, stated simply, decrees that there must be a
certain level of unemployment to ward off inflation. This allegedly
necessary *level* has been rising since 1970. Back then, it was about
4 percent; now (1986) it is about 7 percent.

   Since a certain level of unemployment is deemed necessary for
the proper functioning of our society, economists no longer speak
of a "full employment" society since, by definition, it will induce
the inflationary evil; instead they substitute the phrase "high
employment" society—a change that implies a required level of
unemployment. Thus when Washington economists speak of a
"structural deficit," they mean a budget deficit in a "high employment economy," which—at the time of this writing—is about 7
percent unemployment, a level that costs the federal treasury
about $245 billion a year in lost income and associated expen-
ditures. In a truly full employment economy there would be a
surplus.

Although NAIRU is one of those *givens* among policymakers, no economist has even tried to explain why NAIRU has risen from 4 percent to 7 percent. Nor can any economist demonstrate why inflation will inevitably follow if the unemployment rate falls to 2 percent, or one percent, or zero. If it is permissible to view much of economics as pure apologia, then it would not be beyond concluding that what some economists do is watch the graphs, note the unemployment rate when the media announce "recovery," and then ordain that the jobless rate at that happy moment is irreducible. Thus do some of our most celebrated Doctors of Philosophy think, like Dr. Pangloss, that whatever is is what must be in this best of all possible worlds.

NAIRU is the ritualized apologia for a society that may soon announce that its economy is in a state of "recovery" although the unemployment rate is double-digit. And, in doing so, these apologists will be confirming the conclusion of the committee that we are living in a "labor surplus society," that—may I add—is becoming ever more so, not only in the U.S. but in the world.

Confronted with this frightening fact, the committee lists its traditional program to cope with unemployment, with proposals ranging from enforcement of the Humphrey-Hawkins Act to a "rational industrial policy." Part of that program calls for a "realistic trade policy," a euphemism for another euphemism called "fair trade," as distinguished from "free trade."

This plank is but one-half a point in an eleven point program, but it may be expected that in the coming years labor—and the nation—will have to give more and more attention to the *international* aspects of our economy. The traditional Keynesian formulas will no longer work in a world where domestic economies are inescapably affected by and dependent on global factors. Like it or not, the modern economy is international. And unless that bothersome fact is recognized, no program to cope with domestic economies is "realistic."

A Global Setting

Consider what happens to the simple Keynesian device to stimulate the economy through government expenditures when applied in the current global setting. In the 1930s, government expenditures for New Deal reconstruction projects went to American residents who, in turn, spent the money to buy things and services from American residents who, in turn, did the same thing. The impact of each dollar spent by Uncle Sam was multiplied as the dollar moved through the system.

In 1984, the federal government ran a deficit of some $200 billion—a spur that should have driven the economy forward at a breakneck pace. What happened? In the first quarter, the stimulant worked as the economy leaped forward at the brisk pace of 10.4 percent. But, in the second quarter, the pace slowed to 8.5; in the third quarter to 1.6. The fourth quarter showed some quickening to 4 percent growth and was hailed as a forerunner of steady and solid growth in 1985. But in the first quarter of the new year, the pace came to a near standstill at 1.3 percent growth. The year ended with growth of only 2.3 percent.

What happened was that government stimulants were being poured into a leaky bucket. The federal government poured money out to its residents who, in turn, bought items made overseas. The trade deficit was, as an order of magnitude, just about equal to the federal deficit. The Keynesian cure that was effective for nations at a time when, as in the case of the U.S., overseas trade was a minuscule portion of Gross National Product was no longer able to work its magic with nations where trade was one-quarter of their total business.

By classical theory, of course, the U.S. should automatically benefit from a reversal of the process, turning deficits into surpluses, because of certain laws of equilibrium held in balance by an invisible hand. Since Americans would be demanding goods made overseas, our demand would boost the value of overseas currencies. Since foreign markets would not be buying our wares, the value of our currency would fall. At some point, we could not buy from them because their goods would be too expensive. They would start buying from us because our goods would be cheap to them, and all would right itself—as Dr. Pangloss might have told them from the beginning.

But in the real world of the early 1980s—not the Adam Smithian world of the 1780s—things did not behave necessarily as they should. America ran the greatest deficits any nation has ever run and its currency continued to climb until 1986. Why? It was because the American dollar was in demand. Why? First, because during the 1970s and the first half of the 1980s the rate of interest was high. Second, because the U.S. was a political safe-haven—as contrasted with the rest of the world. Investors holding marks, francs, pounds, or lire wanted to own dollars; their demand for the buck boosted the price. What drove the value of the dollar was not *trade* but *capital* flows.

All this would have been inconceivable in the time of Smith and Ricardo, when it was assumed that capital would rarely cross material boundaries. "Every individual endeavors to employ his capital as near home as he can," noted Smith. Ricardo insisted that it would be most imprudent for a merchant to allow his capital to operate out of his sight for any length of time. Yet today, the movement of capital across national boundaries is many, many times greater than the movement of goods.

In the twentieth century, the phrase "comparative advantage" has lost just about all its meaning, if viewed in terms of the "natural attributes" of a nation. The factors of production are portable: capital, technology, raw materials, and managerial know-how. They can be moved easily and swiftly. Multinational corporations scour the planet to find out where best to allocate their resources to produce most cheaply, to pay the least taxes, to maximize after-tax returns. They do this even when they may not, as patriotic persons, want to do it, for the alternative is to be destroyed by a competitor who has no such qualms.

Capital, Labor, Mobility

This internationalization of the economy gives capital an almost unbeatable advantage over labor: the former is mobile, the latter is not. A global corporation can say to its employees: here are our terms; take them or else. The company can always relocate, labor cannot.

Indeed, capital—whether in the form of an industrial producer or in liquid form—can play the same game with governments: do as we say—or else. Billions of dollars can be moved from one nation to another in a few seconds with a few taps on the keys of a terminal. Technology can be transmitted electronically in words and diagrams and codes in a matter of moments. Managers can be transported physically to the other side of the globe within twenty-four hours. Unions and nations are flat-footed losers in a contest with these fleet-footed financial folk.

A second Keynesian measure for stimulating the economy is to have the central bank—the Federal Reserve Board in the United States—loosen the money supply. But how much of a stimulus will such easier credit be if consumers purchase goods made in other countries? As Raymond T. Dalio, president of Bridgewater Associates, an economic consulting firm, sees it—according to the 4/28/85 *New York Times*—"if the Fed eases credit to spur the economy, it may have limited impacts. Consumers may borrow more money, but—with the dollar still strong—spend more on imports."

The third Keynesian measure is to reduce taxes to spur buying and investing. But if such cuts do not stimulate the economy—in part for reasons already noted—then the government ends up with greater deficits, with an ever rising portion of the federal income going to service debts, with rising interest rates, with an overvalued dollar, with falling exports and rising imports, with greater unemployment—in sum, with even more of a "labor surplus society."

The trio of Keynesian cures was prescribed for domestic economies that were, more or less, self-contained. While the remedies are not totally invalid for countries today, they have lost much of their earlier potency.

But even at an earlier time, the Keynesian trio had only limited value—as Keynes himself noted in *The General Theory.* If the government was not to be called upon too often to borrow to save the system, it was necessary to rectify the inherently irrational and inequitable distribution of income under capitalism. Without income redistribution, the system would overtax the state. A more just distribution was not only desirable for ethical reasons but was necessary for economic reasons.

Labor's Power

A degree of such redistribution has taken place in the capitalist world because of the economic and political presence and power of organized labor. The so-called "iron law of wages"—a virtual *given* for Adam Smith and Karl Marx—was repealed by the struggles of unions. Minimum wage laws, unemployment insurance, social security, housing supplements, and family support were additional ways in which working people were able to lift themselves out of the iron cage. The question is whether there will be, in the future, any force strong enough to play the role that organized labor has played in the past.

American labor is concerned—as are unions in other countries—for the very obvious reason that it is their very own life that is involved. But viewed more conceptually and comprehensively, our total society ought to be worried because, in the absence of a presence pushing for distributive justice, we can indeed expect what Marx predicted: an immiserization of the masses that may not end up with socialism but with bloody anarchy.

The elimination of a counterforce to capitalist "greed" is more of a possibility today than it has ever been—thanks to the robot and to the globalization of the economy. The "robot" can give us the "labor surplus society." The same technological magic that sires the "robot" is giving us a world economy in which giant multinational multi-product corporations need not listen to the plaints of their employees. Indeed, they dare not listen, lest their competitors beat them in the marketplace or pirates drive them from control of their own corporations. The same technology, however, can also pulverize, atomize, castrate the "working class."

The notion of "alienation" at work has been stirred by automation, cybernation, and Charlie Chaplin. Man is a whirling speck on huge gears. In recent years, mountains of manuscripts have described this dehumanization of the person as a process where man must move to the tempo of the machine, define his or her chore by the machine, and—now—learn to think like the machine.

"Alienation" and the Worker

But this notion is not new. In 1844, several years before he and Engels wrote *The Communist Manifesto*, Marx noted "The Alienation of Labor" in an essay by that name.

What then do we mean by the alienation of labor? First that the work he performs is extraneous to the worker, that is, it is not personal to him, is not part of his nature; therefore he does not fulfill himself at work, but actually denies himself; feels miserable rather than content, cannot freely develop his physical and mental powers, but instead becomes physically exhausted and mentally debased....Through his work, the laborer loses his identity.

The "alienation" of labor was the loss of identity by workers as "spiritual" (a word that Marx would have abhorred) beings. But, as Marx would reason just a few years later in *The Manifesto*, workers would rediscover their identity as part of a collective in the camaraderie of the work site where they would be compelled to unite. Capitalism would bring workers together under one roof where they would experience a common life, express common complaints, develop common aspirations, organize common voices in the form of unions and political parties. The work site would become a community that, in due time, would replace the oppressive domination of that alien being, the capitalist.

Whether the Marxist millennium—the collective commonwealth—was a misreading or not, there can be no denying that capitalism did produce labor movements in every country in the world, and that these labor movements have profoundly affected economic, political, and social relations across the globe. While the factory fostered spiritual alienation, it also gave birth to a sense of economic, political, social, and ideological solidarity that— as an active element in a capitalist world—tamed, civilized, modified, and ultimately rescued capitalism from its own suicidal compulsions.

That positive force can be eliminated or, certainly, much lessened by modern technology. The work site—as we have come to know it—may no longer be a work site. The work force may be scattered and strewn, many workers never leaving their homes if they so choose, many of them paying only casual visits to the workplace. Even those who have a fixed job at a fixed place are not likely to stay there for any great portion of a lifetime.

Consider this possibility: two hundred machines are packed tightly into an underground box where there is no light, no space for humans, no need for steady ventilation. These robots are set up for flexible manufacture. They can produce a variety of products since, upon instruction, they can drop some tools and pick up other ones. These smart little inorganic imps respond quickly and cleverly to instructions that are fed into the "factory" from a terminal operated by a woman in another county or another country.

The robots run twenty-four hours a day and never strike. Is this really the future?

Extend the paradigm: in some other part of the world, another person is operating a telephone "central" from home, a job requiring not much more skill than that of the old-fashioned telephone "operator." Still another equally isolated being is keeping the books for a bank where clients are making their daily deposits and withdrawals. Other invisible workers are taking orders for products seen on video screens.

Or consider this: a thousand workers who were members of the steel workers' unions because they were employed in factories making steel are suddenly unemployed—not because of imported steel or even because their corporation opted to move production to another country, but because steel has been replaced by glass, ceramics, plastics, paper, or eeg-wags (gee-gaws spelled backwards). New materials, new forms of transportation, new ways of communicating, new ways of building—all these obsolesce entire careers. The persons who can identify themselves as steel workers, linotypists, designers, or individuals dedicated to any given occupation or line become fewer as the economy finds itself in constant flux. Add the high number of transients and part-timers in such an economy—indeed, in our present economy. How does one organize such a protean, elusive, atomized "working class," many of whom—operating out of their own homes—will be legally listed as "independent contractors"?

The Need for Unions

In the past, most workers were attached to an employer or, at least, to an industry or occupation. For such people, unions were a necessity—the way in which workers could help to define the future—income, work rules, working conditions, leisure, and the securities expressed in fringes. Such workers were prepared to make sacrifices today—even a long strike and major loss of income—to win a better future.

But if workers do not see themselves attached to anything for any length of time, and if, in addition, there are few if any opportunities for employees to meet, why and how would they form a union? And if they do not form unions as a countervailing power to their employers, what force will there be to win a more equitable and rational distribution of income to keep the inverted pyramid of such an unbalanced society from collapsing?

The robotized, globalized, atomized society we have under consideration is not with us—not yet. But its coming is highly likely and perhaps inevitable. Is there anything that can be done to bring order to a future economy in which a large portion of the population, possibly a majority, will be without work or will be suffering with work in isolation in good times, and in which "good times" will be brief and repeatedly disrupted by massive economic crises and social anarchy?

Two ready answers come to mind: Luddism (anti-technology violence) and the dole.

Not all Luddites act outside the law. In 1596, the City of Danzig hired an assassin to kill the man who invented a machine to save labor on a ribbon loom. Since man was made to work, by God's edict after The Fall, anyone who contravened that commandment was a sinner against the Lord and properly condemned to die. In our time, such unabashed truculence and righteousness would not be acceptable. But we do have our legal Luddites who would like to halt or at least brake the onrush of technology. Their ideas are not without merit, in the abstract, but difficult to implement in the concrete. Should any country put a halt to the march of the "robot," it would easily be invaded by the monster as it spewed out its goods in another land whose hunger or ambition made it less sensitive to the macro perils of the mini chip.

The other alternative—the dole—is rejected forthrightly by the Committee on the Evolution of Work in its first report. Bluntly, it states: "We do not accept the dole as a realistic or desirable alternative to gainful employment in productive jobs."

This flat statement is timely, coming at a moment when many, if not most, Americans identify "liberalism" with the dole—in whatever form. For such people, the phrase "welfare state" refers to a society in which many people are "on welfare."

To unions, the term "welfare state" refers to a society that seeks, as the Preamble to the Constitution suggests, to "promote the general welfare" and not to a nation where there is a large and growing portion of the population "on welfare." After all, who supports the people on the dole if not working people? The poor are too poor to pay taxes and the rich too smart to pay taxes, so the working stiff—in the final analysis—is Mr. and Ms. Tax-Payer.

But however working people may feel about a society that carries an ever bigger part of the nation on the dole, the dole per se is bad. It becomes economically impossible when the burden gets too heavy; it is bad for the recipients who are doomed to an empty life of dependence. Historically, it has been the way that great and overly rich empires, with income from their external vassals, bought off riots and revolutions at home.

Economically, politically, psychologically, and ethically, the dole is bad. The term "dole" does not refer to assistances extended to persons who are physically, mentally, or otherwise in personal distress. A society's commitment to care for its unfortunate is what makes a collection of human animals a civilized citizenry. But an economy so structured that it turns to a dole to "take care of" an ever-growing horde of jobless in a "labor surplus society" is inhuman, unrealistic, and ultimately doomed.

Labor's Agenda Endangered

Labor's agenda includes a nation (a world) where people have jobs—without which life is economically endangered and spiritually tortured. How, then, does one construct a society in which all those who wish to and can work do work?

For the owners of the economy this is not an important question. Employment is not their bottom line. A return, preferably a handsome return, on investment is. To working people, employment—a useful life—is the *sine qua non* of their existence. Until now, the pressure of organized labor has resulted in a measure of distributive justice to allow capitalism to balance demand with supply. But what happens from now on?

A realistic scenario—an agenda for the years from now until the year 2000—falls into two time segments: the near and the distant future. In the distant future, we will be confronted with a social order fraught with the problems of robotization, globalization, and atomization. But we are not there yet. And in the interim, as we slip toward such a new world, what shall labor do so that it can be an effective voice, both economically and politically, in humanizing the necessary changes?

"Humanizing" is not used here as an act of *noblesse oblige*, compassion, or charity. By humanization of social policy I mean that the economy should serve the people—and not vice versa. If the economy becomes our *end* and people become our *means* to satisfy that end, then we will suicidally have reversed ends and means. The purpose will have been lost and the process will have perverted the purpose.

Will labor be able to play an effective role in creating an economy that will serve people?

The bad news is that labor does not have the answers to two prime questions: First, what social policies can provide employment to people in a globalized and robotized economy? Second, what can labor do right now to conserve or compose the necessary strength to influence future policies?

The good news is that labor knows what it does not know and, in this act of wisdom, has undertaken an inquiry into its necessary, proper, and feasible role in the coming decades.

As in the case of Vatican II, the labor movement will—like the church—continue its commitment to its historic principles, without which its soul is lost. But again, as in the case of the church, its soul searching is likely to unleash forces of unpredictable directions and proportions. Meanwhile, the process is under way—a process that by its generation of new attitudes and acts will change the character of American labor—and, perhaps, of the total society.

The Pace of Change

The one sentence in the committee's report that caught the most public attention was a blunt admission: "Unions find themselves behind the pace of change." Enemies of labor read this to mean that unions were now obsolete; friends of labor read this to mean that unions would now become more relevant than ever. The press, in general, featured the line because, as in the case of Vatican II, a large, established, seemingly rigid organization was issuing a top-down call to its members to think anew.

It was this line in the second report, entitled, "The Changing Situation of Workers and Their Unions," issued in February 1985, that made the headlines and set the heads of labor in motion. Report recommendations went beyond urging unions to do what they had always done but to do it better. "We must expand our notions of what it is that workers can do through their unions," says the report. Ends as well as means, objectives as well as methods, should be reevaluated.

What is an appropriate way to reevaluate? The answer: back to basics. For unions, the basic is the worker—his or her needs, wants, desires, hopes, and dreams. Some hundred years ago, when the American Federation of Labor was founded, those animal impulses and human aspirations found expression in the ancient trinity of "wages, hours, and working conditions." Today, workers want more: "to have a say in the 'how, why, and wherefore' of their work." That old phrase, "industrial democracy," has become an emotional entity at a time when it seems to have lost much of its ideology. Whether this urge to be a "somebody" instead of just a "something" is a revolt against the "dehumanization" of the workplace, or whether it is an expression of a new self-image perceived by this generation, the fact is that working people increasingly do wish to have a greater say over what happens to them on the job.

Traditionally, unions have been very suspicious of arrangements that come under the rubric of "quality-of-work-life" programs. Such schemes were viewed as gimmicks to lure employees away from unions, a view that is now changing. "Several major unions have developed such [quality-of-work-life] programs and report a positive membership response," notes the committee, that "the labor movement should seek to accelerate their development."

This recommendation, as well as others, however, are all issued with a caveat. These suggestions are not edicts. "A new orthodoxy is the precise opposite of the proper approach," notes the report.

In this spirit, "back to basics" is less a return to some program than a return to the grass roots. The idea is for the leadership to put its ear to the ground: to talk less and to listen more, to be less oral and more aural, to find out how workers feel and think and act—whether unionized or nonunion.

It is in this open spirit that the report makes a series of suggestions on organizing, bargaining, internal democratization, and getting the union message out to the public. They are all somewhat novel, presented as an agenda for discussion rather than as directions for action. The action—for the moment—is to engage in one big pow-wow, a massive discussion about what is to be done.

The suggestion that seems to get the most attention is the desirability of merger among unions. Indeed, in the report there is a special appendix (the only item with an appendix) entitled, "Merger Guidelines." In part, the merger movement is under way because several national unions do not have enough members to justify independent existence or, more pragmatically, to carry the overhead. A merger offers the advantages of large scale economies. But there is another reason why mergers are desirable as well as necessary. Companies historically identified with a product are no longer producing that product or have taken on a protean existence as they turn out dozens or hundreds of different lines. The giants who grew horizontally have gone vertical and conglomerate. While companies move from turf to turf or over many different turfs, unions remain stuck in their jurisdiction. To overcome this, some unions have diversified. Some have tried multi-union bargaining. Others have merged.

Inevitable Adjustments

Viewed historically, it is inevitable that there will be macro adjustments in union structure. When business was local, unions were local. When corporations and industries went national, unions went national. When business goes conglomerate, so must unions.

The various suggestions of the report are all ways to get labor thinking about how to minimize its losses and maximize its potential, to give labor muscle, to enable unions to be a reasonably effective voice in the shaping of national economic policies.

Having such input, however, does not mean that labor and labor alone will be able to grapple with the meta-macro challenge of a robotized globe. The macro solutions will have to be political; collective bargaining alone cannot do the big job. Consider a hypothetical circumstance: a company employs 1,000 workers—under union contract. At expiration, the company introduces robots and discharges 900 workers; the other 100 are union members.

The union solution is to cut work time so that all 1,000 will have jobs. To do so the forty-hour work week will have to be cut to the four-hour work week, or something like that, without a reduction in weekly pay.

The employer refuses to go along. He is ready to double the pay of the 100 employees he is retaining.

The union asks these 100 to strike. They are reluctant. But, being good loyal unionists who love their brothers, they do go on strike.

The employer moves his robots to Portugal.

There, in an exaggerated nutshell, is the problem of a union in a robotized planet.

As I see it—this thought is quite personal and highly tentative—the titanic struggle in the last decade of this century or the first decade of the next will be between mega-multinational corporations and sovereign states—not unlike the historical conflict between church and state in the past. Who's the boss? What the little corporation mentioned in the frightening fantasy above could do to a union, global corporations could do to nations. They could dictate both economic and political policies to governments under the threat to remove capital, technology, employment, and sources of revenue from any country that did not do the bidding of the corporate overlords. The "sovereignties" could lose their sovereignty. The whole world could just be a colony ruled by corporations headquartered in the Cayman Islands, Crete, or the Isle of Man.

Should this fantasy ever become fact, what can nations do?

My guess—perhaps, my unthinking wish—is that they will do what unions have been doing in the past: they will unite. They have the power to refuse companies the right to import or export capital, to locate or relocate facilities, to employ labor, to tap raw materials. Above all else, they have the power to close their markets—both to goods and services emanating from hostile exploiters.

A country like the United States could probably do this on its own. It could do it better with the help of a few natural allies. But if nations, large and small, take collective action to defend their sovereignty against the alien dictator, then the world will witness the reenactment of an earlier drama when governments of "industrial democracies" evolved policies to civilize and "socialize" their domestic capitalisms. This time the grand drama will be replayed on a global stage.

Should such a worldwide movement of nations in some not too distant future search for a proper rubric, it might try: "Nations of the world unite, you have nothing to lose but your pains and a world to gain."

15

LANE KIRKLAND

"It Has All Been Said Before . . ."

Any analysis of the state of American unions, especially one pointing to or predicting their decline, should include the following disclaimer in the interest of accuracy: It has all been said before.

Labor's obituary has been written at least once in every one of the 105 years of our existence, and nearly that many causes of death have been diagnosed. Some of our most prominent labor journalists have earned their keep by writing of our demise each Labor Day, just as some of our better-known labor economists and academics have earned tenure by publishing predictions that unions would perish. It seems we must be forever perishing so that others may be forever publishing.

Reading these gloomy clairvoyants, I am reminded of the eminent professor who told the American Economic Association that trade unionism was of

lessening importance . . . in American economic organization . . . . I see no reason to believe that American trade unionism will so revolutionize itself within a short period as to become in the next decade a more potent social influence than it has in the past . . . .

The professor's prognostications were as wrong when they were uttered, in 1932, as they would be if they were repeated today. And they are being repeated today, in slightly different form.

The most popular contemporary explanation for labor's condition is that times are changing, and the labor movement cannot figure out how to cope with change. This analysis conveniently ignores the fact that the sole reason that men and women organize unions is to bring about change. Unions are not institutions to be forever defended but instruments designed to change for the better the quality of the lives of their members, through collective bargaining and legislative and political action.

Unlike corporations, unions have no independent life of their own apart from their members. They come and go, grow and decline, with changes in the conditions that produced them. The Cornice Workers, the Umbrella and Walking-Stick Dressers, and the Broom and Whisk Makers served the workers who needed them as long as they needed them, then closed up shop and surrendered their charters. But while the Horse Collar Makers may have vanished with the jobs of its members, the members themselves did not disappear. They looked for new ways to earn a living and new unions to represent them, and so the United Auto Workers was born to meet new circumstances and needs.

None of this is to minimize the difficulties facing the labor movement today, only to put them in perspective. Yes, unions have had and continue to have lots of problems. But they cannot be separated from the problems of the American worker. And the foremost problem facing the American worker and American unions in any era is the problem of unemployment.

To some, it may seem strange to talk about high unemployment when we have seen the official jobless rate drop by one-third over the last three years and when the administration boasts of having created millions of new jobs. But the current employment picture itself should be placed in perspective. Even in the midst of a supposed boom, unemployment is higher than at the very depths of the 1971 recession. The official rate has hovered around 7 percent in 1985–86, down from double-digit levels in 1982. But the official figures fail to include those who have become too discouraged to look for work. And they do not count part-time workers who want full-time jobs. Include them, and the real rate of unemployment begins to approach 14 or 15 percent.

A reserve army of the unemployed makes it difficult for unions to organize and bargain. It always has. And it tempts employers to indulge their fantasies of getting rid of unions. Years ago, the robber baron Jay Gould claimed he could hire half the working class to kill the other half. Some employers apparently still believe that, and they see heavy unemployment as the ideal condition for testing the theory.

Unfortunately, the shortfall of employment opportunities is likely to persist. To provide full employment by 1990, we would have had to create 20 million jobs between 1984 and 1990. In the past seven years, we have created 12.5 million. If we continue at that same rate, the shortfall would be 7.5 million jobs.

These employment statistics and trends are evidence of other forces at work on the American economy and society. The labor movement may feel their effects most acutely, but the problems they create touch each and every American. Three decades ago, a third of the work force was directly engaged in manufacturing. Today, only a fifth of the work force earns its paychecks in our basic industries. During the same period, the number of Americans in service jobs has nearly doubled, from 12 percent three decades ago to 22 percent today. Some of this is the irreversible result of technological change. The steel mills and assembly plants that were the Second World War's arsenal of democracy can today be manned by fewer soldiers. In the last few years alone, more than 2 million jobs have been lost in the manufacturing sector.

At the beginning of 1986, the United Steelworkers of America assembled their basic steel negotiating committees for collective bargaining and laid out a plan for contracts covering some 170,000 workers, not all of them in production jobs. At the start of this decade, the same body of steelworkers would have been planning for contracts covering about 550,000 workers in basic steel. Yet, given proper market conditions, the 170,000 workers of today could produce just about the same amount of steel. A great many of those lost jobs in steel and in other basic industries belonged to union members. They *all* belonged to Americans.

Technology is not the only source of the problem. Many of the jobs that have been lost in America have turned up in foreign countries, because we have surrendered to the aggressive mercantilism of other nations. In 1980, our trade surplus in goods were $40 billion. In 1985, our trade deficit passed $140 billion. That deficit represents almost 4 million jobs that have left this country, possibly never to return.

What has happened to these jobs and the unions in those trade-ravaged industries is a measure of what has happened to America. The steady erosion of America's industrial base is depriving millions of young American workers of the stable, well-paying jobs that sustain our standard of living and offer admission to the working middle class.

While it is true that new jobs are being created, what kind of jobs are they? The twenty most rapidly expanding occupations are paying, on average, $100 a week less than the twenty occupations in most rapid decline. The expanding occupations are largely in the service economy, the declining ones in manufacturing. Thus, we have one possible explanation for the recent decline in real family income, despite the rise in two-income families.

This is not a union problem, but a national problem. No one should believe himself immune from the damage. The shopkeepers of Johnstown suffered along with the steelworkers when the mills closed. The realtors of Flint suffered along with the auto workers when the assembly lines shut down: How many homes could they sell to people earning the minimum wage flipping hamburgers in fast-food franchises? And those who earn their living from high technology should wonder where they will sell their mainframes, robots, or lasers when their biggest customers—our basic industries—are forced to shut down.

All this says nothing about what will happen to the tax base that supports our public schools and universities and the avenues of opportunity they open up for bright, young students, no matter what their circumstances of birth.

Who We Are

While these trends would appear to bode ill for the labor movement's future, a closer examination of who we are and how we have changed tells a different story. Yes, we have fewer steel and auto workers in our ranks, because there are fewer of them. But at the same time, we have more than eleven times as many teachers, ten times as many state, county, and municipal workers, four times as many pilots, three and one-half times as many service employees, three times as many actors and artists, and more than twice as many postal workers, fire fighters, and communications workers than we did thirty years ago when the American Federation of Labor and the Congress of Industrial Organizations merged.

More than 40 percent of our members today work in white-collar and technical jobs. Another 23 percent are craftsmen and supervisors. Less than 40 percent of our members work in blue-collar jobs. Unions affiliated with the AFL-CIO have a higher proportion of members with college degrees than the population at large, and we also have a higher proportion of members with graduate degrees. As the composition of our membership shows, trade unionists are nothing more—and nothing less—than the American middle class and those who aspire to it. That should give even those who delight in labor's troubles some cause for concern.

At the same time, there is no evidence that trade unionism is not serving its members well and no evidence that it has suffered any real loss of membership because of the disaffection of current members. If anything, the evidence is all to the contrary. Decertifications of unions by their members, while numerically higher than in prior years, remain statistically insignificant at less than one-tenth of one percent of current membership. More than 75 percent of trade unionists reported themselves as extremely well satisfied or reasonably well satisfied with their union and their union's services in a recent poll conducted by Louis Harris and Associates.

A report issued in January 1985 by the Bureau of Labor Statistics, analyzing wages and benefits in the United States, noted that trade union members averaged 33 percent more than their nonunion counterparts. So, the value of organization in wage and benefit terms remains as great today as ever.

Our critics have been fond of pointing out, as an indication of union weakness, that most of the labor movements of other industrialized Western nations have reached a higher proportion of their potential membership. Such comparisons should take into account differences in the degree of government encouragement and industry acceptance that unions are accorded. New Zealand law requires union membership of every worker as a condition of employment. Scandinavian countries have for generations valued unions as benign and effective instruments of social and economic policy, on equal terms with industry. In some other countries union membership is open to anyone who cares to tender a dues payment as a badge of social philosophy or to gain entree to the political machinery of those labor movements that have linked their fortunes to political parties.

The situation in the United States is quite different. Unions do not admit anyone but workers who have bona fide employer-employee relationships in which union membership can be beneficial to the workers. While union members participate in partisan affairs as citizens, they have rejected all temptations to form a party of their own or to establish institutional links with any and all parties. Above all, there was never a time when U.S. unions were not hampered by discriminatory laws and militant opposition from employers and public officials, misrepresentation by the news media, and obloquy on the part of community financial and social arbiters.

Professor Paul Weiler, of Harvard University Law School, recently analyzed the conduct of American employers. Weiler traced "the skyrocketing use of coercive and illegal tactics by employers" back to 1957, the period when union representation was at its zenith. In all of the United States that year, 922 workers were fired for union activity and then reinstated by the National Labor Relations Board. By 1965, the number of workers illegally fired during organizing campaigns had reached 6,000. In 1980, the NLRB ordered a stunning 10,000 reinstatements for illegal firings during certification campaigns. If the Board ordered 10,000 reinstatements, one can only imagine how many discharges there were in total.

From experience, the American labor movement has developed a toughness and resilience unknown elsewhere in the world. Despite its numbers, it has succeeded, through determined political, economic, and legislative action, in bringing about social reforms and economic gains that exceed the achievements of labor movements many times more highly organized on paper.

That is not to say that the path for trade unionists will be free and clear in the future. Yes, we face changes—changes in technology, changes in the makeup of the work force, changes in materials and production and job patterns, changes in our relations with our employers and our government. A new labor force has grown up around us, and the trade union share of it has dropped.

The Future of Work

But once again, for the labor movement, that is nothing new. We have survived and prospered in the past by offering the working men and women of America not what the administration in power wanted, not what politicians wanted, not what their bosses wanted, not even what the labor movement's leaders may have thought working Americans should have wanted, but what they themselves really wanted. In that spirit, the AFL-CIO Executive Council created its Committee on the Evolution of Work and Its Implications. The committee issued its first report in August 1983 entitled "The Future of Work," analyzing the changes that have occurred and are occurring in the work force and the workplace, and attempted to draw the nation's attention to the continuing shortfall of employment opportunity. Its second report, "The Changing Situation of Workers and Their Unions," was issued in February 1985 and has formed the basis for a continuing and serious discussion within the labor movement. The second report offered a series of recommendations for the consideration of affiliates with respect to new methods of advancing the interests of workers, increasing members' participation in their unions, and improving labor's communications, both internally and externally. Further recommendations deal with improving union organizing activity and with structural changes to enhance the labor movement's overall effectiveness.

Since its issuance, the report has formed the basis for self-analysis, discussion, and planning by the AFL-CIO, affiliated unions, state federations, and central labor councils. A number of national unions have established special committees to analyze the report and to discuss how its ideas might best be applied. The committee continues to function as a working group reviewing the implementation of several of its recommendations, such as the development of television "performance workshops" for union leaders; the creation of a pilot program, entitled "One-on-One," to increase the level of membership participation; the establishment of a membership "benefit program" consisting of various forms of consumer and insurance programs and other services to affiliated unions, their members, and union associates; and the launching of a coordinated organizing campaign in the health care insurance industry. The report has even occasioned considerable interest abroad. It was reported on at length in the publications of the International Confederation of Free Trade Unions and was reprinted in Japanese by the Japanese Federation of Commercial Workers' Union and the Japan Labor Institute.

In this country the report has been much commented on— favorably for the most part—although it should be noted that some commentators have been gleeful about finding among our admissions an echo of some criticism they have offered in the past and now are prepared to concede that we are brilliant for agreeing with them. America's unions will surely be affected by the report and by the suggestions for change and new programs which will arise from the consideration and discussion the report has engendered.

The American union tomorrow will be far more technically competent. Its leaders, conditioned to see the past as a learning device, will focus on the present and future which confronts them. Its spokespersons, now being trained in performance workshops, will be more open and accessible to the media and hopefully will explain our actions and goals better. Its activists, now being trained in one-on-one communication skills, will prod discussion and review of union and union-related issues among a better informed, and therefore more involved, membership.

Its specialists, skills honed in the universities and in the shops, will deal with the myriad complexities of pension administration, stock ownership and options, workplace democracy, buyouts and takeovers, worker ownership, international competition, corporate campaigns, affirmative action, career ladders, safety and health, attrition agreements, coalitions, political action, and a thousand other involvements. Its organizers' car trunks will be filled not just with leaflets and picket signs but with video cassettes and corporate analysis data.

Its members, better informed and more involved, will enliven the internal political life of their unions, strengthen trade union democracy, and continue to insist on a primary focus on job-related conditions. Those members will maintain positions ranging from tolerance to understanding to support for the secondary activities of their unions, while the general public will judge union activities on an inverse scale—caring least about the primary activities and most about the impact of the secondary activities such as community, legislative, and political activism.

Interestingly, it is because of this inversion that the general public should be most concerned about the future of our unions. Almost without regard to the percentage of the work force represented (though there are obviously limits), unions will continue to carry out their primary role of representing workers' interests on the job. In this role, even at a one percent level of organization, the union would remain the most significant force in the work life of its members (even admitting the obvious limitations on its market power).

Union Progress

A year after adopting its landmark report, "The Changing Situation of Workers and Their Unions," the AFL-CIO has realized substantial progress in eight key areas affecting the scope and effectiveness of the labor movement. The federation has put in place a variety of structures to deal with such issues as organizing and collective bargaining; communicating with its members and the general public; providing new services and benefits for existing members and developing programs, benefits and services for union members, supporters, and associates not covered by union contracts; mobilizing community support; and strengthening its internal structure.

Three new offices have been created within the AFL-CIO to help move the labor movement toward its goal of meeting the changes occurring in the workplace and the economy:

- The office of Comprehensive Organizing Strategies and Tactics, established in the Department of Organization and Field Services, to help affiliates develop nonworkplace strategies in their campaigns to win recognition and first contracts from recalcitrant employers.

- A membership benefits corporation to develop and administer a program of consumer benefits and services for members of affiliates, such as low-cost credit cards; group life, health, and other insurance; discounted legal services; and IRA and other investment programs. Eventually these benefits will extend to former members and union supporters not covered by collective bargaining agreements, as the federation's program to establish new associate and other categories of membership takes hold among affiliates.

- A new position to mediate potential organizing conflicts and prevent "wasteful" competition among unions in signing up presently unorganized groups of workers. Two permanent arbitrators have been appointed to hear cases that cannot be resolved through voluntary agreements.

In addition, a temporary office has been established to assist nine AFL-CIO unions in their effort to organize Blue Cross/Blue Shield workers across the country. The health insurance firm has eighty separate operating companies with about 39,000 employees eligible for union membership. About 10,000 are already organized. Operating within the organizing department, the Blue Cross/Blue Shield program will serve as a demonstration project for other multi-union organizing efforts.

Forward strides in other areas covered in the 1985 report prepared by the AFL-CIO Committee on the Evolution of Work include:

- Expanded use of electronic media to get labor's message across, through training sessions conducted by the Labor Institute of Public Affairs in four states, as well as in states where unions face the challenge of compulsory open-shop legislation.

- Inauguration of "one-on-one" programs involving scores of affiliates in three pilot states. Under this system, local officers, shop stewards, and other union activists trained as canvassers talk with members to get their input on community, legislative, and social issues and involve them in local, state, and federal legislative activities.

- Strengthening state and local central bodies and increasing their effectiveness. The AFL-CIO convention last fall voted to make a major effort over the next three years to increase the level of voluntary affiliation with central bodies.

A year ago, the committee expressed confidence that the labor movement "has the capacity to continue the never-ending process of renewal and regeneration that has enabled unions to remain the authentic voice of workers." After one year of activity, there is strong evidence that, in the words of the report, "the labor movement can thrive amidst changing conditions." All in all, the prophets of doom have badly misgauged both the present strength and the future prospects of trade unionism in America. That view is probably shared by America's union-busting business leaders. If unions were dead or dying, they would save their energy and money. Instead, many are pouring unprecedented resources into efforts to frighten and bully workers into abandoning their human and statutory rights to form or join unions of their own choosing and to frustrate the workings of federal and state laws designed to protect those rights.

There are two things to be said about those efforts. One is to point out that every action generates an equal and opposite reaction, and that this is no less true in issues involving human freedom than in the laws of physics. Workers have indeed been frightened by the growing assaults, naked or subtle, on their liberties. Many will succeed in overcoming the threat to their economic and social well-being, and they will be joined increasingly by those who seem, for the moment, to have surrendered their right to a voice in their own wages and working conditions.

Trade unionists would like to see the fullest degree of labor-management cooperation in this country, but it must be cooperation based on mutual acceptance of the other side's right to exist. Trade unionists accept corporations' needs to be productive and to generate capital for investment, production, payroll, and profit. But corporations also need to accept workers' needs to be undisturbed and unintimidated in their rights to form unions or to participate in forms of industrial democracy that would guarantee their dignity and the decency of their living and working conditions. Until those things are an accepted part of the labor-management scene, it makes little sense to speak about labor-management cooperation in the main and to pretend it is anything more than an abstract principle.

The persistence on a course of "union avoidance" (such as the National Association of Manufacturers' adventures with a "Committee for a Union-Free Environment") can only engender continuing conflict. While it may seem appropriate for academics and journalists to lecture the trade union movement on the need to abandon a confrontational approach and to deal more cooperatively with employers, the very real problem that we confront is in finding employers, public or private, who wish to deal cooperatively with us.

The second point is that the union-busters, in their efforts to destroy basic instruments of democracy, are following a path that most Americans will sooner or later perceive as a threat to democracy itself. It is increasingly clear that in pursuing a heaven on earth in the guise of a "union-free environment," businessmen have been seduced by the dream of total power that American workers overwhelmingly rejected a hundred years ago in turning their backs on the dream of a "paradise for workers."

Both schemes are pursued with passionate intensity by the same sort of people—people who embrace tyranny in the name of freedom and who stand ready to jettison democracy in the name of efficiency. Both look on their fellow citizens as objects, not persons. Both seek to rob them of their human dignity and representative institutions and subject them to the arbitrary "guidance" of an elite. The promise that workers would be treated honorably or even humanely by the economic masters once their unions are crushed is as empty as the promise of the "withering away of the state" once the opponents of communism are liquidated.

In creating their trade unions, American workers cast aside all parties, conspiracies, and secret societies whose aim was to create any sort of "dictatorship of the proletariat." They committed themselves to work within the system, acknowledging the rights of others while asserting their own. They seek no more than that today, and they will settle for nothing less.

16

ALEXANDER B. TROWBRIDGE

A Management Look at Labor Relations

With a FY 85 deficit of over $212 billion, a 1985 trade deficit of $113 billion in manufacturing, work stoppages at their all-time low, union membership as a percentage of manufacturing employment less than half what it was in 1953, wages paid in nonunion companies continuing to exceed in percentages those negotiated in unionized companies, and the very survival of some industries and their unions at stake, it would be foolish to argue that the labor-management relationship in the manufacturing industry has not changed—and changed permanently. Predicting the direction of future changes is a far different issue. But assuming that both labor and management want to survive, and even to prosper, there are viable options, some of which will require changes in public policy.

The Way It Was—The Good Old Days

The two decades following World War II were characterized on the whole by domestic stability and American dominance of the world economy. The United States accounted for over one-third of the world gross national product and was recognized as the unchallenged technological leader of the world. International economic growth during these two decades assured a ready market for U.S. products.[1]

Unions grew and prospered substantially during this period. The impact of the War Labor Boards during World War II and the Korean War, as well as growing employer acceptance of the collective bargaining process as prescribed by the National Labor Relations Act, were major contributing factors to that growth. Our dominance of the world economy permitted, even up to the 1970s, labor and management to negotiate generous contract settlements, the costs of which could be passed on to the consumer. During these years cost-of-living adjustments (COLAs), inflexible work rules, overmanning, and other provisions were incorporated into labor contracts.

By the 1970s, our labor-management relations system had three basic characteristics.[2] First, union membership and strength had been maintained in the then dominant sectors of the economy such as manufacturing, construction, extractive industries, printing, and transportation, and such status was accepted as a given by many of the employers in those industries. Secondly, there was widespread acceptance of a formula approach to compensation. Wage increases were linked to macroeconomic factors rather than company or industry-specific performance. Its components included an annual improvement factor (AIF), or some variation thereof with a different name. The AIF was first adopted in the 1948 GM-UAW contract and was based on national productivity increases, which were then 3 percent. There was no explicit linkage to corporate or industry performance. The next component was the COLA, whose purpose was to protect the increase achieved by the AIF by ensuring that it was not eroded by inflation. Although there were variations, it generally equaled 70 percent of the inflation rate. The final component was the fringe benefit package that was negotiated on a benefit level and not on a cost basis. Fringe benefits started out as a relatively modest concept but grew rapidly to be a major cost item—ranging from 30 to 50 percent of wages.

The third and final characteristic was the development and

maintenance of two highly consolidated bargaining structures. One was multi-employer in nature and included steel, railroad, transportation, construction, and mining. All parties agreed to the same contract. The other structure was pattern bargaining, which occurred in the rubber, retail food, auto, and other industries. Some deviations for individual company problems were permitted in this arrangement, but generally wage and benefit levels were the same.

Facing Reality

My opening paragraph mentioned some of the changes and realities that today confront manufacturers and unions. The simple fact is that American manufacturers, with some exceptions, are not competing successfully in today's global economy. Furthermore, even in domestic markets, some companies are unable to keep up with nonunion competitors.

The Report of the President's Commission on Industrial Competitiveness puts it succinctly:

The four key indexes of national competitiveness reveal the following long-term trends for the United States: insufficient productivity growth compared to our major competitors, stagnating growth in real wage levels, inadequate real returns on assets invested in the manufacturing base, lackluster trade performance in manufactured goods (even when the value of the dollar was low), and eroding world market shares in many industrial sectors critical to our future economic development. While the economic recovery has masked many of these trends recently, we cannot afford to take a short-term viewpoint and assume that there has been a permanent reversal. It is vital that the United States take steps to ensure a long-term reversal of our declining competitiveness.[3]

The deep and long recession of the American economy during 1979–1982 has left some visible scars and permanent impressions with American manufacturers. Some did not survive this era, and those who are striving to survive as viable, profitable companies are becoming permanently lean and tough, but they are also fair and pragmatic. They have no choice faced with the following realities:

- Our average rate of productivity, as measured by real gross domestic product per employed person was one-seventh that of most of our major trading partners in the 1973–1983 period.

- From 1963–1973, the real wages paid to American workers increased at an annual rate of 2.6 percent, but since then real wages have stagnated. While real wages are still high compared to our major trading partners, the economy is not supporting an increasing standard of living for our workers equal to what the United States was able to achieve historically.

- As the National Commission's Report notes:

  Over the past twenty years, real returns on assets invested in manufacturing have declined...indicative of the inability of U.S. firms to produce goods profitably....[T]he relative attractiveness of investing in our vital manufacturing core has been compromised. It is no wonder that needed investments have gone unmade and a short-term bias has crept into business and investor decisionmaking.[4]

- Our trade balance in manufacturing has declined from a surplus of $3.4 billion in 1970 to a deficit of $113 billion in 1985. Furthermore, the U.S. share of high technology exports declined precipitously between 1960 and 1985. A Department of Commerce study on high technology exports concluded that between 1965 and 1980, U.S. export shares had declined in eight of the ten high technology sectors remaining. These trends, when viewed in their totality, indicate a weakening in the ability of U.S. corporations to produce products that meet the test of international markets.[5]

Impact on Labor-Management Relations

In recent years collective bargaining has in many instances been characterized as "concession bargaining." That term has been applied to settlements in steel, auto, transportation, meat packing, electrical, textiles, aerospace, etc. In fact, such bargaining characterizes a recognition by both labor and management of changes in the marketplace, and it would be more appropriate to call it "competitive," "survival," or "reality" bargaining.

Most of these settlements have incorporated many of the following:[6]

1. Two-tier wage systems.
2. Lump sum payments in lieu of, or combined with, modest wage increases.

3. Back-loading—where most of the wage and benefit increases are in the final year of a three-year contract, as contrasted to the historical practice of beginning in the first year.
4. Increased flexibility for management, which means the elimination of restrictive work or plant rules and a reduction in job classifications.
5. Increased control over benefit cost increases, particularly in health care.

The highly consolidated bargaining of the past has been severely and probably permanently fragmented. A number of new subjects have appeared in recent collective bargaining contracts, including provisions relating to job security, job training, quality-of-work-life programs, and advance notice and severance provisions relating to plant closing situations.

The competitive nature of collective bargaining today is also reflected in a number of developments that a few years ago would have been unimaginable. For example, the number of work stoppages (involving a thousand workers or more) has continued a decline that began in 1980. In 1984 there were only sixty-two, the fewest in thirty-seven years. Today, even after a contract expires workers increasingly continue to work either under the terms of the old contract or the employer's last offer. In September 1985, 95 percent of employees under private industry contracts that had expired and had not been renewed were at work and not on strike.

Wage settlements reflect this survival bargaining. The third quarter of 1985 was the seventh consecutive quarter in which wages and benefits increased substantially more for nonunion than for union workers. Finally, assuming the current trends in the Consumer Price Index continue, 1986 will be the fourth consecutive year during which total adjustments in collective bargaining with COLAs will be less than adjustments in those contracts without COLAs.[7]

These developments show that companies and unions are now bargaining benefit and wage increases based on microeconomic factors related to company or industry specific performance. The formula approach to compensation with wage increases linked to macroeconomic factors no longer exists. That is also the reason for the decline in highly consolidated bargaining structures.

Some of these changes grew out of sheer survival necessity for companies: the need to curb labor and production costs, the need to restore production incentives to compensation, the need to reduce unemployment costs and archaic processes by shifting laid off workers into training opportunities. Incumbent unions have had to learn along with their employers to roll with the same punches. For those that have not adjusted, collective bargaining is certain to have weakened.

A number of dynamic new approaches by management and labor at least promise the opportunity of stability and perhaps even new growth.[8]

- *Gainsharing.* Bonuses, profit sharing, and a variety of other productivity enhancement techniques attract new attention. Heading the list are those in the UAW—General Motors, and Ford labor agreements. A Conference Board survey found that fifty-six firms had plans for profit sharing that covered union employees. One out of five firms was looking at proposals to establish such plans.

- *Employee participation.* In the 1970s companies began to experiment with new ways to make effective communications with employees work hand in hand with productivity. One result was the quality circle, now the best known form of a labor-management sharing of responsibility. Teams of workers typically work with a supervisor to improve work methods. As a result workers are given new chances to develop their talents and skills.

- *Employment security and productivity.* A concomitant to employee participation plans is the concept that there really is no job security if the firm is not successful. Establishing the "common fate culture" means that a manager communicates to his employee team that their jobs are no more secure than his. "If you do well, you share in the benefits." Gainsharing and participative management plans may work in tandem.

- *Union and employee identification with productivity and profits of the company.* Employees are regularly given meaningful information on personal productivity and company performance. Again, an outgrowth of participation plans may be tied to gainsharing.

- *Corporate acceptance of the union.* These new approaches to labor management relations see the legal representative of the employees as a necessary partner in cooperative programs. This tactic is frequently a companion piece to concession agreements.

Some specific examples of these innovative approaches to collective bargaining and employment security include:

- *Saturn Subsidiary.* This new agreement covering future production of small cars provides that UAW members, active and inactive, will be the primary source for recruitment of the 6,000 member work force. UAW members initially employed at Saturn will be protected by permanent job security. New workers will achieve permanent job security based on seniority. Contrary to a traditional automobile collective bargaining agreement, there will be one productive classification and three to five skill classifications in the work force. Premiums will be added to the base pay rate based on performance, productivity, and quality. All workers will be salaried at this new plant. The retirement plan will not be the traditional one but rather will be a defined contribution, individual account type, following the pattern adopted at the New United Motor Manufacturing, Inc. (NUMMI) plant in California. Decision making at the Saturn plant will require the full participation of workers in the union and the free flow of information in the organization. The union will be represented at all levels of the organization and will participate in all decisions at all levels.[9]

- *New United Motor Manufacturing, Inc.* A joint venture of Toyota and General Motors at Fremont, California, the former GM plant hired mostly displaced GM union employees. It practices a nonadversarial form of labor management relations based on the Japanese model. Stressing cooperation and team work rather than confrontation, the plan involves no cuts in wages and calls for sharing management rights with workers, elimination of executive perks, listening to employee suggestions, full information sharing, sharing the rewards and prosperity that are expected to result, and allowing employees to stop the assembly line for problems. The contract guarantees against layoffs except as a last resort. Formal dispute procedures are not invoked unless necessary. In the first six months of operation there had not been a single grievance filed among NUMMI's 1,800 employees.[10]

- *Xerox.* Faced with a need to cut operating costs at four manufacturing plants by $3.2 million, through the layoff of 180 employees, the company agreed with its Amalgamated Clothing and Textile Workers Union (ACTWU) employees to assign the problem of reducing costs without layoffs to an eight member study action team. The team conducted walk-around investigations and interviews, took trips to competitors, tested new equipment, and redesigned plant and work procedures. Out of forty possible cost saving projects, nine were selected for intense study. After six months, the team submitted its plan to top union officials and corporate managers, for $3.8 million targeted savings. Adopted plans challenged a number of accepted labor management practices. The plan called for self-managing work groups with control over job decisions. Supervisors become resource persons linking work groups and technical services. The resultant savings precluded the necessity for any of the planned layoffs.[11]

Impact on Unions

Global competition has had a severe impact not only on collective bargaining but also on union membership, though other factors have contributed to the prolonged decline in union numbers.

As Professor Leo Troy has put it, summing up his analysis in Chapter 3:

Membership at the beginning of 1985 is the same as it was twenty years ago, about 18 million; the proportion of workers employed in non-farm industries, including government, who were members of unions had fallen to fewer than one in five, a proportion first attained in 1937–38, and that at a time when the union movement was growing rapidly; the percentage of the total labor market organized had declined to rates far below the peak rates of penetration of 1953; the number of union mergers is unparalleled in union history: what exhortation by leaders could not achieve is being forced upon many unions by their dwindling strength; throughout 1984 unions failed to participate in the most vigorous economic recovery since 1951; very few unions show growth, while the giants, with few exceptions, show decline, especially in relation to their record highs; losses in most National Labor Relations Board representation elections for new units, accompanied by continuing defeats in decertification elections. The national polity, with significant support of union members, rejected unions' political policies in the presidential election of 1984, while the public holds union leaders in low esteem. It is no exaggeration, therefore, to characterize the current position of unions as of crisis proportions.[12]

This decline, noted earlier, is not unique to the United States. It is also occurring in Britain, France, West Germany, Italy, and Japan, though there are contrary opinions in the academic community.[13]

Manufacturing was, at one time, one of the more heavily organized sectors—42 percent at its peak in 1953. By 1980 it had declined to 32 percent and to only 26 percent by 1984. Historically, union membership has declined during cyclical business downturns and has increased with business upturns. This is no longer true, however, as between 1983 and 1986—a period which represented a strong economic recovery—unions regained none of their substantial loss.[14]

Other factors have also contributed to this decline, including marketplace changes with particular emphasis on very modest employment opportunities in manufacturing and, concurrently, the significant growth in service industries, which unions have traditionally been unable to organize to any significant degree. Most job creation in the United States today is occurring in small businesses, which historically have not been a cost-effective target for union organization. The composition of today's work force, including many more female workers, young workers, part-time workers, and independent contractors, is not susceptible to the traditional appeals by unions. Certainly, deregulation has had a severe impact in such industries as transportation and communications. Troy, Freeman, and Medoff all agree that unions simply are not devoting enough financial and other resources to their organizing efforts and, in fact, expenditures for organizing have declined sharply during the 1950s, 1960s, and 1970s.[15]

Unions, of course, contend that their losses are due to employer opposition and inadequate enforcement of labor laws. Although it is difficult to conclusively deny the latter as a significant factor, it is interesting to note that the decline in union membership began in the 1950s and has continued under both Republican and Democratic administrations, some of which have been pro-union in their philosophy.

In any event, Troy, Audrey Freedman, and others argue that union membership is in a permanent state of decline and will not recover.[16] I do not agree with this prediction, as it assumes that unions will not act in their own self-interest to reverse this trend. The recent searching self-analysis of the trade union movement, as well as the adoption of a number of the recommendations contained in that report, indicates that unions are looking for new approaches to organizing, ones which reflect the realities of the marketplace and demographics of the work force.[17]

The Human Resource Function and Growth of Union-Free Companies

It started in the mid-1960s, when many senior labor relations professionals gave primary attention to the stability of their collective bargaining relationships and when their union counterparts were achieving the age and outlook of statesmen. The most important force for change was the rise of laws and government regulations mandating nondiscrimination and affirmative action in employment. Affirmative action planning brought many managers to be honest about rational personnel policies and practices. Compliance meant focusing thoughtful attention on every aspect of the employment relationship. The same type of process took place in occupational safety, pension planning, and health care cost containment. All brought increased responsibility to the personnel department, which grew in corporate power and importance.

As businesses expanded into high technologies, needs developed for finding and developing people with unusual skills. Performance became more dependent on attracting, holding, and motivating individual workers. Managers with a personnel psychology background began to supplant the labor relations manager.

The Conference Board survey on labor management relations in 1979 showed that preventing the spread of unionism had become more important to managers than achieving sound collective bargaining results.

The possibility of union-free operations, combined with psychology based, or employee-oriented policies, gave management an alternative to the adversary labor relations system. As a union-free approach, this new human resource system was expected to bypass the union and deal directly with the worker and his needs. While matching the compensation and benefits obtained in collective bargaining, the human resource executive was also interested in the design of the organization and the workplace, the leadership performance of supervisors, and the engagement of individuals and small groups of workers in workplace problems and decisions. Top executives began to rely on the human resource function, giving it the same importance that the labor relations function had once received. Kochan and Cappelli, who have done some impressive work documenting this development, note that the more advanced human resource programs "are concentrated in the same type of 'cutting edge' firms that...were the heaviest users of union substitution policies in the 1920s; namely, the largest, fastest growing, and most profitable firms and industries." This kind of program, they observe, has contributed to the decline of the traditional industrial relations unit.[18]

Although a number of academic studies have been done on the characteristics of union-free companies, the recent best seller, *The 100 Best Companies to Work for in America*, by Robert Levering, Milton Moskowitz, and Michael Katz, summarizes such policies quite well. In addition to competitive pay and strong benefits, they contend that the best companies also share the following programs:

1. Make people feel that they are part of a team or, in some cases, a family.
2. Encourage open communications, informing their people of new developments and encouraging them to offer suggestions and complaints.
3. Promote from within; let their own people bid for jobs before hiring outsiders.
4. Stress quality, enabling people to feel pride in the products or services they are providing.
5. Allow their employees to share in the profits, through profit sharing or stock ownership or both.
6. Reduce the distinctions of rank between the top management

and those in entry-level jobs; put everyone on a first-name basis; bar executive dining rooms and exclusive perks for high-level people.

7. Devote attention and resources to creating as pleasant a workplace environment as possible; hire good architects.
8. Encourage their employees to be active in community service by giving money to organizations in which employees participate.
9. Help employees save by matching the funds they save.
10. Try not to lay off people without first making an effort to place them in other jobs within the company or elsewhere.
11. Care enough about the health of their employees to provide physical fitness centers and regular exercises and medical programs.
12. Expand the skills of their people through training programs and reimbursement of tuition for outside courses.

Although some of these companies are totally or partly organized, the vast majority of them are union free. For the human resource professional, David Metz of the Union Carbide Corporation has conducted a study of its internal practices and those of other major corporations. He also identified twelve key factors that were necessary for a company to remain union free. These are:

1. Top management commitment.
2. Resources dedicated to employees.
3. Critical policies and procedures.
4. Effective supervision.
5. Open communications.
6. Competitive wages and benefits.
7. Effective detection of and response to employee concerns/ problems (grievance procedure).
8. Management credibility and predictability.
9. Role of the facility manager.
10. Relative treatment of employees.
11. Security.
12. Attitude survey.[19]

What is the future of the union-free trend? The answer to that really depends on future responses by both management and labor. To remain union free requires a strong commitment by all of management in a company and a totally communicative and open environment. In many ways it requires a much more demanding effort by the human resources department than in an organized company. Some companies may not sustain that commitment in communications quality in the future and to that extent they will be vulnerable. Similarly, unions will be adopting new organization efforts to counter this trend and will be alert to any management deficiencies which create vulnerability. The old maxim is still true "unions don't organize employees, managers do"—through mistakes, neglect, and, unfortunately, plain old greed.

The Future of Collective Bargaining in a Global Economy

Labor and management are at the crossroads in collective bargaining. They may choose to maintain their traditional adversarial relationship and let "good times" return to the manufacturing community or revert to the old habits of highly structured bargaining linking wages and benefits to macroeconomic factors rather than company-specific performance. Global competition will no longer permit this option. The recent developments in collective bargaining such as two-tier systems, bonuses, lump sum payments, and increased management flexibility, would seem to conclusively guarantee against this option. Certainly, the growth of participative management mechanisms, gainsharing, employment security, and employee identification with productivity and profits of a company justify some optimism that both labor and management have seen the realities of global competition and its impact, as well as the responses that are necessary to successfully face this competition.

Assuming the latter response will be the prevailing trend in the future, a number of public policy changes will be needed. The President's Commission on Industrial Competitiveness summarized such changes.

- Labor management cooperation. New cooperative relationships must be established between labor and management that will maximize productivity by involving employees and their elected representatives in the decision-making process in the workplace, as well as encouraging participative management throughout the organizing. This assumes the National Labor Relations Board and the courts agree that some changes in the basic labor laws may well be necessary to ensure that these innovations are not in violation of the National Labor Relations Act.

- Employee incentives must be strengthened to reward the efforts of individual employees and to emphasize the linkage between pay and performance. Particular attention should be paid to incentive stock options and employee stock ownership plans. This will require changes in the Internal Revenue Code.

- Displaced workers. Employers must be encouraged to provide early notification of planned closings and to strengthen their commitment to employee security. Some considerations should be given to changing the unemployment insurance system so as to allow benefits to be converted to reemployment/training vouchers. The United States employment service must devote much more effective effort to its labor exchange functions. Federal assistance, through the National Job Training Partnership Act or other appropriate vehicle, should be provided for a comprehensive range of services to further the goal of reemployment.

- Improve work skills. Employer investment in employee training should be encouraged through macroeconomic strategies designed to maintain economic expansion and reduce unemployment; balanced tax treatment of employer investments in human and physical capital; strengthened capacity of vocational education institutions and community colleges to provide customized training programs; and removal of tax disincentives for individuals being trained through employer-financed education programs. Employers should also be encouraged to take a more systematic approach in their training activities.[20]

The times have changed, and both labor and management must respond to that change with innovative and thoughtful responses. Certainly neither party can afford the luxuries and excesses of the past in today's global economy.

VII

Conclusion

17

SEYMOUR MARTIN LIPSET

North American Labor Movements: A Comparative Perspective

The efforts in this volume to come to grips with the American union movement at the start of the labor federation's second century have examined the sources of its growing weakness. Why, one hundred years after the founding of the AFL, are trade unions unable to retain and recruit members and to bargain effectively?

There is no easy or definitive answer, as the earlier chapters make clear. The best way to deal with the question is through comparative analysis. The puzzle as to why the United States has, in proportionate numerical terms, the weakest labor movement in the industrialized world is akin to Sombart's classic query voiced in 1906, "Why is there no socialist movement in the United States?"[1] Hypotheses bearing on both can be evaluated only by reference to the situation elsewhere. In this concluding chapter, therefore, I try to judge the adequacy of different explanations by reference to comparable countries, particularly Canada. The latter makes a particularly useful counterpart to the United States, as Huxley, Kettler, and Struthers demonstrate in Chapter 4, since most of her unions emerged as part of one North American movement, have similar sets of employers, and the economy resembles and is closely linked to that of the United States. Hence the fact that Canadian unions have grown while those in America have declined since the mid-1950s forces awareness that an analysis limited to the American situation cannot provide the answer to the conundrums.[2]

The high point in union density in the United States, according to Leo Troy, was 33 percent in 1953. As of 1986, Canadian unions include close to 40 percent of the nonagricultural labor force, while American ones encompass about 18 percent. "The major characteristic distinguishing the two countries is that in Canada more workers are organized within virtually every industry and in particular within government, manufacturing, and construction."[3] The problems facing Canadian unions are somewhat different from American, as M. Bradley Dow points out, since from the 1960s to the 1980s,

over two million workers [comparable to 20 million Americans] joined trade unions . . . , more than doubling total membership. . . . Having organized much of the potentials in public administration, education and health, transportation, communications and utilities as well as among blue-collar workers in manufacturing, construction, mining and forestry, labour must re-orient its organizing energies and methods towards office, technical, and professional workers in the private sector.[4]

Explanations for the decline in the United States in union membership and power in the labor market, drawn from internal analyses of American society, suggested by different authors in this book and elsewhere, generally fall into three broad categories—the structural transformation of the economy, changes in the legal environment, and the ways the basic values of society interact with these to affect attitudes and behavior.

Structural Changes

The "structuralist" approaches divide between the economic and sociological. The former point to the way economic transformations have weakened the bargaining power of unions. The latter stress the effect of changes in the distribution of occupational settings on the behavior and feelings of workers.

The economic argument notes falling levels of productivity from the mid-1960s onward among the heavily unionized smokestack industries, the impacts first of inflation and then of rising unemployment; the ways also in which domestic deregulation and freer international trade adversely affected important unionized industries and encouraged the growth of nonunion companies in the rapidly expanding high tech and service sectors. The latter reflects the shift from a goods-producing to a service-providing economy. These developments, as Galenson and Raskin note in earlier chapters, seemingly have weakened the ability of unions to provide benefits which would enable them to win over prospective new members and to retain the loyalty of old ones, and have encouraged employer anti-union militancy.[5]

Sociological interpretations point to the effects of changes in the distribution of occupations on class behavior and values. Central to the sociological argument are the ways in which thirty or forty years of relative prosperity and economic growth following World War II, and the general rising levels of education and living standards, have been accompanied by a reduction in the proportion of the work force in traditionally union-prone environments, particularly blue-collar workers in the factories, mines, and maritime industry, with a concomitant increase in white-collar, service, and university-trained positions. The latter development has enlarged the constituency for nonmaterialist social reform movements, e.g., feminism, ecology, peace, and civil rights causes. But apart from public employees, those in such pursuits have shown much less interest than manual workers in labor organizations.[6]

Both approaches identify structural economic changes, particularly the increased emphasis on service and high technology, as heavily responsible for the decline of American unions. Since comparable shifts have been occurring in the rest of the developed world, the consequences for unions should be similar. In fact, however, an examination of changes in the industrialized OECD economies challenges the explanatory emphasis on the growth of these sectors.[7] Between 1963 and 1973, the proportion of the total labor force working in industry declined for all countries except

Austria, Finland, Italy, and Japan. Conversely, during the same period, the proportion employed in services increased in each. Over the post-OPEC oil shock decade, 1973 to 1983, every industrialized OECD state experienced both a decline in industrial and an increase in service employment. Thus, from 1973 to 1983, all of the major OECD economies were undergoing similar transformations.[8]

Table 1 examines the relative size of the service sector (tertiary) compared to the industrial sector (secondary) at three points in time, 1963, 1973, and 1983. As Cameron notes, "a tertiary/secondary sector ratio of more than 1.50 indicates that the tertiary sector is 50 percent larger than the secondary. Likewise, a ratio of 0.80 indicates that the tertiary sector is only 80 percent as large as the secondary."[9] The ratios reveal two relevant important points.

First, in 1963, Canada was the *leading* service-producing economy in the OECD, slightly ahead of the United States. By 1983, Canada had widened the gap between itself and the United States.

Table 1
Service/Industrial Sector Ratios
Selected OECD Countries
1963, 1973, 1983

Country	Ratios[a]			Change 1963/83[a]
	1963	1973	1983	
Canada	1.71	2.05	2.71	1.00
Denmark	1.02	1.68	2.26	1.24
France	1.02	1.25	1.72	.70
Germany	.84	.95	1.25	.41
Italy	.94	1.08	1.43	.49
Japan	1.33	1.33	1.61	.28
Netherlands	1.24	1.58	2.41	1.17
Sweden	1.12	1.52	2.16	1.04
Switzerland	.81	1.09	1.47	.66
United Kingdom	1.06	1.29	1.90	.84
United States	1.65	1.89	2.45	.80

[a]See text for interpretation of ratios.

Source: Organization for Economic Cooperation and Development, *Labor Force Statistics, 1963–1983* (Paris: OECD, 1985), pp. 36–39.

Second, in 1963, three countries—Germany, Italy, Switzerland—had slightly larger industrial sectors, while in four others—Denmark, France, Sweden, and the United Kingdom—service was greater. By 1983, the service sectors in all of the major OECD nations were considerably larger than their industrial ones. Clearly, between 1963–1983 these countries had shifted from a goods-producing to a predominantly service-producing economy, with only Germany completing the transformation after 1973.

Thus, if these structural changes play a major role in reducing union density, membership rates should be declining throughout the OECD countries. But, as Table 2 reveals, there is no consistent pattern regarding the *degree* and *direction* of union density across eleven structurally similar societies. Over two decades, 1960 to 1980, the proportion of union members in the labor force increased significantly in Canada (1), Denmark (4), Sweden (5), and Italy (10); it decreased in the United States (2), The Netherlands (3), and Japan (8), remained relatively stable in Switzerland (9) and Germany (11), and moved up and down in Britain (6).[10]

Union density in Canada, the top-ranked country in terms of service/industrial sector ratio, increased sharply, while it fell in the United States, which ranks second. But organized labor is weaker in both than in lower-ranked Denmark, Sweden, and the United Kingdom, all of which, incidentally, gained in proportionate membership between 1960 and 1980. On the other hand, Germany, Italy, Japan, and Switzerland, which are among the lowest in terms of service-sector employment, that is, having a relatively larger industrial sector compared to the other OECD countries, varied inconsistently, stable in Germany and Switzerland, down in Japan, up in Italy. These comparisons reinforce the findings of Henry Farber and Richard Freeman.[11] In the words of the latter, "structural changes in the economy are not the *prime* cause of declining union" strength.

Other explanations point to factors which produced a decline in the competitive position of the unionized sector, as compared to both foreign and domestic competition, as the major reasons for the erosion in the bargaining position of American labor. Thus, Jack Barbash lists a number of ad hoc changes in the situation of American manufacturing that supposedly have "impaired American competitiveness in world markets."[12] Among these are

Table 2

Rank-order of Selected OECD Countries by Service/Industrial Sector Ratio for 1983 and Percent Union Membership in Total Labor Force for Selected Countries, 1960 to 1982.[a]

Country	Rank[b]	Percent Union Membership						
		1960	1965	1970	1975	1980	1981	1982
Canada	1	23.5	23.2	27.2	29.8	30.5	30.6	31.4
United States	2	22.3	24.5	25.4	23.7	19.9	19.0	17.8
Netherlands	3	38.7	37.4	37.5	38.4	37.1	35.7	35.0
Denmark	4	59.6	60.8	64.3	68.4	75.2	73.9	—
Sweden	5	—	—	72.3	78.1	87.7	87.0	—
United Kingdom	6	44.2	44.2	48.5	51.1	53.1	49.9	47.8
France	7	—	20.8	23.1	22.9	19.2	19.0	—
Japan	8	32.2	34.8	35.4	34.4	30.8	30.8	30.5
Switzerland	9	30.3	—	29.2	33.4	33.5	30.3	33.4
Italy	10	26.5	27.4	33.1	42.4	43.3	41.4	39.6
Germany	11	37.1	36.5	36.3	37.9	38.6	38.3	37.1

[a]Note that this table deals with the proportion in the total labor force, not the non-agricultural labor force to which other statistics refer.

[b]For rank order see Table 1

Sources: For union membership data see Leo Troy and Neil Sheflin, *Union Sourcebook: Membership, Structure, Finance, Directory* (West Orange, NJ: IRDIS, 1985), pp. 7–17, A1–A2.

"lowered worker productivity, flagging entrepreneurship, insufficient investment, investment and work disincentives in the tax system, persisting two-digit inflation, an overextended welfare state, overrepresentation of the inexperienced and unmotivated young in the work force, a declining work ethic, high interest rates, [and] the energy crisis." Similarly, John Parrish suggests that "when productivity gains slowed, then stagnated after 1965, the consequences were serious. Wage gains went into cost push and rising prices . . . .Industry found itself saddled with not only very high wage and benefit costs, but uneconomic work rules, overmanning, slow work paces, and limitations on overtime."[13] While the demand for American manufactured goods declined in the late 1970s, wages actually increased, according to a recent Brookings study.[14]

To resist further unionization of their factories and offices or to avoid unions altogether was a natural response to this predicament. Richard Freeman and James Medoff conclude that "part of the increased management opposition to unions is attributable to the increased union wage differential . . . [M]ultivariate statistical analysis shows that about 40 percent of the rise in management unfair labor practices is due to the rise in the union premium. When unions are more costly to employers, employers are more hostile to unions."[15]

These efforts to explain the decline of American unions make logical sense. But as with the focus on the effects of changes in occupational composition, the argument weakens when looked at in comparative context. The American economy and particularly its smokestack industries, have, of course, suffered from increased foreign, and in some cases greater domestic, competition. But other countries, such as Britain and Canada, whose union movements are in a much stronger position than the one in the United States, have experienced more severe economic problems, higher rates of inflation and unemployment.

As the data in Table 3 indicate, the misery index, the sum of inflation and unemployment rates, has been higher in these countries than in the United States for almost every year in the 1970s and 1980s.

During most of this period the Canadian and British economies have performed relatively poorly as Pradeep Kumar notes:

Table 3
The Misery Index in Canada, the United Kingdom, and the United States, 1970–1984

Year	Canada	United Kingdom	United States
1970	9.1	9.5	10.7
1971	9.0	13.3	10.1
1972	11.0	11.4	8.8
1973	13.2	12.5	11.0
1974	16.3	19.1	16.5
1975	17.7	28.8	17.4
1976	14.6	22.5	13.4
1977	16.1	22.2	13.4
1978	17.3	14.6	13.7
1979	16.7	19.0	17.1
1980	17.7	24.9	20.5
1981	20.1	22.5	17.9
1982	21.8	20.9	15.9
1983	17.8	17.7	12.7
1984	15.0	17.8	11.4

Sources: *Historical Statistics 1960–1983, OECD Economic Outlook* (Paris: OECD, 1985), p. 39, 83; "The OECD Member Countries 1985 Edition," *The OECD Observer* 133 (March 1985), special insert.

Canada's poor wage-productivity-labour cost performance relative to other major industrial countries, in particular the United States—our most important trading partner, has been a source of serious concern among policy-makers and in the business community. Productivity levels in Canada have been persistently lower than in the United States, Japan, and major European countries as Germany for decades. Our trend rate of growth since 1973 has been the lowest among the major industrialized countries with the exception of the United Kingdom. At the same time Canadian rates of increase in hourly compensation have been considerably higher than in the United States and Japan. Consequently, unit labour cost has exceeded the average of most industrialized countries.[16]

The recession of the early 1980s affected both North American countries, but it was

far deeper and broader based [in Canada] than in the United States. ... Aside from the difference in the magnitude of the decline in output, income and employment, there was also a sharp divergence in wage-price-cost productivity behaviour. As a broad generalization, while the U.S. recession followed the pattern of a typical business cycle, the Canadian downturn was a serious stagflation, i.e., recession combined with cost-price inflationary pressures.[17]

It should also be noted that the decline of American labor as judged by the proportion of the nonagricultural labor force belonging to unions, which began in 1954 and continued through 1985, started during a period of prosperity and labor peace. Not even the current economic recovery, the strongest of the postwar era, has reversed the trend. "Union membership has not risen, but rather has declined both absolutely and as a percentage of the employed wage and salaried workers between 1983 and 1984."[18]

If the shift from a goods-producing economy to a service-producing one and the cost pressures on unionized industries do not explain why American unions have fared worse than the Canadian or most others in the developed world, then what does? One of the most frequently advanced explanations, particularly by those who recognize that the greater strength evidenced by unions in Canada since the mid-1950s undermines the structural analyses, deals with variations in the legal environment.

The Legal Environment

The legal environment is particularly important in North America since, unlike the situation elsewhere, the law in the United States and Canada prescribes the conditions under which labor organizations gain a government protected right to represent employees exclusively in collective bargaining. These involve unions demonstrating to a labor relations board that they have the support of a majority of workers. Depending on jurisdiction, such boards, as in much of Canada, may authorize representation rights when presented with union endorsements (signed cards) by a majority of those affected, or, as is generally true in the United States, call for a representation election. The laws also define what employers and unions may or may not do to advance their goals.

Given the presumed importance of government involvement, some suggest that unions have declined in the United States because the basic legislation, enacted during the 1930s under Roosevelt, the Wagner Act, has become less supportive of or even unfavorable to unions as a result of revisions, particularly those contained in the Taft-Hartley Act, passed by a Republican-con-

trolled Congress in 1947. It has also been argued that labor boards
appointed by Republican presidents have administered the legislation in ways which have made it more difficult for labor
organizations to organize than in the past. The evidence suggests
the matter is more ideological than partisan. A study by the AFL-
CIO Lawyers Coordinating Committee reports on the distribution
of NLRB decisions made in the first year that the boards operated
with a majority appointed by each of the last three presidents —
Gerald Ford, Jimmy Carter, and Ronald Reagan. There was
almost no difference in the percent of cases decided in the
employer's favor by the Republican Ford board, 29 percent in
1975–76, and the Democratic Carter one, 27 percent in 1979–80.
The Reagan appointed board, however, ruled 60 percent of the
time against the union during 1983–84. David Silberman, the Associate General Counsel of the AFL-CIO, notes that the latter "is
radically different from its predecessors, Republican and Democratic alike."[19] Since the NLRB did not acquire a Reagan majority
until 1983, the current "tilt" does not help explain the falloff in
union strength from 1953 on.

In retrospect, the decade following the passage of the Wagner
Act, 1935–1945, represents the heyday of the American labor
movement. These years span the institutionalization of government protections of the right to organize under the National Labor
Relations Act (which is the model for Canadian labor law), and the
creation and dissolution of the War Labor Board which legitimized
unions as a responsible political actor. In "the period 1933–39
union growth was never less than 6 per cent a year and in one year
exceeded 20 per cent."[20] Between 1935 and 1945, as Leo Troy
notes in Chapter 3, the proportion of the nonfarm labor force
organized rose from 13 to 31 percent. Many students of labor
would agree with Richard Block and Steven Premack that "Never
before, or since, has the government been so helpful to the process
of unionization."[21]

The American legal framework was largely set in the Roosevelt
and first Truman administrations, when "the government established and interpreted the basic rules that have since governed
the collective bargaining system in the United States."[22] Since the
revisions enacted in 1947 in the Taft-Hartley Act, "the legal environment surrounding the recruitment of new members by

unions has remained virtually constant."[23] Consequently, Block and Premack argue that "union growth is now primarily a function of factors *internal to the collective bargaining system itself.* Although external factors still do play an important and, on occasion, a crucial role, it seems reasonable to believe that union growth is now a function of the behavior of the parties and of the legal environment."[24] This assumption both serves to reduce other social factors to secondary importance and legitimates union demands for sweeping reforms in the legal environment, that is, labor law reform.

The critical issue that needs to be assessed is the effect of variations in labor legislation across national boundaries, particularly in North America. Efforts to specify the reasons for the varying situation of unions in Canada and the United States have suggested that unions north of the border have experienced greater success due to the greater legal protections afforded them as compared to those operative in the United States. Weiler, Meltz, and Freeman and Medoff contend that the divergence in the trends of union density in the two countries results in large part from the fact that, unlike the situation in the United States, federal and provincial legislation in Canada has continued to encourage labor organization.[25] In Chapter 4, Huxley, Kettler, and Struthers also emphasize that, in distinction to Canada, "the American legal scheme *allows* rather than *encourages* [collective] bargaining, and that it also allows comparatively free play to the very considerable forces opposed to it."

Seemingly, American labor groups are handicapped by the need to win representation elections, often held months after the unions have submitted the requisite number of *authorization cards*, or *petitions*, signed by at least 30 percent of the employees. By the mid-1980s, unions were winning less than half (45 percent) of all such contests, down, it should be noted, from three-fifths in 1965, two-thirds in 1955, and three-quarters immediately after the war. In most of Canada, on the other hand, unions are certified on demonstrating that they have enrolled a majority, 50 to 60 percent depending on jurisdiction, as *dues-paying members.* Where elections are required, as in British Columbia and Nova Scotia, they are almost invariably held within two weeks.[26] Hence, Canadian employers have little or no opportunity to try to change their employees' pre-filing decision to join a union, while American companies can and often do conduct lengthy anti-union campaigns prior to the election. Canadian legislation, however, is more stringent in requiring that unions produce evidence of membership rather than of endorsement of an application for an election as in the United States. Still, in spite of these policies, unions failed to win certifications through elections in approximately one-quarter of the cases in Nova Scotia between 1977 and 1982 and in British Columbia in 1984–85.[27]

The most sweeping proposal to facilitate unionization in the United States to emerge from this comparative perspective has been put forward by Paul Weiler, who suggests "the elimination of the representation campaign through a system of instant elections."[28] The suggestion is premised on the assumption that prolonged delay between the filing of authorization cards and certification elections, which current American law makes possible, enables employers to wage effective campaigns to reduce union support among their employees. This belief is sustained by a number of American studies of the effect of employer opposition to unions in certification elections which indicate that such activities play a major role in preventing union victories. Reviewing the literature, Freeman and Medoff conclude that "opposition, broadly defined, is a major cause of the slow strangulation of private sector unionism."[29]

Though these conclusions make logical sense, Weiler himself, however, has questioned the extent to which legal changes can affect the situation: "One should be wary of any claim that a mere variation in legal procedure could actually influence larger trends in union organization."[30] Such contradictions in the evaluation of the effect of law largely result from uncertainty about its relative importance compared to larger social forces. The findings of a comprehensive and methodologically sophisticated study of the consequences of variations in election timing and employer tactics on the outcomes of representation elections, published since Freeman's and Medoff's review, sustain Weiler's doubts, and suggest the need for more research.

To test the effect of these factors, Laura Cooper examined 760 one-union elections in Region 18 of the NLRB (all of Minnesota, North Dakota, South Dakota, and parts of Iowa and Wisconsin) from 1978 to 1980.[31] The key indicator of campaign effect in the study was the difference between the percentage of employees signing authorization cards and that voting for the union at the election. She found that:

In contrast to popular wisdom, the union's support dropped to a substantially greater degree—15.5 percent—in elections held the shortest period of time after the petition, between 15 and 30 days. Also contrary to expectations, in elections with the greatest delays between petition and election—more than 90 days—unions lost only 10.1 percent of their support.[32]

Another way of examining the effect of delay, albeit indirectly, is to consider the relationship between union victories in elections and the percentage of workers signing authorization cards. Cooper reported that unions which turned in cards signed by from 30 to 59 percent of the work force failed to win more than two-fifths of the elections. "Only when a union had cards from more than 60 percent of employees did it achieve at least an even chance of winning the election." By submitting authorizations from 70 percent or more, unions increased their winning percentage to 65 percent.[33] Seemingly, what determines victory in American representation elections is the extent of support unions are able to mobilize *prior* to requesting an election.

Cooper's most surprising finding challenges

the assumption that employer unfair labor practices committed during a campaign decrease employee support for the union. This study found no evidence to support such an assumption . . . .In none of the regression analyses did unfair labor practices appear to have even the slightest influence upon the percentage of union vote, union vote loss, or election outcome. The only evidence of a statistically significant relationship between the commission of unfair labor practices and voting behavior . . . showed that in close elections, unions actually gained support when employers engaged in unlawful conduct.[34]

The difference in results between Cooper's research and other efforts to estimate the impact of factors in the campaign situation may be a function of the variation in the dependent variable. Cooper deals with the shift in percentage of employees who signed cards and of those who subsequently voted for the union. Most of the other studies deal with the success rate, i.e., the proportion of elections won by labor organizations. Cooper's approach seems a better way to evaluate campaign effects.

An examination of long-term trends in the extent of unionization in Canada and the United States, also serves to counter the
emphasis on the explanatory weight of differences in legal
systems. As reported earlier by Huxley, Kettler, and Struthers,
Canadian union density exceeded the American from 1924 to
1936. A more comprehensive set of estimates of union membership by George Bain and Robert Price reports even greater cross-
national differences and indicates that Canadian union membership was proportionately larger from 1918 to 1938.[35] Prior to
World War II, however, the Canadian legal environment was extremely hostile to unions, more so than the American.[36]

Although the main focus of the discussion on the effects of the
legal procedures affecting certification has been on variations in
North America, it should not be forgotten that European trade
unions, almost invariably more successful than North American
ones in recruiting members (Table 2), operate without the sanction of certification by a government agency. As Derek Bok
emphasizes:

What is distinctive about our law is the active part it plays in regulating
the process by which the union achieves recognition from the employer.
In other countries, . . . the laws create no formal machinery [certifying
unions] . . . ; no provision has been made for representation elections, nor
does the law require the selection of a union to serve as exclusive
bargaining agent for any given group of employees.[37]

The British experience, typical of that in Europe, assumes "that
trade unions must be allowed to operate informally, in a legal
vacuum. . . . The unions of manual workers had very generally
gained recognition by their ability to strike in the works of
employers who refused it. . . ."[38] And except for the British, European labor organizations also secure and hold members without
contractual provisions, common on this continent, to require
workers to join or remain in labor organizations. As Everett
Kassalow notes, "formal arrangements, through collective
bargaining (or other) arrangements to make union membership a
condition of employment, are largely absent in continental
Western Europe. Indeed, *under a number of continental West European national constitutions, or in separate labor statutes, such com-
pulsion is illegal.*"[39] And again, unlike the situation in North
America, Western European unions are not involved in "the han-

dling of workers' grievances or the administration of the labor-management contract."[40]

The effect of legislation on the potential for unionization is, of course, not limited to the procedural rules. Other changes in American labor law passed since the mid-1960s designed to increase workers' legal rights as well as improve conditions affecting health and safety may have weakened the appeal of unions. Legislation defining the rights of employees in the workplace has created a direct competitor to unions in their role as protector of workers.[41] As Joseph Garbarino suggests, the expansion of such protections, together with the growth of special interest groups working to make the new laws viable, pose a direct threat to unions:

> The legal system's expansion in the 1960s and 1970s into the areas of discrimination, health and safety, income protection, and other phases of employment relations may be the most serious threat to the labor movement's future growth . . . .The existence of numerous organized interest groups working on issues related to employee relations combined with an activist Congress and an accessible judicial system responsive to individual concerns represents a threat to collective bargaining as a method of achieving gains.[42]

Unions must deal with the fact that protective regulatory legislation and judicial decisions such as those which have eroded the employment-at-will doctrine, the unlimited power of the employer to discharge, "have given many workers most of the benefits and protections commonly provided by unionization."[43]

AFL-CIO president Lane Kirkland has acknowledged the improvement in the legal position of individual workers, which the labor movement helped to secure, but emphasizes that unions still have a major role to play in implementing these rights.

> There's one vacuum that exists between the existence of those rights and the attainment of them by the individual employees. They need somebody to represent them, somebody to speak for them in the various tribunals that make those laws effective. If you don't have that, the law is worthless. And that's a role, it seems to me, that the trade union can play during that period before they're quite ready to, let's say, face the conflict with the employer as a group.[44]

Kirkland, in effect, says that legal guarantees and judicial rulings must be enforced, may have to be litigated. Individual workers, therefore, are still dependent on organizations to secure these rights. The argument is a realistic one, although individuals can and do bring complaints before various regulatory boards. But there is little evidence to sustain or contradict the thesis that the expansion of legal protections has reduced the appeal of American unions. Logically this outcome is possible. Workers, particularly those who have never belonged to a union, may feel less need for one than in the past. But we simply do not know. In any case, there have been similar developments in Canada. Again a comparison with Canada undercuts the argument, both because Canada has stronger protective regulation and a larger union movement than the United States, and the increase in such protection has not weakened Canadian unions. As Joseph Rose and Gary Chaison note:

> It has been suggested that the expansion of regulatory schemes, e.g., occupational health and equal employment opportunity laws, has made union organizing more difficult . . . .Canadian public policy provides considerably broader protection for unorganized workers than is the case in the United States. In several jurisdictions, binding arbitration is available to resolve disputes involving unjust dismissal and redundancies and layoffs. . . . There is no empirical evidence that these innovations have retarded union growth.[45]

Employer Policies

American unions also have suffered in recent decades from the use by many employers, particularly in the rapidly expanding high tech and other unorganized industries, of pre-emption policies, as well as from sophisticated tactics designed to constrain union support. A pre-emption strategy is designed to avoid a union by "buying off" or preventing labor discontent. Barbash suggests, "Much of the relative decline has been due to the pursuit by large corporations of a union-substitution policy; that is, buying out their employees' union impulse, so to speak, and doing for them everything a union would do but without having to suffer the active presence of a union." Wrenn notes,

> If an employer pays essentially the same wages as unionized employers in the area and adds to that a promotion system that gives serious consideration to seniority, some sort of limited grievance procedure and, for

good measure, a quality-of-work program, unions will tend to have a hard time convincing workers to join, especially if the process of forming a union, winning an election, and negotiating a first contract is a process likely to take several years. . . .[46]

Cornfield points to "the rapid diffusion of private welfare plans in the nonunion large corporate sector during the post–World War II era" as the explanation for the decline of unions in this sector and their success in small shops which do not have such plans.[47]

It should be obvious that the thesis that the falloff in union strength in the United States is a function of increased resistance by employers, the greater use of legal and illegal methods to intimidate or otherwise undermine support for labor organization, cannot be dismissed by the evidence and logic presented thus far. As noted earlier, it has received some support from academic research. Freeman concludes that "studies of the causes of the decline suggest that perhaps 40% is due to increased management opposition."[48]

Yet, these emphases also may be challenged by reference to the comparative data. Large Canadian employers appear to be as sophisticated or as generous as American in providing assorted benefits. In any case, although there is an impressionistic consensus that Canadian employers are less hostile to unions than American, there has not been a systematic evaluation of the behavior of employers on the two sides of the border.[49] It may be noted, however, with the authors of the report of the AFL-CIO Committee on the Evolution of Work, that many of the major companies and other conditions in the two countries are the same. "Canada has roughly the same type of economy, *many similar employers*, and has undergone the same [structural] changes" as the United States.[50] And as indicated earlier, the economic pressures on Canadian employers to cut costs are at least as great, if not greater, than on Americans. Whatever the variation in the behavior of private management in the two countries and in their ability to affect union representation campaigns, any comparative evaluation must take into account that Canadian unions, like American, have had their greatest success in recent decades in organizing government workers. But the Canadians have done more than twice as well in this sector as their American counterparts.[51] It would be hard to argue that the much greater strength of public employee unions north of the common border reflects a significant difference in the degree of employer opposition, although, as Huxley, Kettler, and Struthers point out, the scope of collective bargaining in the public sector is greater in Canada.

The Impact of Public Opinion

In seeking to supplement these emphases, I would reiterate the point made earlier in Chapter 12, "Labor Unions in the Public Mind," that the evidence drawn from American opinion polls indicating loss in public support for unions from the mid-1950s to the present, argues strongly against the thesis that the fluctuations in union density during the past three decades are a function of changes in socioeconomic or legal structures. Public appreciation of trade unions has fallen steadily during that period and it is, therefore, not surprising that workers have shown a lesser willingness to join or vote for them in representation elections over the same period. As I noted in the earlier chapter, from an all-time low percentage of 14 in 1957, "the proportion expressing disapproval continued to move up to a record high of 35 percent in the summer of 1981. These losses in approval ratings between the late 1950s and the early 1980s correspond to the steady falloff in the proportion of the nonagricultural labor force who belong to unions in those years." Basically, American labor organizations have declined in their ability to recruit or retain members for the same reasons that the American public generally has become less sympathetic to them.[52]

To test the hypothesis that the falloff in union strength is associated with the decline in public support for trade unions, I have correlated the approval rates in Gallup Polls, as reported in Table 5 in Chapter 12, for various postwar years with union density and the percentage of union victories in NLRB certification elections in the same years. The Pearson correlations are presented in Table 4, below.

The four correlations range between .68 and .81. These are strong relationships and clearly indicate that the ability of unions to maintain or gain members and to win certification elections is closely linked to the public's view of them. A somewhat different

Table 4
Correlations Between Public Approval of Unions
and Union Support, 1947–1981

I.	Approval and Union Density	r = .76
II.	Net Approval and Union Density	r = .81
III.	Approval and Win Rate	r = .68
IV.	Net Approval and Win Rate	r = .70

Note: Approval refers to percent answering "approve" to the question, "In general, do you approve or disapprove of unions?" Net Approval refers to the percent difference between approve and disapprove. Union Density is the percent of the non-agricultural labor force belonging to unions as estimated by Troy and Sheflin, op. cit., pp. 7–17, A1–A2. Win Rate is the percent of union victories in NLRB certification elections.

way to test the relationship is to use a statistical formula, the least-squares equation, which permits a "prediction" of union density in any given year by entering the Gallup approval and net approval percentages into the equation. The results, which indicate a close fit, are given in Table 5.

Table 5
Least-Squares Equation Predictions of Union Density

Year	Actual Union Density	Union Density Predicted by Approval Rate	Union Density Predicted by Net Approval Rate
1947	32.1	28.8	28.7
1949	31.9	28.0	28.9
1953	32.5	33.0	32.5
1957	31.2	31.1	31.9
1959	29.0	30.3	30.8
1961	28.5	29.9	30.4
1962	30.4	28.8	28.9
1963	30.2	29.9	29.7
1965	30.1	31.5	31.4
1967	29.9	29.5	29.5
1973	28.5	26.8	27.4
1978	25.1	26.8	26.3
1979	24.5	25.3	25.0
1981	22.6	25.3	24.6

The same findings are presented in graph form in Figure 1. These illustrate the ways in which changes in the indicators of union strength move in tandem with variations in public approval of organized labor. These occur in spite of the irregularity with which Gallup asks the approval question and the probability that there is a time lag in the impact of changes in public opinion on union strength.

Obviously, Pearson correlations and linear regression equations are not the only ways to test or model the relationships. Public approval of unions may be a function of other unmeasured variables, such as the misery index. Perhaps, when the misery index increases, public approval of unions declines. In that case, some of the variance the Gallup data explains is overestimated, since it would include some of the explained variance due to the effect of the misery index. But the heuristic value of these models outweighs the negative characteristics of their simplicity. Clearly, as public approval of unions declines, so too do union density and the certification win rate of unions.

Each of the findings reported above is congruent with the assumption that a major, if not the major, factor affecting union growth or decline and ability to win certification elections is variation in the public estimation of unions. The opinion of workers varies almost totally in tandem with that of Americans as a whole. And knowing the distribution of public attitudes in a given year permits a fairly close prediction of the actual union density and winning percentage of unions in NLRB certification elections. These changes in public opinion from 1947, the year the Taft-Hartley Act was passed, to 1981, the most recent year for which a Gallup measure and membership and certification rates both exist, are clearly not affected by changes in the labor law environment, the composition of labor relations boards, delays in calling certification elections, employer tactics, or variations in the structure of the labor force.[53] The fact that the relationships are so high strongly suggests that the explanations for the decline of American unions lies in the larger aspects of American social structure, those which determine its basic social values. As noted at the start of this chapter, the studies that seek to explain the decline of labor organizations by reference to the factors which differentiate union members from nonmembers, or environments that are

Figure 1

**Relationships Between Gallup Union Approval Rates and Union Density and Percentage Wins in
Certification Elections, and Between Predicted Union Densities and Actual Density**

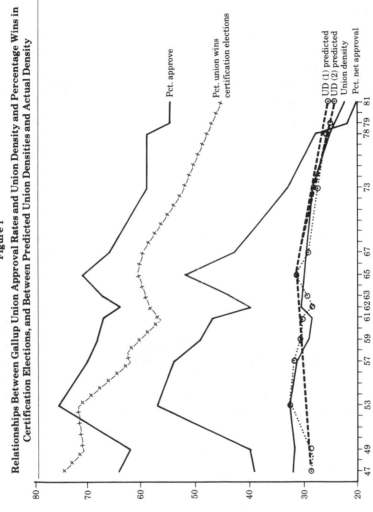

Note: UD(1) = predicted by approval rate; UD(2) = predicted by net approval rate.

more or less conducive to union strength, clearly cannot solve the conundrum of why American workers are so much less organized than their compeers elsewhere.[54]

To account for the lack of appeal of trade unions in the United States to the public and also to the employed labor force and to explain the growth in union density in the 1930s and 1940s and subsequent decline from the mid-1950s on, can only be done comparatively. It is necessary to specify what is unique, "exceptional," about America.

In seeking to do this, I return to a more detailed comparison of the United States and Canada. I hope to demonstrate that a major part of the answer, largely ignored by legal scholars and labor economists, lies in the ways in which the effects of structural changes on the strength of their labor movements are mediated by diverse national values.

Canadian and American Values

Canada and the United States differ in many ways, as I have tried to document and explain in earlier publications.[55] Most relevant to the concerns of this book are the variation in trade union strength and the presence or absence of electorally viable socialist or social democratic parties. While Canada falls behind much of Europe on both items, its trade union movement has encompassed a significantly larger proportion of the nonagricultural labor force than has the American one for most of the years between 1918 and the present, and class oriented or social democratic third parties have had significant electoral strength in federal and a number of provincial elections since 1921.[56]

To understand the sources of these differences, it is necessary to recognize that on many value, behavioral, and institutional indicators, Canada falls between the United States and Britain, closer generally to the U.S. than it is to the U.K.[57] As compared to her more populous neighbor, Canada is a more elitist, communitarian, statist, and particularistic (group oriented) society. These variations stem from structural differences, geography, resources, population density, and varying historical experiences. Both language areas of Canada sought to preserve and develop their cultural uniqueness by rejecting revolutionary ideals, those of the American and French Revolutions.

Contemporary America is the outcome of processes which began with an egalitarian, individualistic revolution. The United States remained through the nineteenth and early twentieth centuries the extreme example of a classically liberal or Lockean society which rejected the assumptions of the alliance of throne and altar, of ascriptive elitism, of statism, of *noblesse oblige*, and of communitarianism. This tradition was reinforced by America's religious commitment to the individualist "nonconformist" Protestant sects.

Canada, dominated by a Tory counterrevolutionary ethos, developed a more communitarian orientation. The two major Canadian national groups sought to defend their values and culture by reacting against two classically liberal revolutions. English-speaking Canada exists because she opposed the Declaration of Independence; French-speaking Canada, largely under the leadership of Catholic clerics, sought to isolate herself from the anti-clerical, democratic values of the French Revolution.[58] The leaders of both cultures, after 1783 and 1789, consciously attempted to create a conservative, monarchical, ecclesiastical, and statist society in North America. Canadian elites saw the need to use the state to protect minority cultures, English Canadians against Yankees, French Canadians against Anglophones, and also to provide services in a sparsely settled continent-spanning nation which private capital failed to supply.

These Canadian traditions are reinforced by the country's religious history. Harold Innis may have said it all when he wrote that a "counter-revolutionary tradition implies an emphasis on ecclesiasticism."[59] The majority of Canadians adhere to the Roman Catholic or Anglican churches, each of which is hierarchically organized and continued until recently to have a strong relationship to the state.

Both Canadian cultures fostered a variant of the Tory paternalistic view of the world. As Phelps Brown notes, "no tradition or doctrine inculcated an abhorence of collectivism such as prevailed south of the border. A Tory tradition ... stressed authority and hierarchy, but with these went solidarity and benevolence, which occupy some common ground with collectivism."[60] The United States, on the other hand, as Marx and Engels and assorted academic political theorists have emphasized, has been the classic or extreme example of a "born modern" bourgeois or classically liberal society, stressing anti-statism, individualism, and competitive meritocracy.[61]

Leftist collectivist, communitarian (welfare) and particularistic movements have emerged in western society in response to conservative emphases on elitism and statism. A tradition of state paternalism fostered by national elites has served to legitimate efforts by the less privileged strata to mobilize resources to improve their position through government action. Conversely, as a number of analysts, both socialists and others, such as H. G. Wells, Leon Samson, Michael Harrington, and Louis Hartz, have emphasized, the fact that the American national tradition is anti-Tory, anti-elitist, classically liberal, i.e., anti-statist, has weakened efforts to mobilize workers and others on behalf of socialist and collectivist objectives. Prior to the Great Depression, the American labor movement, both in its moderate AF of L form and radical Industrial Workers of the World (IWW) guise, opposed programs to extend the role of the state. The former was syndicalist, the latter anarcho-syndicalist. The majority of both, like other American groupings, were suspicious of government and, therefore, also rejected socialism and socialist parties.[62]

This larger framework of national differences in North America does not, of course, explain variations in the strength of different movements at varying times. Social democratic forces lacked significant strength in Quebec until the emergence of the *Parti Quebecois* in the 1970s, a development which paralleled a sharp increase in trade union density in the province. But as two Canadian political scientists, William Christian and Colin Campbell, have pointed out, these changes are linked to the province's past. The emergence of social democracy (the *Parti Quebecois* applied for membership in the Socialist International, but was denied it because the New Democratic Party objected)

is hardly surprising . . . for . . . Quebec's stock of political ideas includes a strong collectivist element. This collectivism is deeply embedded in Quebec's institutions. From the earliest days of New France, the government actively intervened on a broad scale in economic affairs. . . . Quebec's collectivist past provided receptive and fruitful soil for socialist ideas once the invasion of liberal capitalism had broken the monopoly of the old conservative ideology.[63]

The big anomaly in the comparison between the two countries is the growth in union density in the United States from the mid-1930s to the mid-1950s which, as we have seen, temporarily placed the American labor movement ahead of the Canadian. The same period also witnessed a change in the political and ideological behavior of much of organized labor. The American movement became deeply involved in political action, largely in support of the Democratic party, while the CIO and sections of the AF of L adopted political programs calling for a high level of state involvement in planning the economy, as well as sharp increases in welfare and health programs.

These changes reflected the impact of the Great Depression. That unprecedented event undermined traditional American beliefs among large sectors of the population, led to the acceptance by a majority of the need for state action to reduce unemployment and to assist those adversely affected by the economic collapse and to support trade unionism. As Richard Hofstadter noted, it introduced "a social democratic tinge" in American major party politics that had never been present before.[64] Analyses of public opinion polls and election results noted that class factors had become highly differentiating variables. Samuel Lubell, who conducted in-depth interviews of many voters, concluded that the electoral support for Roosevelt and New Deal programs constituted "a class-conscious vote for the first time in American history. . . . The New Deal appears to have accomplished what the Socialists, the I.W.W. and the Communists never could approach. It has drawn a class line across the face of American politics."[65]

The growth of class divisions and anti-capitalist feeling is attested to by the strong electoral support given to leftist third parties and to organized radical factions within the major parties in New York, Washington, Wisconsin, Minnesota, North Dakota, Oregon, California, and other states, as well as the socialist views expressed by large minorities in the opinion surveys. In 1937, Gallup indicated that 21 percent of those with opinions voiced a readiness to join a new Farmer Labor party. In a Roper poll taken in 1942, 25 percent of the respondents agreed that "some form of socialism would be a good thing . . . for the country as a whole." No other survey conducted in the 1930s, or shortly after, explicitly inquired about socialism. A 1936 Roper/*Fortune* poll, however, found

that a majority of respondents favored public ownership of various
utilities; 56 percent supported public ownership of electric lights;
55 percent for such ownership of gas; 50 percent for telephones;
and 49 percent for trolleys and buses. A Gallup survey taken in
1937 reported that 41 percent of the respondents favored government ownership of banks.[66]

Moreover, a clearly identifiable class-based division in attitudes
emerged; the less affluent strata, measured by both socioeconomic
status and occupation, perceived redistributionist policies, government ownership, and welfare policies more favorably than did the
well-to-do. The Great Depression produced a substantial change in
the attitudes of many Americans toward the traditional economic
system, which included increased support for, and willingness to
join, trade unions.

The "social democratic tinge" introduced during the 1930s
declined under the impetus of the postwar economic miracle,
which while still subject to the business cycle, basically involved a
steadily growing economy, with increased rates of social mobility
and higher living standards. From 1973 to 1983, "almost 18
million jobs were created in North America, while the six Western
European countries [France, Germany, Great Britain, Italy, the
Netherlands, and Sweden] experienced a net loss of 840,000 jobs.
Japan and Australia also gained jobs over the period, but not
nearly as fast as North America." During 1983, the United States
created more than "1.3 million jobs ... in continued sharp contrast with the six European countries which lost 715,000 jobs."[67]

There is considerable evidence from election results (six Republican victories in the nine Presidential elections held from 1952
on) to the findings of opinion polls that the postwar resurgence led
Americans to regain their faith in the promise of America as an
open meritocratic society. Support for statism/nationalization of
various industries and socialism in general declined greatly. A
1975 Cambridge Reports, Inc. poll asked, "Some people have proposed nationalization—or government takeover—of particular
industries which they feel have too much influence over U.S. life
and should be controlled. Would you favor or oppose government
takeover of any of the following industries?" Respondents were
asked how they felt about nationalization of each of eight major
industries. In every case, decisive majorities were opposed: Televi-

sion and radio networks (87 percent), automobiles (81 percent), banks (79 percent), steel (76 percent), telephone (72 percent), electric power (70 percent), railroads (67 percent), and oil (61 percent). Similar results to other related questions have been reported by a number of pollsters. Harris has repeatedly found in the 1970s and 1980s that only a tenth have favored "the federal government taking over and running most *big* businesses in this country."[68]

Strong left state third parties and organized social democratic factions within the major parties have disappeared. The electoral strength of socialist parties in the United States has been at an all-time low, well below one percent, in all presidential elections held since World War II. This pattern is also reflected in opinion polls which have inquired about attitudes toward socialism. As compared to the 1942 Roper poll, which found that 25 percent felt that "some form of socialism would be a good thing," less than half this proportion, 10 percent in 1976 and 12 percent in 1981, told pollsters that they would "favor . . . introducing socialism in the U.S." Almost everyone, 90 percent, reacted positively to "free enterprise."[69] Given the evidence of the restoration of faith in traditional American values, it is perhaps understandable, as noted earlier, that support for and membership in trade unionism have also fallen considerably.

The effects of the Great Depression and subsequent postwar economic growth on Canada have been quite different from those experienced south of the border. These variations reflect the fact that, as noted above, the political and social traditions, the values, the basic organizing principles, of the two societies have differed.

Flowing from Canada's cultural and political links to Britain, to monarchy, the Canadian conservative tradition, elaborated in modern times by her major philosophers like George Grant, has been Tory, one which Harold Macmillan has described as a "form of paternal socialism." It derives from the communitarian *noblesse oblige* values of the manor, of aristocracy. Canadian Toryism originally rejected and still opposes the anti-statist liberalism of the American Revolution, of Jefferson and Jackson. To foster Tory objectives and to prevent or reduce dependence on the United States, Canadian politicians have created a large state sector.

Canadian scholars have emphasized, in the words of Herschel

Hardin, that "Canada, in its essentials, is a public enterprise country, always has been, and probably always will be," while the
United States has a "private enterprise culture."[70] Or, as political
scientist J.T. McLeod notes, "the pervasiveness of state intervention, regulation, and the frequent appearance of public ownership" characterizes Canada, where "the State has always dominated and shaped the economy." Unlike "the United States,
[Canada] has never experienced a period of pure unadulterated
laissez-faire market capitalism."[71] The period since 1960 has witnessed a particularly rapid expansion in the number of crown corporations; fully 70 percent of them were created in the past
quarter of a century.[72]

Research based on opinion poll interviews indicates that Canadians, at both elite and mass levels, are more supportive than
Americans of state intervention. Summarizing surveys of high-
level civil servants and federal, state, and provincial legislators,
Robert Presthus reported

the sharp difference between the two [national] elites on 'economic liberalism,' defined as a preference for 'big government'. . . . Only 17 percent of the American legislative elite ranks high on this disposition, compared with fully 44 percent of their Canadian peers. . . . This direction is
the same among bureaucrats, only 17 percent of whom rank high among
the American sample, compared with almost 30 percent among Canadians.[73]

He also noted that differences related to party affiliation in both
countries emphasize the crossnational variations. Canadian
Liberal legislators score much higher than American Democrats
on economic liberalism and Canadian Conservatives score much
higher than Republicans. Conservatives and Republicans in each
country are lower on economic liberalism than Liberals and Democrats, but *Canadian Conservatives are higher than American
Democrats*.[74]

Mass attitudinal data reinforce the thesis that Canadians are
more collectivity oriented than Americans and therefore more
likely to support government intervention. Commenting on
1968–70 studies of American and English Canadian attitudes,
Stephen Arnold and James Barnes noted: "Americans were found
to be individualistic, whereas Canadians were more collectivity
oriented," more supportive of state provision of medical care or a

guaranteed minimum income.[75] A variety of opinion data gathered in the 1970s and 1980s reveal that Canadians are both more elitist than Americans *and* more disposed to reject competitive and business values and to support income redistributive measures.[76]

The existence of an electorally viable social democratic party, the New Democrats (NDP), in Canada has been taken by various analysts as an outgrowth of the greater influence of the Tory-statist tradition and the stronger collectivity orientation north of the border.[77] British labor economist Henry Phelps Brown points out that "the strong tradition of Toryism in Canada laid its stress on solidarity and against individualism and the fissiparous impact of market forces. Here it found common ground with socialism, and implicitly, with the propensity of the worker to organize for the protection of the conditions of his working life."[78] Conversely, the absence of a significant socialist movement to the south is explained in part by the vitality of the antistatist and individualistic values in the United States. There is, of course, good reason to believe, as Louis Hartz, Gad Horowitz, Henry Phelps Brown, and I, among others, have argued, that social democratic movements are the other side of statist conservatism, that Tories and socialists are likely to be found in the same polity, while a dominant Lockean liberal tradition inhibits the emergence of socialism as a political force. Socialism is strong where Tory and monarchical statism legitimated strong government, and where elitism fostered organized counter reactions by the less privileged strata.

Although the great majority of Canadian and American trade unionists have belonged to the same international unions, part of the AFL until the CIO split in the mid-1930s, the affiliates in the two countries have varied in ways which have reflected the diverse national traditions.[79] The leaders of American workers, as noted earlier, were anti-statist and opposed a separate labor or socialist party. The Canadian labor officials, though not formally socialists, repeatedly endorsed the principle of independent labor political action from the turn of the century on and were much more favorable to state intervention than their counterparts to the south. As Gad Horowitz notes:

The TLC [Trades and Labour Congress], though it consisted almost entirely of Canadian locals of AFL unions, and was greatly influenced by

Gompers, never adopted the Gompers approach *in toto* . . . .[Unlike the AFL] the TLC . . . never took a stand *against* socialism. Unlike the AFL, it never adopted the phraseology of *laissez-faire* and Lockean individualism.[80]

During the 1930s, many labor activists took part in the formation of the country's first nationally viable social democratic party, the Cooperative Commonwealth Federation (CCF). The relationship became stronger over the years. A poll of labor leaders in 1958 revealed that 45 percent of the TLC (AFL) officials surveyed supported the CCF, as did an overwhelming 93 percent of the Canadian Congress of Labor (CCL-CIO) executives.[81] The two labor federations, the TLC and the CCL merged into the Canadian Labour Congress in the mid-1950s and then went on to join with the CCF to transmute the socialist movement into the New Democratic Party (NDP) in the early 1960s. The united Canadian union movement has continued to officially support the NDP.

Although the Canadian economy has been weaker than the American, the postwar boom, extensive growth, upgrading of the occupational structure, higher income and standards of living, also occurred in Canada. But in spite of such improvements, which, of course, fell off in the early 1980s, Canadian socialism held its own nationally, generally obtaining between a fifth and a quarter of the vote in English Canada. Social democracy gained a new bastion in French Canada with the rise of the *Parti Quebecois* to major party status in the 1970s. And, of course, unlike the situation in the United States, the Canadian labor movement reached new heights in membership in the 1970s and 1980s. As noted earlier, this difference is not a function of structural variations in the two economies. In fact, Meltz documents that if "the industrial distribution of employment between the two countries had been the same and if . . . the rates of union organization [by industry] were the ones that actually existed, the overall union rate would have been even higher [in Canada] than it was in 1980 by approximately 10 percent."[82] That is, structurally the Canadian economy is less union-prone than the American.

Canadian unionists, the majority of whom are still in AFL-CIO affiliates, as well as the general public and political elites, have remained to the left of their American counterparts down to the present. As Mark Thompson and Albert Blum note: "With the exception of apolitical craft unions, Canadians invariably are in the left wing of the internationals. Canadians favor broader public health insurance plans, government ownership of basic industries. . . ."[83]

Prosperity has not undermined social democratic electoral strength or trade union membership in Canada. Unlike the situation in the United States, there has not been a return to the values of classical liberalism, because they have never been the national tradition. Canadian political parties, including the now governing Tories, remain committed to an activist welfare state, to communitarianism.[84] In the United States, on the other hand, the postwar boom revived belief in traditionally libertarian antistatist American values, and class became less salient ideologically. The weakness of socialism and of trade unionism are associated. The divergence in the trajectories of union density across the border reflect the undermining of the social democratic forces unleashed by the Great Depression in the south, and their maintenance in the north. If union density in the United States is declining to its pre-1930s level, it is because the social forces which emerged in the 1930s have experienced a steady decay over the post–World War II era.

The greater strength of the Canadian unions is linked to a more union friendly legal environment, more cooperative politicians, less hostile employers, but more important than these, to the greater propensity of workers to join than in the United States. As Phelps Brown notes, in Canada, "the atmosphere of social solidarity coming down from its conservative tradition might have been expected to let the trade unionist breathe more freely than he could south of the border."[85] All of these factors reflecting different political cultures and national values are interrelated. As Noah Meltz emphasizes, they "combine to explain why the percentage of workers organized in Canada was higher than in the United States before the Wagner Act of 1935 and after the late 1950s."[86] They also help to account for the results of a crossnational comparison of the attitudes toward trade unions among employees. "[T]here is at least one striking difference between the two countries. Specifically, there appears to be a higher level of latent unionism in Canada as measured by willingness of nonunionists to take out union membership."[87]

Robertson Davies, Canada's greatest living novelist, and a Tory, emphasizes that in spite of Canadians exhibiting a greater "decorum in the discharge of social and political affairs [than Americans] . . . beneath all of this we are a people firmly set in the socialist pattern."[88] The American social structure and values foster the free market and competitive individualism, an orientation which is not congruent with class consciousness, support for socialist or social democratic parties, or a strong trade union movement.

Notes
Contributors
Index

NOTES

2. Walter Galenson, "The Historical Role of American Trade Unionism"

1. John R. Commons et. al., *History of Labor in the United States* (New York: The Mac-Millan Co., 1918–1935), vol. 2, p. 195.
2. Ibid., p. 307.
3. American Federation of Labor, *Proceedings of the 18th Annual Convention, 1898*, p. 105.
4. *The Carpenter*, March 1889, p. 4.
5. Quoted in U.S. Department of Labor, Bureau of Labor Statistics, *Characteristics of Company Unions*, 1935, Bulletin 634, 1937, p. 160.
6. Draft letter from William Green to Frank Duffy. Files of the United Brotherhood of Carpenters and Joiners.
7. For a good recent analysis of the system in operation see W. Streeck, *Industrial Relations in West Germany* (New York: St. Martin's Press, 1984).

3. Leo Troy: "The Rise and Fall of American Trade Unions: The Labor Movement from FDR to RR"

1. Orley Ashenfelter and John Pencavel, "American Trade Union Growth: 1900–1960," *Quarterly Journal of Economics* 83 (August 1969), pp. 13–23; and George Bain and Farouk Elsheikh, *Union Growth and the Business Cycle: An Econometric Analysis* (Oxford: Blackwell, 1975).
2. Neil Sheflin, Leo Troy, and C. Timothy Koeller, "Structural Stability in Models of American Trade Union Stability," *Quarterly Journal of Economics* 96 (February 1981).
3. Ibid.
4. Alfred Marshall, *Principles of Economics*, eighth edition, (London: Macmillan, 1952), pp. 316–321.
5. Gordon Bloom and Herbert R. Northrup, *Economics of Labor Relations*, seventh edition, (Homewood: Irwin, 1973).
6. Leo Troy and Neil Sheflin, *Union Sourcebook* (W. Orange: IRDIS, 1985).
7. Leo Wolman, *Ebb and Flow in Trade Unionism* (New York: National Bureau of Economic Research, 1936).
8. Leo Troy, *Trade Union Membership, 1897–1962* (New York: National Bureau of Economic Research, 1965).
9. Ibid.
10. Wolman, op. cit.
11. Membership figures exclude Canadian membership of international unions headquartered in the United States.

12. Jack Steiber, *Public Employee Unionism: Structure, Growth, Policy* (Washington: Brookings, 1973).

13. Wolman, op. cit.

14. Charles J. Janus, "Union Mergers in the 1970s: A Look at the Reasons and the Results," *Monthly Labor Review* 101 (October 1978).

15. Larry T. Adams, "Changing Employment Patterns of Organized Workers," *Monthly Labor Review* 108 (February 1985), pp. 25–31.

16. Janus, op. cit.

17. Larry T. Adams, "Labor Organization Mergers, 1979–1984: Adapting to Change," *Monthly Labor Review* 107 (September 1984), pp. 21–27.

18. Gregory Stricharchuk, *Wall Street Journal*, Friday, January 18, 1985, p. 1.

19. Walter Galenson, *The CIO Challenge to the AFL* (Cambridge: Harvard University Press, 1960).

20. Stricharchuk, op. cit.

21. Victor R. Fuchs, *The Service Economy* (New York: National Bureau of Economic Research, 1968).

22. Arthur Burns, *Production Trends in the United States Since 1870* (New York: National Bureau of Economic Research, 1934).

23. Adams, op. cit.

24. Neil Sheflin, "Transition Function Estimation of Structural Shifts in Union Growth," *Applied Economics* 16 (February 1984), p. 81.

25. Leo Troy, "The Convergence of Public and Private Industrial Relations Systems in the United States," *Government Union Review*, Summer, 1984.

26. Paul Weiler, "Promises to Keep: Securing Workers' Rights to Self-Organization Under the NLRA," *Harvard Law Review* 96 (June 1983).

27. Solomon Barkin, *The Decline of the Union Movement* (Santa Barbara: Fund for the Republic, 1961).

28. Weiler, op. cit.

29. Cited in *Wall Street Journal*, November 6, 1984, p. 31.

30. Richard A. Epstein, "A Common Law for Labor Relations: A Critique of the New Deal Labor Legislation," *Yale Law Journal* 92 (July 1983), pp. 1357–1408.

31. Ibid.

32. Julius G. Getman and Thomas C. Kohler, "The Common Law, Labor Law, and Reality: A Response to Professor Epstein," *Yale Law Journal* 92 (July 1983), pp. 1915 ff.

33. Richard B. Freeman and James L. Medoff, *What Do Unions Do?* (New York: Basic Books, 1984) p. 239.

34. William T. Dickens and Jonathan S. Leonard, "Accounting for the Decline in Union Membership, 1950–1980," *Industrial and Labor Relations Review* 38 (April 1985), p. 333.

35. James L. Medoff, "The Public's Image of Labor and Labor's Response," December 1984, Unpublished mimeo, p. 7.

36. Ibid. See chapter 17 of this book for a more detailed report.

37. Ibid., p. 3.

38. Ibid., p. 9.

39. Stephen M. Hills, "The Attitudes of Union and Nonunion Male Workers Toward Union Representation," *Industrial and Labor Relations Review* 38 (January 1985), p. 181. The Medoff report, which does not have a breakdown for government, shows no group of workers in any private industrial sector in favor of unions as of 1977. Table 4 A, p. 10.

40. A.H. Raskin, "Comments" in the discussion of "Unions and Politics: 1984 and Beyond," Industrial Relations Research Assoc. Meetings Dec. 30, 1985, New York, Mimeo, p. 1.

41. Freeman and Medoff, op. cit., p. 229.

42. AFL-CIO Executive Council, *Report to the Sixteenth Convention*, Oct. 28, 1985, p. 66; Freeman and Medoff, op. cit., p. 237.

43. Milton Friedman, "Some Comments on the Significance of Labor Unions for Economic Policy," in David McCord Wright, ed., *The Impact of the Union* (New York: Harcourt, 1951), p. 231.

44. George R. Neuman and Ellen Rissman, "Where Have All the Union Members Gone?" *Journal of Labor Economics* 2 (1984).

45. Cited in *New York Times*, Jan. 29, 1986, p. D 1.

46. Leo Troy, "The Impact of Public Employee Unionism on the Philosophy and Policies of Organized Labor," *Government Union Review,* Spring, 1982.

47. Cited in *Wall Street Journal,* January 18, 1985, p. 8.

48. *The Changing Situation of Workers and Their Unions,* A Report by the AFL-CIO Committee on the Evolution of Work (Washington, D.C.: AFL-CIO, February, 1985).

4. Christopher Huxley, David Kettler, and James Struthers: "Is Canada's Experience 'Especially Instructive'?"

1. *The Changing Situation of Workers and Their Unions,* A Report by the AFL-CIO Committee on the Evolution of Work (Washington, D.C.: AFL-CIO, February, 1985), p. 15.

2. Ibid.; Richard B. Freeman, "Why are Unions Faring Poorly in NLRB Representation Elections," in Thomas Kochan, ed., *Challenges and Choices Facing American Labor* (Cambridge, Mass.: MIT Press, 1985); Paul Weiler, "Promises to Keep: Securing Workers' Rights to Self-Organization under the NLRA," *Harvard Law Review* 96 (June 1983), pp. 1769–1827. Himself a Canadian, a prominent labor arbitrator, and former Chairman of the Labour Relations Board in British Columbia, Weiler is not embarrassed to speak of "the Canadian model," in both senses of the latter term; for a more publicistic use of the same comparison, see Bob Kuttner, "Can Labor Lead?" *The New Republic*, March 12, 1984.

3. Robert White, "Report of UAW Director for Canada and International Vice President Robert White," December 1 and 2, 1984, unpublished document, p. 33.

4. UAW Canada, *Building a New Union in Canada,* p. 11.

5. For illustrative contrasting journalistic assessments, see James Bagnall, "UAW's White takes next step in independence fight," *Financial Post*, December 15, 1984, p. 12 and Wilfred List, "Little Change in Store for Independent Canadian UAW," *The Globe and Mail*, April 15, 1985, p. B5. The head of the Canadian Labour Congress, himself a member of the UAW, welcomed White's move with the following statement: "The facts are that we are not clones of Americans. We do have a different society, and a different culture, a different political system and a different judicial system. As workers, our economic and social goals in the collective bargaining system are distinctly different..." *Canadian Labour*, January, 1985, p. 7. But this brought a quick warning against overstatement from a meeting of Directors of other Canadian international industrial unions, assembled by the Canadian director of the United Steel Workers. See Wilfred List, "Autonomy issue creates a stir on the labour scene," *Globe and Mail*, February 18, 1985, p. B8. For background on recent developments in relations between Canadian unionists and international unions, see Mark Thompson and Albert A. Blum, "International Unionism in Canada: The Move to Local Control," *Industrial Relations* 22 (Winter 1983). Additional sources of internal conflict, undermining the capacity of the CLC to speak for all Canadian unions, are illustrated in Joseph B. Rose, "Some Notes on the Building Trades-Canadian Labour Congress Dispute," *Industrial Relations* 22 (Winter 1983), pp. 97–111. The actions taken by the UAW and the support for them from the head of the CLC (as well as the head of the Ontario Federation of Labour, another UAW member) are indicative of something very important, but they are not representative for the complex movement in any simple sense.

6. Joseph B. Rose and Gary N. Chaison, "The State of the Unions: United States and Canada," *Journal of Labor Research* 6 (Winter 1985), pp. 97–111, at p. 108. In average annual totals of days lost per thousand workers, Canada was second only to Italy among major industrial nations during 1960–1970 as well as 1971–1982. But it should be noted that there has been a dramatic decline, with 1983 totals only 50% of the 1981 figure and 28% of the 1982 one. Bradley M. Dow, "The Labour Movement and Trade Unionism: Summary Outline (June 1984)" in W.D. Wood and Pradeep Kumar, eds., *The Current Industrial Relations Scene in Canada, 1984* (Kingston: Queen's University Industrial Relations Centre, 1984). Rose and Chaison naturally weigh economic as well as other legal and political factors, as does another respected Canadian specialist, who has also published a recent valuable analysis and comparison. See also Noah M. Meltz, "Labor Movements in Canada and the United States," in Kochan, op. cit. We are greatly indebted to both of these earlier publications.

7. Stephen D. Krasner, "Structural causes and regime consequences: regimes as intervening variables," *International Organization* 36 (Spring 1982), p. 185. Labor lawyers already use the term "regime" as an alternative to the concept of public labor policy, which is more common among industrial relations specialists, but we would like to extend the political references of the concept. It is chosen first of all because it gives full weight to the autonomous practices of the two principal participants in dependent employment relationships without, as the "systems" concept does, treating the operations of state policy as an "environmental" factor and thus as a function of factors external to the relationships of principal interest. Unlike the "policy" concept, moreover, it is a political concept which nevertheless avoids reducing the special character of norm-governed processes to the parallelogram of forces embodying the concrete interests immediately at issue from situation to situation. As a constituted pattern, a regime embodies a measure of resistance to disruptive change; it places constraints upon the forms and exercises of power deployed; but these characteristics differ significantly in degree from regime to regime. A regime may be said to intend a preferred type of outcome, but this design will be established in a structural tendency, subject to even quite important exceptions, and not in a purely instrumental manner. Regimes differ as to complexity, flexibility, and tolerance of inner inconsistency or conflict, but all display that visible blend of legal manner and power factors which mark the "law of war and peace" which is the paradigm for the concept itself. Krasner and others expressly cite Hugo Grotius in connection with their development of the concept; and parallels between the Grotian concept of a "law of war and peace" and the effective reality of partially legalized labor relations have been noted in the past. See also Karl Korsch, "Jus belli ac pacis im Arbeitsrecht," *Kritische Justiz* 5 (1972) pp. 142ff. The reconstitution of a regime—i.e., a change in its structural tendency—requires a shift in the underlying power constellation, but this may be an unintended consequence of the operations of the former regime itself. For a less recondite formulation of the need for a political science framework for the study of international relations, see Peter Gourevitch, Peter Lange, and Andrew Martin, "Industrial Relations and Politics: Some Reflections," in Peter Doeringer, ed., *Labor Relations in International Perspective* (New York: Holmes & Meier Publishers, Inc., 1981).

8. Leo Panitch and Donald Swartz, "Towards Permanent Exceptionalism: Coercion and Consent in Canadian Industrial Relations," *Labour/Le Travail* 13 (Spring 1984), pp. 133–157. Recent changes and proposals in British Columbia, Alberta, and Quebec may indicate some shift towards the American design, but this is by no means clear, and the force of the resistance makes these exceptions, which on the whole prove the rule. David McMurray, "Labour and Policy: Summary Outline," in Wood and Kumar, op. cit., pp. 93ff. More characteristic of the longer-term pattern is the fact that the Ontario legislation, which for a time replaced all negotiated salary settlements of public employees (very broadly defined) with a standard increment, constructively interpreted a considerable variety of arrangements as if they were col-

lective agreements, and expressly put those who could not be said to be under such agreements at a possible disadvantage. It is arguable of course that such a design, since it binds unions to discipline its members to comply with the settlements imposed in the guise of collective agreements, is eventually more damaging to the integrity of the labor movement than almost anything else. The question plays an important part in debates about the failure of the German trade union movement to resist Hitler, since very similar legislation was a recurrent feature of Chancellor Bruening's policy between 1930 and 1932. See Hans-Hermann Hartwich, *Arbeitsmarkt, Verbaende und Staat, 1918–1933* (Berlin: Walter de Gruyter, 1967); Andreas Kaiser, "Probleme gewerkschaftliche Politik in der Endphaese der Weimarer Republik," *Blaetter fuer deutsche und Internationale Politik* 9 (September 1980), pp. 1099–1114.

9. An astute introduction to the American debate is provided in James A. Craft, "Post-Recession Bargaining: Mutualism or Adversarial Relations?" *Labor Law Journal* 34 (July 1983), pp. 431–439. See also Jean Mayer, "Workers' Well-being and Productivity: the Role of Bargaining," *International Labour Review* 122 (May-June 1983), pp. 343–353 and somewhat surprisingly, Bob Kuttner, "Can Labor Lead?" *The New Republic*, March 12, 1984. During the decline of the 1920s, confronted with anti-union "welfare capitalism," the American Federation of Labor proclaimed the "American Plan" as a non-adversarial strategy for survival. Except for some of the railway unions, Canadian organizations were little influenced by this conception.

10. The total union density series used for Canada is based on official data provided by Labour Canada. This series includes all unions and employee associations that engage in collective bargaining. It is calculated on the basis of labor force data for the total number of nonagricultural paid workers, which includes all full- and part-time wage and salary earners in nonagricultural employment. The total union density series used for the U.S. are those published by the Bureau of Labor Statistics (BLS), giving union membership as a percentage of nonagricultural employment. A number of problems have been identified with the accuracy of the union membership figures used by the BLS, especially between 1936 and 1952, when the rivalry between the AFL and the CIO resulted in inflated membership claims. Further problems have been found with the concept of union membership. For example, see George Sayers Bain and Robert Price, *Profiles of Union Growth* (Oxford: Blackwell, 1980), p. 81. The procedure adopted here of comparing union densities for the two countries on the basis of the Labour Canada and the BLS series follows the approach of Weiler, op. cit., and others. In addition to the BLS aggregate union membership series for the U.S., there exists one compiled by the National Bureau of Economic Research. It was begun by Leo Wolman, extended by Leo Troy, and most recently revised and updated through 1984 by Leo Troy and Neil Sheflin, *Union Sourcebook* (West Orange: Irdis, 1985). This most up-to-date series was unavailable to us at the time of writing, except for the total density figures for 1983 and 1984, which we have included, notwithstanding the differences between the BLS series and that of Troy and Sheflin. See further Troy's contribution to this volume in chapter 3.

11. Bain and Price, op. cit., p. 163.

12. Milton Derber, "Comment," on A. Rees, "The size of union membership in manufacturing in the 1980s," in H. A. Juris and M. Roomkin, eds., *The Shrinking Perimeter* (Lexington, Mass.: Lexington Books, 1980), pp. 55–58.

13. Meltz, op. cit., p. 322.

14. Weiler, op. cit., p. 1818, n. 171.

15. Rose and Chaison, op. cit., p. 98–100.

16. Meltz, op. cit., p. 321–322. As noted by Bain and Price, op. cit., p. 168, comparisons of changes in the level of union density in particular sectors "are made difficult by variations between countries in the way in which trade unions, trade union members, potential union members, and industries are defined." Nevertheless, comparisons of disaggregated data for Canada

and the U.S. have been attempted by Bain and Price, op. cit.; Weiler, op. cit.; Meltz, op. cit.; and, most recently, Rose and Chaison, op. cit.

17. A major emphasis in much recent research on trade union growth has been on the influence of economic variables, such as employment growth, the rate of unemployment, price changes, and the level or rate of profits. Interestingly, an influential initial contributor to this body of research did suggest the value of testing for political variables based on political representation in government. See Orley Ashenfelter and John H. Pencavel, "American Trade Union Growth: 1900–1960," *Quarterly Journal of Economics* 83 (1969), pp. 434–448. And this has been taken up in a few attempts in Canada. See Dennis R. Maki, "Political Parties and Trade Union Growth in Canada," *Industrial Relations/Industrielles* 37 (1982) pp. 876–885. The comparative questions asked by this paper appear to us to require comparative historical research.

18. David Brody, *Workers in Industrial America: Essays on the Twentieth Century Struggle* (New York: Oxford University Press, 1980) and David Brody, "The Expansion of the American Labor Movement: Institutional Sources of Stimulus and Restraint," in David Brody, ed., *The American Labor Movement* (New York: Harper & Row, 1971).

19. Joseph Rayback, *A History of American Labor* (New York: The Free Press, Collier-Macmillan Ltd., 1966), pp. 396–400.

20. Laurel Sefton MacDowell, "The Formation of the Canadian Industrial Labour Relations System during World War Two," *Labour/Le Travail* 3 (1978). The consequence of Ottawa's refusal to enact compulsory union recognition and collective bargaining during the war became evident during the Kirkland Lake Gold miners' strike of 1941 in northern Ontario. Despite the recommendation of a government-appointed conciliation board, mine owners in Kirkland Lake refused to recognize or bargain with the Mine, Mill, and Smelter Workers Union. Forced into a strike position during the worst months of winter by lengthy government conciliation procedure, the miners eventually lost a bitterly fought three month strike. This conflict almost bankrupted the fledgling CIO organization in Canada and proved to be a turning-point in mobilizing organized labor's resistance against the King administration's war labor policy. For an excellent analysis of the strike and its significance, see Laurel Sefton MacDowell, *"Remember Kirkland Lake": The History and Effects of the Kirkland Lake Gold Miners' Strike, 1941–42* (Toronto: University of Toronto Press, 1983).

21. Stuart Jamieson, "Times of Trouble: Labour Unrest and Industrial Conflict in Canada, 1900–1966," Study No. 22, *Task Force on Labour Relations* (Ottawa: Information Canada, 1968), p. 348.

22. Convincing evidence that the federal government shared this concern came from the appointment in 1966 of a major Task Force on Labour Relations, chaired by one of the leading Canadian authorities in industrial relations, McGill University dean, H.D. Woods. The 23 background studies of the task force subsequently published between 1966–69 constitute the most comprehensive analysis of labor relations yet undertaken in Canada. The task force concluded that "signs of ... rebellions have been unmistakeable. They include increasing turnover among senior union leaders, especially at the international level, a number of cases in which workers have refused to ratify collective agreements, a spate of wildcat strikes, and seemingly greater willingness on the part of workers to change their union allegiance." Although recognizing that Canada's "adversarial system" of industrial relations was undoubtedly flawed, the task force concluded that it was nonetheless well suited to the country's political culture and consequently did not recommend major changes in government policy. Michael R. Smith, "Industrial Conflict in Post-War Ontario or One Cheer for the Woods Report," *Canadian Review of Sociology and Anthropology* 18 (August 1981), p. 371; Morton, op. cit., p. 362.

23. For strike data, see Jamieson, op. cit., p. 371.

24. Lewin and Goldenberg, op. cit., pp. 243, 246; Mary Lou Gillis, "Trade Unionism: Sum-

mary Outline," in *The Current Industrial Relations Scene 1980* (Kingston: Industrial Relations Centre, 1981), p. 219.

25. Kenneth P. Swan, "Public Bargaining in Canada and the U.S.: A Legal View," *Industrial Relations* 19 (Fall 1980), pp. 276–78; George Hildebrand, *American Unionism: An Historical and Analytical Survey* (Reading, Mass: Addison Wesley, 1978), pp. 91–93.

26. Lewin and Goldenberg, ibid., pp. 239–40.

27. AFL-CIO Committee on the Evolution of Work, op. cit.

28. Jamieson, op. cit., pp. 391–92.

29. Desmond Morton, op. cit. p. 258.

30. Lewin and Goldenberg, op. cit., p. 242.

31. Panitch and Swartz, op. cit.

32. Compare Christopher Huxley, "The State, Collective Bargaining, and the Shape of Strikes in Canada," *Canadian Journal of Sociology/Cahiers Canadiens de Sociologie* 4:3 (1979); Panitch and Swartz, op. cit.; and James B. Atleson, *Values and Assumptions in American Labor Law* (Amherst: University of Massachusetts Press, 1983).

33. Swan, op.cit.

34. Weiler, op. cit.; Freeman, op. cit.; AFL-CIO, op. cit.; compare Meltz, op. cit. and Rose and Chaison, op. cit.

35. McMurray, op. cit.; Weiler, op. cit.; Jeffrey Gandz and Darryl Slywchuck, "The Implications of Developments in the Legal-Administrative Framework of Canadian Industrial Relations," *Business Quarterly* 46 (Summer 1981), pp. 64–75.

36. Weiler, op. cit.; Rose and Chaison, op. cit.; Jules Bernstein, "Union-Busting: From Benign Neglect to Malignant Growth," *U.C.D. Law Review* 14 (Fall 1980), pp. 3–77. A measure of the most recent American development is the trend in the ratios between employees newly covered by certifications granted and decertifications granted. The indices were as follows: for 1978, 8.9; for 1980, 8.98; for 1981, 8.2; for 1982, 3.9; for 1983 (first half), 2.97. Ratios computed from data in Dow, op. cit., p. 226. Despite some downward fluctuations in certifications in Canada, there are no signs of anything resembling such a turn.

37. McMurray, op. cit.; Gandz and Slywchuck, op. cit.; Trevor Bain and Allan D. Spritzer, "Private Sector Industrial Relations in the South," Proceedings of the 1981 IRRA Spring Meeting, *Labor Law Journal* (August 1981), pp. 536–544; Joseph Krislov and J. Lew Silver, "Union Bargaining Power in the 1980s," in ibid., pp. 480–484.

38. Canada Limited v. UE Local 504 (1980) OLRB Repr. Apr. 577, see Gandz and Slywchuck, op. cit.

39. McMurray, op. cit.; Gandz and Slywchuck, op. cit.; Rose and Chaison, op. cit.

40. J. David Greenstone, *Labor in American Politics*, Phoenix edition, (Chicago: University of Chicago Press, 1977); Vernon Coleman, "Labor Power and Social Equality: Union Politics in a Changing Economy," Mimeo, American Political Science Association, 1984.

6. Alain Touraine: "Unionism as a Social Movement"

1. Clark Kerr and Abraham Siegel, "The Inter-industry Propensity to Strike: An International Comparison," in A. Kornhauser, ed., *Industrial Conflict* (New York: McGraw Hill, 1954); Charles Tilly, *From Mobilization to Revolution* (Reading, MA: Addison-Wesley, 1978); Seymour M. Lipset, "Radicalism or Reformism: The Sources of Working Class Politics," in *Consensus and Conflict: Essays in Political Sociology* (New Brunswick, NJ: Transaction Books, 1985).

2. Heinrich Popitz and H. P. Bahrdt, et al., *Das Gesellschaftsbild der Arbeiter* (Tübingen: Mohr, 1957).

3. Victoria Bonnell, *Roots of Rebellion: Workers' Politics and Organizations in Saint Petersburg and Moscow, 1900–1914* (Berkeley: University of California Press, 1983).

4. Alain Touraine, *La Conscience Ouvriere* (Paris: Seuil, 1965).

5. Miklos Haraszti, *A Worker in a Workers' State* (London: Penguin Books, 1976); Alain Touraine, Michel Wieviorka, Francois Dubet, Jan Strzelecki, *Solidarity* (New York: Cambridge University Press, 1983).

6. Touraine, op. cit.

7. Fritz J. Roethlisberger and W. G. Dickson, *Management and the Worker* (Cambridge: Harvard University Press, 1939).

8. Alain Touraine, Michel Wieviorka, Francois Dubet, *Le Mouvement Ouvrier* (Paris: Fayard, 1984).

9. Sidney Webb and Beatrice Webb, *Industrial Democracy* (London: Longmans, 1897).

10. Edward P. Thompson, *The Making of the English Working Class* (London: Penguin Books, 1968); Richard Hoggart, *The Uses of Literacy* (London: Chatto and Windus, 1957); Yves Lequin, *Les Ouvriers de la Region Lyonnaise, 1848–1914* (Lyon: PUL, 1977); Jacques Ranciere, *La Nuit des Proletaires* (Paris: Fayard, 1981).

11. Georges Sorel, *Reflexions sur la Violence,* new edition, (Geneva and Paris: Slatkine, 1981).

12. Adolf Sturmthal, *The Tragedy of European Labor* (New York: Columbia University Press, 1943).

13. Serge Mallet, *La Nouvelle Classe Ouvriere,* new edition, (Paris: Seuil, 1969).

14. Georges Couffignal, *Les Syndicats Italiens et la Politique* (Grenoble: PUG, 1978); Alessandro Pizzorno, *Lotte Operaie e Sindicato in Italia, 1968–1978,* six volumes, (Bologna: Il Mulino, 1974–1978).

15. Antonio Negri, *Dall' Operaio Masa All'operaio Sociale, Intervista sull' Operaismo Cura di Paolo Pozzi e Roberta Tomasini,* multiplia edizioni, 1979. See also his *La Classe ouvriere contre l'etat* (Paris: Gallilee, 1972) and *Domination and Sabotage* (London: Red Books, 1977).

16. Philippe Schmitter, "Corporatism and Policy-making in Contemporary Western Europe," *Comparative Political Studies* (April 1977), pp. 7–38.

7.   Richard B. Freeman: "Effects of Unions on the Economy"

1. For examples of economists with generally negative views of labor unions, see Henry C. Simons, *Economic Policy for a Free Society* (Chicago: University of Chicago Press, 1948); Gottfried Haberler, "Wage Policy and Inflation," in P. D. Bradley, ed., *The Public Stake in Union Power* (Charlottesville, Va.: University of Virginia Press, 1959), pp. 63–85; Milton Friedman, *Capitalism and Freedom* (Chicago: University of Chicago Press, 1962), pp. 123–25, and *Free to Choose* (New York: Harcourt Brace Jovanovich, 1980), pp. 228–47; W.H. Hutt, *The Theory of Collective Bargaining* (London: P.S. King, 1930); Fritz Machlup, *The Political Economy of Monopoly* (Baltimore: Johns Hopkins University Press, 1952).

For examples of economists with generally positive outlooks on labor unions, see Lloyd G. Reynolds and Cynthia H. Taft, *The Evolution of Wage Structure* (New Haven: Yale University Press, 1956); Sumner H. Slichter, James J. Healy, and E. Robert Livernash, *The Impact of Collective Bargaining on Management* (Washington, D.C.: The Brookings Institution, 1960); and Derek C. Bok and John T. Dunlop, *Labor and the American Community* (New York: Simon and Schuster, 1970). Alfred Marshall's views are expressed in *Elements of Economics,* 3rd Edition, (London: MacMilllan, 1899).

2. The research findings are presented in detail in R. B. Freeman and J.L. Medoff, *What Do Unions Do?* (New York: Basic Books, 1984).

3. Charles E. Lindblom, *Unions and Capitalism* (New Haven: Yale University Press, 1949), p. 4; Henry C. Simons, "Some Reflections on Syndicalism," *Journal of Political Economy* 52 (March 1944); and Gottfried Haberler, "Wage Policy and Inflation," in Bradley, op. cit., p. 63.

4. The general procedure for estimating welfare loss or gain is described in detail in Arnold C. Harberger, "Three Basic Postulates for Applied Welfare Economics: An Interpretive

Essay," *Journal of Economic Literature* 9 (September 1971), pp. 785–97. Under the assumptions of this approach, the economic cost of the resource misallocation associated with the union monopoly wage effect is:

	decline in employment		fraction of		fraction of
1/2 x union wage	x in union sector due	x labor force		x total costs	
effect/100	to wage effect/100	in unions		associated	

This formula estimates the size of the triangle under the demand curve for union labor, which provides an estimate of what social loss would be if all output were produced under collective bargaining, and then multiplies this amount by an estimate of the fraction of all output produced in unionized settings. Our calculations assume a union wage effect of 20 to 25 percent, a decline in employment of workers of 13 to 17 percent, a union share of the work force of 25 percent, and a labor share of GNP of three-fourths. Using the formula above we obtain for the social cost:

$$1/2(.20)(.13)(.25)(.75) \quad = \quad .0024 \qquad (1)$$
$$1/2(.25)(.17)(.25)(.75) \quad = \quad .0040 \qquad (2)$$

Albert Rees' calculations in "The Effects of Unions on Resource Allocation," *The Journal of Law and Economics* 6 (October 1963), pp. 69–78, yield a similar result, as do those of Robert DeFina using a more complex model in "Unions, Relative Wages, and Economic Efficiency," *Journal of Labor Economics* 1 (October 1983).

    5. Pencavel and Hartsog find essentially *no* effect of unionism on employment. John Pencavel and Christine Hartsog, "A Reconsideration of the Effects of Unionism on Relative Wages and Employment in the U.S., 1920–80," National Bureau of Economic Research Working Paper No. 1316, 1984; and for a good review of the recent theories see Henry S. Farber, "The Analysis of Union Behavior," in *Handbook of Labor Economics* (Amsterdam: North Holland Press, forthcoming).

    6. An early analysis of the relationship between the union/nonunion Wage differential and the rate of unemployment and the rate of inflation is found in H. Gregg Lewis, *Unionism and Relative Wages* (Chicago: University of Chicago Press, 1914), chapter 5. The impact of these two variables on the wage effect through the 1970s has been analyzed by George E. Johnson in "Changes Over Time in the Union/Nonunion Wage Differential in the United States (University of Michigan, February 1981, mimeographed). More discussion of union wage policy through the business cycle is provided by Marten S. Estey, *The Unions: Structure, Development, and Management*, 3rd edition (New York: Harcourt, Brace, Jovanovich, 1981), p. 137.

    7. Robert Flanagan, "Wage Concession and Longterm Union Wage Flexibility," *Brookings Papers on Economic Activity* 1 (1984), pp. 183–222. Robert Flanagan, "Wage Interdependence in Unionized Labor Markets," *Brookings Papers on Economic Activity* 3 (1976), pp. 635–673. George Johnson, "The Determination of Wages in the Union and Nonunion Sectors," *British Journal of Industrial Relations* 15 (July 1977), pp. 211–225. Daniel J. B. Mitchell, *Unions, Wages and Inflation* (Washington, D.C.: Brookings Institution, 1980).

    8. Friedman, op. cit., p. 124.

    9. Reynolds and Taft, op. cit.

    10. R. B. Freeman, "Union Wage Practices and Wage Dispersion Within Establishments," *Industrial and Labor Relations Review* 36 (October 1982).

    11. Freeman and Medoff, op. cit., p. 90.

    12. The quit rate is much lower for unionized workers than for similar nonunionized workers. See, for example, Francine D. Blau and Lawrence M. Kahn, "Race and Sex Differences in Quits by Young Workers," *Industrial and Labor Relations Review* 34 (July 1981), pp. 563–77; Richard N, Block, "The Impact of Seniority Provisions on the Manufactur-

ing Quit Rate," *Industrial and Labor Relations Review* 22 (January 1978), pp. 199–216; Richard B. Freeman, "Individual Mobility and Union Voice in the Labor Market," *American Economic Review* 66 (May 1976), pp. 361–368; Richard B. Freeman, "The Effect of Unionism on Worker Attachment to Firms," *Journal of Labor Research* 1 (Spring 1980), pp. 29–61; Richard B. Freeman, "The Exit-Voice Tradeoff in the Labor Market, Unionism, Job Tenure, Quits, and Separations," *Quarterly Journal of Economics* 94 (June 1980), pp. 643–673; Freeman and Medoff, op. cit.; Lawrence M. Kahn, "Union Impact: A Reduced Form Approach," *The Review of Economics and Statistics* 59 (November 1977), pp. 533–507; Duane E. Leigh, "Unions and Nonwage Racial Discrimination," *Industrial and Labor Relations Review* 33 (July 1979), pp. 439–450; J.E. Long and A.E. Link "The Impact of Market Structure on Wages, Fringe Benefits, and Turnover," *Industrial and Labor Relations Review* 33 (January 1983); and Olivia S. Mitchell, "Fringe Benefits and Labor Mobility," *Journal of Human Resources* 17 (Spring 1982), p. 293.

The quit rate is much lower for unionized industries than for nonunionized industries. See, for example, Charles Brown and James Medoff, "Trade Unions in the Production Process," *Journal of Political Economy* 86 (June 1978), p. 355–378; John Burton and John Parker, "Interindustry Variation in Voluntary Labor Mobility," *Industrial Labor Relations Review* 22 (January 1969), pp. 199–216, revised by Freeman; John Pencavel, *An Analysis of the Quit Rate in American Manufacturing*, Industrial Relations Section (N.J.: Princeton University, 1970); V. Stoikov and R. Raimon, "Determinants of the Differences in Quit Rates Among Industries," *American Economic Review* 63, pt. 1 (December 1968), pp. 1283–1298.

The job tenure for unionized workers is higher than for nonunionized workers. See, for example, Freeman, "The Exit Voice Tradeoff...," op. cit.; Freeman and Medoff, op. cit.

13. Freeman and Medoff, op. cit., pp. 96–97.

14. Ibid., pp. 114–115.

15. Bok and Dunlop, op. cit., p. 260.

16. Harry Katz, Thomas Kochan, and Kenneth Gobeille, "Industrial Relations Performance, Economic Performance and the Effects of Quality of Working Life Efforts: An Inter-Plant Analysis," Sloan School Working Paper 1329–82 (Massachusetts Institute of Technology, July 1982), Bernard Ichniowski, "How Do Labor Relations Matter? A Study of Productivity in Eleven Paper Mills," National Bureau of Economic Research (Summer Workshop, August 1983); Michael Schuster, "The Impact of Union-Management Compensation on Productivity and Employment," *Industrial and Labor Relations Review* 36 (April 1983) pp. 415–30.

17. John T. Dunlop, "Labor-Management Response to Productivity Change," a lecture delivered at Utah State University, April 1, 1982, and published in "George S. Eccles Distinguished Lecture Series, 1981–82" (Logan, Ut.: Utah State University, 1982), p. 34.

18. Freeman and Medoff, op. cit., p. 183.

8. Daniel K. Benjamin: "Combinations of Workmen: Trade Unions in the American Economy"

1. Much of the historical background and institutional setting I describe draws heavily on three important works in the field of labor economics: Albert Rees, *The Economics of Trade Unions* (Chicago: University of Chicago Press, 1962); H. Gregg Lewis, *Unionism and Relative Wages in the United States* (Chicago: University of Chicago Press, 1963); and Richard B. Freeman and James L. Medoff, *What Do Unions Do?* (New York: Basic Books, 1984). In addition, my discussion of the impact of unions on workplace productivity relies importantly on the work of Charles Brown and James Medoff, "Trade Unions and the Productive Process," *Journal of Political Economy* 86 (June 1978), pp. 335–378.

2. Brown and Medoff, op. cit., pp. 369–371, found that capital accounted for a larger share of output in union than in nonunion firms. Another way of representing this result is that a given percentage increase in the use of capital yields a larger percentage increase in output in union firms than in nonunion firms. This differential productivity of capital in union firms could be due to a variety of causes, including differences in the type of capital used or in the nature of the outputs produced. Whatever the cause, assuming away its existence, as Freeman and Medoff do, necessarily forces an overstatement of the estimates of labor productivity in union firms. Allowing for the differential productivity of capital in union firms yields the conclusion that unions reduce the productivity of labor inputs.

9. Morgan Reynolds: "The Case for Ending the Legal Privileges and Immunities of Trade Unions"

1. Roscoe Pound, "Legal Immunities of Labor Unions," in Philip D. Bradley, ed., *Labor Unions and Public Policy* (Washington, DC: American Enterprise Institute, 1958); reprinted in *Journal of Labor Research* 1 (Fall 1979), p. 46.

2. Ludwig von Mises, *Socialism* (Indianapolis: Liberty Classics, 1981 [1922]), p. 435.

3. Pound, op. cit., p. 69. Dean Pound also emphasized the fact that labor unions persistently and successfully resisted suggestions that they be incorporated; as unincorporated associations they are either unsueable or if sueable, enforcement of the judgment is complicated and a doubtful remedy. Although unions occasionally lose in civil damage suits, there are chronic problems in sueing unincorporated associations and applying the "implied authorization" or doctrine of agency to the acts of union officials and members. For more on this issue, see Morgan Reynolds, *Power and Privilege: Labor Unions in America* (New York: Universe, 1984), p. 285.

4. Reynolds, op cit., p. 265.

5. Richard A. Epstein, "A Common Law for Labor Relations: A Critique of the New Deal Labor Legislation," *The Yale Law Journal* 92 (July 1983), p. 1386, n. 91.

6. Philip Taft, *Organized Labor in American History* (New York: Harper and Row, 1964), p. 454.

7. Quoted in Reynolds, op. cit., 109.

8. See Thomas Haggard and Armand J. Thieblot, Jr., *Union Violence: The Record and the Response by Courts, Legislatures, and the NLRB* (Philadelphia: Ind. Research Unit, Wharton School, U. Penn., 1983), p. 250; also see Morgan Reynolds, "Union Violence: A Review Article" *Journal of Labor Research* 5 (Summer 1984), pp. 237–46.

9. United States v. Enmons, 410 U.S. (1973) at p. 401.

10. Ibid., at p. 418.

11. Edwin Witte, *The Government in Labor Disputes* (New York: McGraw-Hill, 1932), p. 266.

12. Friedrich A. Hayek, *Law, Legislation, and Liberty* (Chicago: University of Chicago Press, 1976), vol. 2, ch. 8.

13. Milton Friedman, *Capitalism and Freedom* (Chicago: University of Chicago Press, 1962), p. 22.

14. Haggard and Thieblot, op. cit., p. 114.

15. Ibid, p. 116.

16. Morgan Reynolds, "An Interview with W.H. Hutt," *Journal of Labor Research* 6 (Summer 1985), p. 320.

17. Dan C. Heldman, James T. Bennett, and Manuel H. Johnson, *Deregulating Labor Relations* (Dallas: The Fisher Institute, 1981); Also see Mark Pulliam, "Monopoly Union Power, Wage Competition, and the Labor Antitrust Exemption: 'Which Side Are You On?'" *Pacific Law Journal* 13 (1981); Howard Dickman, "Exclusive Representation and American Industrial Democracy: An Historical Reappraisal," *Journal of Labor Research* 5 (Fall 1984), pp. 325–50.

18. Leonard M. Apcar, "Kirkland's Call to Void Labor Laws Ignites a Growing National Debate," *Wall Street Journal*, November 6, 1984, p. 29.

10. David Lewin: "Public Employee Unionism in the 1980s: An Analysis of Transformation"

1. David Lewin, "Collective Bargaining and the Right to Strike in the Public Sector," in A. Lawrence Chickering, ed., *Public Employee Unions: A Study of the Crisis in Public Sector Labor Relations* (San Francisco: Institute for Contemporary Studies, 1976), p. 160.

2. U.S. Bureau of the Census, *1982 Census of Governments, Volume 3, Public Employment, Number 2, Compendium of Public Employment* (Washington, D.C.: Government Printing Office, 1984); Leo Troy and Neil Sheflin, *Union Sourcebook: Membership, Structure, Finance, Directory, First Edition* (West Orange, New Jersey: Industrial Relations Data Information Service, 1985).

3. Union membership differs from the proportion of employees covered by collective bargaining agreements. For example, in 1982, when 45.7 percent of all full-time state and local government employees belonged to labor organizations, only 34.8 percent were covered by contractual agreements (U.S. Bureau of the Census, op.cit.). For further distinctions among union membership, bargaining unit representation, and contractual agreement coverage among public employees, see Richard B. Freeman, "Unionism Comes to the Public Sector," National Bureau of Economic Research, Working Paper No. 1452, September 1984; and John F. Burton, "The Extent of Collective Bargaining in the Public Sector," in Benjamin Aaron, Joseph R. Grodin, and James L. Stern, eds., *Public-Sector Bargaining* (Washington, D.C.: Bureau of National Affairs, 1979), pp. 1–43. Burton also presents data on federal sector union membership. Such membership approaches 90 percent of all Postal Service and blue-collar (Federal Wage System) employees, and exceeds 60 percent of all white-collar (General Schedule) employees. Also see Sar A. Levitan and Alexandra B. Noden, *Working for the Sovereign: Employee Relations in the Federal Government* (Baltimore: Johns Hopkins University Press, 1983); Daniel J.B. Mitchell, "The Impact of Collective Bargaining on Compensation in the Public Sector," in Benjamin Aaron, Joseph R. Grodin, and James L. Stern, eds., *Public-Sector Bargaining* (Washington, D.C.: Bureau of National Affairs, 1979), pp. 118–149; and Leo Troy, "The Agenda of Public Sector Unions and Associations," *Government Union Review* 4 (Spring 1983), pp. 15–35.

4. U.S. Bureau of the Census, op. cit.

5. Lewin, op. cit., pp. 145–163.

6. Herbert R. Northrup, "The New Employee Relations Climate in Airlines," *Industrial and Labor Relations Review* 36 (January 1983), pp. 167–181.

7. David Lewin, Peter Feuille, and Thomas A. Kochan, *Public Sector Labor Relations: Analysis and Readings,* 2nd ed. (Sun Lakes, AZ: Horton and Daughters, 1981).

8. B.V.H. Schneider, "Public Sector Labor Legislation—An Evolutionary Analysis," in Benjamin Aaron, Joseph R. Grodin, and James L. Stern, eds., *Public-Sector Bargaining* (Washington, D.C.: Bureau of National Affairs, 1979), pp. 191–223; and Freeman, op. cit.

9. The 1962 Presidential Order, Number 10988, was issued by President Kennedy; the 1969 Presidential Order, Number 11491, was issued by President Nixon; and the Federal Civil Service Reform Act of 1978, adopted during the Carter administration, codified the federal government's system of labor relations.

10. Gregory Saltzman, "Bargaining Laws as a Cause and Consequence of the Growth of Teacher Unionism," *Industrial and Labor Relations Review* 38 (April 1985), pp. 335–351; and David Lewin, "The Effects of Regulation on Public Sector Labor Relations: Theory and Evidence," *Journal of Labor Research* 6 (Winter 1985), pp. 77–95.

11. Wes Ulman, Mayor of Seattle, provides but one example of this phenomenon. Converse-

ly, an elected official may subsequently receive campaign support from public employee unions after initially opposing—and being opposed by—such unions and their leaders. Ed Koch, Mayor of New York City, provides an example of this phenomenon.

12. David Lewin and Mary McCormick,"Coalition Bargaining in Municipal Government: New York City in the 1970s," *Industrial and Labor Relations Review* 34 (January 1981), pp. 175–190. Quality-of-work-life agreements usually supplemented "normal" labor contracts and, in some cases, reflected a conversion from adversarial or "distributive" bargaining to cooperative or "integrative" bargaining and labor relations—see Richard E. Walton and Robert McKersie, *A Behavioral Theory of Labor Negotiations* (New York: McGraw-Hill, 1965). On concession bargaining, see David Lewin, "Public Sector Concession Bargaining: Lessons for the Private Sector," *Proceedings of the Thirty-Third Annual Meeting of the Industrial Relations Research Association* (Madison, WI: IRRA, 1983), pp. 383–393.

13. For a more complete analysis of sanitation labor relations in the U.S., especially the effects of technological change on such relations, see David Lewin, "Technological Change in the Public Sector: The Case of Sanitation Service," in Daniel B. Cornfield, ed., *Workers, Managers, and Technological Change: Emerging Patterns of Labor Relations* (New York: Plenum, 1986). The emphasis in this section is on municipal refuse collection and labor relations.

14. Also, in the early 1980s, only about two-thirds of all organized public sanitation employees were covered by collective bargaining agreements. See U.S. Bureau of Labor Statistics, *Work Stoppages in Government, 1980* (Washington, D.C., 1981) and U.S. Bureau of the Census, 1984, op. cit.

15. Barbara J. Stevens, "How Management Decisions Explain Cost Differences Between City Pickup Systems," *Solid Wastes Management* 22 (September 1977), pp. 32, 36, 72, 98, 100, and 103–105.

16. Eileen Brettler Berenyi, "Union Opposition Could Not Overcome Movement Toward Contract Collection," *Solid Wastes Management* 25 (October 1980), pp. 14–16 and 105–106, and Lewin, 1986, op. cit.

17. These and other recent changes in the technology of refuse collection discussed below were drawn from accounts published in various issues of *American City and County, Public Works, Solid Wastes Management, Waste Age,* and *World Wastes* between 1971 and 1984.

18. Lewin, 1986, op. cit.

19. Lewin, ibid., found technological change to have a large, statistically significant negative effect on changes in municipal sanitation employment, and a smaller but still significant negative effect on changes in sanitation unionization between 1975 and 1983.

20. U.S. Bureau of Labor Statistics, 1981, op. cit. In 1980, for example, 8.3 percent of all organized full-time sanitation employees were involved in strikes, compared with 5.0 percent of all organized teachers, 3.6 percent of all organized firefighters, 1.7 percent of all organized police, and 5.0 percent of all organized full-time local government employees.

21. Lewin, 1986, op. cit.

22. Ibid.

23. David Lewin, Peter Feuille, and Thomas A. Kochan, op. cit.; Mary McCormick, "Labor Relations," and James M. Hartman, assisted by Linda Mitchell, "Sanitation," in Charles Brecher and Raymond D. Horton, eds. *Setting Municipal Priorities, 1982* (New York: Russell Sage, 1981), chapters 10 and 7.

24. For supporting evidence, see Jack Barbash, "The Impact of Technological Change on Labor-Management Relations," in Gerald G. Somers, Edward L. Cushman, and Nat Weinberg, eds., *Adjusting to Technological Change* (New York: Harper and Row, 1963), pp. 44–60; Harold Levinson, Charles R. Rehmus, Joseph P. Goldberg, and Mark L. Kahn, *Collective Bargaining and Technological Change in American Transportation.* (Evanston, IL: The Transportation Center, Northwestern University, 1971); Neil W. Chamberlain and James W. Kuhn, *Collective*

Bargaining, 3rd ed. (New York: McGraw-Hill, 1985); Sumner Slichter, James J. Healy, and E. Robert Livernash, *The Impact of Collective Bargaining on Management* (Washington, D.C.: Brookings, 1960); Paul T. Hartman, *Collective Bargaining and Productivity: The Longshore Mechanization Agreement* (Berkeley: University of California Press, 1969); Chester A. Newland, ed., *MBO and Productivity Bargaining in the Public Sector* (Chicago: International Personnel Management Association, 1974); and Melvin H. Osterman, "Productivity Bargaining in New York—What Went Wrong?" in Lewin, Feuille, and Kochan, op. cit., pp. 162–174.

25. Newland, op. cit.

26. Examples of this research are contained in Ann Bartel and David Lewin, "Wages and Unionism in the Public Sector: The Case of Police," *The Review of Economics and Statistics* 63 (February 1981), pp. 53–59; David Lewin and Harry C. Katz, "Payment Determination in Municipal Building Departments Under Unionism and Civil Service," in Werner Z. Hirsch, ed., *The Economics of Municipal Labor Markets* (Los Angeles: Institute of Industrial Relations, University of California, 1983), pp. 90–121; David Lewin, "The Effects of Civil Service Systems and Unionism on Pay Outcomes in the Public Sector," in David B. Lipsky, ed., *Advances in Industrial and Labor Relations, Volume 1* (Greenwich, Conn.: JAI Press, 1983), pp. 131–161; Linda N. Edwards and Franklin R. Edwards, "Wellington-Winter Revisited: The Case of Municipal Sanitation Collection," *Industrial and Labor Relations Review* 35 (April 1982), pp. 307–318; William H. Baugh and Joe A. Stone, "Teachers, Unions, and Wages in the 1970s: Unionism Now Pays," *Industrial and Labor Relations Review* 35 (April 1982), pp. 368–376; and Peter Feuille, John T. Delaney, and Wallace A. Hendricks, "The Impact of Interest Arbitration on Police Contracts," *Industrial Relations* 24 (Spring 1985), pp. 161–181. Because the availability of large data sets trails far behind actual events, virtually no study has as yet examined the effects of unionism on public sector compensation during the late 1970s and early 1980s.

27. David Lewin, 1983, IRRA, op. cit.; D. Quinn Mills, "When Employees Make Concessions," *Harvard Business Review* 61 (May-June 1983), pp. 103–113; and Peter Capelli, "Concession Bargaining in the National Economy," *Proceedings of the 35th Annual Meeting of the Industrial Relations Research Association* (Madison, WI: Industrial Relations Research Association, 1983), pp. 362–371.

28. Allen M. Ponak and C.R.P. Frasor,"Union Members Support for Joint Programs," *Industrial Relations* 18 (May 1979), pp. 197–209.

29. Troy and Sheflin, op. cit.

11.   Joseph M. Garbarino: "Faculty Collective Bargaining: A Status Report"

1. These data are from Joel Douglas (with L. DeBona), *Directory of Faculty Contracts and Bargaining Agents in Institutions of Higher Education* (New York: National Center of Collective Bargaining in Higher Education and the Professions, Baruch College, 1984). Hereafter cited as *Directory, National Center*. In three states and the District of Columbia the governing boards of public colleges recognized unions without the support of a collective bargaining law.

2. *National League of Cities v. Usury* [44USLW4974 (1976)].

3. There are three major dimensions for evaluating the record of unionization. One is the number of persons in organized units. A second is the number of institutions organized. The third is the number of bargaining units that are represented. A bargaining unit often includes more than one institution so that there are more institutions unionized than there are units. Some researchers use "campuses" as synonymous with institution but this is a separate designation. There are many more campuses than there are institutions. An institution is considered organized only if a majority of its regular faculty are represented.

4. The reader is cautioned that the year-to-year changes reported in Table 1 result mainly

from additions or deletions of units. There is no continuing record of year-to-year changes in the size of existing units. Number of faculty represented in a unit is usually reported for the year of organization.

5. In some member institutions a separate law school unit has organized (e.g., New York University) or a subsidiary campus has organized (e.g., the Duluth campus of the University of Minnesota).

6. *Academe,* Bulletin of the AAUP, December 1972, p. 1.

7. Membership data are from Government Employee Relations Report, *Special Report on Higher Education,* Bureau of National Affairs, 1982 and ibid., *Daily Labor Report,* July 2, 1984. The AAUP has another 12–13,000 members in inactive status.

8. The Los Angeles Community College System (AFT), with 4800 members was the only two-year unit with more than 2500 members. The nine units account for 42 percent of all organized faculty.

9. *Academe,* Bulletin of the AAUP, March/April, 1984, p. 15a and Nov./Dec. 1984, p. 15a.

10. For a more detailed account of this period, see J. W. Garbarino, *Faculty Bargaining: Change and Conflict* (New York: McGraw-Hill, 1975), pp. 84–92. Current information is primarily from the reports in *Academe,* Bulletin of the AAUP.

11. *Digest of Educational Statistics, 1983–84* (Washington, D.C.: National Center for Educational Statistics, 1975), Table 91, p. 103.

12. An example of this situation is provided by the University of California's Berkeley chapter. An independent Faculty Association affiliated with the AAUP at the time of a bargaining election. A payment of $1.00 a month per member was agreed to in exchange for AAUP membership from a payment of about $12.00 a month to the local group, itself a relatively low dues level for a traditional union.

13. In 1981 the range of dues from bargaining chapters was reported as from 0 to $54 a year with an average of $16. *Academe,* March/April 1984, p. 9.

14. See the double page ad of the Committee for an Open AAUP and the statement of the candidate withdrawing from the race in *Academe,* March/April, 1984, pp. 4, 5, and 9 for one view of the issues.

15. There is a very large literature in this area; one of the most succinct and useful summaries is found in J. Victor Baldridge and Frank R. Kemerer and Associates, *Assessing the Impact of Collective Bargaining,* AAHE-ERIC/Higher Education Research Report No. 8, 1981 (cited hereafter as BK report).

16. BK report, p. 1

17. BK report, however, the Florida Board of Regents replaced the Faculty Senate Council with a body made up of the presidents of the several faculty senates because they felt the Council had been dominated by union activists (BK report, p. 23). At the Minnesota Community Colleges, the faculty union chose to exercise its right to function as the faculty representative on professional issues, excluding nonunion faculty from participation. This issue, incidentally, led to an open conflict between the Collective Bargaining Congress and the AAUP national leadership. *Academe,* March-April 1984, pp. 4–5.

18. BK report, p. 4.

19. BK report, p. 38.

20. In the 1960s a major state university system was reported as awarding tenure to over 90 percent of those reviewed. In 1971 the Commission on Academic Tenure found that 45 percent of public and 36 percent of private institutions responding to a survey awarded tenure to over 80 percent of those considered. Garbarino, op. cit. p. 238.

21. Richard B. Freeman, *Should We Organize? Effects of Faculty Unionism on Academic Compensation,* Working Paper No. 301, National Bureau of Economic Research Inc., November, 1978.

22. The most recent report shows a 9.4 percent advantage of unionized over nonunion public institutions as of 1984. This is compatible with an increase in the union-nonunion differential which has been variously estimated in the early years of organization as either insignificant or positive to a minor degree. However, the study is a simple comparison of averages with no controls for other variables. (*The Chronicle of Higher Education*, May 1, 1985.) For earlier data, see Garbarino, op. cit., p. 81.

12. Seymour Martin Lipset: "Labor Unions in the Public Mind"

1. Derek C. Bok and John T. Dunlop, *Labor and the American Community* (New York: Simon and Schuster, 1970), p. 12.

2. Seymour Martin Lipset and William Schneider, *The Confidence Gap: Business, Labor and Government in the Public Mind* (New York: The Free Press, 1983).

3. The others are Congress, education, the executive branch of the federal government, medicine, military, organized religion, press, and the Supreme Court.

4. Bok and Dunlop, op. cit., pp. 18–19.

5. Thomas A. Kochan, "How American Workers View Labor Unions," *Monthly Labor Review* 102 (April 1979), pp. 23–31.

6. National Family Opinion Surveys, 1975; Cambridge Reports, Inc., 1976.

7. Kochan, op. cit., p. 24.

8. For comparison with other institutions see Seymour Martin Lipset, "Feeling Better: Measuring the Nation's Confidence," *Public Opinion* 8 (April/May 1985), pp. 7–8.

9. Kochan, op. cit., p. 25; Stephen M. Hills, "The Attitudes of Union and Nonunion Male Workers Toward Union Representation," *Industrial and Labor Relations Review* 38 (January 1985), pp. 180, 183.

10. AFL-CIO Committee on the Evolution of Work, *The Changing Situation of Workers and Their Unions* (Washington, D.C.: American Federation of Labor and Congress of Industrial Organizations, 1985), pp. 12–13.

11. Kochan, op. cit., p. 24.

12. Ibid., p. 29.

13. Brian Heshizer and Harry Graham, "Are Unions Facing a Crisis? Labor Officials are Divided," *Monthly Labor Review* 107 (August 1984), p. 24.

14. Kochan, op. cit., p. 24.

15. Lipset and Schneider, op. cit., pp. 257–274.

16. John Hoerr, "Beyond Unions. A Revolution in Employee Rights in the Making," *Business Week*, July 8, 1985, p. 72.

17. Kochan, op. cit., p. 30.

18. Hills, op. cit., pp. 181–183.

19. Ibid., p. 193.

20. Quoted in Hoerr, op. cit., p. 74.

13. Herman Benson: "The Fight for Union Democracy"

1. Clark Kerr, "Foreword," in the ITU study, Seymour Martin Lipset, Martin A. Trow, and James S. Coleman, *Union Democracy* (New York: Free Press, 1956), p. vii.

2. *Union Democracy Review*, No. 8 (Spring 1975), p. 4.

3. A.J. Hayes, Hearings before the Senate Labor Subcommittee, Transcript of Proceedings, "Union Financial and Administratice Practices and Procedures," May 8, 1958, GPO document 25738, p. 584.

4. John Herling, *Right to Challenge* (New York: Harper & Row, 1972), pp. 361, 401.

5. See 29 CFR 452.76 and Department of Labor, "Statement of Reasons," Carl Rolnick to Lloyd McBride, 11/11/77, p. 9.

6. *Union Democracy in Action*, No. 26 (June 1967), p. 4.

7. Joseph Rauh, *Union Democracy Review*, No. 42, (September 1984), p. 4.

8. Charles Craypo, "The National Convention as an Internal Appeals Tribunal," *Industrial and Labor Relations Review* 22 (July 1969), pp. 487–511.

9. Cited in *New York Times*, November 2, 1957.

10. Walter Reuther, Speech at CIO Executive Board, February 24, 1955. Quoted in H.W. Benson, *Democratic Rights for Union Members* (New York: Association for Union Democracy, 1979), p. 193.

11. Neil W. Chamberlain, *Sourcebook on Labor* (New York: McGraw-Hill, 1958), p. 215.

12. Walter Galenson, *The CIO Challenge to the AFL* (Cambridge, Mass.: Harvard University Press, 1960), p. 624.

13. Max Ascoli, "Editorial," *Reporter*, April 1959.

14. Arthur Goldberg, "Proceedings: May 1958 Fund for the Republic Conference," *Labor in a Free Society* (Berkeley: University of California Press, 1964), p. 104.

15. *Union Democracy Review*, No. 43 (November 1984), p. 1.

16. City Club of New York, Subcommittee of Labor Unions, 1937. Quoted in Chamberlain, op. cit.

17. Herbert S. Parnes, *Union Strike Votes* (Princeton: Princeton University Press, 1956).

18. Robert Kennedy, *The Enemy Within* (New York: Harper & Row, 1960), p. 217.

19. Joseph Rauh, "Twenty-Five Years of Landrum-Griffin," *Union Democracy Review*, No. 42 (September 1984), p. 1.

20. John Brophy, *A Miner's Life* (Madison: University of Wisconsin Press, 1964), p. 218.

21. Melvin Dubofsky and Warren Van Tine, *John L. Lewis* (New York: Quadrangle/Times, 1977), p. 1.

22. IBEW constitution, 1956.

23. Ibid.

24. Sylvia Kopald, *Rebellion in Labor Unions* (New York: Boni & Liveright, 1924).

25. Harold Seidman, *Labor Czars* (New York: Liveright Publishing Corp., 1938).

26. Edward Sadlowski, *Union Democracy Review*, No. 21 (February 1981), p. 7.

27. 316 F2d 445 (1963) and *Union Democracy in Action*, No. 9 (May 1963).

28. "Blowing in the Wind," *Union Democracy Review*, No. 23 (June 1981), p. 3.

29. U.S. Bureau of Labor Statistics, "Education of Workers: Projections to 1990," Special Labor Force Report 160, 1974.

30. William Leiserson, *American Trade Union Democracy* (New York: Columbia University Press, 1957), p. 75.

31. Robert Michels, *Political Parties* (New York: Free Press, 1949), p. 405.

32. Ibid.

16.   Alexander B. Trowbridge: "A Management Look at Labor Relations"

1. *Global Competition: The New Reality*, Vol. 2, Report of the President's Commission on Industrial Competitiveness, (Washington, D.C.: U.S. Government Printing Office, 1985), p. 16.

2. Arnold Weber, "Lifeboat Labor Relations," in *Across the Board*, May, 1984, The Conference Board, New York, N.Y., pp. 29–35.

3. Report of the President's Commission on Industrial Competitiveness, op. cit., p. 16.

4. Ibid., pp. 8–12.

5. Ibid., p. 14.

6. Richard Bellous, "Labor and Management: The Situation in 1986," updated January 21, 1986, *Issue Brief*, Economics Division, Congressional Research Service, Library of Congress, pp. 1–11.

7. David J. Schlein, et al., "Collective Bargaining During 1986: Pressures to Curb Costs Common" report from *Monthly Labor Review* and as printed in *Daily Labor Report*, No. 133, Bureau of National Affairs, Washington, D.C., February 9, 1986, pp. D1–D3.

8. Randolph M. Hale, "Managing Human Resources — A Challenge for the Future," *Enterprise*, National Association of Manufacturers, Washington, D.C., June, 1985, pp. 6–9.

9. "Auto Workers Board Approve Agreement for Saturn Subsidiary," *Daily Labor Report*, No. 145, July 29, 1985, Bureau of National Affairs, Washington, D.C., pp. AA1–AA3.

10. *Daily Labor Reports*, No. 89, 124, and 132, respectively May 8, 1985, June 27, 1985, and October 3, 1985.

11. Peter Lazes and Susan Costanza, "Xerox Cuts Costs Through Labor-Management Collaboration," Labor-Management Cooperation Brief, U.S. Department of Labor, Bureau of Labor-Management Relations and Cooperative Programs, July, 1984.

12. Leo Troy, "The Rise and Fall of American Trade Unions," chapter 3, this volume.

13. Ibid. Also, Richard B. Freeman and James L. Medoff, *What Do Unions Do?* (New York: Basic Books, 1984) p. 222.

14. Troy, *op. cit.*

15. Ibid., and Freeman and Medoff, op. cit.

16. Troy, op. cit.; also Audrey Freedman, "What Has Happened to Unions?" *Bell Atlantic Quarterly* 2 (Autumn 1985).

17. "The Changing Situation of Workers and Their Unions," A Report by the AFL-CIO Committee on the Evolution of Work (Washington, D.C.: AFL-CIO, 1985).

18. Thomas Kochan and Peter Cappelli, "The Transformation of the Industrial Relations Function," in Paul Osterman, ed., *Employment Policies of Large Firms* (Cambridge, Mass: MIT Press, 1983).

19. David C. Metz, "12 Key Factors in Staying Union Free-A Checklist for Employers," *30, CUE, Washington, D.C.*

20. Report of the President's Commission on Industrial Competitiveness, op. cit., pp. 137–160.

17.   Seymour Martin Lipset: "North American Labor Movements: A Comparative Perspective"

1. I have dealt with the question in a number of publications. See especially Seymour Martin Lipset, "Why No Socialism in the United States?" in S. Bialer and S. Sluzar, eds., *Radicalism in the Contemporary Age*, vol. 1, *Sources of Contemporary Radicalism* (Boulder, CO: Westview Press, 1977), pp. 31–149, 346–363; "Socialism in America," in P. Kurtz, ed., *Sidney Hook: Philosopher of Democracy and Humanism* (Buffalo, NY: Prometheus Books, 1983), pp. 47–63. For comparative analyses of the factors affecting the strength and content of radical politics, see Lipset, *Consensus and Conflict* (New Brunswick, NJ: Transaction Books, 1985), pp. 187–252, chapters 5 and 6, "The Industrial Proletariat and the Intelligentsia in Comparative Perspective" and "Radicalism or Reformism: The Sources of Working-Class Politics."

2. Noah M. Meltz, "Labor Movements in Canada and the United States," in Thomas A. Kochan, ed., *Challenges and Choices Facing American Labor* (Cambridge: MIT Press, 1985), p. 318. Depending on which of the sources Meltz reports, Labour Canada or the recalculation of Canadian data by Bain and Price, which involves adding in union-like associations, Canadian unions have encompassed a larger percentage of the nonagricultural labor force than the American ones from 1946 or 1956 on. Most observers date the Canadian lead from the mid-1950s.

3. Ibid., p. 322.

4. M. Bradley Dow, "The Labour Movement and Trade Unionism: Summary Outline," in

W.D. Wood and Pradeep Kumar, eds., *The Current Industrial Relations Scene in Canada 1983* (Kingston, Ont.: Industrial Relations Centre, Queen's University, 1983), p. 235.

5. Richard E. Ratcliff and David Jaffe, "Capitalists Vs. The Unions: An Analysis of Anti-Union Political Mobilization Among Business Leaders," *Research in Social Movements, Conflict and Change* 4 (1981), pp. 95–121; John B. Parrish, "U.S. Labor Relations in Revolution," *The Journal of the Institute for Socioeconomic Studies* 9 (Winter 1985), pp. 23–36; Rob Wrenn, "The Decline of American Labor," *Socialist Review* 15 (April/May 1985), pp. 89–118.

6. Ronald Inglehart, *The Silent Revolution. Changing Values and Political Styles Among Western Publics* (Princeton: Princeton University Press, 1977); "Post-Materialism in an Environment of Insecurity," *American Political Science Review* 75 (December 1981), pp. 880–900; "The Changing Structure of Political Cleavages in Western Society," in Russell J. Dalton, Scott C. Flanagan, and Paul Allen Beck, eds., *Electoral Change in Advanced Industrial Democracies: Realignment or Dealignment?* (Princeton: Princeton University Press, 1984), pp. 25–69, and other articles in Dalton, et al.; Lipset, op. cit., pp. 187–218.

7. The approach was developed by David Ross Cameron, *Postindustrial Change and Secular Realignment* (unpublished doctoral dissertation, Department of Political Science, University of Michigan, 1976), pp. 72–103.

8. The less industrialized OECD countries, Greece, Iceland, Ireland, Portugal and Turkey, are omitted from consideration here. Austria, Australia, Belgium, Finland, Luxembourg, New Zealand, and Norway are not included in Tables 1 and 2 because I do not have data on their union membership.

9. Cameron, op. cit., p. 87.

10. The numbers in parentheses refer to the rank order in the first column in Table 2.

11. Henry S. Farber, "The Extent of Unionization in the United States," in Kochan, ed., op. cit., p. 22; Richard B. Freeman, "Why Are Unions Faring Poorly in NLRB Representation Elections," in ibid., p. 50.

12. Jack Barbash, "Trade Unionism from Roosevelt to Reagan," *The Annals* 473 (May 1984), p. 16.

13. Parrish, op. cit., p. 25.

14. Colin Lawrence and Robert Lawrence, "Manufacturing Wage Dispersion: An Endgame Interpretation," *Brookings Papers in Economic Activity* 1 (1985), p. 48.

15. Richard B. Freeman and James L. Medoff, *What Do Unions Do?* (New York: Basic Books, 1984), p. 239.

16. Pradeep Kumar, "Wages, Productivity and Labour Costs: Summary Outline," in W.D. Wood and Pradeep Kumar, eds., *The Current Industrial Relations Scene in Canada 1985* (Kingston, Ont.: Industrial Relations Centre, Queen's University, 1985), p. 413.

17. Pradeep Kumar, "The Economy: Summary Outline," in Wood and Kumar, eds., op. cit., p. 10.

18. Wrenn, op. cit., p. 110.

19. "NLRB Tilts Sharply Against Unions, Study Finds," *AFL-CIO News*, June 1, 1985, pp. 1, 3.

20. Orley Ashenfelter and John H. Pencavel, "American Trade Union Growth: 1900–1960," *Quarterly Journal of Economics* 83 (August 1969), p. 434.

21. Richard N. Block and Steven L. Premack, "The Unionization Process: A Review of the Literature," *Advances in Industrial and Labor Relations* 1 (1983), p. 49.

22. Ibid., p. 65.

23. Ronald L. Seeber, "Union Organizing in Manufacturing: 1973–1976," *Advances in Industrial and Labor Relations* 1 (1983), p. 3.

24. Block and Premack, op. cit., p. 66, emphasis added. See also Herbert G. Heneman III and Marcus H. Sandver, "Predicting the Outcome of Union Certification Elections: A Review of the

Literature," *Industrial and Labor Relations Review* 36 (July 1983), pp. 537–559; Barbash, op. cit., pp. 11–22; William T. Dickens and Jonathan S. Leonard, "Accounting for the Decline in Union Membership, 1950–1980," *Industrial and Labor Relations Review* 38 (April 1985), pp. 323–334; William J. Moore and Robert J. Newman, "The Effects of Right-To-Work Laws: A Review of the Literature," *Industrial and Labor Relations Review* 38 (October 1984), pp. 38–51.

25. Paul Weiler, "Promises to Keep: Securing Workers' Rights to Self-Organization Under the NLRA," *Harvard Law Review* 96 (June 1983), pp. 1805–1821; Freeman and Medoff, op. cit., pp. 242–243; Meltz, op. cit., pp. 322–325.

26. Unlike the situation in the United States, labor relations are largely under provincial jurisdiction in Canada.

27. This information was provided by staff of the Labor Relations Boards in both provinces. As might be expected, the union win rate increases with the percent of the work force who are members of unions prior to petitioning for certification in Nova Scotia, which has data so classified. It is well under 50 percent when less than 50 percent belong, and is overwhelming when 70 percent or more are enrolled.

28. Weiler, op. cit., p. 1770.

29. Freeman and Medoff, op. cit., pp. 233–239. For an earlier comprehensive review see Heneman and Sandver, op. cit., pp. 537–559; see also William T. Dickens, "The Effect of Company Campaigns on Certification Elections: Law and Reality Once Again," *Industrial and Labor Relations Review* 36 (July 1983), pp. 560–575.

30. Weiler, op. cit., p. 1820.

31. Laura Cooper, "Authorization Cards and Union Representation Outcome: An Empirical Assessment of the Assumption Underlying the Supreme Court's *Gissel* Decision," *Northwestern University Law Review* 79 (March 1984), pp. 87–141.

32. Ibid., p. 121.

33. Ibid., p. 118.

34. Ibid., pp. 139–140.

35. George Sayers Bain and Robert Price, *Profiles of Union Growth. A Comparative Statistical Portrait of Eight Countries* (Oxford: Basil Blackwell, 1980), pp. 88–91, 107–109. They do not give percentage estimates for Canada prior to 1921, since there are no useful labor force measures. It is clear, however, from looking at the absolute figures for union membership that Canadian union density must have been higher than the American from 1918 on.

36. J.A. Frank, Michael J. Kelly and Bruce D. MacNaughton, "Legislative Change and Strike Activity in Canada, 1926–1974," *Relations industrielles* 37, no. 2 (1982), p. 272.

37. Derek C. Bok, "Reflections on the Distinctive Character of American Labor Laws," *Harvard Law Review* 84 (April 1971), p. 1426. This is a comprehensive article which not only details variation in the laws, but seeks to relate national differences in the behavior and strength of unions to variations in social structure, values and institutional history.

38. Henry Phelps Brown, *The Origins of Union Power* (Oxford: Clarendon Press, 1983), p. 215.

39. Everett M. Kassalow, "The Closed and Union Shop in Western Europe: An American Perspective," *Journal of Labor Research* 1 (Fall 1980), p. 328. Emphasis added.

40. Ibid., p. 332.

41. Joseph W. Garbarino, "Unionism Without Unions: The New Industrial Relations," *Industrial Relations* 23 (Winter 1984), pp. 40–51; George Strauss, "Industrial Relations: Time of Change," *Industrial Relations* 23 (Winter 1984), pp. 1–15.

42. Garbarino, op. cit., pp. 48–49. A detailed review and summary of the "growing web of laws and court rulings" established to protect workers may be found in John Hoerr, "Beyond Unions: A Revolution in Employee Rights is in the Making," *Business Week*, July 8, 1985, pp. 72–77.

43. Strauss, op. cit., p. 5.

44. Lane Kirkland, News Conference, Tulsa, Oklahoma, *News AFL-CIO*, July 13, 1985, p. 9.

45. Joseph B. Rose and Gary N. Chaison, "The State of the Unions: United States and Canada," *Journal of Collective Negotiations in the Public Sector* 6 (Winter 1985), p. 105.

46. Barbash, op. cit., p. 12; Wrenn, op. cit., p. 113.

47. Daniel B. Cornfield, "Declining Union Membership in the Post-World War II Era: The United Furniture Workers of America, 1939–1982," *American Journal of Sociology* 91 (March 1986), pp. 1122–1125.

48. Freeman, op. cit., p. 62.

49. One of the leading Canadian students of industrial relations asserted as recently as 1973 that "Canadian employers have been less willing than their counterparts in the United States to recognize and make concessions to unions." Stuart Jamieson, *Industrial Relations in Canada* (Toronto: Macmillan of Canada, 2nd ed., 1973), pp. 2–3.

50. AFL-CIO Committee on the Evolution of Work, *The Changing Situation of Workers and Their Unions* (Washington, DC, AFL-CIO, 1985), p. 15 (emphasis added); see also Weiler, op. cit., p. 1819.

51. Meltz, op. cit., p. 319.

52. Different labor economists interpreting findings that "political factors are significant in a union growth equation" also "argue that legislation is not the cause but only the symbol of public attitudes toward trade unions ... [and] that party in power is merely a proxy for unavailable public opinion poll data on the attitudes of the public toward unions." Dennis R. Maki, "Political Parties and Trade Union Growth in Canada," *Relations industrielles* 37, no. 4 (1982), pp. 878–879. He cites Ashenfelter and Pencavel, op. cit., pp. 438–439, and Neil M. Chamberlain, *The Labor Sector* (New York: McGraw-Hill, 1965), p. 129.

53. Gallup repeated the union approval question in 1985 for the first time in four years. As reported in Chapter 12, the approval percentage increased by three points, the first such improvement in 22 years, while union density appeared to be still declining. This finding, however, may be due to chance variation, since other surveys taken in 1985 by ORC, Cambridge Reports, Inc., and Harris do not show any upswing in the public view of organized labor.

54. For a comprehensive analysis of domestic factors see Dickens and Leonard, op. cit., pp. 323–334.

55. Seymour Martin Lipset, *Revolution and Counterrevolution. Change and Persistence in Social Structures* (Garden City: Doubleday/Anchor Books, 1970; revised edition), pp. 37–75; *The First New Nation: The United States in Historical and Comparative Perspective* (New York: Norton Library Edition, 1979; third edition), p. 248–268; "Revolution and Counterrevolution: Some Comments at a Conference Analyzing the Bicentennial of a Celebrated American Divorce," in R.A. Preston, ed., *Perspectives on Revolution and Evolution* (Durham: Duke University Press, 1979), pp. 22–45; "Canada and the United States: The Cultural Dimension," in Charles F. Doran and John H. Sigler, eds., *Canada and the United States* (Englewood Cliffs, NJ: Prentice-Hall, 1985), pp. 109–160.

56. Some readers may note that the data reported in Table 2 suggest that France appears to compete with the United States for the bottom slot. But the low level of formal union membership in France is deceiving. Many French workers who take part in strikes and vote for union centers in assorted administrative and social security elections rarely pay dues. This lack of organizational support may flow from traditions and institutions formed in the pre–World War I anarcho-syndicalist movement, the CGT, which is the ancestor of the different contemporary union centers, or simply reflect an anarchic strain in French culture. In any case, as the national election results indicate, French workers are much more class conscious than the Americans or Canadians. For analyses of the elections to grievance committees

(prud'hommes) among all French workers which suggest that three-fifths vote for union lists, see Gerard Adam, *Le Pouvoir Syndical* (Paris: Bordas, 1983), pp. 87–107.

57. Lipset, *The First New Nation*, op. cit., pp. 248–268.

58. Hugh MacLennan, "A Society in Revolt," in Judith Webster, ed., *Voices of Canada. An Introduction to Canadian Culture* (Burlington: Association for Canadian Studies in the United States, 1977), p. 30; Northrop Frye, *Divisions on a Ground: Essays on Canadian Culture* (Toronto: Anansi, 1982), p. 66.

59. Harold A. Innis, *Essays in Canadian Economic History* (Toronto: University of Toronto Press, 1956), pp. 384–385.

60. Phelps Brown, op. cit., p. 249; Gad Horowitz, *Canadian Labour in Politics* (Toronto: University of Toronto Press, 1968), pp. 9, 15–16.

61. The most comprehensive statement of this thesis is Louis Hartz, *The Liberal Tradition in America* (New York: Harcourt, Brace, and World, 1955). See also H.G. Wells, *The Future in America* (New York: Harper and Brothers, 1906), pp. 72–76.

62. For an analysis of the ways in which American trade unionism has reflected "the basic values of the larger society," see Lipset, "Trade Unionism and the American Value System," Chapter 5 in *The First New Nation*, op. cit., pp. 170–204.

63. William Christian and Colin Campbell, *Political Parties and Ideologies in Canada* (Toronto: McGraw-Hill Ryerson, 1983), p. 36.

64. Richard Hofstadter, *The Age of Reform* (New York: Vintage Books, 1967), p. 308; see also S. M. Lipset, "Roosevelt and the Protest of the 1930s," *Minnesota Law Review* 68 (December 1983), pp. 273–298.

65. Samuel Lubell, "Post-Mortem: Who Elected Roosevelt?" *Saturday Evening Post*, January 25, 1941, p. 9; see also Lubell, *The Future of American Politics* (New York: Doubleday Anchor Books, 1965), pp. 55–68.

66. Lipset, "Roosevelt and the Protest ... ," op. cit., pp. 278–279.

67. Joyanna Moy, "Recent Trends in Unemployment and the Labor Force, 10 Countries," *Monthly Labor Review* 108 (August 1985), p. 11.

68. Seymour Martin Lipset and William Schneider, *The Confidence Gap: Business, Labor and Government in the Public Mind* (New York: The Free Press, 1983), pp. 265–266.

69. Ibid., pp. 285–287.

70. Herschel Hardin, *A Nation Unaware. The Canadian Economic Culture* (Vancouver: J.J. Douglas, 1974), pp. 62, 140.

71. J.T. McLeod, "The Free Enterprise Dodo is No Phoenix," *The Canadian Forum* 56 (August 1976), pp. 6, 9.

72. Marsha A. Chandler, "The Politics of Public Enterprise," in J. Robert S. Pritchard, ed., *Crown Corporations in Canada* (Toronto: Butterworth, 1983), p. 187.

73. Robert Presthus, *Elites in the Policy Process* (London: Cambridge University Press, 1974), p. 463.

74. Robert Presthus, "Aspects of Political Culture and Legislative Behavior: United States and Canada," in Presthus, ed., *Cross-National Perspectives: United States and Canada* (Leiden: E.J. Brill, 1977), p. 15. For a discussion of the continuation of this pattern on the policy level by Canadian parties, see Richard Gwyn, *The 49th Paradox: Canada in North America* (Toronto: McClelland and Stewart, 1985), pp. 157–187.

75. Stephen Arnold and James Barnes, "Canadian and American National Character as a Basis for Market Segmentation," in J. Sheth, ed., *Research in Marketing*, vol. 2 (Greenwich: JAI Press, 1979), p. 32.

76. Lipset, "Canada and the United States," op. cit., pp.148–151.

77. For an earlier effort to account for a socialist party in Canada and the absence of one in the U.S., see S.M. Lipset, "Radicalism in North America: A Comparative View of the Party

Systems in Canada and the United States," *Transactions of the Royal Society of Canada*, Series IV, 16 (1976), pp. 19–55. In that paper, I stress the role of diverse electoral and constitutional structures in facilitating a multi-party system in Canada and a two party one in the U.S. Analyzing the reasons for greater union density in Canada has convinced me that political cultural values are much more important than electoral systems in determining the relative strength of socialist forces in the two countries, although variations in constitutional structures, the presidency elected by the entire country versus constituency contests for Parliament, affect the number of viable parties.

78. Phelps Brown, op. cit., p. 240.

79. For a general historical analysis of the tensions between the two since the formation of the AFL, see Robert II. Babcock, *Gompers in Canada: A Study in American Continentalism Before the First World War* (Toronto: University of Toronto Press, 1974).

80. Horowitz, op. cit., p. 59; Charles Lipton, *The Trade Union Movement of Canada* (Toronto: University of Toronto Press, 1973), pp. 75–76, 118–121, 233–236; Harold A. Logan, *The History of Trade-Union Organization in Canada* (Toronto: University of Toronto Press, 1928), pp. 245–248, 274–286; Babcock, op. cit., pp. 60–66, 160–162, 179–182.

81. Horowitz, op. cit., p. 184.

82. Meltz, op. cit., p. 322.

83. Thompson and Blum, op. cit., p. 83.

84. During the provincial election campaign in Manitoba in March 1986, the leader of the Conservative opposition to the incumbent NDP, Gary Filmon, told an American reporter that he decided not to campaign against socialism because "the talk of socialism doesn't seem to have a sting" in Canada. In fact, he accused "the socialist government of 'neglecting' and 'starving' Manitoba's elaborate health and social welfare system." He promised to restore services cut by the NDP. Herbert H. Denton, "Socialists Seek Reelection in Manitoba," *The Washington Post*, March 18, 1986, p. A 21.

85. Phelps Brown, op. cit., p. 235.

86. Meltz, op. cit., p. 325.

87. Harvey Krahn and Graham S. Lowe, "Public Attitudes Towards Unions: Some Canadian Evidence," *Journal of Labor Research* 5 (Spring 1984), pp. 160–161.

88. Robertson Davies, "Dark Hamlet with the Features of Horatio: Canada's Myths and Realities," in Webster, ed., op. cit., p. 43.

CONTRIBUTORS

DANIEL K. BENJAMIN, formerly chief of staff at the U.S. Department of Labor, is professor of economics at Clemson University. He did his undergraduate work at the University of Virginia and received his Ph.D. in economics from the University of California, Los Angeles. In addition to having served on the faculties of the University of California and the University of Washington, he has been a national fellow at the Hoover Institution and a visiting scholar at Liverpool University. His numerous publications range across a broad spectrum of topics in the field of economics.

HERMAN BENSON, one of the founders of the Association for Union Democracy, is its executive director and editor of its periodical, *Union Democracy Review*. Originally a toolmaker by trade, he was a member of the United Auto Workers, the United Rubber Workers, the United Electrical Workers, and the International Union of Electrical Workers. He published the newsletter, *Union Democracy in Action*, from 1959 to 1972. Between 1967 and 1973 he was public relations consultant for Painters District Council 9 in New York City and managing editor of its newspaper. He is author of *Democratic Rights for Union Members*.

RICHARD B. FREEMAN is professor of economics at Harvard University. He received his Ph.D. from Harvard University in 1969 and his B.A. from Dartmouth College in 1964. He is also director of labor studies at the National Bureau of Economic Research. He previously taught at Yale University and at the University of Chicago. He is author of the following books: *What Do Unions Do?*, with James L. Medoff; *The Overeducated American*; and *The Minority Unemployment Crisis*, with Harry Holzer.

WALTER GALENSON is Jacob Gould Schurman Professor Emeritus at Cornell University. Among his many publications are the books, *Labor in Norway, The Danish System of Labor Relations, Labor Productivity in Soviet and American Industry, The CIO Challenge to the AFL, Trade Union Democracy in Western Europe, The Chinese Economy Under Communism, The International Labor Organization: An American View, The United Brotherhood of Carpenters and Joiners*, and *A Welfare State Strikes Oil: The Norwegian Experience*.

JOSEPH W. GARBARINO is professor of business administration; director of the Institute of Business and Economic Research at the University of California, Berkeley; and a labor arbitrator. In the area of faculty collective bargaining, he is the author of *Faculty Bargaining: Change and Conflict* and a contributor to *Higher Education and the Labor Market* and *Faculty Bargaining in Public Higher Education.*

CHRISTOPHER HUXLEY completed his Ph.D. at the University of Toronto in 1979. His research has included studies of strike activity in Canada and Britain. He has published in the *Canadian Journal of Sociology* and in *Labor/Le Travail.* He is currently associate professor of sociology at Trent University where he teaches organization theory and industrial sociology.

DAVID KETTLER is professor in the Department of Political Studies at Trent University in Peterborough, Ontario. His recent publications include *Karl Mannheim, Works Community and Workers' Organization: A Central Problem in Weimar Labour Law* and *Recht und Verfassung im Wohlfahrtsstaat.*

LANE KIRKLAND has been president of the AFL-CIO since 1979. He previously had served for ten years as secretary-treasurer, the labor federation's second-highest office. Member of the International Organization of Masters, Mates, and Pilots; vice-chairman, Trade Union Advisory Committee, OECD; vice-president, International Confederation of Free Trade Unions; and a fellow of the American Association for the Advancement of Science, he has also served on many presidential commissions and advisory boards and is the director of numerous nongovernmental organizations.

DAVID LEWIN is professor of business, director of the Industrial Relations Research Center, and faculty coordinator of the Ph.D. program at the Columbia Business School. His articles on collective bargaining, human resource management, and wage determination appear in numerous scholarly and professional journals. He has recently completed papers on "Technological Change, Employment, and Unionism in Municipal Sanitation Service," "The Effects of Divestiture on Bargaining Structure at A.T.&T.," "Conflict Resolution in the Nonunion High Technology Firm," "The Effects of Regulation on Public Sector Labor Relations," and "The National Labor Relations Act at 50: A Research Assessment and Agenda." His book (with Richard B. Peterson), *The Modern Grievance Procedure in the Private and Public Sectors: A Theoretical and Empirical Analysis*, is forthcoming.

SEYMOUR MARTIN LIPSET is the Caroline S.G. Munro Professor of Political Science and Sociology and senior fellow of the Hoover Institution, Stanford University. He is also co-editor of the journal, *Public Opinion.* He has been president of the American Political Science Association, the International Society for Political Psychology, and the

Sociological Research Association. He is currently president of the World Association for Public Opinion Research. He has written extensively on comparative politics, American and Canadian societies, and trade unions. His many books include *Union Democracy, Political Man, The First New Nation, The Confidence Gap: Business, Labor, and Government in the Public Mind*, and most recently, *Consensus and Conflict*.

RAY MARSHALL holds the Audre and Bernard Rapoport Centennial Chair in Economics and Public Affairs at the University of Texas, where he is also director of the Center for the Study of Human Resources. He serves on the boards of directors and steering councils of numerous organizations and institutes. Past positions include U.S. Secretary of Labor, 1977–1981, and president of the Industrial Relations Research Association and the Southern Economic Association. He has written extensively on labor economics and economic policy. His most recent books include *The Jobs Challenge; The Role of Unions in the American Economy;* and *Labor Economics: Wages, Employment, Trade Unionism, and Economic Policy*.

A. H. RASKIN was for many years chief labor correspondent of the *New York Times*. He also served as a member of that paper's editorial board, as assistant editor of the editorial page, and as labor columnist until his retirement in 1977. He has been an adjunct professor at Columbia, Stanford, and Pace Universities and a Woodrow Wilson Visiting Fellow at Union College, Lawrence University, Gustavus Adolphus College, and Trinity University. During World War II he served as chief of the labor branch of the Army's Industrial Services Division, with the rank of lieutenant colonel, and received the Distinguished Service Medal. He is also the recipient of many journalistic awards. He is co-author with David Dubinsky of *David Dubinsky, A Life With Labor*.

MORGAN O. REYNOLDS is professor of economics at Texas A&M University. He received his Ph.D. from the University of Wisconsin in 1971 and has held appointments at the University of California and the Institute for Research on Poverty. He is the author of many articles in academic journals and of the books *Public Expenditures, Taxes, and the U.S. Distribution of Income; Power and Privilege: Labor Unions in America*; and *Crime By Choice*. Forthcoming work includes an edited volume on the work of W. H. Hutt and a book on productivity and unions.

JAMES STRUTHERS is associate professor in the Canadian Studies Program at Trent University, Peterborough, Ontario. He is the author of *No Fault of Their Own: Unemployment and the Canadian Welfare State, 1914–1941*.

ALAIN TOURAINE is Directeur d'Etudes at the Ecole des Hautes Etudes en Sciences Sociales in Paris. He is past president of the French Sociological Association and vice-president of the International Sociological Association. He has also been visiting professor at the universities of California at Berkeley, New York, Montreal, Geneva, Santiago, São Paulo, and Mexico. His main fields of interest are industrial sociology, social movements, social theory, and Latin American problems. Among his books translated into English are *The May Movement, The Post-Industrial Society, The Academic System in American Society, The Self-Production of Society, The Voice and the I, The Anti-Nuclear Prophecy,* and *Solidarity.*

ALEXANDER B. TROWBRIDGE has served as president of the National Association of Manufacturers since 1980. His extensive background in industry, government, and associations has included positions as vice-chairman of Allied Chemical Corporation (now Allied-Signal Corporation); president of The Conference Board, Inc., New York City; president of the American Management Association; and U.S. Secretary of Commerce, 1967–1968. A member of the Council on Foreign Relations, he has recently been appointed to the President's Board of Advisors on Private Sector Initiatives.

LEO TROY is professor of economics at Rutgers University. He obtained his Ph.D. and M.A. in economics at Columbia University and his B.A. at the Pennsylvania State University. An expert on union statistics, Professor Troy has been teaching and doing research for more than thirty years. For many years he was a member of the research staff of the National Bureau of Economic Research. His work has been published widely.

GUS TYLER is the assistant president of the International Ladies' Garment Workers Union. He is also a nationally syndicated columnist and the author of nine books on subjects as diverse as the economy, politics, crime, Mexican Americans, and urban affairs. He has written hundreds of magazine articles, dozens of which have been reprinted in anthologies, and many book reviews and critiques for major publications. Mr. Tyler is senior fellow of and regular moderator for the Aspen Institute for Humanistic Studies and board member of numerous institutes, funds, and councils.

INDEX

Abel, I. W., 328, 330, 334
Abortion issue, 66
Addison, Joseph, 338
Adversarial bargaining, 25,
    115–116, 131, 136, 147–148,
    262, 264, 415
Affirmative action, 414
AFL. *See* American Federation of
    Labor
AFL-CIO. *See* American Federation
    of Labor and Congress of
    Industrial Organizations
AFSCME. *See* American Federation of
    State, County, and Municipal
    Employees
Agnelli, Giovanni, 167
Air travel industry, 10, 35–36, 64,
    90, 221–222, 248
Akron, 160, 344
Alienation, 383–385
Amalgamated Clothing and Textile
    Workers Union (ACTWU),
    26–27, 412
"Amalgamated" unions, 92
Ambivalence, of union members,
    303–309
American Association of University
    Professors (AAUP), 272,
    273–275, 276, 277, 278–280
American Civil Liberties Union
    (ACLU), 348, 349, 362–363
American Economic Association,
    393
American Federation of Labor
    (AFL), 41–62 passim, 159,
    203, 231, 275, 343, 389
  Canadian, 449–450
  CIO merger with, 12–14, 16,
    60–61, 90, 105, 204, 205, 343

construction unions in, 88, 90
  and corruption, 342, 357
  finances of, 80
  membership of, 13, 46, 50, 52, 57, 73
  philosophy of, 56, 90, 105, 152,
    444, 445
  during World War II, 4, 57
American Federation of Labor and
    Congress of Industrial
    Organizations (AFL-CIO),
    3–4, 10–40 passim, 60–67,
    206, 324, 325, 376, 401–403
  and Canadian unions, 131–132,
    324, 450
  and corruption, 14–15, 342, 343,
    357, 358
  education level of members of,
    397
  Lawyers Coordinating Committee
    of, 430
  merger forming, 12–14, 16,
    60–61, 90, 105, 204, 205, 343
  mergers within and without, 90,
    91, 92, 93, 343–345
  no-raiding pact of, 12, 275, 344
  organizing innovations
    recommended by, 108–109
  in presidential campaigns,
    30–33, 34, 64–67, 102–103
  public opinion of, 33, 101,
    302–303, 306–308
  public sector groups in, 22–23,
    29, 90, 272–273, 275, 276
  See also Committee on the
    Evolution of Work; Kirkland,
    Lane
American Federation of State,
    County, and Municipal
    Employees (AFSCME), 93, 344

American Federation of Teachers
    (AFT), 82, 93, 266, 271–272,
    273–275, 276–277, 280
American Plan, 51, 160
American Revolution, 442–443,
    447
American Telephone and Telegraph
    Corporation, 96
Anaheim convention, AFL-CIO, 19,
    22, 34, 103
Anarchists, 158, 167
Anarcho-syndicalism, 39, 444
Anglicanism, 443
Annual improvement factor (AIF),
    7, 406
Annual Report, 1979 (NLRB), 222
Anti-Racketeering Act (1934), 228,
    231
Anti-unionism, 45–46, 50–51, 68,
    122, 160. *See also* Employer
    opposition
Antonini, Luigi, 45
Appeals, union, 337–339
Argentina, 171
Arnold, Stephen, 448–449
Ascoli, Max, 347–348
Ashenfelter, Orley, 77
Association for Union Democracy,
    329, 363, 364
Association of American
    Universities (AAU), 271
Association of Catholic Trade
    Unionists, 364
Association of Western Pulp and
    Paper Workers (AWPPW), 339
Associations
    vs. full-scale unions, 108
    professional, 85, 108
As Unions Mature (Lester),
    365–366
Attorneys, union, 336–337
Australia, 446
Austria, 148, 166, 424
Automation, 255–257, 377
Automobile industry, 54–55,
    114–115, 160, 162, 196, 216.
    See also United Auto Workers
Avery, Sewell, 58

Back-loading, 409

Bain, George Sayers, 77, 117, 434
Baldridge, Kemerer, and Associates
    (BK), 281, 283
Bal Harbour white paper, 23–26,
    29, 32, 35, 36, 37–38
Barbash, Jack, 425–427, 436
Barnes, James, 448–449
Belmont, August, 46
Benefits. *See* Fringe benefits
Benjamin, Daniel K., 201–220
Benjamin, Ernst, 280
Bennett, James T., 237
Benson, Herman, 323–369
Berry, George L., 53
Beverly Enterprises, 27
Bill of Grievances, 49
"Bill of Rights," ACLU, 363
Bill of Rights, LMRDA, 334
Birmingham, 344
Blacks, 16–19, 20, 32, 44, 57, 66
Block, Richard, 430, 431
Bloom, Gordon, 78
Blue-collar workers, 69, 86,
    105–106, 397, 423
    in goods industries, 94–95, 206
    union wage advantage of, 181,
    188, 219
Blue Cross/Blue Shield, 402
Blum, Albert, 450–451
Board of director representation,
    employee, 71–72
Boilermakers union, 343
Bok, Derek C., 194, 288, 434
Bolsheviks, 114
Bonnell, Victoria, 152
Bonuses, 37, 139–140, 146
Boston police strike, 51
Boston University, 270
Boswell, Dan, 354–355
Boycotts, 26–27, 58, 109, 149
Boyle, W. A. (Tony), 353, 365
Brazil, 171, 172
"Bread-and-butter" unionism, 7, 19,
    34, 104
Bretton Woods institutions,
    137–138
Brillancourt, 160
Britain, 168, 169, 172, 425,
    427–428, 434, 446
    Canada and, 442, 447

coal strike in, 165
decline of unionism in, 76, 107,
 160
immigrants from, 41, 44
jurisdiction disputes in, 48
wages in, 43
wildcat strikes in, 72
in World War II, 56
British Columbia, 354–355, 431, 432
British Joint Production
 Consultative and Advisory
 Committee, 169
British Trade Union Congress, 169
Brookings study, 427
Borphy, John, 352
Brotherhood of Carpenters, 42, 330,
 343
Brotherhood of Electrical Workers
 Local 3, 330
Brotherhood of Painters and Allied
 Trades, 344. *See also* Painters
 unions
Brotherhood of Painters,
 Decorators, and Paperhangers,
 344
Brotherhood of Railway Carmen, 50
Brotherhood of Sleeping Car
 Porters, 16, 57
Brown, Charles, 217
Brown, Henry Phelps, 443, 449, 451
Brown, John Y., 232
Budget deficit, federal, 22, 378, 380
Building Service Employees union,
 344
Bullock Report, 169
Bureaucratization, faculty unions
 increasing, 280, 284
Bureau of Census, 80
Bureau of Labor Statistics, 10,
 58–59, 69, 91, 397
Business agents (BA), 327
Business cycles, 41, 45, 58, 93–94,
 96–97, 374–375, 413. *See also*
 Depressions; Recessions
Business leaders
 public opinion of, 294–296, 297,
 299
 See also Employer opposition
Business power, public opinion of,
 312–313

Business responsibility for inflation,
 public opinion of, 316–317
Business Roundtable, 28
Business unionism, 45–50, 115,
 153, 157, 158, 159, 164–165

California, 84, 245, 267, 338, 351,
 411
California Faculty Association
 (CFA), 275–276, 277
California State Employees
 Association (CSEA), 275–276
California State Universities and
 Colleges (CSUC), 268, 275, 276,
 277–278
Cambridge Reports, Inc. (CRI),
 330–302, 305, 310, 313,
 315–316, 446–447
Cameron, David Ross, 424
Campbell, Colin, 444
Canada, 113–132, 205, 324,
 422–452 passim
 auto workers of, 114–115, 162
 electrical workers of, 354–355
 governmental policy in, 30, 114,
 116, 436
Canadian Congress of Labor (CCL),
 450
Canadian Labour Congress, 115,
 450
Capital, 217–218, 381–382
Capitalism, 40, 153
 Marx on, 384
 neo-, 171
 radical unions and, 46, 163, 164
 socialist parties and, 166
 welfare, 51
Capitalism and Freedom
 (Friedman), 184
Cappelli, Peter, 415
Carlough, Edward F., 331
Carlough, Edward J., 331
Carpenters union, 42, 330, 343
Car salesmen, public opinion of, 297
Carter, Jimmy/Carter
 administration, 28, 64, 65, 67
 deregulation by, 9
 Humphrey-Hawkins Full
 Employment and Balanced
 Growth Act by, 18

"national accord" by, 19–20
NLRB decisions during, 430
Castro, Fidel, 22
Catholics, 66, 162, 167, 443
CBS News/*New York Times* poll,
    309–310
Center for Political Studies (CPS),
    309, 314–315
Centralization, faculty unions
    increasing, 281, 284
Central States Teamster Fund, 341
Certification. *See under* Elections
Chaison, Gary N., 115, 120, 436
Chamberlain, Neil, 343
"Changing Situation of Workers
    and Their Unions" (Committee
    on the Evolution of Work),
    388–389, 399–400, 401
Chicago, 367–368
China, 22, 62
Christian, William, 444
Christianity, 162, 167, 442, 443
Chrysler company, 6, 55, 72
CIO. *See* Congress of Industrial
    Organizations
Citizens' Industrial Alliance, 45
City University of New York
    (CUNY), 265, 274–275, 276,
    277
Civic Service, Inc., 290
Civil rights, 16–19, 20, 57, 66
Civil service. *See* Public
    employment
Civil Service Reform Act, 98, 245
Civil War, 203
Class consciousness, 43–45, 48, 66,
    136, 151–170 passim,
    445–446, 452
Clayton Act (1914), 49, 230
Coal industry, 154, 165, 195, 232
Coalitions, faculty union, 276–278
Co-determination, 37, 71–72, 160.
    See also Decision-making,
    employee participation in
Coercion, 228, 232–233. *See also*
    Violence
Coleman, James S., 329, 347, 362,
    367, 368
Collective Bargaining Congress
    (CBC), 279–280

"Collegiality," 281
Committee for Industrial
    Organization, 54. *See also*
    Congress of Industrial
    Organizations
Committee on Fair Employment
    Practices, 57
Committee on Improper Activities
    in the Labor Management
    Field. *See* McClellan
    Committee
Committee on Political Education
    (COPE), 30, 63, 206
Committee on the Evolution of
    Work (AFL-CIO), 129, 373,
    377, 388–389, 399–400, 401,
    402–403
  on ambivalence of workers, 303
  on Canada, 114, 115, 117, 437
  on the dole, 386
  on public sector unionism,
    126–127
*Commonwealth of Massachusetts v.
    Hunt,* 78
Communications Workers of
    America (CWA), 96, 344
Communist Manifesto, The (Marx
    and Engels), 383, 384
Communists, 40
  AFL-CIO and, 22, 62–63
  British, 168
  CIO and, 13, 55–56, 60–61, 62
  Eastern European, 161
  Foster with, 50
  French, 39, 159, 164, 165, 168,
  Haywood and, 47
  Italian, 39
  See also Soviet Union
Company unions, 51, 71, 91, 160,
    227, 230
"Comparative advantage," 381
Compensation packages, 37,
    139–140, 146, 207–214, 218,
    406. *See also* Fringe benefits;
    Profit sharing; Wages
Competition
  domestic, 137, 146
  international, 96, 141, 142, 146,
    148, 214, 412–413, 417
  labor market, 136, 200

Comprehensive Organizing
Strategies and Tactics (COST),
109, 401–402
Concession bargaining, 194,
213–214, 251, 262, 408–409,
411
Confederacion de Trabajadores
Mexicanos (CIM), 171
Confederation Francaise et
Democratique du Travail
(FDT), 162, 167–168, 170
Conference Board survey, 410, 414
Confidence, public, in unions, 33,
288–299, 304, 305, 320
Confidence Gap, The (Lipset and
Schneider), 313
Conglomerates. *See* Mergers
Congress, 6–7, 40, 49, 64, 103, 238
and Anti-Racketeering Act, 228,
231
and civil rights, 16, 17, 20
elections to, 32, 40, 53, 65–66
and federal employee bargaining,
126
Hobbs Act by, 228, 231
and Humphrey-Hawkins Full
Employment and Balanced
Growth Act, 18
Labor Management Reporting
and Disclosure/Landrum-
Griffin Act enacted by, 61, 204,
347–352
minimum wage law by, 59
and National Industrial Recovery
Act, 203, 225
and NLRA/Wagner Act, 54, 56,
203–204, 225, 231, 267
Norris-LaGuardia Act enacted
by, 52, 203, 225
Taft-Hartley Act passed by, 58,
122, 204, 231, 429–430
See also Senate; *individual laws*
Congress of Industrial
Organizations (CIO), 5, 54–56,
88, 89–90, 123, 204, 343, 449
AFL merger with, 12–14, 16,
60–61, 90, 105, 204, 205, 343
Canadian affiliates of, 449, 450
and Communists, 13, 55–56,
60–61, 62

and corruption, 14, 342, 343, 357
membership of, 13, 57, 81, 122
politics of, 55–57, 67, 105, 160,
161, 445
Steelworkers Organizing
Committee of, 91
during World War II, 4, 55–56,
57
Consensus building, 147, 148
Conservative government, British,
169
Conservative Party, Canadian, 116,
448
Constitutions, union, 61, 324–325,
327, 339, 341, 351–354
passim, 365
Construction industry, 70, 88, 90,
102, 206
union corruption in, 343
union locals in, 325, 327
Consultants, anti-union, 26, 68, 130
Consumerist benefits, 25, 108–109,
402
Consumer Price Index, 7, 409
Contracting, private, of public
services, 252–257, 260, 261
Conventions, union, 339–341
"Convergence," 98
Coolidge, Calvin, 51
Cooper, Laura, 432–433
Cooperation, 116, 147–148, 404,
411, 417–418
GM and, 8, 411
in public sector bargaining, 262,
264
See also Worker participation
Co-operative Commonwealth
Federation (CCF), 123, 125,
450
Coordinated corporate campaign,
26–27
Cornfield, Daniel B., 437
Corporatism, 170–172
Corruption, 14–15, 341–343, 349,
357–366 passim
election, 345–347, 352–353, 364
LMRDA and, 15, 61–62, 204,
349, 357
public's perceptions of, 204, 288,
296–298, 305, 315

Cost-of-living adjustments
   (COLAs), 7, 8, 19, 406, 409
Cost, public/private-contract
   services, 252–255, 260, 261
Courts, 51–52, 202, 336, 418
   and Hobbs Act, 228–229
   Norris-LaGuardia Anti-
      Injunction Act and, 52, 78, 225
   and union official elections, 351,
      354–355, 364, 365
   See also Supreme Court, U.S.
Craft unionism, 13, 45, 54,
   119–121, 164, 202, 344
Credit cards, 25, 109
Cuba, 22
Curran, Joe, 358
Czechoslovakia, 161

Dalio, Raymond T., 382
Danzig, 386
Data files, computerized, 79–80,
   178
Davies, Robertson, 452
Decertification elections, 95, 100,
   288, 397
Decision making, employee
   participation in, 26, 37, 69,
   72–73, 169, 412, 417
*Decisions and Orders of the National
   Labor Relations Board,* 222
Declaration of Independence, 443
Defense budget, national, 22, 63
Defensive unionism, 69, 152–165
   passim
Delgado, Charles, 355
Demand, First Law of, 207
Democracy
   industrial, 389
   national, 39, 160, 404
   union, 323–369
   See also Social democracy
"Democracy in Labor Unions"
   (Summers), 348, 363
"Democracy in Trade Unions"
   (ACLU), 362
Democractic Party, 33–34, 63, 131,
   230, 445, 448
   NEA influence in, 273
   in 1932 elections, 53
   in 1952 elections, 67

   in 1972 elections, 64
   in 1976 elections, 64
   in 1980 elections, 64
   in 1984 elections, 32, 34, 65–66,
      104
   in 1986 elections, 32
   in 1988 elections, 102–103, 104
   and NLRB appointments, 99
Demography
   in union membership, 85–86
   wage advantage by, 181
Denmark, 425
Density, union, 75–90 passim, 95,
   107–108
   Canada/U.S., 116–121, 122,
      125–126, 422, 425, 431, 434,
      444, 445, 451
   in manufacturing, 88, 90, 95, 107,
      120–121, 413
   in OECD countries, 425
   private sector (general), 80–82,
      84, 99, 266
   public opinion affecting, 438–442
Department of Commerce, 196, 408
Department of Labor, 53, 87, 104
   financial reports filed with, 80, 82
   NEA reports filed with, 82
   Secretary of, 53, 64, 103
   Survey Research Center Quality of
      Employment, Survey sponsored
      by, 306–307, 308
   and union election complaints, 330,
      333, 346, 353, 365
Depressions, 41, 106. *See also* Great
   Depression
Derber, Milton, 117–118
Deregulation, 9, 96, 141, 214,
   221–238, 413
Detroit, 160
Dickens, William T., 100
Direct action unionism, 167
Discrimination, racial, 17–18, 44,
   57
Disinflation, 103
Dole. *See* Welfare state
Dollars, demand for, 214, 381
Domestic content law, 21
Douglas, William, 229
Dow, M. Bradley, 422
Draper Laboratories, 196

Dual unionism, 48, 275
Due process, 337–338
Dues, 80, 277, 279
Dunlop, John T., 28–29, 177, 194,
     196, 288
Duplessis, Maurice, 127

Eastern Airlines, 36, 72
Econometric models, 77–78, 97
Economic policy. *See* Public policy
"Economism," 153
Economy, 50, 151, 169–170,
     177–200, 374–382, 422–429
     cost-of-living adjustments based
     on, 7, 8, 19, 406, 409
     international, 9, 96, 140–148,
        214, 379–381, 383, 406
     public employee unionism
        affected by, 248–249,
        252–255, 260, 261, 262–263
     See also Business cycles;
        Compensation packages;
        Financial systems;
        Government expenditures;
        Market forces; Prices;
        Productivity
Educational level, of union
     members, 361–362, 397
Education-field unions, 265–284
Education system, Japanese, 144
Efficient contracts, 182
Eisenhower, Dwight D., 13, 63, 99,
     300
Elections
     decertification, 95, 100, 288, 397
     NLRB union
        representation/certification,
        28, 68–69, 100–102, 103, 130,
        204, 205, 226, 287, 288,
        302–303, 320–321, 429–441
        passim
     See also Political elections
Electrical workers. *See*
     International Brotherhood of
     Electrical Workers
Eliot, Charles, 45
Elitism, 449
Elsheikh, Farouk, 77
Ely, Richard T., 362
Employee-operated enterprise, 93,
     146. *See also* Self-management

Employee participation. *See* Worker
     participation
Employer opposition, 26–29, 45–58
     passim, 95, 100–102,
     135–136, 202, 205, 436–438
     and NLRB representation
        elections, 68–69, 100, 102,
        205, 432, 433
     with unfair labor practices, 203,
        205, 227, 398, 427, 433
     for union-free environment,
        68–69, 116, 148–149, 404,
        414–417
     wages accounting for, 209–210,
        427
Employment security, 69–70,
     140–148 passim, 164, 168,
     410, 411, 418
Engels, F., 383, 443–444
Entente cordiale, 8, 35
Enterprise management, 139
Enterprise union, 71
Epstein, Richard, 99–100, 226
Equality
     income, 183–188, 199, 219, 234
     privileges and immunities and,
        223
Equal opportunity, racial, 16–18
Ethical-moral practices, public
     opinion of, 288, 296–298, 305,
     315. *See also* Corruption
Ethical practices codes, 14, 15, 357
Ethnic groups, 44, 45, 66. *See also*
     Race
Europe, 9, 70, 77, 104, 134–148
     passim, 160–172 passim,
     434–435
     Canada compared with, 442
     class consciousness in, 45, 66
     ethnic homogeneity in, 66
     jobs lost in, 446
     jurisdiction disputes in, 48
     Leninism in, 156
     service employee unionization in,
        68
     socialism in, 40, 59, 65, 68, 105,
        165
     See also Scandinavian countries;
        individual countries
Evolution, regressive, 159

Executive Council, AFL-CIO, 18,
    21, 23–26, 30, 109, 373, 399
Executive Order 8802, 57
Executive Order 10988, 79, 82–83,
    98, 266

Faculty unions, 265–284
Fair Labor Standards Act, 56, 225
Farber, Henry, 425
Far East, 9. *See also* Japan
Fascism, 62, 160, 170
Federal Anti-Injunction Act. *See*
    Norris-LaGuardia/Federal
    Anti-Injunction Act
Federal Civil Service Reform Act,
    98, 245
Federalism, Canadian, 122–123
Federal Reserve Bank, 382
Federation of Organized Trades and
    Labor Unions, 41–42
Finances, union, 79–80, 336–337
    corruption with, 204, 341–342
    faculty union, 277, 279
    for organizing activities, 103, 413
Financial pressures
    on public employee unionism,
    248–249, 260, 262–263
    textile workers using, 27
Financial systems
    Japanese, 143
    U.S., 142, 382
Fingerhut/Granados, 299
Finland, 424
Finnegan v. Leu, 334
Firefighters, municipal, 252, 254
Firefighters Union, 50
Fitch, John, 362–363
Flexibility, American/Japanese
    system, 138–140, 146, 147, 148
Florida, 84, 85
Florida State Universities, 275
Food and Commercial Workers, 93
Food prices, in–plant, 227
Force Ouvriere, 170
Ford, Gerald, 64, 430
Ford, Henry, 55, 154, 155
Ford company, 6, 55, 410
Ford Motor v. NLRB (1979), 227
Foreign policy, AFL-CIO, 22–23,
    62–63

Fosco, Angelo, 330
Fosco, Peter, 330
Foster, William Z., 50
Fox, Arthur, 351
France, 152–172 passim, 425
    Communists of, 39, 159, 164, 165,
    168, 170
    decline of unionism in, 76, 107
    jobs lost in, 446
    wildcat strikes in, 27
Frankfurter, Felix, 52
Fraud
    union election, 345–347,
    352–353, 364
    union fund, 341
    See also Racketeering
Freedman, Audrey, 414
Freeman, Richard B., 177–200,
    214–219, 320–321, 425
    on Canada/U.S. union density,
    431
    on employer opposition, 100, 427,
    432, 437
    on faculty compensation, 283
    on organizing activity, 103, 413
French General Confederation of
    Labor (CGT), 159, 164, 167,
    170
French Popular Front, 160, 169
French Revolution, 442, 443
Friedman, Milton, 103, 177, 184,
    232
Fringe benefits, 8–9, 58–59, 183,
    188–191, 199, 207, 218, 406
    Bureau of Labor Statistics
    reports on, 58–59, 397
    concessions over, 213, 409
    for public employees, 261, 283
    public opinion of, 308
Frontier Airlines, 36
Fuch, Victor, 94
Full employment, 17–18, 105, 137,
    138, 145, 378, 395
Funds, union, 204, 336, 341–342.
    See also Finances, union
Furriers union, 344
"Future of Work" (Committee on
    the Evolution of Work), 377,
    399–400

Galenson, Walter, 39–73, 343, 423
Gallup polls, 101, 299, 300, 301,
    309, 320, 438–440
  on Canadian Co-operative
    Commonwealth Federation,
    123
  on confidence in unions, 289, 304
  on corruption in unions,
    296–297, 315
  on inflation, 316
  on socialist institutions, 445, 446
  on union threat, 313
Garbarino, Joseph W., 265–284,
    435
Garvin, Clifton C., Jr., 29
Gary, Elbert, 46
Gasoline prices, 216
General Motors (GM), 4–7, 55, 115,
    196, 410, 411
General Motors formula, 7–9, 19,
    406
General Theory, The (Keynes), 382
German immigrants, 41
Germany, 62, 152, 160. *See also*
    West Germany
"Givebacks," 211, 213–214. *See also*
    Concession bargaining
Glenn, John, 31
GNP. *See* Gross national product
Goldberg, Arthur, 65, 348
Goldwater, Barry, 63, 224
Gompers, Samuel, 3, 10–11, 41–42,
    49, 69, 105, 159
  and open-shop campaign, 46
  Trades and Labour Congress and,
    450
  on War Labor Board, 50
Goods industries, 94–95, 96, 206,
    375. *See also* Construction
    industry; Manufacturing
    industries; Mining industries
Gotbaum, Victor, 23
Gould, Jay, 395
Government employment. *See*
    Public employment
Government expenditures, 22, 63,
    378, 379–380. *See also* Welfare
    state
Government intervention, 56,
    78–79, 86, 109, 169, 448–449

Canadian, 128, 448–449
"more," 77, 104–107
  See also New Deal; Regulation;
    Socialism; Welfare state
Government policy. *See* Public
    policy
Government responsibility for
    inflation, public opinion of,
    316, 317
Grand Coalition, 169
Grant, George, 447
Great Britain. *See* Britain
Great Depression, 52–57, 203–204,
    211, 230, 231
  Canadian effects of, 447, 451
  competition causing, 137
  political radicalism evoked by,
    43, 105, 445–446, 451
Green, Lloyd, 341, 364
Green, William, 13, 53, 57, 159
Greene, Nathan, 52
Griffuelhes, Victor, 159
Gross national product (GNP), 9,
    97, 137–138, 218, 407
  annual improvement factor
    related to, 7
  monopoly wage gains affecting,
    182–183
  quit rates affecting, 215
  strikes affecting, 212–213
Gubernatorial elections (1984), 32,
    65–66
"Guild" unionism, 153

Haberler, Gottfried, 177, 180
Hall, Burton H., 351, 364
Hanna, Mark, 46
Hapgood, Powers, 352
Haraszti, Miklos, 153
Hardin, Herschel, 447–448
Harold, John, 364
Harper's, 45
Harrington, Michael, 444
Harris (Louis) and Associates polls,
    24, 299–300, 397
  on confidence in unions, 33, 290,
    305, 320
  on corruption in unions, 296
  on government intervention, 447
  on union power, 309, 310

on union representation
    elections, 302–303
on wage demands, 317, 318
Hart, Gary, 31, 65
Hartz, Louis, 444, 449
Harvard University, 45
Hawthorne Plant, Western Electric
    Company, 155
Hayek, Friedrich von, 229, 231
Hayes, A. J., 331, 332, 363
Haywood, William (Big Bill), 47
Health care industry, 267
Health insurance, 58–59, 409
Health issues, 69
Healy, James J., 177
Hechler, Ken, 365
Heldman, Dan C., 237
Hereditary union leadership,
    330–331
Herling, John, 332
"High employment," 378
High-technology industries, 85, 162,
    164, 287, 408, 423
Hillman, Sidney, 57
Hills, Sidney, 320
Histradut, 63
Hobbs Act (1945), 228–229, 231
Hoffa, Jimmy, 15, 36
Hofstadter, Richard, 445
Hoggart, Richard, 158
Hollywood, Florida, convention,
    AFL-CIO, 23
Hoover, Herbert, 52–53, 225
Hormel strike, 109
Horowitz, Gad, 449–450
Horse Collar Makers, 394
Hospital employees, 252
Hospital Local 1199, 346
Hotel and Restaurant Workers, 343, 358
Hotel Local 6 decision, 348
Hours, working, 42, 69
House of Representatives, 66, 103
    Labor Committee of, 347, 349
Humanization, 387–388
Human resource programs, 144,
    414–417
Humphrey, Hubert, 63, 65
Humphrey-Hawkins Full
    Employment and Balanced
    Growth Act (1978), 18

*100 Best Companies to Work for in
    America, The* (Levering,
    Moskowitz, and Katz),
    415–416
Hungary, 153
Hutcheson, Maurice, 330
Hutcheson, William L., 53, 69, 330
Hutt, W. H., 223, 234
Huxley, Christopher, 113–132, 422,
    431, 434, 438

Ideology, of industrial relations
    system, 134, 151. *See also*
    Philosophy, union
Illinois, 267–268
Immigrants, 41, 44, 45, 375
Immunities, legal, 105, 223–238
Income, national, 235
Income redistribution, 106,
    382–383. *See also under*
    Compensation packages;
    Equality
Independent Steel Workers Union,
    93
Industrial democracy, 389
Industrial Disputes Investigation
    Act (1907), Canadian, 123
Industrial policy, national, 21
Industrial Relations and Disputes
    Investigation Act (1984),
    Canadian, 124
Industrial unions, 13, 89–90, 203,
    204, 344
Industrial Workers of the World
    (IWW), 46–47, 167, 444
Inflation, 10, 19, 36, 103, 138,
    141–142, 181–183
    cost-of-living adjustment and, 8,
    19, 406
    General Motors strike/formula
    and, 5, 8, 19, 406
    Japanese, 139
    public opinions about, 316–318
    Reagan administration and, 9,
    20, 316
    unemployment and, 20, 141,
    378–379, 427–429
Information occupations, 140
Injunctions, labor, 51–52, 203, 225,
    230

Innis, Harold, 443
Insurgency, 333, 353–369 passim
Interest group unionism, 161–162, 170
Interest rates, 172, 214, 381
Internal Revenue Code, 418
International Association of Machinists (IAM), 337, 338, 363
International Association of Machinists and Aerospace Workers, 23
International Brotherhood of Electrical Workers (IBEW), 96, 335, 336, 353–355, 367–368
International Brotherhood of Teamsters, 91, 198, 272–273, 344, 345
  corruption in, 14–15, 61, 341, 342, 343
  insurgent groups in, 352, 358, 359
  ITU takeover attempt of, 91
  membership of, 55, 93, 96
  Presser family and, 331
  Reagan endorsed by, 31
  and sanitation workers, 259
  and taxes, 106
  violence by, 228
International Confederation of Free Trade Unions, 62, 400
Internationalization, 96, 133, 140–148, 379–381, 383. *See also* Trade
International Labor Organization, 141
International Ladies' Garment Workers Union, 45
International Longshoremen's Association (ILA), 14, 343, 347
International Organization of Masters, Mates, and Pilots, 90, 357–358, 364
International Typographical Union (ITU), 91, 329, 344, 359, 362, 367, 368
International Union of Electrical Workers (IUE), 346, 352, 358
Interstate Commerce Commission, 198
Irish unionism, 167

"Iron law of wages," 382–383
Israel, 63, 66
Italy, 167, 170, 172, 424, 425, 446
  decline of unionism in, 76, 107
  fascism in, 62
  radical unions in, 39, 152, 158, 162–163
ITU. *See* International Typographical Union

Jackson, Jesse, 32
James, Ed, 351, 365
Jamieson, Stuart, 124, 127
Japan, 9, 133–149, 172, 192, 424, 425
  decline of unionism in, 76, 77, 107, 108
  jobs gained in, 446
  "spring offensives" in, 163–164
Japanese Federation of Commerical Workers' Union, 400
Japanese model, 70–71, 144–145, 411
Japan Labor Institute, 400
Jews, 66
Job conditions. *See* Working conditions
Job security. *See* Employment security
Johnson, Lyndon B., 17, 63, 67, 378
Johnson, Manuel H., 237
"Joint" union, 92
Judiciary. *See* Courts
Jurisdiction, union, 12, 48, 54, 61, 275, 344
Justice, 231–233

Kassalow, Everett, 434
Katz, Michael, 415
Kennedy, John F., 67
  and civil rights, 16, 17
  and corruption, 61, 349, 357
  election of, 63, 126
  Executive Order 10988 of, 79, 82–83, 98, 266
Kennedy, Robert F., 61, 350
Kerr, Clark, 151, 329
Kettler, David, 113–132, 422, 431, 434, 438
Keynes, J. M., 382

Keynesianism, 106, 107, 134,
    381–382
  full employment with, 137
  internationalization and, 140,
    141, 142, 145, 379–380
King, Mackenzie, 124
King, Martin Luther, Jr., 20
Kirk, Paul G., Jr., 33
Kirkland, Lane, 11–35 passim,
    68–69, 73, 99, 237, 393–404,
    435–436
Knights of Labor, 41
Kochan, Thomas A., 24, 305–306,
    310, 415
Kopald, Sylvia, 356–357
Korean airline shootdown, 23
Korean War, 59, 79, 80, 81, 406
Kumar, Pradeep, 427–428

Labor Czars (Seidman), 357
Labor Department. *See* Department
    of Labor
Laborers union, 330, 331, 341, 343
Labor government, British, 169
Labor Injunction, The (Frankfurter
    and Greene), 52
Labor injunctions, 51–52, 203, 225,
    230
Labor Institute of Public Affairs,
    402
Labor Management Group, 28–29
Labor Management Relations Act,
    235
Labor Management Reporting and
    Disclosure Act (LMRDA), 15,
    61, 226, 347–355, 357
  constitutions affected by, 61,
    324–325, 351, 352, 354
  elections affected by, 61, 204,
    331, 348, 351, 352–353
  financial reports received by, 80,
    204
  immunities in, 227
  and staff civil liberties, 333–334
"Labor movement," 151, 152, 153,
    154, 155–156, 157–173
Labor Reform Act (1977), 109
Labor's Non-Partisan League, 56
"Labor surplus society," 378–379,
    382, 383

Landrum-Griffin Act. *See* Labor
    Management Reporting and
    Disclosure Act
Landsorganisasjon (LO), 164, 169
Lapp, John, 363
Larkin, James, 167
Latin America, 9, 122, 167, 171, 172
Laws, 39, 149
  Canadian/U.S., 128–132,
    429–436
  domestic content, 21
  privileges and immunities under,
    105, 221–238
  affecting public employee
    unionism, 249
  right-to-work, 8, 28, 88, 131, 235
  for union democracy, 347–355,
    362, 369
  See also Congress; Courts;
    individual laws
Lawyers, union, 336–337
Lawyers Coordinating Committee,
    AFL-CIO, 430
Layoffs, 193–194, 209, 211, 283, 412
Leaders, union, 102–103, 328–369
    passim
  elections of, 61, 325–353 passim,
    364–365
  opinions by, 308–309
  public opinion polls about, 24, 33,
    290–299, 304–305
Leapfrogging, 138
Leftism. *See* Radicalism, political
Legal environment. *See* Courts;
    Laws
Leiserson, William, 363
Leninism, 156, 163, 165–166
Leonard, Jonathan S., 100
Lequin, Yves, 158
Lester, Richard A., 366
Levering, Robert, 415
Levy, Paul Alan, 351
Lewin, David, 241–264
Lewis, John L., 4, 53–56 passim, 61,
    195, 352, 353, 366
Liberal Party, Canadian, 116,
    127–128, 448
Liberty, 233–234
"Lifetime employment" system,
    140, 142

Lindblom, Charles E., 180
Lipset, Seymour Martin, 151,
    287–321, 329, 347, 362, 367,
    368, 421–452
Lip watch company, France, 162
Little, Frank H., 47
Litton Industries, 27
Livernash, E. Robert, 177
LMRDA. *See* Labor Management
    Reporting and Disclosure Act
Local government, 49–50
Local government employees,
    126–127, 245–246. 251–261,
    262
Local unions, 206, 325–327, 403
Lockouts, 210
Longshoremen, east coast, 14, 343,
    347
Los Angeles Times polls, 294, 303,
    317
Loyal Legion of Loggers and
    Lumbermen, 230
Lubell, Samuel, 445
Luddism, 386

McBride, Lloyd, 334
McClellan, John L., 14, 16
McClellan Committee, 14, 61, 342,
    347, 350, 357
McDonald, David J., 13
McDonnell plant, St. Louis, 337
McGovern, George, 34, 64
McGuire, Peter J., 42, 49
Machinists' Union, 50–51, 55, 68,
    93, 96, 358
Machlup, Fritz, 177
McKee, Frank, 334
McLeod, J. T., 448
Macmillan, Harold, 447
Madden v. Atkins, 364
Mallet, Serge, 162
Management opposition. *See*
    Employer opposition
Manufacturing industries, 79, 206,
    395, 396, 407–408, 425–427
    locals in, 325
    union density in, 88, 90, 95, 107,
       120–121, 413
    white-collar workers increasing
       in, 94–95

worker opposition to unions in,
    102
Marchand, Jean, 127
Marches
    civil rights, 57
    Solidarity Day (1981), 20–21, 35
Marginalized workers, 161–162
Marine Engineers union, 358
Market forces, 94–97, 99, 136. *See*
    also Business cycles;
    Competition
Market share, 144, 146
Marshall, Alfred, 78, 177
Marshall, Ray, 133–149
Marshall Plan, 60–61
Marx, Karl, 154, 165, 382, 383–384,
    443–444
Massachusetts, 44, 85
Masters, Mates, and Pilots, 90,
    357–358, 364
Matignon agreements, 169
Mayers, Lewis, 363
Meany, George, 10–11, 20, 23, 33, 34
    and civil rights, 16–17, 20
    and Communists, 22, 34, 62
    on corruption, 14–15, 342, 357
Meat Cutters union, 344
Mechanics, airline, 35
Mechanization, 152–153, 156. *See*
    also Technological change
Media use, 335–336, 402
Mediterranean countries, 167
Medoff, James L., 24, 214–219
    on Canada/U.S. union density,
       431
    on employer opposition, 100, 427,
       432
    on organizing activity, 103, 413
    on worker opposition, 101
Meltz, Noah M., 120, 121, 431, 450,
    451
Membership, union, 60, 67–69,
    75–100 passim, 203, 204, 230,
    287, 412–414, 429
    AFL, 13, 46, 50, 52, 57, 73
    AFL-CIO, 12, 25, 29–30
    Canadian union, 422, 450
    CIO, 13, 57, 81, 122
    Machinists' Union, 50–51, 68, 93,
       96

Mine Workers, 53
OECD union, 425, 426
private sector (general), 29–30,
    80–82, 84, 85–86, 99, 266
public sector, 29–30, 79–90
    passim, 242, 244, 245,
    268–274 passim, 279
Steelworkers, 68, 92–93, 96
Teamsters, 55, 93, 96
See also Density, union
Men, 19, 31, 45, 205–206
Mergers
    corporate, 95
    union, 12–14, 16, 60–61, 75–76,
        90–94, 105, 204, 205, 263,
        343–345, 390
Metz, David, 416
Mexican migrants, 47
Mexico, 171
Michels, Robert, 329, 347, 366–367
Michigan, 84, 85
Middle class
    American, 138, 397
    French, 166–167
Migratory workers, 46–47
Militancy, Canadian union, 115
Miller, Arnold, 365
Milwaukee Technical Institute, 266
Miners for Democracy, 353, 365
Mining industries, 88, 102, 154, 165,
    195, 206. *See also* United Mine
    Workers
Minimum wages, 56, 59, 109
Minnesota, 351
Misery index, 427–429, 440
Mises, Ludwig Von, 223
Mondale, Walter F., 30–32, 65
Monetarism, 142
Monetary-fiscal policies
    Japanese, 143
    U.S., 142, 382
Monopolies, 137
"Monopoly wage-setting" face, 178,
    179–188, 189, 192, 200
Montgomery Ward, 58
Morality. *See* Ethical-moral
    practices, public opinion of
"More", 10, 77, 104, 105
Morgan, J. P., 46
Moskowitz, Milton, 415

"MPG effect," 216
Multi-employer bargaining, 185,
    189, 407
Multinational corporations, 140,
    381, 383. *See also*
    Internationalization
Multi-plant bargaining, 185
Municipal employees. *See* Local
    government employees
Murphy, Frank, 55
Murray, Philip, 5–6, 13, 61
Musicians union, 358

Nader, Ralph, 365
"National accord," 19–20
National Association of
    Manufacturers, 28, 404
National Center for Educational
    Statistics, 268, 270, 284
National Civic Federation, 46
National Education Association
    (NEA), 68, 82–83, 85, 93, 108,
    272, 273–275, 276
National Industrial Recovery Act
    (1933), 53–54, 203–204, 225,
    231
National Job Training Partnership
    Act, 418
National Labor Relations (Wagner)
    Act (NLRA), 54, 56, 99, 105,
    137, 149, 160, 222, 225–226,
    235, 237, 375, 429–430
    and associations (union-friendly),
        108
    Canada and, 121, 124, 131
    and cooperation, 418
    and educational institutions, 266,
        267, 270
    Great Depression and, 54,
        203–204, 231
    Japan and, 133
    majority rule under, 48
    nonprofit health care under, 267
    Taft-Hartley Act and, 58, 98, 99,
        204, 226, 227, 231, 429–430
    on unfair labor practices, 203,
        227
    union growth linked to, 78, 88,
        97–98, 109, 169, 204, 406
National Labor Relations Board

(NLRB), 98–99, 203–204, 226, 237, 287–288, 418, 430
Annual Report (1979) of, 222
on Boston University faculty, 270
and employer opposition, 68–69, 100, 102, 205, 398, 432, 433
Reagan administration, 64, 430
union representation/certification elections of, 28, 68–69, 100–102, 103, 130, 204, 205, 226, 287, 288, 302–303, 320–321, 431–441 passim
National Longitudinal Survey, 303, 320
National Master Freight Agreement, 198
National Opinion Research Center (NORC), 290, 292
National Steel, 93
NBC News poll, 317
NDP. *See* New Democratic Party, Canadian
NEA. *See* National Education Association
Negotiation, 129, 163–164, 169–170, 206, 319
Negri, Antonio, 163
Neo-capitalist state, 171
Neo-corporatism, 170–172
Neo-fascism, 170
Neo-Leninism, 163
Netherlands, 425, 446
New Bedford, Massachusetts, 44
New Deal, 52–57, 78, 99, 160, 222, 224, 380
  CIO during, 4, 54–56, 57
  mining unionization during, 53, 54, 56, 88
  public opinion of unions during, 300
  social democratic tinge and, 445
  union growth linked to, 55, 117, 169
New Democratic Party (NDP), Canadian, 116, 123, 125, 128, 131, 444, 449, 450
New Jersey, 85, 342, 354
New United Motor Manufacturing, Inc. (NUMMI), 411–412

"New working class," 162
New York City
  garment workers in, 45
  public sector unionism in, 79, 249, 259, 267
  Teamster violence in, 228
  union corruption in, 346, 347, 357–358
  union insurgency in, 357–358, 364
New York state
  union corruption in, 341, 346, 351
  union density in, 84, 85
  union insurgency in, 362, 364, 367
  See also New York City
New York State Crime Commission, 14
New York Times, 309–310, 382
New Zealand, 398
Nixon, Richard M., 19, 34, 62, 378
NLRA. *See* National Labor Relations Act
NLRB. *See* National Labor Relations Board
Non-Accelerating Inflation Rate of Unemployment (NAIRU), 378–379
Nonprofit organizations, 266–267
No-raiding agreement, 12, 275, 276, 344
Norris-LaGuardia/Federal Anti-Injunction Act (1932), 52, 78, 99, 105, 203, 225, 235
Northrup, Herbert R., 78
Norway, 160, 161
Nova Scotia, 130, 431, 432

OECD, 423–425, 426
"Official family," 328–369 passim.
  See also Leaders, union
Ohio, 84, 85, 267–268
Oligarchy, 324, 329, 345, 359–360, 366, 367, 368
Oligopolies, 136–137, 146
Olympic Games (1936), 62
Omnibus Civil Rights Act, 16–17, 20
O'Neal, Frederick, 18
"One-on-one" programs, 402–403

Ontario, Canada, 123, 124, 131
Open-shop campaigns, 45–46, 51,
    68, 122, 160
Operating Engineers union, 344,
    358
Opinion Research Corporation
    (ORC) polls
    on confidence in unions, 289, 304,
        305
    on corruption in unions, 296, 297,
        305, 315
    on inflation, 316
    on union power, 311–312
Opinion Research Surveys (ORS),
    306–307
"Oracle Social Club," 368
Organization for Economic
    Cooperation and Development
    (OECD), 423–425, 426
Organization of Petroleum
    Exporting Countries, 8
Organized crime, 14–15, 341, 342,
    358
Organizing activities, 53, 55, 91,
    103, 108–109, 205, 413
Organizing staff, union, 331–334

Packinghouse union, 344
Painters union, 344
    corruption in, 341, 343, 346
    insurgents in, 341, 351, 352, 358,
        364
    Raftery family running, 330
Pan American World Airways, 35
Papermakers union, 358
Paper mills, 196
Paris, 160
Parrish, John, 427
Parti Quebecois, 444, 450
Part–time workers, 69, 245–246
PATCO. *See* Professional Air
    Traffic Controllers
    Organization
Pattern bargaining, 146, 206, 407
Pencavel, John, 77
Penn and Schoen, 310
Pennsylvania, 84, 85
Pennsylvania State College System,
    276, 277
Pensions, 58–59, 189

Pentagon, 22
"Per capita tax," 277
Perkins, Frances, 53
Perlman, Selig, 41, 48, 362–363
Peronist unionism, 171
Personnel departments, 414–417
Petro, Sylvester, 223
Philosophy, union, 77, 90, 104–107.
    See also Government
    intervention; Politics
Pillard, Charles, 355
Poland, 23, 63, 153, 161, 172
Police, municipal, 51, 252
Polish Americans, 66
Political elections, 33–34, 49–50
    Canadian, 442
    1984, 32–33, 40, 65–67
    1986, 32
    See also Presidential elections
Political parties, 39, 40, 42, 49, 156,
    165–166, 173
    Canadian, 116, 123, 125,
        127–128, 131, 442–451
        passim
    European, 59, 166–167, 168, 169,
        366
    U.S., 65, 99, 447, 448 (*See also*
        Democratic party)
    See also Communists
Political Parties (Michels), 366–367
Politics, 104, 105, 122, 136,
    161–173 passim, 229–231,
    237–238
    AFL, 49–50, 56–57, 105, 237,
        445
    AFL-CIO, 12, 29–34, 63–67,
        206
    Canadian, 115, 127–128,
        131–132
    CIO, 55–57, 67, 105, 160, 161,
        445
    NEA in, 273
    and public employee unionism,
        29–30, 128, 249
    utopian, 158–159
    See also Political elections;
        Political parties; Radicalism,
        political
Polytechnic Institute, 270
Popitz, Heinrich, 152

Population
    union, *see* Membership, union
    U.S., 41
Portuguese immigrants, 44
Postal Reorganization Act (1970),
    98
Postal Service, U.S. (USPS), 89, 98
Postal workers
    Canadian, 127–128
    U.S., 89, 98
Pound, Roscoe, 223, 224
Power, union, public opinion of, 33,
    309–316
Pre-emption strategies, 436
Pre-industrial societies, 166
Premack, Steven, 430, 431
Presidential elections, 446, 447
    1932, 53
    1936, 56
    1940, 56–57
    1944, 57
    1952, 63
    1956, 63
    1960, 63, 126
    1964, 63
    1968, 63–64
    1972, 34, 64
    1976, 64
    1980, 64
    1984, 30–33, 34, 64–67, 76, 102,
        103, 104, 106
    1988, 103, 104
President's Commission on
    Industrial Competitiveness,
    407–408, 417–418
Press, union, 335–336
Presser, Jackie, 331
Presser, William, 331
Pressmen's union, 349
Presthus, Robert, 448
Price, Robert, 117, 434
Price controls, 7, 58, 59
Prices, 8, 50, 58, 140, 141, 208, 217
    European, 140, 148
    gasoline, 216
    GM, 5, 6–7
    Japanese, 140, 148
    oligopolies and, 137, 146
    See also Inflation
Printing Pressmen, 331

Private contracting, of public
    services, 252–257, 260, 261
Private employment growth, 243.
    See also under Membership,
    union
Private sector unionism, 92, 94, 98,
    106–107, 108, 109
    Canadian, 152
    college, 267, 268–271, 283–284
    membership trends in, 29–30, 79,
        80–82, 84, 85–86, 99, 266
Privileges, legal, 223–238
Privy Council Order-in-Council
    1003, Canadian, 124
Proctor and Gamble market
    research sector, 290
Productivity, 148, 194–197, 199,
    215–218, 235, 410, 423
    in Canada, 428
    in Europe, 138, 140
    in Japan, 142–143, 146
    in U.S., 137–138, 140, 142–143,
        195–196, 221–222, 427
    See also Gross national product
Productivity bargaining, 259
Professional Air Traffic Controllers
    Organization (PATCO), 35, 90,
    248
Professional associations, 85, 108
Professional staff, union, 334–337
"Professional" unionism, 153, 162
Profit maximization, 144, 146,
    197–199
Profit sharing, 37, 194, 410
Progressive Conservatives,
    Canadian, 116
Progressive Party, 13
"Progress sharing," 7
Promotion policy, faculty unions
    and, 282
Proposition 13, California's, 245
Prosperity, 234–235
Protestants, 443
Proudhon, Pierre Joseph, 156
Provenzano family, 342
Public administration workers, 102
Public Agenda survey, 143
Publications, union, 335–336
Public Citizen Litigation Group, 365
Public Employees Federation, 362, 367

Public employment, 243–245, 377.
  See also Public sector unionism
Public Interest Opinion Research, 316
Public opinion, 24, 101, 204,
    287–321, 397, 438–442
  on confidence in unions, 33,
    288–299, 304, 305, 320
  on corruption in unions, 204, 288,
    296–298, 305, 315
  on French workers, 152–153,
    154, 156
  on productivity, 143
  on socialist institutions, 123,
    445–447, 448–449
  of union power, 33, 309–316
Public policy, 21, 103, 418
  Canadian, 30, 114, 116, 436
  European, 134, 138, 160,
    169–170
  Japanese, 139, 143, 144,
    148–149
  U.S., 60, 78–79, 97–100,
    105–106, 107, 134, 138, 142,
    148–149, 160
  See also Government
    intervention; Laws; *individual
    presidents*
Public sector unionism, 70, 77, 98,
    104, 105–107, 109, 241–284
  in AFL-CIO, 22–23, 29, 90,
    272–273, 275, 276
  Canadian/U.S., 120–121,
    125–128, 130, 437–438
  corruption in, 341
  defensive unionism by, 162
  locals in, 325, 326
  membership in, 29–30, 79–90
    passim, 242, 244, 245,
    268–274 passim, 279
  mergers in, 91, 92, 344
Public Service Staff Relations Act
    (1967), Canadian, 128
Pulp, Sulphite, and Paper Mill
    Workers, 358

Quality
  faculty union institution,
    271–272
  and productivity, 146
Quality circle, 410

Quality of Employment Survey, 296,
    303, 305, 306–307
Quality-of-worklife programs, 26,
    37, 389
Quebec, Canada, 124, 127, 131, 444
Quits, 191–193, 199, 209, 211,
    215–216

Race, 16–19, 20, 31–32, 44, 57, 66,
    205–206
Racketeering, 14, 342–343, 349,
    357, 360–361, 364
Radicalism, political, 43, 90,
    151–152, 161, 163, 165–166,
    445–446. *See also*
    Communists; Socialism
Raftery, Lawrence, 330
Raftery, S. Frank, 330
Railway Labor Act (1926), 78, 88,
    235
Railway unions, 78, 89, 202
Ranciere, Jacques, 158
Randolph, A. Philip, 16, 20, 57
Raskin, A. H., 3–38, 102–103, 423
Rauh, Joseph, 330, 337, 351, 365
Reagan, Ronald/Reagan
    administration, 20, 21, 34, 77,
    104, 238, 289
  AFL-CIO conventions criticizing,
    22, 23
  and air traffic controllers, 10, 64
  deregulation policies of, 9
  election campaigns of, 30–32, 34,
    64–66, 106
  employer opposition and, 68
  inflation during, 9, 20, 316
  NLRB of, 64, 430
Rebellion in Labor Unions (Kopald),
    356–357
Recessions, 146
  1870s, 41
  1958–62, 125
  1970s, 378, 407
  1980s, 32, 69, 97, 213–214, 375,
    407, 428–429
Red Brigades, 163
Reed, John, 47
Regulation, 89, 137, 222, 226, 233,
    267, 435. *See also*
    Deregulation; Laws

Religion, 162, 167, 442, 443
Relocation, plant, 95
Reporter, The, 347–348
Report of the President's
    Commission on Industrial
    Competitiveness, 407–408,
    417–418
Republican Party, 65, 99, 448
Retail Clerks union, 344
Retail employees, 206
Retirement plans, 58–59, 189, 411
Reuther, Walter P., 4–7, 13, 20, 61,
    332, 340, 342
Review boards, union appeal,
    338–339
"Revolutionary defeatism," 35
Revolutionary ideals, national,
    442–443
Revolutionary unionism, 152, 158, 167
Revolutionary vanguard parties,
    156, 165–166
Reynolds, Lloyd, 177
Reynolds, Morgan, 221–238
Ricardo, David, 381
"Right-to-work" laws, 8, 28, 88, 131,
    235
Robots, 376, 377, 383, 384–385,
    386, 390–391
Rockefeller, Nelson, 65
Roethlisberger, Fritz, 155
Roosevelt, Franklin Delano, 77, 104,
    225, 375, 429, 430. *See also*
    New Deal
Roosevelt, Theodore, 49, 62
Roper/*Fortune* poll, 445–446
Roper polls, 289–290, 302
    on ethical standards, 296, 297
    on socialist institutions,
        445–446, 447
    on union leaders, 292–296, 297
    on union power, 310–311,
        312–313
    on wage demands, 318
Rose, Joseph B., 115, 120, 436
Rubber industry, 6, 160, 344
Russia
    prerevolutionary unions in, 152
    See also Soviet Union

Sadlowski, Edward, 330, 333, 337, 358

Safety issues, 69
St. Louis, 337
Saint-Simon, C. de, 166
Saltsjobaden agreements, 169
Salzhandler, Solomon, 360–361
Salzhandler v. Caputo, 361
Samson, Leon, 444
San Antonio, Texas, 109
San Francisco, 267, 364
San Francisco Bay Area Painters
    Union, 341
Sanitation service, 251–261, 262
Sanitation Workers' Union, 259
Saturn plant, 411
Save the Union movement, 352
Scandinavian countries, 19, 160,
    164, 165, 168, 171, 398. *See
    also individual countries*
Scanlon Plan, 198–199
Scargill, Arthur, 165
Schecter Poultry Case, 225
Schmitter, Philippe, 170
Schnitzler, William, 357
Schonfeld, Frank, 364
Schwab, Charles, 46
Scientific management, 135–136,
    154–155, 157–158
Screen Actors' Guild, 64
Secretary of Labor, 53, 64, 103
Seidman, Harold, 357
Self–management, 162, 412
Senate, 28
    Committee on Education and
        Labor of, 43
    Labor Committee of, 331, 347
    McClellan Committee of, 14, 342,
        347, 350, 357
Senates, academic, 281–282, 284
Seniority clauses, 70
Service Employees International
    Union (SEIU), 92, 106, 276,
    278, 335, 344, 345
Service industries, 77, 94, 95–96,
    206, 423
    and class consciousness, 161
    employment growth in, 68, 89,
    120–121, 287, 375, 395, 396,
    413, 424
    union density in, 68, 89, 107–108
    See also Public sector unionism

Sheet Metal Workers, 331
Sheflin, Neil, 97
Sherman Anti–Trust Act, 49, 230
Shoe industry, 85
Siegel, Abraham, 151
Silberman, David, 430
Simons, Henry C., 177, 180, 223
Slichter, Sumner, 177
Slowdowns, 210
Smith, Adam, 219–220, 381, 382
Smith–Connally Act (1984), 350
"Social contract," 168–170, 171
Social democracy, 170, 449
    Canadian, 115, 442, 444, 449, 450
    European, 59, 168, 169, 366
    U.S. and, 445–446, 447, 451, 452
Socialism, 166–167
    Canadian, 116, 123, 444,
        449–450, 452
    European, 45, 105, 159–160, 162,
        165, 168
    U.S. and, 40, 45, 46, 105, 107,
        159, 421, 444, 445–446, 447,
        452
    See also Social democracy
Social movement, unionism as,
        151–173
Social role, of unions, 72
    public opinion of, 299–303
    See also Civil rights; Foreign
        policy, AFL-CIO
Social security, 59, 168
Social services, 40, 106, 168. *See
    also* Welfare state
Social values, American/Canadian,
        440, 442–452. *See also* Class
        consciousness
Sociological interpretations,
        151–173, 422–429
"Sociological intervention" method,
        155
"Solidarity" (concept), 35
Solidarity Day march, 20–21, 35
Solidarnosc (Solidarity), Polish, 23,
        63, 66, 172
Solzhenitsyn, Aleksandr, 63
Sombart, Werner, 421
Sorel, Georges, 159
Soviet Union, 13, 22, 23, 47, 56, 60,
        62–63

Spain, 158
Spanish-Portuguese neo-fascism,
        170
Staff, union
    organizing, 331–334
    professional, 334–337
Stagflation, 140, 141, 182–183, 429
State central bodies, union, 325, 403
State Coalition for a Democratic
        Union (SCDU), 362
State intervention. *See* Government
        intervention
State, 49
    gubernatorial elections in, 32,
        65–66
    union-control legislation by, 231
    union density among, 84–85
    unionized employees of, 126–127,
        245–246, 267, 284, 325, 326
        (*See also* Public sector
        unionism)
    See also individual states
State University of New York
        (SUNY), 277
Statism, 446, 449
Steel industry, 385
    CIO and, 54, 91
    strikes in, 6, 9–10, 46, 50, 60
    Truman and, 6, 59–60
    See also United Steelworkers of
        America
Steelworkers Organizing
        Committee, 91
Stevens (J.P.) textile company, 27,
        109
Stevenson, Adlai, 63
Stillman, Don, 365
Strasser, Adolph, 41–42, 43
Strikes, 9–10, 122, 160, 202, 210,
        212–213, 409
    airline workers, 10, 35–36, 64,
        248
    auto workers, 4–5, 6, 7, 55
    Canadian, 115, 123, 124, 125,
        127–128, 129
    for eight-hour day, 42
    during Great Depression, 52, 225
    Hormel, 109
    Industrial Workers of the World
        and, 46, 47

miners, 127, 232
public employee, 51, 246–248,
   257, 261, 263, 272
rubber worker, 344
steel workers, 6, 9–10, 46, 50, 60
textile and garment workers,
   26–27, 45
violence with, 223–224, 232
wildcat, 8, 72, 125, 127–128, 344
during World War II, 58, 344
Structuralism, 422–429
Struthers, James, 113–132, 422,
   431, 434, 438
Sturmthal, Adolf, 160
Summers, Clyde, 348–349, 351,
   355, 363, 365
Supply-side economics, 142
Supreme Court, U.S., 267
   and LMRDA, 334, 348
   minimum-wage ruling of, 109
   NIRA ruled unconstitutional by,
      54, 203, 225, 231
   and NLRA, 78, 97, 98, 226, 227,
      265–266, 267, 269–270
   and Truman seizing steel mills,
      60
   on union coercion, 228, 229
   on union shop agreements, 88
   Yeshiva case of, 267, 268–270
Survey Research Center (SRC), 296,
   299, 304, 305, 306–308, 310
Sweden, 160–172 passim, 425, 446
Switzerland, 425
Syndicalism, 39, 46–47, 167, 444

Taft, Philip, 227, 362–363
Taft-Hartley Act (1947), 28, 58, 64,
   122, 204, 231, 287–288, 440
   Korean War and, 59
   and NLRA, 58, 98, 99, 204, 226,
      227, 231, 429–430
   politics of labor after, 63
   Smith-Connally Act and, 350
Taxes, 106, 243–245, 382
Taylor, Frederick H., 154
Taylor, Myron C., 54
Teamsters. *See* International
   Brotherhood of Teamsters
Teamsters for a Democratic Union,
   367

Teamsters Local 560, 342
Teamsters Local 807 (1942), 228
Technological change, 133,
   152–153, 156, 395
   by automation, 255–257, 377
   and internationalization, 140
   by robots, 376, 377, 383,
      384–385, 386, 390–391
   in sanitation service, 252,
      255–261
Telecommunication industries, 96
Temporary layoffs, 193–194, 211
Terrorism, 163
Texas, 84, 85, 109, 355
Textile industry, 26–27, 85
Thatcher, Margaret, 165, 171
Theory of the Labor Movement
   (Perlman), 48
Thomas, Norman, 363, 364
Thomas, R. J., 7
Thompson, E. P., 158
Thompson, Mark, 450–451
Tilly, Charles, 151
Tobin, Daniel, 53
Toryism, 442–443, 447, 449, 451
Touraine, Alain, 151–173
Townsend, Willard, 16
Toyota, 411
Trade, 9, 380, 396, 408
Trades and Labour Congress (TLC),
   449–450
Training, employee, 418
Transportation industries, 88–89,
   141. *See also* Air travel
   industry; Trucking industry
Trans World Airlines, 36
Trentin, Bruno, 167
Trials, union, 337–338
Trotsky, Leon, 152
Trow, Martin A., 329, 347, 362, 367,
   368
Trowbridge, Alexander B., 405–418
Troy, Leo, 75–109, 412–413, 414,
   422, 430
Trucking industry, 198, 228, 325.
   See also International
   Brotherhood of Teamsters
Truman, Harry S., 4, 5, 6, 13, 58,
   59–60, 61, 430
Turnover. *See* Quits

Two-tier wage agreements, 70, 185,
     194, 408
Tyler, Gus, 373–392
Typographers union. *See*
     International Typographical
     Union

UAW. *See* United Auto Workers
Unemployment, 18, 37, 69, 138, 147,
     374, 378–379, 394–395
   Canadian, 124–125, 427–429
   during Great Depression, 52, 54
   inflation and, 20, 141, 378–379,
     427–429
   Japanese, 139
   Keynesianism and, 134, 141
   on misery index, 427–429
   Reagan administration and, 9
   from robot displacement, 377
   during World War II, 57
Unemployment compensation, 59,
     138, 418
Unfair labor practices, 203, 205,
     227, 398, 427, 433
Union Carbide Corporation, 416
Union-free environment, 68–69,
     116, 148–149, 404, 414–417
Union Nationale government,
     Canadian, 127
Union shop, 8, 28, 88, 122, 315–316,
     350
Union-substitution policies
   by business, 95, 436–437
   by government, 103
United Airlines, 35
United Auto Workers (UAW), 204,
     326, 394, 410, 411
   Canadian, 114–115
   elections of, 332, 340
   GM contracts with, 4–7, 406,
     410, 411
   and LMRDA, 348
   membership reductions of,
     67–68, 93, 96
   pensions won by, 58
   Reuther of, 4–7, 61, 332, 340
   review board of, 339

United Electrical, Radio, and
     Machine Workers, 6

United Faculty of Florida (UFF),
     275
United Food and Commercial
     Workers, 344
United Kingdom. *See* Britain
United Mine Workers (UMW), 53,
     54, 195, 203, 323–324
   coercion used by, 232
   election fraud in, 346, 352–353,
     364
   insurgent groups in, 353, 358,
     364, 366
   Lewis over, 53, 54, 56, 195, 352,
     353, 366
United Mine Workers Journal,
     365
United Professors of California
     (UPC), 275–276
United Rubber Workers, 6
United States Chamber of
     Commerce, 28
U.S. News and World Report, 317
United States Merchant Marine
     Academy, 266
U.S. Steel Corporation, 46, 54, 91
United Steelworkers of America,
     5–6, 204, 328, 335, 395
   membership reductions in, 68,
     92–93, 96
   elections in, 330, 332, 333, 334,
     337, 346, 352
   insurgents in, 330, 333, 337, 358
   Reuther and, 5–6, 13, 61
   strikes by, 6, 9–10
U.S. v. Enmons (1973), 228
United Transport Service
     Employees, 16
University of Alaska, 270
University of California, Los
     Angeles, 271–272
University of Florida, 271
University of Hawaii, 276, 277
University of Michigan, 296
Ure, Andrew, 154
Usery decision, 267, 268
Utopian politics, 158–159

"Value added," 217
Values, Canadian and American,
     442–452

Van Arsdale, Harry, 330
Van Arsdale, Tommy, 330
Vargas government, 171
Vietnam War, 8, 22, 63, 79, 81
Violence, 158, 163, 223–233
passim, 352, 353, 364
Voice/response face, 178, 179,
189–191, 193
Voss, Paula, 103

Wage controls, 7, 59, 128
Wages, 10, 19, 36–37, 42–43, 50,
69, 70, 137–141 passim, 146,
164, 168, 179–191, 199, 20,
207–218 passim, 406, 427
Bureau of Labor Statistics
analysis of, 10, 69, 397
Canadian, 428
concessions in, 194, 213–214,
408–409
in 1870s, 41
equality in, 183–188, 199, 219,
234
European, 43, 138, 140, 141, 148,
168
General Motors/GM formula and,
5, 6–9, 19, 406
during Great Depression, 52–53,
211
minimum, 56, 59, 109
postal workers', 98
and presidential election voting,
31
public employee, 261, 283
public opinion polls on, 308, 318
quits and, 192, 209, 211, 215–216
taxes and, 106
two-tier, 70, 185, 194, 408
Wagner Act. *See* National Labor
Relations Act
Wallace, George, 64
Wallace, Henry A., 13, 61
Wall Street Journal, 93
Walsh-Healey law, 225
War Labor Boards, 4, 50, 57–58,
122, 137, 406, 430
War Measures Act, Canadian, 123
Wayne State University, 280
Webbs, 184
Weiler, Paul, 398, 431, 432

Weimar period, Germany, 160
Welfare capitalism, 51
Welfare state, 40, 57–59, 171,
386–387, 451
Wells, H. G., 43, 444
Western Electric Company, 155
Western Federation of Miners, 46
West Germany, 19, 70, 163, 169,
172, 425
co-determination of, 37, 71, 72
decline of unionism in, 76, 107
job losses in, 446
Social Democratic Party of, 169,
366
West Virginia, 364
What Do Unions Do? (Freeman and
Medoff), 214–219
Whipsawing, 138, 141
White, A. J., 355
White, Byron, 227
White, Robert, 114–115
White–collar workers, 69, 86, 397,
423
and employment security, 69, 70
in goods industries, 94–95
union wage advantage of, 188,
219
See also Service industries
White males, 19, 31, 205–206
Wholesale workers, 206
Wichita State University, 270
Wildcat strikes, 8, 72, 125,
127–128, 344
Williams, Lynn, 334
Willkie, Wendell, 56
Wilson, Charles, 7
Wilson, Dow, 341, 364
Wilson, Woodrow, 49, 50, 78, 223
Wilson Labor government, 169
Winpisinger, William W., 23
Wisconsin, 79, 266
Wisconsin school, 362–363
Witte, Edwin, 230
Wolman, Leo, 79, 80
Women, 18, 19, 45, 86, 140
Work councils, 71
Worker opposition, to unionization,
100–102
Worker participation, 37, 148,
159–160, 410, 417–418

in decision making, 26, 37, 69,
     71–72, 169, 412, 417
  See also Employee-operated
     enterprise
"Work ethic," 24
Working conditions, 159, 164, 168,
     308
Work rules, 208–209, 215, 409
World Federation of Trade Unions,
     62
World War I, 50, 78, 79, 81, 159, 230
World War II, 4, 57–58, 79, 81, 117,
     122, 395
  Akron rubber strike during, 344
  Canadian labor during, 123–124
  Communists during, 55–56

public opinion of unions during,
     300
War Labor Board during, 4,
     57–58, 122, 137, 406
Wrenn, Rob, 436–437

Xerox, 412

Yablonski, Chip, 351
Yablonski, Joseph (Jock), 353,
     364–365
Yankelovich, Skelly, and White,
     299, 310
Yellow dog contract, 52, 225
Yeshiva University, 267, 268–270,
     284